COMPUTED ELECTRON MICROGRAPHS AND DEFECT IDENTIFICATION

A. K. HEAD, P. HUMBLE, L. M. CLAREBROUGH,
A. J. MORTON and C. T. FORWOOD

CSIRO Division of Tribophysics,
University of Melbourne, Australia

v.7

1973

NORTH-HOLLAND PUBLISHING COMPANY – AMSTERDAM • LONDON
AMERICAN ELSEVIER PUBLISHING COMPANY, INC. – NEW YORK

Library of Congress Catalog Card number: 72-93092
North-Holland ISBN for the series: 0 7204 1750 3
North-Holland ISBN for this volume: 0 7204 1757 0
American Elsevier ISBN: 0 444 10462 3

Publishers:

North-Holland Publishing Company - Amsterdam
North-Holland Publishing Company, Ltd. - London

Sole distributors for the U.S.A. and Canada:

American Elsevier Publishing Company, Inc.
52 Vanderbilt Avenue
New York, N.Y. 10017

Printed in The Netherlands

PREFACE

For the last few years at Tribophysics, we have been using a technique of computer simulation of electron micrographs for the identification of defects in crystalline solids. Theoretical micrographs are computed for a range of possibilities for the unknown defect and identification is made by the visual matching of experimental and theoretical micrographs. The technique was developed initially in order to overcome the difficulty of assimilating the information in the large number of intensity profiles needed to identify the Burgers vectors of dislocations in highly elastically anisotropic materials. Subsequently, the technique has proved invaluable for the identification of single dislocations and complex configurations of dislocations and stacking faults in many other materials regardless of the degree of elastic anisotropy.

Since the initial development, there have been many requests for the computer programs we have used so that it was considered worthwhile to publish them and all the information essential for their use in defect identification.

The book is written for the post graduate student or research worker using transmission electron microscopy for studying defects in crystalline solids. Crystallography, diffraction theory and elasticity theory form the background on which the technique is based. These topics are not covered completely but, for each, sufficient detail is given to enable their use in the technique to be followed.

The programs are based on the Howie–Whelan two-beam theory of diffraction for distorted crystals, but the displacement field of the defect is treated in linear anisotropic elasticity rather than isotropic elasticity. The technique can thus be used for defects in crystals of any degree of anisotropy. The programs can be used to compute theoretical micrographs of single dislocations in cubic, tetragonal or hexagonal crystals and more complex configurations. involving up to two dislocations and three stacking faults, in cubic crystals. Further, detailed background information necessary for understanding the programs is given so that alterations of programs, for particular situations not covered by the programs presented, will be facilitated.

In Tribophysics, the technique has been applied to electron microscopy of metals at 100 kV where the experimental conditions have been set to approximate to the theoretical two-beam case. For these conditions it has been successful on all occasions on which it has been used. In many instances it has been possible to obtain accurate quantitative information and the technique has proved to be extremely useful, in some cases invaluable, for the types of problem in which we have been interested. It is hoped that, with the aid of the information in this book, the method may prove of similar utility to others.

We wish to thank the Executive of CSIRO for permission to prepare this volume and the staff of the CSIRO Division of Computing Research for efficient service. Particular thanks go to Mr. E.G. Beckhouse of this Division for the preparation of photographic material.

CONTENTS

1 | INTRODUCTION

This book describes a technique which has been evolved over the past few years for identifying defects in crystalline solids by comparing the images they produce in the electron microscope with corresponding theoretical images (Head, 1967a). The defects for which the technique is most useful are those which are visible in the microscope because of the effect their displacement fields have on the diffraction of electrons by the crystal. Dislocations and stacking faults are by far the most common defects of this type. Stacking faults, as a result of the simple discontinuous nature of their displacement field, produce images which are reasonably well understood and interpreted. Dislocations, on the other hand, have displacement fields which are continuously distributed throughout the crystal and an electron micrograph of a dislocation results from this whole displacement field and not just the dislocation core. Thus there is no intuitive relation between a dislocation and its image. Objects such as large precipitates and inclusions are usually visible in the electron microscope because of their different absorption and we may use their diffraction patterns and the techniques of conventional optical microscopy to identify their structure and obtain their morphologies. It is because dislocations have images which are not susceptible to direct interpretation by normal 'intuitive' processes such as those used in metallography that their identification is difficult.

Since the formulation of the two-beam dynamical theory of electron diffraction for imperfect crystals by Howie and Whelan in 1961, it has been widely applied to crystals containing defects. The equations which describe this theory contain a term for the displacement field around a defect. The standard form of this term for a dislocation, derived on the basis of linear isotropic elasticity theory, is dependent upon the factors $g \cdot b$, $g \cdot b_e$ and $g \cdot b \wedge u$ (where g is the diffracting vector, b is the Burgers vector, b_e is the edge component of the Burgers vector and u is a unit vector along the dislocation line) in such a way that if a value of g can be found which makes these factors zero, the whole displacement term is zero. In this case, the electrons are diffracted by the crystal as if it were perfect, and the dislocation (i.e. its displacement field) is invisible. If any of these factors is non-zero, the dislocation will exhibit some contrast, the amount of which can only be determined by numerical integration of the diffraction equations.

Since g may be determined by indexing the diffraction patterns, the occurrence of invisibility has formed the basis for a practical method of determining the Burgers vectors of dislocations. Detailed examination of the displacement function (see expression (2.31)) shows that the requirement that all three factors be zero, can only be satisfied for pure screw or pure edge dislocations and in these cases the conditions for invisibility in isotropic materials reduce to the familiar criteria; $g \cdot b = 0$ for screw dislocations and $g \cdot b = 0$, $g \cdot b \wedge u = 0$ for edge dislocations.

These criteria are thus very restrictive and in the practical determination of Burgers vectors of dislocations, it has usually been assumed that the term $g \cdot b$ is dominant and $g \cdot b = 0$ has been identified with weak images as well as with images which are experimentally invisible. The justification for identifying $g \cdot b = 0$ with weak images within the framework of isotropic elasticity, has been that the terms $g \cdot b_e$ and $g \cdot b \wedge u$ are not zero. However, the exact effect of these terms on the intensity of an image is seldom calculated. The $g \cdot b = 0$ condition has been used in this way to determine the Burgers vectors of mixed dislocations despite the fact that the invisibility criteria only strictly apply to pure screw and pure edge dislocations in isotropic materials. Moreover, most crystals are not elastically isotropic, but are anisotropic. The form of the displacement field around dislocations in elastically anisotropic media is different from that for isotropic media and it is known that (except in special circumstances) even pure screw and pure edge dislocations cannot be made truly invisible. The experimental observation of invisibility in real crystals for most dislocations is, therefore, somewhat fortuitous and probably occurs because many images for which $g \cdot b = 0$ are weak and they fall close to, or below, the threshold of visibility against the background noise. However, weak images can occur when $g \cdot b$ is not zero; for instance, when the crystal is set at large deviations from the Bragg condition. On the other hand, even when $g \cdot b = 0$, dislocations of mixed character can have quite strong images for isotropic elasticity, as can both pure screw and pure edge dislocations in moderately anisotropic crystals.

Thus the use of experimentally invisible or weak images to detect instances in which $g \cdot b = 0$ is open to the criticism that in practice it is never possible to know when a mistake might be made. On the other hand, the invisibility criteria are simple to use, and there seems to be no doubt that in the majority

of cases examined up till now, experimental invisibility has coincided with
$g \cdot b$ = 0. Thus the $g \cdot b$ rules have been a useful substitute for determining the
Burgers vectors of dislocations in the absence of specific contrast calculations.
Nevertheless, since crystals are in general elastically anisotropic, since dislocations are in general neither of screw nor edge orientation, and since true
invisibility is impossible to determine experimentally, there appears to be a
need for other, more certain methods of dislocation identification.

In the technique to be developed in this book, the displacement fields
around dislocations are calculated using linear anisotropic elasticity theory
and therefore better represent dislocations in real crystals. However, the displacements have to be calculated numerically and are specific to a particular
dislocation in a particular crystal. Nothing can be implied, for instance from
these specific calculations, about a similar dislocation in a different crystal.
In addition, except when dislocations lie in particular symmetry directions
in crystals, the term in the Howie–Whelan formulation representing the
displacement due to the dislocation, is never zero. Thus, in order to know
what the theoretical image of the dislocation looks like, the Howie–Whelan
equations must be numerically integrated through the thickness of the
specimen over the region occupied by the dislocation. It is apparent, therefore,
that the increase in reliability of dislocation identification obtained by using
anisotropic elasticity is at the expense of the simple invisibility rules with the
consequent necessity to use computing methods at several stages in the process.
Indeed, unless these disadvantages were reduced considerably, this method of
identification would not be worth-while in practice. We have offset these disadvantages first by finding faster (and therefore, cheaper) methods of computing images and secondly by making the comparison between computed
and experimental information easier for the observer.

Previous methods of computing defect images have been mainly of the
intensity profile type in which a graph is constructed of the electron intensity
as a function of position along a line crossing the defect. Such profiles are
typically formed from 50 or 60 discrete intensity values, each requiring an
integration of the Howie–Whelan equations through the thickness of the
foil. Each profile takes about 15 sec to calculate on our computer and usually
about 10 profiles, computed for several depths in the foil, corresponding to
various positions along the length of the defect, are required to obtain a
reasonable basis for comparison with the experimental image.

In comparing the computed profiles with the experimental micrograph,
the observer is presented with information in two different forms. He has
either to synthesise the information contained in the profiles to form a
theoretical micrograph, or to analyse the experimental image in terms of
virtual microphotometer traces. We have chosen to present the computed
information in the form of theoretical micrographs so that the comparison

(a)

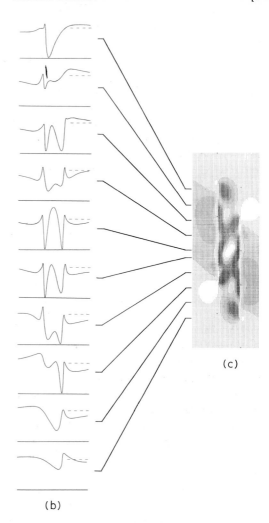

(c)

(b)

Fig. 1.1. Experimental micrograph (a) of a dislocation dipole in nickel compared with a matching set of computed profiles (b) and a matching theoretical micrograph (c). The theoretical micrograph and the profiles were computed using the same data (that corresponding to the particular circumstances of (a)). The rows of the micrograph exactly corresponding to each of the profiles are indicated by the lines between (b) and (c).

between theory and experiment is more direct. Moreover, we have employed a more efficient way of organizing the integration procedure so that the time for one theoretical micrograph (which is equivalent to 129 profiles) computed on our CDC 3600 computer is typically 40–50 sec.

Fig. 1.1(a) shows an experimental image of a dislocation dipole in nickel and figs. 1.1(b) and (c) show the two ways of presenting the corresponding computed image. The profiles in fig. 1.1(b) and the corresponding rows of the theoretical micrograph indicated in the figure are constructed from the same values of intensity, but it will be apparent that the comparison between theory and experiment is much more readily made using the theoretical micrograph in fig. 1.1(c) rather than the profiles in fig. 1.1(b).

The general method of identification of defects using the computed micrographs may be stated as follows. Firstly, experimental micrographs of the unknown defect are taken under a number of different diffracting conditions e.g. different diffracting vectors taken in different electron beam directions. Then informed guesses are made as to what the unknown defect might be and theoretical micrographs are computed for these under the same diffracting conditions as the experimental micrographs. When the theoretical and experimental micrographs match consistently for one guess, the defect is identified.

Unlike the use of invisibility criteria, this technique does not involve only the choice of weak or invisible images. On the contrary, the images which are best suited to the comparison technique are those which have easily distinguished topological features; that is, images with 'character'. When sorting through the guesses initially, an effort to match the most characteristic images is made first. Usually, four or five such images are sufficient to eliminate all the guesses except one and this one remaining possibility is tested further with the remaining images.

By now the reader will probably have some idea of what the technique offers for problems he might have in mind and how it may be used in practice. It is the purpose of this book to put forward in detail all the ingredients which will enable him to obtain the required experimental information and set up and run the required computer programs. The following chapters give an introduction to the theory, describe the way in which the electron microscope is used to obtain the data for the computer programs, give the principles behind the programs, list the programs themselves, show how they may be modified to suit individual needs and describe several examples of the way in which identification is made.

When the procedures which will be described in this book are followed, the effort involved in identifying defects is by no means excessive and it is more than balanced by the increased confidence the user will have in the identification he has made. It is true, of course, that for identifying the Burgers vector of a single dislocation, the technique is more sophisticated than the use of simple $g \cdot b$ rules. The authors now use $g \cdot b$ rules mostly as a guide to eliminate some of the initial guesses and the identification is finally made with the aid of computed micrographs. However, on reading the examples contained in ch. 8, it will be apparent that these are not solely straightforward Burgers vector determinations of dislocations in moderately anisotropic materials, but concern, in the main, more complex situations. They include, for instance, the determination of Burgers vectors of dislocations in highly anisotropic materials or the identification of configurations consisting of several dislocations and stacking faults. These are all cases which require some form of image computation and $g \cdot b$ rules are entirely inappropriate.

It is important to realise that once the experimental images of a composite type of defect have been matched by the computed ones, not only have the dislocations and stacking faults been identified, but also the full geometry of the defect has been determined. This complete specification of a defect is what is meant by 'identification' and the identification of composite defects has already led to a better understanding of the mechnism of some defect interactions in crystalline solids.

2 | INTRODUCTION TO THE BASIC THEORY

2.1. Introduction

In this chapter the parameters and notation necessary for an understanding of the computer programs are introduced. It should be understood that it is not the intention here to given an exhaustive or rigorous presentation of the various theories or the approximations inherent in them. For this, the reader will be referred to the original papers and recognised texts *. However, points which relate to the accuracy or understanding of the programs or to the reliability of some of the parameters are discussed in some detail. For example, the basic two-beam diffraction equations are merely written down, whereas the way in which the displacements around a dislocation are treated for an aniso- tropic solid, is outlined in detail. The derivation of the Howie—Whelan equa- tions is well documented in the original papers and is contained in most standard text books on electron microscopy. Once derived, they tell us very little about the contrast from defects since in general they have to be inte- grated numerically for specific cases. On the other hand, the cases in which dislocations in anisotropic media give rise to no contrast, or the reasons why the electron beam direction and the dislocation line direction have to be specified before computations of contrast can be performed, are not well covered in the literature and so they are dealt with more fully.

The equations which describe the two-beam dynamical diffraction of electrons by crystals are introduced and these are used as a basis on which to discuss successively the parameters which appear in them. Thus, the first

---

* For a comprehensive treatment of electron diffraction in distorted crystals, see Hirsch et al. (1965). For the specific topic of anisotropic elasticity, see the relevant chapters of Nye (1960) and Hirth and Lothe (1968).

sections of this chapter deal mainly with the parameters relating to diffraction theory. The parameter in the equations which represents distortion of the crystal from the perfect state is considered in a later section (§ 2.7) where the discussion deals mainly with linear elasticity theories of infinite continuous media.

2.2. The diffraction of electrons by a crystal

A rigorous treatment of the theory of electron diffraction in crystals is not within the scope of this book, but it is extremely useful when using the image matching technique to have a background knowledge of the diffraction processes which can occur, the theories which have been formulated and the approximations and limitations contained in them. In the present context, of course, interest is centred on the two-beam dynamical theory of electron diffraction using a column approximation (Howie and Whelan, 1961) which is used to compute the electron micrographs.

The two-beam dynamical theory was probably formulated originally because it is the simplest case of its type to consider. However, its subsequent widespread use has arisen not only because of its simplicity but also because the experimental conditions can usually be manipulated to approximate to the theory. That is, it is usually possible to set up the experimental conditions so that only two of the diffracted beams * contain most of the intensity. Practical experience has shown that the application of the theory to such experimental situations is remarkably successful. In addition to the two-beam theory, however, we are also concerned with some other diffraction processes which occur in real crystals (e.g. inelastic scattering processes and the formation of Kikuchi lines), since use is made of these in obtaining the parameters necessary to run the computer programs.

The introduction which follows is mainly a qualitative description based on the experimental appearance of diffraction patterns and the effects on these of tilting the crystal.

Examination of a diffraction pattern from a thinned metal foil, for example, shows that the processes concerned in the passage of the electrons through the crystal are many and complex. In addition to the bright central spot corresponding to the electrons which are undeviated by the presence of the crystal, there are many others which are arranged in a regular array. These arise from the diffraction of part of the incident beam into specific directions and represent diffraction by various sets of crystal planes accord-

---

* In this, and similar contexts, the term 'diffracted beams' includes the beam in the incident direction.

ing to Bragg's law. These spot patterns are used to obtain the diffracting vector g and give an approximate value for the electron beam direction B. *

Superimposed on the grid of spots there is usually a diffuse background and a system of diffuse lines. These Kikuchi lines are used to obtain many of the parameters needed to run the program. Kikuchi lines occur in pairs, and in general, one of the pair is lighter (i.e. contains fewer electrons) than the diffuse background, and the other is darker (i.e. contains more electrons). These are called the deficient and excess lines respectively. Kikuchi line pairs originate from the scattering of some of the electrons in the incident beam with the loss of only a small amount of energy. These electrons effectively form a secondary source of electrons distributed throughout the crystal. The source radiates in all directions, although there is a strong peak in the forward (incident beam) direction. The Kikuchi lines are formed by the subsequent Bragg diffraction of electrons from this distributed source. Since Kikuchi lines and diffraction spots result from the Bragg diffraction of electrons with very similar energies, the spacing between a Kikuchi line pair can be taken to be the same as that between the central spot and the particular Bragg spot formed by diffraction from the same set of planes. When the crystal orientation is altered, the planes causing the Bragg diffraction are rotated and this results in a movement of the Kikuchi lines (Hirsch et al., 1965, p. 121). In contrast, the spot pattern remains stationary when the crystal is tilted, although the intensities of the spots change and some spots may disappear altogether, whilst new ones may appear. Thus, the spot pattern cannot be used to determine the precise orientation of the crystal, whereas the Kikuchi lines may be used both for this purpose and to follow changes in orientation of the crystal.

The Kikuchi lines, the diffuse background, and some of the diffuseness in the Bragg spots, all arise from electrons which have suffered some energy loss (~ 20 eV) during their passage through the crystal. This energy excites some particular degree of freedom of the crystal, that is, some specific mode of vibration of the crystal or electrons in it. Electrons interacting with the crystal in this way are said to have suffered an inelastic scattering process. The diffraction spots, on the other hand, arise from interactions between the electrons and the crystal as a whole. Since the mass of the electrons is negligible compared with that of the crystal, the electrons lose virtually no energy during the process and they are said to be elastically scattered.

Because of the number and complexity of the scattering processes, it is necessary to look for some simplification when formulating a theory. A guide to which approximations are reasonable may be obtained by examining what

---

* The convention for the electron beam direction B adopted in this book is that it is anti-parallel to the direction of electron flow. That is, it is the upward drawn normal to the diffraction pattern.

happens in practical electron microscopy. Electron micrographs are usually formed by placing an aperture around either the spot representing the directly transmitted beam or one of the spots representing a diffracted beam. When the spot selected in this way is magnified it forms either the bright field image of the area on which the beam is incident, or one of the dark field images. By placing the aperture in this way the diffuse background of the diffraction pattern is largely excluded and, to a first approximation, attention may be confined only to the spots *. However, even when no account is taken of the inelastically scattered electrons, it is apparent that a diffraction pattern taken at random will contain a large number of diffraction spots and the distribution of electrons in any one of them will be influenced to a greater or lesser degree by the electrons coming from all of the others. That is, the problem is one of elastic scattering in which each scattered beam is coupled to every other.

In practice, it is usually possible to tilt the crystal relative to the incident electron beam to reduce the intensity of the outer spots to a very low level compared with the central spot and those close to it. Indeed, it is often possible to reduce the scope of the pattern to the point where the central beam and only one other neighbouring spot are intense. It is this which is the usual experimental approximation to, and is generally called, the two-beam case. However, even then it will be found that there is always some intensity in the other spots, especially in those contained in the row defined by the two brightest ones, the so-called systematic row. Calculations carried out for a many-beam case (Fisher, to be published) involving only the systematic reflections, show that the first two beams contain about 98% of the total intensity, in the case of crystals containing atoms of small to medium atomic numbers (e.g. aluminium and copper) and about 90% in the case of crystals of large atomic number (e.g. gold). Although it is not strictly valid to equate the amount of intensity in a beam with the information it may contain, on the basis of calculations such as these and the appearance of diffraction patterns which can be obtained by suitable tilts of the crystal, it would seem reasonable

---

* This simplification involves two assumptions: (i) that the overall background outside the aperture has little effect on the information in the beam selected by the aperture and (ii) that the part of the background in the neighbourhood of the spot which is selected by the aperture does not unduly influence the information carried by the beam. The first assumption is difficult to assess, but it can be said that the theory which results, appears to be quite adequate for most purposes. Considering the second assumption it can be shown (see, for example, Kamiya and Uyeda, 1961; Howie, 1963) that the inelastically scattered electrons selected by the aperture, give rise to either a more or less uniform background in the image, or to contrast which is in phase with the information contained in the spot itself. Thus, since we here consider only the topology of an image and not its absolute intensity, no serious error is likely to arise from the second assumption.

that a two-beam approximation is not only the simplest approach which can be made to the problem of the diffraction of electrons by crystals, but a suitable one for many situations.

There have been several attempts to describe mathematically the physical processes which occur on the assumption that only two beams are excited in the crystal. One of the first of these was the kinematical theory (e.g. Hirsch et al., 1960). In this, it is considered that the interaction between the electrons and the crystal is weak, so that only a small number of the incident electrons are scattered into the diffracted beam. Since the number is small, the main beam is considered to have constant intensity as it passes through the crystal, and the probability that the electrons in the diffracted beam will be scattered again either into other directions, or back into the original direction, is neglected. This type of theory has the advantage of relative simplicity and has some application to very thin crystals, or to crystals which are oriented a long way from the exact Bragg reflecting position. However, it has been shown to be a poor approximation for many of the effects observed experimentally, especially in thick crystals and it has been largely replaced by dynamical theories.

In the two-beam dynamical theory, full account is taken of the scattering of electrons from the main beam into the diffracted beam and the subsequent scattering from the diffracted beam back into the main beam. It is the dynamical balance of electrons scattered to and fro between the two beams which gives this type of theory its name. In this book, we will be concerned with two ways of formulating the two-beam dynamical theory, and although they lead to the same (or an equivalent) pair of coupled differential equations, the derivation and interpretation of the parameters which appear in these equations (particularly the extinction distance and absorption parameters) differ. The first way is the wave-optical formulation. In this, the electrons are considered to be waves and they are assumed to be diffracted by the crystal in much the same way as monochromatic light is diffracted by a grating. The wave-optical formulation draws heavily on some aspects of kinematic theory and the absorption of the electron beams is brought into the formulation in a phenomenological way. In the second formulation, the wave-mechanical approach, the electrons are considered to be particles moving in the potential field of the crystal and the appropriate Schrödinger equation for this situation is set up and solved. Since the lattice potential is periodic, it may be expressed as a Fourier series, and on this formulation, absorption is introduced into the theory, again in a phenomenological way, by supposing that the Fourier coefficients of the series are complex. The extinction distance is found to be inversely proportional to the real part of the appropriate Fourier coefficient.

In what follows, it will be seen that from time to time it is convenient to draw upon these alternative formulations and their different interpretation of the parameters, but in the main we will follow the wave-optical approach.

2.3. The two-beam dynamical equations

The theory of electron diffraction on which the micrograph programs are based is the two-beam dynamical theory formulated by Howie and Whelan (1961) for centrosymmetric crystals. This itself follows the form of a two-beam theory for X-rays by Darwin (1914).

Consider an electron beam incident on a crystal which is oriented close to the Bragg diffracting condition for a particular set of planes. As the beam passes through the crystal it will generate a diffracted beam which, in turn, can be re-diffracted back into the incident direction. This dynamic exchange of electrons between the incident and diffracted beams may occur several times if the crystal is sufficiently thick. We will define T and S to be the amplitudes of the electron waves in the directions of the incident and diffracted beams respectively; both T and S are functions of position in the crystal.

The formulation of Howie and Whelan uses a column approximation in which the crystal is visualised as being divided up into parallel, independent columns, with dynamic exchange between T and S within a column, but no exchange of electrons between columns. This approximation is suggested by the particularly small Bragg angles involved in electron diffraction ($\sim\frac{1}{2}°$). On this column approximation, because the exchange of electrons between beams in adjacent columns is neglected, the intensity of an image may be computed point by point (i.e. column by column). The approximation can be applied to distorted crystals, but may become inaccurate in regions where the strains are large (for example, close to a dislocation core). This point will be discussed further in §9.4 where it is concluded that the large strains close to the core of a dislocation do not, in practice, significantly affect the images obtained.

The equations which may be used to describe the two-beam dynamical diffraction of electrons by an isolated column of a crystal are a pair of coupled, first-order differential equations in T and S. One such pair of equations relating to a distorted crystal is:

$$dT/dz = (\pi i/\xi_0)T + (\pi i/\xi_g)S \exp(2\pi isz + 2\pi i g \cdot R),$$

$$dS/dz = (\pi i/\xi_0)S + (\pi i/\xi_g)T \exp(-2\pi isz - 2\pi i g \cdot R),\qquad(2.1)$$

where g is the diffracting vector *; z is in the direction of the incident beam **; R is the displacement field at depth z in the column; s is a parameter which measures the deviation of the crystal orientation from the exact Bragg position; ξ_0 is a parameter which represents the mean refractive index of the crystal; and ξ_g is a parameter, called the extinction distance, which is a measure of the periodic distance in the crystal over which the diffracted beam builds up and dies away.

In order to obtain results from the theory which are in agreement with observation, the quantities $1/\xi_0$ and $1/\xi_g$ in eq. (2.1) have to be replaced by the complex quantities $1/\xi_0 + i/\xi_0'$ and $1/\xi_g + i/\xi_g'$ respectively. We will see later that this substitution can be related to the use of a complex crystal potential. On making the substitution, the equations become:

$$dT/dz = \pi i(1/\xi_0 + i/\xi_0')T + \pi i(1/\xi_g + i/\xi_g')S \exp(2\pi isz + 2\pi i g \cdot R),$$

$$dS/dz = \pi i(1/\xi_0 + i/\xi_0')S + \pi i(1/\xi_g + i/\xi_g')T \exp(-2\pi isz - 2\pi i g \cdot R). \quad (2.2)$$

The occurrence of ξ_0' and ξ_g' in the equations effectively introduces the phenomena of absorption and anomalous absorption (preferential transmission) into the theory. The quantity ξ_0' determines the mean absorption coefficient of the crystal. Although electrons are never physically absorbed, this parameter takes account of the electrons which undergo large angle (inelastic) scattering and which are subsequently rejected by the positioning of the objective aperture around the selected spot. The importance of the parameter ξ_g' and of anomalous absorption will become clear in the following section.

Eqs. (2.1) or (2.2) do not represent a unique description of the theory, and other pairs of coupled differential equations may be obtained for quantities T' and S' which are related to T and S by phase factors which depend on z. For instance, if we make the substitutions $T' = T \exp(-\pi iz/\xi_0)$ and

---

* The diffracting vector g is defined to be normal to the diffracting planes in the direction in which the diffracted beam is displaced from the direct beam. It is a vector of the reciprocal lattice and is normal to the set of planes in the real lattice from which the electrons are being diffracted. From this definition, it follows that the diffracting vector is acute with the electron beam direction B but since the angle between g and B is usually of the order of $89°$, for many purposes this is taken to be $90°$. The magnitude of g is equal to the reciprocal of the spacing d between the diffracting planes, although if the strict crystallographic definition of d is used, the magnitude of g must be written as n/d where n is the order of diffraction in the Bragg equation, $2d \sin \theta_B = n\lambda$.
** In the column approximation, z is identified with the coordinate down the column.

$S' = S \exp(2\pi i sz - \pi iz/\xi_0 + 2\pi i g \cdot R)$ we obtain the equations:

$$dT'/dz = (-\pi/\xi_0')T' + \pi i(1/\xi_g + i/\xi_g')S' ,$$

$$dS'/dz = \pi i(1/\xi_g + i/\xi_g')T' + S'(-\pi/\xi_0' + 2\pi is + 2\pi i \, d(g \cdot R)/dz) . \qquad (2.3)$$

When written in this form, it may be shown (Hirsch et al., 1965, p. 164) that distortions in the crystal give rise to a local rotation of the lattice and thus the deviation parameter is effectively changed from s to $s + d(g \cdot R)/dz$. However, it should be noted that whilst s is considered to be constant down a column, the term $d(g \cdot R)/dz$ is not.

It is convenient to take the unit of length as ξ_g/π, i.e. to change the variable z in the eqs. (2.3) to Z where $Z = z\pi/\xi_g$; when this is done we obtain:

$$dT'/dZ = -(\xi_g/\xi_0')T' + (i - \xi_g/\xi_g')S' ,$$

$$dS'/dZ = (i - \xi_g/\xi_g')T' + (-\xi_g/\xi_0' + 2is\xi_g + 2\pi i \, d(g \cdot R)/dZ)S' . \qquad (2.4)$$

When using these equations, interest is usually centred on the intensity of the electron waves ($|T'|^2$ or $|S'|^2$) rather than their amplitudes, since intensity is what is recorded by a photographic plate. Thus, the phase difference between T and T' and S and S' can be neglected. The product $s\xi_g$ is dimensionless and in the usual formulation of the theory is denoted by w. The dimensionless quotient ξ_g/ξ_0', termed the normal absorption coefficient, will be denoted by $\mathcal{N}$, and the ratio ξ_g/ξ_g', called the anomalous absorption coefficient, will be denoted by $\mathcal{A}$. The derivative of the scalar product of the diffracting vector g with the displacement vector R is usually written as β' and making all these changes, eqs. (2.4) become

$$dT/dZ = -\mathcal{N}T + (i - \mathcal{A})S ,$$

$$dS/dZ = (i - \mathcal{A})T + (-\mathcal{N} + 2iw + 2\pi i\beta')S . \qquad (2.5)$$

This is the formulation of the two-beam dynamical theory, based on a column approximation and including absorption, which has been used in writing the computer programs. In the following sections, we will discuss various aspects of the parameters which enter into eqs. (2.5) and the additional parameters needed to run the programs.

2.4. The absorption parameters

2.4.1. THE NORMAL ABSORPTION COEFFICIENT $\mathcal{H}$

The normal absorption coefficient $\mathcal{H}$ takes into account the general decrease in the number of electrons in a column as a function of depth in the crystal. As indicated earlier, this decrease is almost entirely due to large angle inelastic scattering processes and the subsequent loss to the image of the electrons so scattered, by the positioning of the objective aperture of the microscope. For a crystal of constant thickness, the parameter $\mathcal{H}$ merely acts as a constant scaling factor for the intensities over the whole area of the image. In order to simulate this scaling effect, the theoretical micrographs have their intensities normalised to that intensity which would be obtained from a perfect crystal set in the identical diffracting conditions *. Thus, the details of the computed image of a defect are independent of normal absorption. The value of normal absorption would be needed if it were necessary to compare absolute intensities with experiment.

On the other hand, in order to maintain accuracy and speed when numerically integrating eqs. (2.5), the value of $\mathcal{H}$ has to be chosen with some care. In order to discuss the effect of $\mathcal{H}$ in this context, it is of course necessary to know something about the numerical integration routine which is used. This is discussed in detail elsewhere (§ 10.3.3 and § 10.2.7) but it is sufficient for the present discussion to say that the routine is one in which the integration interval is adjusted at each step so that a fixed error criterion is satisfied. In our programs this error criterion has been chosen so that the final intensities are correct to $\sim 1\%$ for crystals which are about five extinction distances thick.

An idea as to the best choice for $\mathcal{H}$ may be obtained as follows. Suppose the crystal is undistorted, $\beta' = 0$. Then eqs. (2.5) may be solved analytically and the solutions are of the form $T = \exp(\alpha Z)$. If this is substituted in eqs. (2.5), it may be seen that in fact there are two solutions of this form, $\exp(\alpha_1 Z)$ and $\exp(\alpha_2 Z)$ where α_1 and α_2 are the roots of the equation:

$$\alpha^2 + 2\alpha(\mathcal{H} - iw) + \mathcal{H}^2 - 2i\mathcal{H}w - (i - \mathcal{A})^2 = 0 . \qquad (2.6)$$

That is:

$$\alpha_1, \alpha_2 = -\mathcal{H} + iw \pm [(i - \mathcal{A})^2 - w^2]^{\frac{1}{2}} , \qquad (2.7)$$

---

* This intensity is referred to throughout this book as the background intensity. In the computer programs it is obtained by integrating eqs. (2.5) down a column in the crystal far removed from the defect.

or if $\mathscr{A}$ is small compared with unity ($\mathscr{A}$ is usually of the order of 0.1):

$$\alpha_1, \alpha_2 \approx i[w \pm (1 + w^2)^{\frac{1}{2}}] - \mathscr{R} \mp [\mathscr{A}/(1 + w^2)^{\frac{1}{2}}] . \tag{2.8}$$

Thus a general solution may be written:

$$T = C_1 \exp(\alpha_1 Z) + C_2 \exp(\alpha_2 Z) , \tag{2.9}$$

where C_1 and C_2 are constants which are determined by boundary conditions. Explicitly, we have:

$$T = C_1 \exp\{i[w + (1 + w^2)^{\frac{1}{2}}]Z\} \exp\{[-\mathscr{R} - \mathscr{A}/(1 + w^2)^{\frac{1}{2}}]Z\}$$

$$+ C_2 \exp\{i[w - (1 + w^2)^{\frac{1}{2}}]Z\} \exp\{[-\mathscr{R} + \mathscr{A}/(1 + w^2)^{\frac{1}{2}}]Z\} . \tag{2.10}$$

The form of this solution may be better seen if we put $w = 0$ and so obtain:

$$T = C_1 \exp(iZ) \exp[(-\mathscr{R} - \mathscr{A})Z]$$

$$+ C_2 \exp(-iZ) \exp[(-\mathscr{R} + \mathscr{A})Z] . \tag{2.11}$$

For each of the two components in expression (2.11), the factors $\exp(\pm iZ)$ are phase factors but the other exponential factors correspond to a change in magnitude. The general behaviour of T will be oscillatory because of phase differences between the two components and it will have a general change in magnitude because of the other exponential factors. Indeed, if the normal absorption $\mathscr{R}$ is put equal to zero, as we may be tempted to do, since its value is immaterial for the contrast of the micrographs, then the first component of expression (2.11) dies away as $\exp(-\mathscr{A}Z)$, but the second component grows as $\exp(+\mathscr{A}Z)$. In the case of the second component, therefore, the numbers may become so large that the integration routine will take an excessive amount of time to integrate the function to the stated error. On the other hand, if $\mathscr{R}$ is non-zero, the first component dies away as $\exp(-\mathscr{R} - \mathscr{A})Z$ and the numbers may become comparable with the error itself. Inspection of expression (2.11) shows that the best choice for $\mathscr{R}$ is $\mathscr{R} = \mathscr{A}$. In this case the second component remains constant (apart from the oscillatory term) whilst the first component dies away at the slowest convenient rate. For these reasons, therefore, in the programs the value of normal absorption has always been equated with the value for anomalous absorption. There is an added convenience in this choice, in that some of the expressions to be integrated are simpler to evaluate when these two parameters are equal. This convenience offsets to some extent the fact that, for non-zero values of w (see expression (2.10)), the proper choice for $\mathscr{R}$ would appear on the above reasoning to be $\mathscr{R} = \mathscr{A}/(1 + w^2)^{\frac{1}{2}}$. In any case, it is not clear how the situation changes for non-zero values of β' and it is thought that the choice of $\mathscr{R} = \mathscr{A}$ is the simplest and most convenient one which is likely to cover most contingencies.

2.4.2. THE ANOMALOUS ABSORPTION COEFFICIENT $\mathscr{A}$

The details of the contrast of an image are a function (sometimes a sensitive function) of the anomalous absorption coefficient $\mathscr{A}$, and in order to compute theoretical images of a defect which correspond to those observed experimentally, the appropriate value of $\mathscr{A}$ must be used. As it has been introduced here, $\mathscr{A}$ is defined as the ratio of the two-beam extinction distance ξ_g to the two-beam anomalous extinction distance ξ'_g. An equivalent definition obtained from the wave-mechanical formulation may be given using the notion of a complex crystal potential. If the gth order Fourier coefficient of the complex crystal potential is written as $V_g + iV'_g$, where V_g is the Fourier coefficient of the real crystal potential, then the anomalous absorption coefficient may be written as V'_g/V_g (Humphreys and Hirsch, 1968). Since the gth Fourier coefficient may be identified in diffraction theory with the diffracting vector g, it is immediately apparent from this definition that the value of $\mathscr{A}$ depends on the diffracting vector used, as well as the crystal (potential) which is being examined.

As we will see later in §2.6, values of V_g may be obtained directly (e.g. Radi, 1970) or from the values of the atomic scattering amplitudes for electrons f (e.g. Doyle and Turner, 1968). The quantity V'_g is not so readily determined. It arises from the various forms of inelastic scattering of the electrons by the crystal, by far the largest contribution coming from the thermal or phonon scattering process. Single electron excitation makes a significant contribution only at small angles of scattering (Humphreys and Hirsch, 1968), but the effect of plasmon scattering on V'_g is usually negligible (Howie, 1963). It may be seen, therefore, that V'_g is essentially due to a thermal scattering process, and since V_g also has to be corrected for the effects of the thermal vibration of atoms by using the appropriate Debye–Waller factor, it becomes evident that the anomalous absorption coefficient is also a function of temperature.

Both V_g and V'_g have been calculated and listed by Radi (1970) for most monatomic crystals and for some crystals of the rock salt type at three values of temperature and for several values of g. In these calculations, V'_g includes contributions from both phonon and single electron scattering. Humphreys and Hirsch (1968) have published graphs of V'_g/V_g as a function of reciprocal lattice vector for a number of metals at two temperatures. These graphs include only the phonon contribution to V'_g and are reproduced in fig. 3.20.

When evaluating the phonon contribution to V'_g, both Radi, and Humphreys and Hirsch have made use of the formulation of thermal diffuse scattering theory given by Hall and Hirsch (1965) and this takes no account of the possibility that the inelastically scattered electrons may pass through the objective aperture of the microscope and contribute to the image. That is, the theory essentially assumes a zero aperture size. Experimentally, some of these electrons do pass through the objective aperture and they have the effect of increasing the value of V_g' above the calculated value. Thus, although the published calculations of the anomalous absorption parameter may be used as a guide, they should be increased by some factor to account for the use of a non-zero objective aperture (see §3.11, §8.5).

2.5. The deviation of the crystal from the Bragg reflecting position

It will be appreciated from the discussion in §2.3, that the formulation of the two-beam equations allows for the fact that the crystal may not be oriented at the exact Bragg reflecting position. The amount of the deviation from the Bragg condition may be represented by the parameter s (e.g. eqs. (2.1)) or the dimensionless parameter $w = s\xi_g$ (eqs. (2.5)). The parameter w is the one which has been used in the computer programs and its components s and ξ_g are discussed in the sections immediately following this one. However, it may be asked why it is necessary to consider crystals which are deviated at all from the Bragg reflecting condition. This question will now be discussed in terms of the parameter w.

It may be seen from the discussion concerning the optimum value of $\mathcal{H}$ that the solution to eqs. (2.5) for T in the case of $\beta' = 0$ consists of two components (expression (2.10)). The first,

$$C_1 \exp\{i[w + (1+w^2)^{\frac{1}{2}}]Z\} \exp\{[-\mathcal{H} - \mathcal{A}/(1+w^2)^{\frac{1}{2}}]Z\}, \qquad (2.12)$$

diminishes rapidly with Z, but the second,

$$C_2 \exp\{i[w - (1+w^2)^{\frac{1}{2}}]Z\} \exp\{[-\mathcal{H} + \mathcal{A}/(1+w^2)^{\frac{1}{2}}]Z\}, \qquad (2.13)$$

diminishes less rapidly. This second component is much more slowly attenuated than would be expected from the value of the normal absorption coefficient $\mathcal{H}$, and this is due to the term in $\mathcal{A}$. This component is thus anomalously transmitted through the crystal and it is for this reason that the parameter $\mathcal{A}$ is called the anomalous absorption coefficient.

In practice, the usual interest is in thick crystals (large Z) and let us now consider the intensity transmitted by the crystal in the direction of the undeviated beam (i.e. the bright field intensity) as a function of w. The bright field intensity is given by the product TT^* where T^* is the complex conjugate of T. This product can, of course, also be written $|T|^2$. For sufficiently large Z, the first component of T diminishes to a negligibly small value and the only contribution comes from the second term, expression (2.13). In fact, the coefficient C_2 in this expression is also a function of w and for boundary conditions of $T = 1$ and $S = 0$ at $Z = 0$, is given by:

$$C_2 = \frac{i[w(1 + w^2)^{\frac{1}{2}} + 1 + w^2] - \mathcal{A}}{2[\mathcal{A} - i(1 + w^2)]} . \tag{2.14}$$

It is apparent that at large values of $|w|$, the term $\exp\{[-\mathcal{R} + \mathcal{A}/(1 + w^2)^{\frac{1}{2}}]Z\}$ in expression (2.13) is extremely small and it follows that the bright field intensity will also be small. On the other hand, when w is close to zero, the term $C_2 C_2^*$ which appears in the expression for the bright field intensity is the major consideration and it can be shown that if $w \ll 1$, $C_2 C_2^*$ is given by:

$$C_2 C_2^* \approx \frac{\mathcal{A}^4 + 1 + 2w\mathcal{A}^2}{4(\mathcal{A}^2 + 1)^2} , \tag{2.15}$$

and it can be seen that this increases as w increases from zero. Thus transmission is maximised at some positive value of w.

In summary, therefore, for thick crystals in which there is an anomalous absorption (transmission) effect, the second component of the wave amplitude T is particularly well transmitted and the maximum value of this occurs at a positive deviation of the crystal from the exact Bragg condition. It is probably not an overstatement to say that it is this fact which has made electron microscopy of defects a practical proposition, particularly in the case of thinned metal specimens which are invariably thick in the sense in which that word has been used here.

2.5.1. THE DEVIATION VECTOR s_g

The parameter w is a dimensionless measure of the deviation of the crystal from the exact Bragg reflecting position. It is defined as $s\xi_g$. The extinction distance ξ_g will be discussed in the following section, but the vector s_g and the related quantity s are considered here.

The definition of s_g may be obtained by consideration of the diagrams shown in fig. 2.1. These show a section of reciprocal space with reciprocal lattice points at G_{-1}, O, G_1 and G_2. The diffracting vector g is the vector OG_1. The point O has been chosen as origin and the Ewald construction has been applied. In this construction, the centre C of a sphere is chosen such that the magnitude of the radius of the sphere is $1/\lambda$ (where λ is the wave-

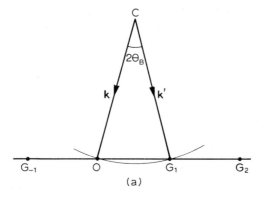

(a)

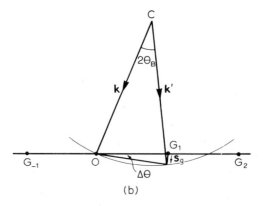

(b)

Fig. 2.1. Portion of reciprocal space illustrating the Ewald construction for a crystal in the exact Bragg diffracting position (a) and for the case where the deviation from the Bragg condition is positive (b).

length of the electrons in the crystal), and the direction CO is in the direction of the incident electrons. The vector **CO** is called the wave vector k of the incident electron wave. The diagrams in fig. 2.1 are not drawn to scale, since CO = $1/\lambda$ = $1/0.037 \approx 27$ Å^{-1} for 100 kV electrons, and OG$_1$ is typically 0.5 Å^{-1}. Thus the section of the Ewald sphere indicated in fig. 2.1 is much flatter than it appears in the diagram.

In defining the deviation of the crystal from the Bragg condition, it is necessary to consider only the relative orientation of the sphere and the reciprocal lattice about an axis through O normal to the plane defined by the centre of the sphere C and the diffracting vector g.

Figure 2.1(a) illustrates the construction for the exact Bragg reflecting case where the sphere not only passes through the origin, but also through the reciprocal lattice point G_1. The wave vector of the diffracted electrons CG_1 is usually represented by k' and this also has a magnitude of $1/\lambda$. The angle subtended at C by the diffracting vector g is twice the Bragg angle θ_B. It may be readily seen from triangle OCG_1, that $\frac{1}{2}|g|/|k| = \sin \theta_B$, or:

$$2d \sin \theta_B = \lambda , \tag{2.16}$$

where $|g| = 1/d$ (see §2.3). Thus the Ewald construction is merely the geometrical representation in reciprocal space of Bragg's law. Since in electron diffraction the Bragg angle θ_B is $\sim\frac{1}{2}^\circ$, it is common to re-state the law as:

$$2d \, \theta_B = \lambda . \tag{2.17}$$

Figure 2.1(b) shows the Ewald sphere construction for the case where the crystal is tilted slightly past the exact Bragg reflecting position. In performing the rotation from the situation depicted in fig. 2.1(a) to that shown in fig. 2.1(b) the angular relation between k and k' has been maintained. The deviation vector s_g associated with the diffracting vector g is defined as the vector drawn from the reciprocal lattice point G_1 to the end of the wave vector k' on the Ewald sphere. It may be seen from the diagram, especially if the true scale of this is recalled, that s_g is very nearly parallel to k and because of this and the way it enters into the theory, s_g is usually replaced by s, its component in the z direction. It is the parameter s which has been used throughout the formulation given here.

It is conventional to take s to be positive if the reciprocal lattice point is inside the sphere, negative if it is outside. The value of s corresponding to the diffracting vector g is positive in fig. 2.1(b) but the values of s corresponding to other diffracting vectors in the systematic row are all negative. Since the extinction distance ξ_g is always positive, the signs of s and w are always the same and this convention for the sign of s is consistent with that used for w in the previous section.

If the tilt of the crystal past the Bragg position is denoted by $\Delta\theta$, then to a very good approximation, since the angles are small, we may write:

$$s = |g| \Delta\theta . \tag{2.18}$$

This relation will be used in §3.9 where the experimental determination of the values of s and w from the relation between the spot diffraction pattern and the Kikuchi line pattern is discussed.

2.6. The extinction distance

The other quantity, besides s, which enters into the evaluation of the dimensionless deviation parameter w is the extinction distance. From the physical description of the dynamical diffraction process, it is apparent that the extinction distance is a basic parameter in the theory. In addition, from the definition of the variable Z used in eqs. (2.5), it follows that all linear dimensions in the programs are normalised to the extinction distance. For a number of reasons, therefore, it is necessary to have an understanding of this parameter.

2.6.1. THE THEORETICAL TWO-BEAM EXTINCTION DISTANCE ξ_g

The extinction distance is usually calculated from theoretical considerations on the assumption that the crystal is made up of non-interacting atoms or ions. If ϕ is the potential of an isolated atom (or ion), the potential of a crystal containing these atoms is considered to be made up by a linear superposition of the individual potentials placed at the lattice points. Since the lattice is periodic, the crystal potential may alternatively be described by an infinite Fourier series whose coefficients are V_g where the subscript g is taken over all reciprocal lattice vectors. If f_t is the Fourier transform of the isolated potential ϕ, it can be shown rigorously that the coefficients V_g are given by

$$V_g = f_t(g) \ . \tag{2.19}$$

It was mentioned earlier that, on the wave-mechanical formulation of the theory, the extinction distance can be described in terms of the appropriate Fourier coefficient V_g, where the subscript may now be identified with the diffracting vector $\boldsymbol{g}$. The explicit expression for ξ_g in terms of V_g is:

$$\xi_g = \frac{(h^2E/2me)^{\frac{1}{2}} \cos\theta_B}{V_g} \ , \tag{2.20}$$

where h is Planck's constant, E is the energy of the incident electrons, θ_B is the Bragg angle, m is the relativistically corrected mass of the electron, and e is its charge. The values of V_g tabulated by Radi (1970) may be substituted in expression (2.20) to obtain values of extinction distance.

The values of V_g which are listed by Radi are discrete values which refer to specific reflections and to specific crystals and, where extinction distances for other cases are needed, it is possible to obtain them using f_t which is a continuous function of the reciprocal lattice vector. Unfortunately, the quantity f_t is not directly listed in tables and reference works. However, the

THE EXTINCTION DISTANCE

values of atomic scattering amplitudes for electrons f are available * and f is related to f_t by:

$$f = Cf_t .$$ (2.21)

The constant C in expression (2.21) is usually chosen so that the form of f is that which would be obtained using the first Born approximation to the scattering of electrons by free atoms. However, it should be emphasised that in this context, f is being used simply to obtain values for the Fourier transform f_t, and the values so obtained are in no way subject to the limitations and assumptions made in the Born approximation. For a monatomic crystal, with one atom per unit cell, the expression for the extinction distance in terms of f is

$$\xi_g = \frac{\pi V_c \cos \theta_B}{\lambda f} ,$$ (2.22)

where V_c is the volume of the unit cell, θ_B is the Bragg angle and λ is the wavelength of the incident electrons.

The atomic scattering amplitude for electrons is a function of the angle of scattering or the diffracting vector g (as indicated by expression (2.19)). However, f is usually tabulated in terms of $(\sin \theta_B)/\lambda$, i.e., $\frac{1}{2}|g|$. The constant C in expression (2.21) includes the mass of the electron and in many tables of f, and in the case of values of V_g listed by Radi, this has been taken to be the rest mass m_0. Since in electron microscopy the incident electrons have energies of the order of 100 kV, their velocities v are an appreciable fraction (≈ 0.55) of the velocity of light c. Thus the values of f or V_g obtained from such tables must be adjusted for the relativistically correct mass of the electron m, by multiplying by the factor $[1 - (v/c)^2]^{-\frac{1}{2}}$.

In cases where f is not listed for the atom or ion of interest, it is possible to obtain a value for it from the atomic scattering amplitude for X-rays, f_x. Once again f_x is linearly related to f_t and the relation between f_x and f is:

$$f = \frac{me^2}{2h^2} \left(\frac{\lambda}{\sin \theta_B}\right)^2 (Z - f_x) ,$$ (2.23)

where Z is the atomic number of the atom and all other quantities are as defined previously.

* See, for example, Hirsch et al. (1965), Appendix 3, p. 489.

In calculating either V_g, f or f_x the potential ϕ of the isolated atom (or ion) has to be estimated and then the assumption is made that this is un-altered when the atoms (or ions) are formed into a crystal. The recent calcu-lations of V_g by Radi and of f and f_x by Doyle and Turner (1968) are based on estimates of ϕ derived from relativistic Hartree–Fock models of the atom which are generally regarded as being reliable. On the other hand, the assump-tion that ϕ has its isolated value when the atom is present in a crystal needs some consideration. In fact, in a crystal, the outer electrons of the atoms are probably quite substantially disturbed from their isolated orbits, but it might be thought that the inner electrons remain almost unaltered. If this is the case, then since the inner electrons are responsible for the deviation of the incident electrons through angles of the order of the Bragg angle, it is to be expected that this assumption will be a good one. Thus it is considered (Doyle, private communication) that for the 111 or 020 diffracting vectors in copper, for example, this approximation introduces only about 5% error into the evaluation of V_g, f or f_x. Values calculated for larger diffracting vectors will be subject to smaller errors.

Values of extinction distance deduced in the ways outlined above are all for crystals at $0°K$. In order to correct the values for the effect of temperature, the values of V_g or f should be multiplied by the Debye–Waller factor. This factor may be written:

$$\exp\left(-M_g\right),\tag{2.24}$$

where

$$M_g = B\left(\frac{\sin\theta_B}{\lambda}\right)^2.\tag{2.25}$$

The thermal Debye parameter B is a constant for a given crystal, and values for several crystals may be found in International Tables for X-ray Crystallo-graphy (1962). The Debye–Waller factor usually results in the reduction of V_g or f (and consequently an increase in ξ_g) by only a few percent, but since it is a function of $[(\sin\theta_B)/\lambda]^2$, it rapidly assumes a greater importance when calculating extinction distances corresponding to large diffracting vectors. It should be pointed out, however, that such cases are not relevant here, since it is very difficult experimentally to set up good two-beam condi-tions for very large diffracting vectors.

If a crystal contains more than one atom per unit cell, or more than one atomic species, the atomic scattering amplitude for electrons f in the expres-sion for the extinction distance (expression (2.22)) must be replaced by $|F_g|$:

$$\xi_g = \frac{\pi V_c \cos\theta_B}{\lambda |F_g|},\tag{2.26}$$

where F_g is the structure factor for the unit cell. A value of F_g may be obtained from the values of f for the atoms in the unit cell using the general relation:

$$F_g = \sum_{j=1}^{N} f_j' \exp[2\pi i(r_j \cdot g)] \, \exp(-M_g)_j \, , \qquad (2.27)$$

where r_j is the position vector of the jth atom in the unit cell, f_j is the atomic scattering amplitude for electrons applying to the jth atom, $(M_g)_j$ is the Debye–Waller factor for the jth atom, and N is the number of atoms in the unit cell.

For centrosymmetric crystals where the origin of position coordinates r_j is taken at a centre of symmetry, this relation reduces to

$$F_g = \sum_{j=1}^{N} f_j \exp(-M_g)_j \cos 2\pi \, (r_j \cdot g) \, . \qquad (2.28)$$

Examples of the use of expressions (2.25), (2.26) and (2.28) to obtain values of ξ_g for alloys are given in §3.8.

2.6.2. THE APPARENT EXTINCTION DISTANCE ξ_{ga}

The discussion in §2.6.1 is based solely on theoretical considerations and at this stage it is necessary to examine the relevance of the theoretically derived values of ξ_g to the experimental case.

Even though every effort is made experimentally to adjust the diffraction conditions so that only two strong beams (the transmitted beam and a single diffracted beam) appear on the diffraction pattern, additional systematic and non-systematic reflections will always make some contribution to the formation of an experimental image. An experimental image, therefore, can only be approximated by the two-beam theory. Since the intensity of the non-systematic beams can be reduced to a very low level, the main experimental deviation from a two-beam condition is usually to be found in the systematic beams. In the cases where images of stacking faults and dislocations formed under n-beam systematic conditions have been investigated, it has been commonly found that the images can be closely approximated by a two-beam theory provided a modified two-beam extinction distance is employed. This modified extinction distance will be referred to as the 'apparent extinction distance' ξ_{ga}. In applying the image matching technique, it has been assumed that the major differences between the experimental (n-beam) image and the two-beam theoretical micrograph can always be accommodated using the apparent extinction distance ξ_{ga}, keeping all other parameters (e.g. $\mathscr{A}$ and s) at their two-beam values. This assumption has two main repercussions: on the absolute evaluation of linear dimensions and on the value of w. Each of these will be considered in turn.

All dimensions in the theoretical images are in units of the extinction distance so that during the visual matching of computed and experimental images, the value of extinction distance is not needed, and the difference between ξ_g and ξ_{ga} is never apparent. Relative values of extinction distance are needed to maintain a constant foil thickness from image to image, but values of ξ_{ga} are only needed when an absolute measurement of some dimension in the defect or its image is required.

The value of ξ_{ga} may be determined using a matching pair of experimental and computed images by comparing the dimension of some feature in the experimental image (for which an absolute measurement can be made knowing the magnification etc.) with the dimension of the same feature in the computed image. This latter length is in units of the apparent extinction distance ξ_{ga}. This technique is demonstrated in ch. 7.

The effect of ξ_{ga} is not taken into account in evaluating w, and the standard expression in terms of the theoretical two-beam extinction distance $w = s\xi_g$ is always used. This has been done because in the cases where values of ξ_{ga} have been determined for experimental two-beam situations, the values obtained are of the order of 15% less than the theoretical values of ξ_g. The corresponding reduction in the value of w is usually within the experimental error in measuring s.

It should be pointed out that since the apparent extinction distance was introduced expressly to accommodate differences between the experimental (n-beam) situation and the theoretical (two-beam) situation, its value can be different for each pair of matching images even if these were taken with the same nominal two-beam diffracting vector. Such variations are usually considered to be small, however, and in most cases the values of ξ_{ga} have been considered to be constant with g. Further, in the general application of the image matching technique, the relative values of ξ_{ga} for different diffracting vectors have been taken to be the same as the relative values of ξ_g. This last assumption is employed in establishing a constant foil thickness for micrographs taken with different diffracting vectors (§3.10).

In summary, therefore, we have found that in the majority of applications, the theoretical two-beam extinction distances ξ_g are adequate and introduce no observable inconsistencies into the image matching process. It is only when absolute length measurements are required that the values of apparent extinction distance ξ_{ga} are needed.

2.7. The displacement vector *R*

The parameters discussed so far in this chapter apply to perfect crystals
and they are assumed to apply also to distorted crystals. Distortion of the
crystal, that is, deviation of the lattice from its perfect regular state, is
introduced into the diffraction theory through the vector displacement
field *R*. Thus, in this section we will not be so much concerned with diffraction theory, but with the geometry of displacements in the crystal due to
various defects. Since the defect of prime interest is the crystal dislocation,
this means that the interest lies in the theory of elasticity as it applies to
crystalline solids.

It may be seen from expression (2.4) that the displacement field enters
into the diffraction equations through the derivative (with respect to the
variable down the column) of its scalar product with the diffracting vector *g*.
Thus, since *g* is very nearly normal to the column (exactly normal in the
column approximation), the electrons as they pass down the column, sample
the component of *R* normal to the column and parallel to *g*. In order that
the column approximation should hold for such a situation, the variation of
$d(g \cdot R)/dZ$ across a column should be small. This is not necessarily always
the case in practice and indeed the variation can be large close to the core of
a dislocation. However, if the column approximation does break down for
this reason, it is not usually important. This is because a typical two-beam
dislocation image is two or three hundred Ångströms wide and since the
detail is spread throughout the image, the overall appearance of the image
is not greatly affected by the small region close to the core. Moreover, because of the characteristics of the integration routine, in writing the computer
programs, care has been taken to keep the columns at a reasonable distance
from the dislocation core (see, for example, § 10.9.2 vii).

The displacement vector *R* which is defined throughout the crystal, may
be a continuous function as in the case of a dislocation, or it may be a discontinuous function, as in the case of a stacking fault. The displacement
associated with a stacking fault occurs by moving one part of the crystal
rigidly with respect to the other across the plane of the fault. In the case of
a fault, the vector which describes the movement is not a translation vector
of the lattice, and thus the potential in which the electrons are moving in one
part of the crystal is out of phase with the potential in the other. It should be
pointed out that the choice of the particular form of the Howie–Whelan
equations (eqs. (2.5)) used in the programs was made on the basis of their
general convenience for numerical evaluation. However, this form of the
equations is not suitable for handling discontinuous displacements of the
above type, since β' becomes infinite. This difficulty is overcome by treating
the problem of a stacking fault as one of an interface between two parts of
an otherwise perfect crystal. This is discussed further in § 2.7.1.

The other type of displacement field we have to consider is a continuous function through the crystal and the main example of this type is, of course, the dislocation displacement field. In dealing with diffraction theory, it will be found in the literature that R is variously defined as being the displacement of a unit cell in a column, or the displacement of atoms from their perfect crystal positions. However, this discrete description is never adhered to when actually calculating R. The displacements are invariably evaluated on a continuum model of the solid, and the definition of R for a dislocation obtained from elasticity theory on such a basis is entirely compatible with the way it is used in diffraction theory.

The displacement field of a dislocation may be calculated using linear isotropic elasticity theory. Until recently, this has been the basis for most interpretations of electron microscope images of dislocations, since, in this case, R may be expressed in an explicit analytic form. This is discussed in §2.7.2(i) where it will be seen that the $g \cdot b$ rules for the invisibility of dislocation images follow quite simply from this expression.

The elastic properties of most crystals are anisotropic, however, and to a good approximation, the displacements due to dislocations in real crystals may be calculated using linear anisotropic elasticity. In the computed micrograph programs, the dislocation displacements are all calculated on this basis. The disadvantage of this approach is that although the functional form of R is known, the various constants which enter into the expression have to be calculated numerically for each specific dislocation. However, this is more than offset by the use of the computed micrograph technique where this better approximation to the displacement field, and hence to the electron diffraction image of a dislocation, is used to the full. Section 2.7.2(ii) deals with the derivation of the displacement field of a dislocation using linear anisotropic elasticity.

2.7.1. THE DISPLACEMENT DUE TO A STACKING FAULT

In order for eqs. (2.5) to take account of a discontinuous displacement function R which occurs in the case of stacking faults, it is necessary to overcome the problem that the term β' in the equations is infinite across the plane of the defect. This may be done by assuming the crystal to be strain-free, as it is everywhere except at the fault, and treating the fault as an interface across which the two parts of the crystal have been translated with respect to each other. The assumption that the crystal is strain-free reduces the term in β' in eqs. (2.5) to zero. To calculate the intensity from a stacking fault, the resulting equations are integrated down to the position of the fault where the current values of the wave amplitudes T and S are adjusted for the presence of the fault, and the integration is then continued. The type of adjustment which has to be made to the wave amplitudes can

be seen from the transformation which was carried out on T and S to obtain
eqs. (2.3) from eqs. (2.2). Whereas the value of T just below the fault is
independent of $\boldsymbol{R}$, the new value of S contains a factor $\exp(2\pi i \boldsymbol{g} \cdot \boldsymbol{R})$. Thus,
across the plane of the defect, T will remain unchanged, but S will become
$S \exp(i\alpha)$ where the phase angle α is given by

$$\alpha = 2\pi \boldsymbol{g} \cdot \boldsymbol{R} \ . \tag{2.29}$$

In this expression, $\boldsymbol{R}$ is the displacement vector of the part of the crystal
which the electrons are about to enter, with respect to the part of the crystal
which they are just leaving.

It can be seen from expression (2.29) that if $\boldsymbol{g} \cdot \boldsymbol{R}$ is an integer, α is an integral multiple of 2π, and the amplitude S as well as T will remain unaltered
across the fault. That is, the fault will be invisible. It will be appreciated that
$\exp(i\alpha)$ is oscillatory and we need only consider values of α in the range
$-\pi < \alpha \leqslant \pi$. The equivalent condition on $\boldsymbol{g} \cdot \boldsymbol{R}$ is that it is to be evaluated
'modulo 1', e.g., $\boldsymbol{g} \cdot \boldsymbol{R}$ is in the range $-\frac{1}{2} < \boldsymbol{g} \cdot \boldsymbol{R} \leqslant \frac{1}{2}$.

So far as diffraction theory is concerned, the vector $\boldsymbol{R}$ may be any displacement vector. However, in practice $\boldsymbol{R}$ must bear some relationship to the crystallography of the lattice. In the case of a stacking fault, $\boldsymbol{R}$ may be a shear
vector in the plane of the defect, as in the case of a fault formed by slip in
the crystal, or it may be a vector normal to the plane, as in the case of a fault
formed by the removal of a plane of atoms in the crystal and the subsequent
closing of the lattice. In the case of face-centred cubic crystals these two ways
of describing the displacement vector give equivalent values for $\boldsymbol{g} \cdot \boldsymbol{R}$, modulo 1.

2.7.2. THE DISPLACEMENT VECTOR *R* FOR A DISLOCATION

In the following sub-sections we consider the displacements caused by a
straight dislocation in an infinite elastic continuum. It will become apparent
that in the case of both isotropic elasticity and anisotropic elasticity, the
displacement vector $\boldsymbol{R}$ is directly dependent on the Burgers vector $\boldsymbol{b}$, and it
is convenient, therefore, to discuss this quantity first.

The Burgers vector is a pseudo vector and depends for its definition on
the sense which is taken for the positive direction of the dislocation line, on
the sense which is taken for a Burgers circuit round the dislocation line, and
on whether the closure failure of the Burgers circuit is taken in good or bad
crystal. This being the case, it is important to state which conventions have
been used in obtaining the value of $\boldsymbol{b}$ used in the definition of $\boldsymbol{R}$.

The convention we have adopted is illustrated for the edge dislocation
depicted schematically in fig. 2.2(a). The arrangement of the lattice is as
shown in the figure and the positive sense of the dislocation line is taken
to be out of the paper. Consider an anti-clockwise circuit in the plane of the

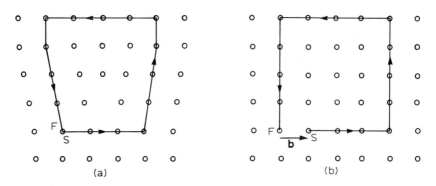

Fig. 2.2. Schematic representation of circuits taken in a simple cubic lattice: (a) around an edge dislocation, and (b) in the perfect crystal, illustrating the FS/RH definition of the Burgers vector. The sense of the dislocation line is out of the paper.

paper which starts at S and goes from lattice point to lattice point around the dislocation line, finishing at F. This circuit is in the sense of a right-handed screw (RH) being screwed along the positive direction of the disloca-tion line. Now consider an undistorted lattice (fig. 2.2(b)) and try to make the same circuit from lattice point to lattice point in this. It will be found that the circuit does not close. The Burgers vector of the dislocation is defined as the vector necessary to close the circuit, that is the vector joining F to S (FS). The convention on which the Burgers vector has been defined here is referred to as FS/RH where the closure failure is specified in good crystal. This is the convention which has been used to define the Burgers vector throughout this book.

   In obtaining the displacements due to a dislocation, the crystal is assumed to be an infinite continuum. Linear elasticity theory is used throughout, that is, it is assumed that Hooke's law is obeyed everywhere and, where the displacements due to several dislocations are required, they may be obtained from the simple vector sum of the displacements due to each individual dislocation. The linear theory is expected to break down close to the dislocation core, but for the reasons stated earlier in this section, this is not expected to produce a marked effect on the images of dislocations.

   The following sub-sections deal mainly with the derivation of R and there are two important points to be borne in mind when these expressions are used to compute the contrast from dislocations. First, it should be remem-bered that the quantity needed for the differential equations (2.5) is β', which is given by:

$$\beta' = \frac{d(\mathbf{g} \cdot \mathbf{R})}{dZ} , \tag{2.30}$$

and the effect of β' has to be integrated down each column of the crystal to obtain an intensity value. Although it may be possible to analyse the effects of the various parameters on R and hence on β', it is not until the eqs. (2.5) have been integrated through the crystal that it is possible to say what effect these parameters have on the intensity of the image. Except in the special case of $\beta' = 0$, eqs. (2.5) cannot be integrated analytically and so, in general, the effects of the parameters may only be assessed by the numerical computation of specific cases. In the special case of $\beta' = 0$, which for a dislocation invariably implies that $g \cdot R = 0$, the intensity obtained is simply that which would be obtained from a perfect crystal under the same diffracting conditions. In short, therefore, except in the case $\beta' = 0$, even though the variation in R may be well-known and understood, it is impossible to predict the resulting variation in image intensity.

The second point concerns the assumption that the medium in which the dislocation lies is infinite. When expressions for R obtained on this basis are used to compute the contrast from dislocations in thin foils, the assumption is implicitly made that the foil has been cut out of the infinite solid and tractions have been applied to the newly formed surfaces to retain the state of strain. In reality, of course, the surfaces of the foil are free and there are no tractions acting on them. The derivation of the displacement field of a general dislocation lying in an arbitrary direction in a finite medium with two free surfaces is extremely difficult and can only be done in rather special cases. However, empirically, the value of R relevant to an infinite medium appears to be a reasonable one for all the cases which have been computed so far.

(i) *Displacement vector R for a dislocation in an elastically isotropic crystal*

In isotropic elasticity and for an infinite medium, it can be shown that a screw dislocation has displacements only in directions parallel to the line of the dislocation and an edge dislocation produces displacements only in the plane normal to the line of the dislocation. Because linear elasticity is being used, the general displacement R for a dislocation of mixed character, may be obtained by a linear combination of these two results. The expression for R in terms of cylindrical polar coordinates (η along the dislocation line, r at right angles to the line, and the angle θ, measured from the slip plane in the sense of a right-handed screw pointing along η) is:

$$R = \tfrac{1}{2\pi} \left[b\theta + b_{\mathrm{e}}(\sin 2\theta/4(1-\nu)) \right.$$

$$\left. + b \wedge u\{((1-2\nu)/2(1-\nu)) \ln r + (\cos 2\theta)/4(1-\nu)\} \right] , \qquad (2.31)$$

where b is the Burgers vector, b_e is the edge component of the Burgers vector, ν is Poisson's ratio, and u is a unit vector along the dislocation line * (i.e. along $+\eta$). Other expressions for R may be found in the literature, but on investigation it will be found that these differ from eq. (2.31) only by a constant which corresponds to a rigid body motion. In the present context, therefore, these expressions are equivalent to eq. (2.31) since for β' we require the derivative of the displacement.

It can be seen from expressions (2.30) and (2.31) that, in general, β' will depend upon the products $g \cdot b$, $g \cdot b_e$ and $g \cdot b \wedge u$. This dependence has been fully exploited in deducing the invisibility rules for screw and edge dislocations in isotropic media. In these special cases $g \cdot b$, $g \cdot b_e$ and $g \cdot b \wedge u$ (and hence β') are zero. In cases other than pure edge or pure screw dislocations at least one of the factors $g \cdot b$, $g \cdot b_e$ and $g \cdot b \wedge u$ will be non-zero and it is not possible to predict what the image of a dislocation will look like.

Because of their widespread use, let us consider for a moment the invisibility rules and what they imply about the physical diffraction situation.

In the case of a screw dislocation, the component b_e and the product $b \wedge u$ are, of course, always identically zero. If a diffracting vector g is chosen such that it is at right angles to the Burgers vector, then $g \cdot b = 0$, $R = 0$ and $\beta' = 0$ and the dislocation will be invisible. That is to say its image will be indistinguishable from the background intensity transmitted by the rest of the (perfect) crystal. A physical interpretation of how this invisibility arises may be obtained in the following way. Since g is normal to the diffracting planes, and b for a screw dislocation is along its line, it follows that the set of planes which are diffracting the electrons are parallel to the direction of the dislocation line. If it is now remembered that a screw dislocation produces displacements only parallel to its line direction, and none in other directions, it is readily seen that any plane containing the dislocation line direction remains flat. In particular, therefore, for a screw dislocation when the criterion $g \cdot b = 0$ holds, the diffracting planes are flat and their perfect crystal spacing is maintained so that it is as if the diffraction were taking place in perfect crystal.

For an edge dislocation ($b_e \equiv b$), the product $b \wedge u$ is never zero and in order for the dislocation to be invisible (i.e. $\beta' = 0$) both $g \cdot b$ and $g \cdot b \wedge u$ have to be zero. These conditions may be fulfilled by choosing a diffracting vector g which is along the line of the dislocation. Here again a little thought will show that in this case also, invisibility occurs because the planes which are diffracting the electrons remain flat even in the presence of the dislocation. If, for an edge dislocation, $g \cdot b = 0$, but $g \cdot b \wedge u \neq 0$, the diffracting planes are

---

* Here u is a *unit* vector. However, throughout this book, unless specifically noted otherwise, u is taken to be any vector in the direction of the dislocation line.

not flat and the dislocation will exhibit some contrast. In the special case of edge dislocations for which only $g \cdot b = 0$, it has been suggested that these will be effectively invisible if the factor m ($\equiv \frac{1}{8} g \cdot b \wedge u$) is $\lesssim 0.08$ (Hirsch et al., 1965, p. 178). However, this suggestion seems to be based on a calculation for an edge dislocation situated in the centre of a foil parallel to the foil surface, in which the effect of the foil surfaces on the displacement function was simulated by the inclusion of one image dislocation in each surface (Howie and Whelan, 1962). It is not clear how generally applicable this specific calculation may be.

If a dislocation is neither pure screw nor pure edge, but is of mixed character, it will be appreciated from the foregoing discussion that it produces displacements in all directions in the crystal. Thus, in general, no planes will remain flat and it will be impossible to find a diffracting vector which will make $\beta' = 0$. It follows that a dislocation of mixed character will always have an image which shows some contrast compared with background, and moreover, since $\beta' \neq 0$, the amount of contrast can only be determined by numerical integration.

(ii) Displacement vector R for a dislocation in an elastically anisotropic crystal

The advantage of the isotropic elasticity description of R has been mainly in its application to the two special cases in which invisibility of the image occurs. As we have seen, in all other cases the amount of contrast can only be decided by numerical computation. In anisotropic elasticity, in general, no planes in the crystal remain flat * (even for pure screw and pure edge dislocations) and so the images in this case always have to be computed. There is an additional complication in anisotropic elasticity in that it is not possible to write down an explicit expression for R and this also has to be computed numerically.

Before considering the derivation of R for an elastically anisotropic solid, it should be noted that what is set out here is only meant as a guide to understanding the micrograph program and is not in any sense a rigorous or complete treatment of the subject. The reader is referred to original papers by Eshelby et al. (1953) and Stroh (1958) and to books by Nye (1960) (chs. 1, 2, 5, 8 and 9) and by Hirth and Lothe (1968) (chs. 2 and 13) for a broader understanding of the subject.

The derivation of the displacements given here is based on the method of Eshelby, Read and Shockley. However, the notation of Stroh has been used,

---

* There are some exceptions to this and these are mentioned later in this section (see also § 8.2).

although it has been extended somewhat and the methods of calculation he suggested have been modified to suit evaluation using a digital computer (subroutine ANCALC, §10.3.1).

Consider a set of cartesian axes * Ox_1, Ox_2 and Ox_3. Let the stress acting in the ith direction on the plane normal to the jth axis be denoted by σ_{ij} where i and j take the values 1, 2 and 3. The most general linear (Hookian) relation between the stresses σ_{ij} and the strains e_{ij} may be written in terms of the fourth rank tensor c_{ijkl}:

$$\sigma_{ij} = c_{ijkl} e_{kl} , \tag{2.32}$$

where i, j, k and l all take values from 1 to 3 and the convention has been assumed that a summation over repeated ('dummy') subscripts is carried out. For example, the expression for σ_{11} would be written explicitly as:

$$\sigma_{11} = c_{1111} e_{11} + c_{1112} e_{12} + c_{1113} e_{13}$$
$$+ c_{1121} e_{21} + c_{1122} e_{22} + c_{1123} e_{23}$$
$$+ c_{1131} e_{31} + c_{1132} e_{32} + c_{1133} e_{33} . \tag{2.33}$$

It can be shown that the 81 elastic constants c_{ijkl} are not all independent, since the conservation of energy requires that:

$$c_{ijkl} = c_{jikl} = c_{ijlk} = c_{klij} . \tag{2.34}$$

Thus in a general elastically anisotropic solid there are 21 independent elastic constants, but in a crystalline solid, the effects of crystal symmetry can reduce this number still further. For example, for an elastically aniso-tropic crystal of cubic symmetry there are only 3 independent constants. In addition, only the ratios of elastic constants appear in the expressions for the displacement fields of dislocations. Thus there are only two independent ratios for cubic crystals **.

---

* Throughout this book, a 'set of cartesian axes' implies an axis system composed of a right-handed set of orthogonal equal unit vectors.

** For an elastically isotropic solid, there are only two independent constants giving a single ratio. This ratio, Poisson's ratio, is given by $\nu = c_{1111}/(c_{1111} + c_{1122})$ where c_{1111} and c_{1122} are the two elastic constants for the isotropic case.

The components of strain e_{kl} are defined as the partial derivatives of the displacements u_i: *

$$e_{kl} = \tfrac{1}{2}\{(\partial u_k/\partial x_l) + (\partial u_l/\partial x_k)\} .$$ (2.35)

Using the symmetry relations between the elastic constants, eq. (2.34), the stresses may be written in terms of the displacements:

$$\sigma_{ij} = c_{ijkl}(\partial u_k/\partial x_l) .$$ (2.36)

If there are no body forces acting, then the equations which must be satisfied for mechanical equilibrium are:

$$c_{ijkl}(\partial^2 u_k/\partial x_j \partial x_l) = 0 .$$ (2.37)

Now consider the situation when the axis Ox_3 is taken to be along the dislocation line. Since we are considering an infinite medium, this choice means that the elastic state is independent of x_3 and we may look for solutions for the displacement u_k to expression (2.37) of the form:

$$u_k = A_k f(x_1 + p x_2) ,$$ (2.38)

where A_k are the components of some vector, f is some function (at the moment, arbitrary) and p is some constant. The problem is to find the function f which satisfies the form required for the displacements around a crystal dislocation and to determine A_k and p in terms of the Burgers vector of the dislocation (components b_k) and the elastic constants of the crystal c_{ijkl}.

Substituting expression (2.38) in the equilibrium eqs. (2.37) we have

$$(c_{i1k1} + c_{i1k2}p + c_{i2k1}p + c_{i2k2}p^2)A_k = 0 .$$ (2.39)

Remembering that the summation convention over k applies, eq. (2.39) is a set of three linear equations in A_k. These have a solution (in which A_k are not all zero) only if p is such that the determinant of their coefficients is zero, i.e. if

$$|c_{i1k1} + c_{i1k2}p + c_{i2k1}p + c_{i2k2}p^2| = 0 .$$ (2.40)

---

* The displacements u_i are the components of the vector displacement R and should not be confused with the vector along the dislocation line u.

This relation is a sextic in p and its six roots provide six values of p for which eq. (2.39) has a non-zero solution for A_k.

In general, the roots of eq. (2.40) can only be determined numerically and so it is not possible to write down an explicit analytic expression for u_k. Eshelby, Read and Shockley showed that eq. (2.40) has no real roots and that the roots occur in conjugate pairs. If one root of each pair is denoted by p_α ($\alpha = 1$, 2 or 3) then the other root of each pair, its complex conjugate, is denoted $\overline{p_\alpha}$. The corresponding notation for the values of A_k obtained by substituting these roots in eq. (2.39) is $A_{k\alpha}$ and $\overline{A_{k\alpha}}$.

Eshelby, Read and Shockley showed further that, for a dislocation in an infinite medium, the function f is in fact the logarithmic function and that the general solution for u_k may be written as a sum over α:

$$u_k = \frac{1}{2\pi i} \sum_\alpha A_{k\alpha} D_\alpha \ln(x_1 + p_\alpha x_2) - \frac{1}{2\pi i} \sum_\alpha \overline{A_{k\alpha} D_\alpha} \ln(x_1 + \overline{p_\alpha} x_2) , \tag{2.41}$$

where D_α are constants which depend on the elastic constants.

As this point, the axis system must be defined more specifically. If the axis Ox_2 is chosen to be in the plane containing the electron beam direction and the dislocation line (the Ox_3 axis), then the derivative of the displacements necessary for the Howie–Whelan equations (2.5) is directly proportional to the derivative of u_k with respect to x_2. If this derivative is taken, and both of the resulting terms (corresponding to the two terms on the right-hand side of expression (2.41)) are combined and multiplied by the diffracting vector, components g_k, it can be shown that

$$\beta' = \frac{d(\boldsymbol{g} \cdot \boldsymbol{R})}{dZ} \propto \frac{\partial(g_k u_k)}{\partial x_2} = \sum_\alpha \frac{P_\alpha x_1 + Q_\alpha x_2}{(x_1 + R_\alpha x_2)^2 + (S_\alpha x_2)^2} , \tag{2.42}$$

where P_α, Q_α, R_α and S_α are constants depending upon the elastic constants and the Burgers vector. The exact expression for β' is given in § 10.3.1, eq. (10.21).

Thus, although the functional form of β' is known and is given by eq. (2.42), the evaluation of the constants P_α, Q_α, R_α and S_α has to be carried out numerically. This is a direct consequence of the occurrence of the sextic equation (2.40). However, there are cases in which a certain amount of analytical manipulation is possible. For example, if the dislocation (i.e. axis Ox_3) lies along any 2-, 3-, 4-, or 6-fold rotation axis of the crystal, or is normal to an even-fold rotation axis, the roots of eq. (2.40) can be found analytically (Teutonico, 1968). Further, if the dislocation is parallel to an even-fold axis in the crystal, or is normal to a plane of mirror symmetry, not only can the

roots of eq. (2.40) be found analytically but the solution for the screw component in eq. (2.39) (A_3) is separable from the solutions for the edge component $(A_1$ and $A_2)$ (Teutonico, 1968; Eshelby et al., 1953). This is the result
which held for the isotropic case and it may be seen that the isotropic result
is a degenerate case of the anisotropic one since, in isotropic elasticity, any
plane in the crystal is a symmetry plane in the sense used here. It follows that,
in anisotropic elasticity, if the dislocation lies normal to a plane of mirror
symmetry in the crystal and if it is in pure screw or pure edge orientation, the
rules for invisibility derived in the previous section will apply. However, in the
general case where Ox_3 is not normal to a symmetry plane, the edge and screw
components of the displacement are not separable even if the dislocation is
in pure screw or pure edge orientation. In other words, in the general case, no
plane in the crystal remains flat, and it is impossible to diffract the electrons
from any set of planes without obtaining some contrast.

At two places in the above outline, directions were specified for the coordinate axes. The choices were: (i) Ox_3 along the dislocation line and (ii) Ox_2
in the plane containing the electron beam direction and the dislocation line.
Of course, the elastic constants c_{ijkl} in the above expressions refer to this
particular set of axes. The elastic constants which are given in reference tables
etc. and which are used as data in the programs refer to axes taken in a specified way in the crystal lattice. Thus for the evaluation of β' in the above
analysis it is necessary to know the orientation of Ox_2 and Ox_3 with respect
to these crystal axes. That is, it is essential to know the dislocation line direction u and the electron beam direction B in crystal axes. Neither of these
was specifically required to determine β' in isotropic elasticity. In the following chapter it will be shown how u and B may be determined in practice.

The elastic constants are needed to determine β' and their values must
be specified as data before the program can be run. As they appear in the
theory here, the elastic constants have a four suffix notation. Although this
is convenient for many of the mathematical operations which have to be
performed, for many other purposes a two suffix notation has advantages.
If the elastic constants on the two suffix notation are denoted by c_{mn}, they
are related to c_{ijkl} by the transformation $ij \rightarrow m$ and $kl \rightarrow n$ in the following
manner: $11 \rightarrow 1$, $22 \rightarrow 2$, $33 \rightarrow 3$, 23 or $32 \rightarrow 4$, 31 or $13 \rightarrow 5$ and 12 or $21 \rightarrow 6$.
Thus there are 36 components of the matrix c_{mn} but because of the sym-
metry relations of eq. (2.34) only 21 are independent and the matrix is symmetrical about the leading diagonal.

The two suffix notation is the one which is used when listing experimental
values in reference tables, e.g. Huntington (1958). Elastic constants are always
measured relative to a set of cartesian axes irrespective of the symmetry of
the crystal concerned. When looking up values of c_{mn} for inclusion in the data
to run the micrograph programs, care should be taken to establish the orienta-

tion of this set of axes with respect to the crystal axes. In cubic crystals, the three independent constants c_{11}, c_{12} and c_{44} are measured relative to the obvious axes, i.e. $Ox_1 /\!/ Ox$, $Ox_2 /\!/ Oy$ and $Ox_3 /\!/ Oz$. However, in hexagonal crystals, the five independent constants $c_{11}, c_{12}, c_{13}, c_{33}$ and c_{44} are referred to axes: $Ox_3 /\!/ Oz$, $Ox_1 /\!/ Ox$. The reader is referred to Appendix B, p. 282 in the book by Nye (1960) for the choice of axes in other crystal systems.

2.8. The foil normal F

A parameter which does not appear explicitly either in the diffraction theory or in the elasticity theory, but which is required in the micrograph program is the direction of the normal to the surface of the foil specimen F. Its importance arises because of the necessity to tilt a specimen in the electron microscope in order to determine the geometry of the defect and to obtain different diffracting vectors as will be seen in the following chapter. In the past, there has been a tendency to identify the foil normal F with the beam direction B but with tilt angles of up to $45°$ available with modern tilting devices, this is usually not a sufficiently good approximation.

The non-coincidence of F and B affects the image of a dislocation in two ways. The first is simply a geometric one concerning the increased thickness of foil presented to the electron beam. If the foil is tilted at an angle to the beam direction so that F and B make an angle δ to each other, then the thickness of specimen which the electrons have to penetrate is $t/\cos\delta$ where t is the thickness of the foil measured normal to its surface. In the micrograph program, the relevant quantities supplied as data are t, F and B and the integration is carried out for the computed thickness $t/\cos\delta$.

The second effect due to the non-coincidence of the foil normal with the beam direction concerns the 'distortion' of the image compared with what would be obtained if F and B were taken as being identical. The image is 'skewed' or 'sheared' about its centre line if F is at an angle to the plane containing B and u or it is changed in width when F, B and u are all in the same plane. Since the technique being presented here is one of identification by a visual matching process, effects such as these are important. Consequently, the programs take due account of the difference between F and B and produce the appropriate images.

3 | EXPERIMENTAL TECHNIQUES

3.1. Introduction

Before any images of a defect can be computed, it is necessary to determine the input data for the programs. In this chapter, the experimental methods used to determine this input data will be described.

In order to obtain the data, micrographs and their corresponding diffraction patterns should be collected in such a way that the crystallography of the defect and of the foil, as well as the diffraction conditions for each micrograph, can be specified as completely as possible. The procedure for obtaining this experimental information involves taking, for the same defect, a series of electron micrographs and corresponding selected area diffraction patterns for a number of different beam directions and diffracting conditions. This is done in the electron microscope by tilting the crystal relative to the electron beam and a method for recording the information in a systematic way is outlined in §3.3. The manner in which this experimental information is used to obtain the data necessary for the programs is described in §§3.4–3.11. In particular:

§3.4 describes the way in which specific indices can be assigned to the operative diffracting vector g for each micrograph;

§3.5 gives a method for determining the beam direction B for each micrograph;

§3.6 outlines a method for determining crystallographic directions characteristic of the defect, such as the line direction u;

§3.7 discusses methods for the determination of the foil normal F;

§3.8 describes methods for obtaining values of theoretical two-beam extinction distances;

§3.9 outlines the method of obtaining a value of the deviation from the Bragg condition w and

§3.10 discusses some methods for the determination of foil thickness t.

In addition, it is necessary to have values of the anomalous absorption co-efficient $\mathscr{A}$ for the particular crystal and diffracting vector. Methods of obtaining values of $\mathscr{A}$ are given in §3.11.

Some of the methods described in this chapter involve well-known techniques, but they are presented here so that a complete procedure is described for obtaining the data needed for image computation. However, it will be assumed that the reader is able to recognise and index low order cross-grating (spot) diffraction patterns and is familiar with the use of stereographic projections. Both of these topics are well documented in several texts (e.g. Andrews et al., 1967) but it should be noted that in some texts cross-grating patterns are not always indexed consistently and in some cases a mixture of left and right-handed axis systems has been used. Throughout this book right-handed axes are used for indexing patterns and the beam direction B is defined to be the upward drawn normal to the diffraction pattern as viewed on the fluorescent screen of the microscope (see §2.2).

Before the experimental information can be analysed, it is necessary to know the relative rotation between the image and the diffraction pattern which occurs as a result of the image forming process in an electron microscope. This rotation must be determined, if it is not already known, and for this reason, before any of the methods listed above are discussed, a procedure for determining such rotations will be described.

3.2. Image-diffraction pattern rotation

Image forming processes using electromagnetic lenses not only involve the usual inversions due to the crossing of ray paths, common to optical lens systems, but in addition rotations of ray paths due to the magnetic fields of the various lenses (electromagnetic rotations). The effect of all optical inversions and electromagnetic rotations must be determined before any quantitative crystallographic information, requiring the relation between an image and its corresponding diffraction pattern, can be obtained. Of course, it will be realised that such a calibration need only be done once for a particular microscope for the operating conditions selected. The operating conditions ﹏ust be such that true selected area diffraction patterns are obtained and throughout this book the discussion assumes that all diffraction patterns are of this type *.

---

* True selected area diffraction is obtained when the lens settings are such that the inter-mediate image (see fig. 3.1) is formed in the plane of the selector aperture. For details see Hirsch et al. (1965) p. 5 and pp. 18–23.

In view of the fact that rotations have to be taken into account, a consistent method of handling plates and positive prints must be adopted. Obviously, the orientation of plates in the microscope must be known and in the examples described in this chapter the orientation of a photographic plate, as viewed in the microscope, is represented by arranging the print squarely on the page with an arrowhead in its top right-hand corner (see fig. 3.2(a)). When relating images and their corresponding diffraction patterns, we will consider that plates are always viewed emulsion side up. Further, for all positive prints, plates have been printed with the emulsion side up so that the prints correspond directly to images as they are observed on the fluorescent screen of the microscope.

Rotations vary, not only with the lens current settings in one microscope, but from one microscope to another. To illustrate this, examples of the determination of such rotations will be given for two microscopes in common use: the Siemens Elmiskop 1A and the Philips EM200 set for selected area diffraction at a magnification of approximately 20,000 times, both microscopes operating at 100 kV *.

The objective lens of an electron microscope forms a diffraction pattern of the specimen at its back focal plane and an image of the specimen in a different plane (the intermediate image plane), as shown schematically in fig. 3.1. The diffraction pattern and intermediate image are subsequently magnified and projected onto the fluorescent screen by differing electron-optical systems, so that there will be a relative rotation ϕ between the final diffraction pattern and the final image.

The usual method of determining the angle ϕ is to use a small vapour deposited crystal of molybdenum trioxide. Such crystals are long laths with their long dimension parallel to the [100] direction. Therefore, if an image of, and a diffraction pattern from, a crystal of MoO_3 are recorded on the same plate, a determination of the angle ϕ can be made by measuring the angle between the long edge of the image of the crystal and the [100] direction in the diffraction pattern **. This experiment, whilst accurate in one sense (the angle can usually be measured to $\pm 1°$) involves an uncertainty of $180°$ in ϕ, since $\pm[100]$ directions in the image cannot be distinguished.

To eliminate this uncertainty of $180°$, it is necessary to consider the formation of diffraction patterns and images in more detail. The diffracting vector g in the specimen is shown in the upper part of fig. 3.1 and defined to be the normal to the reflecting planes of the specimen and acute with the beam

---

* Of course, the particular angles of rotation determined here for the two microscopes will only apply to the lens current settings we have used.
** In the MoO_3 diffraction pattern the [100] direction corresponds to the larger spacing of the rectangular cross-grating pattern.

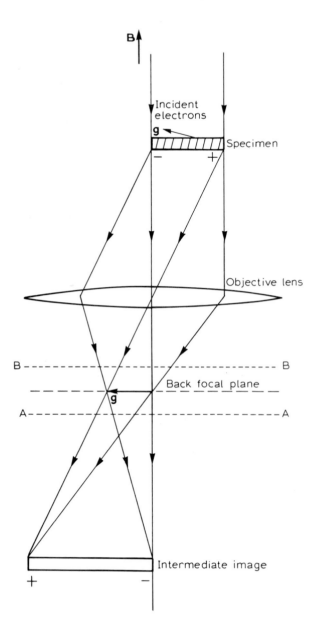

Fig. 3.1. Schematic ray diagram illustrating the formation of a diffraction pattern and an intermediate image by the objective lens of an electron microscope.

direction B (§2.3). This vector is represented in the diffraction pattern in the way shown in the lower part of fig. 3.1 as the displacement of the diffracted beam from the transmitted beam. It can be seen from fig. 3.1 that an objective lens always produces an optical inversion between the specimen and the intermediate image, i.e. directions in the intermediate image are always rotated relative to directions in the specimen by 180°. However, it can be seen that the diffracting vector g in the specimen, is not inverted in the diffraction pattern. Therefore, directions in the intermediate image are inverted with respect to corresponding directions in the diffraction pattern, and this inversion occurs at the back focal plane. If an image of the specimen can be formed on the fluorescent screen from a region such as BB in fig. 3.1, then this image will not be inverted with respect to the diffraction pattern. Imaging a region such as BB produces an out-of-focus diffraction pattern which consists of enlarged diffraction spots, each spot containing an out-of-focus image of the specimen *. Clearly such out-of-focus images will be in their correct orientation with respect to the diffraction pattern apart from a very small rotation introduced by focussing BB rather than the back focal plane. Since the final image is obtained by focussing the intermediate image onto the fluorescent screen, it will be in a different orientation relative to the images in the out-of-focus diffraction pattern. If the final image is rotated so that it is in the same orientation as the images in the out-of-focus diffraction pattern, then the final image will be approximately in its correct relative orientation (i.e. approximately at the angle ϕ) with respect to the diffraction pattern and so the uncertainty of 180° from the MoO_3 experiment is eliminated.

The whole calibration procedure will now be illustrated for the Siemens and Philips microscopes.

Figure 3.2(a) shows for a Siemens microscope an image of the edge of a metal foil enclosed by the diffraction aperture and a defocussed diffraction pattern from a region such as BB (fig. 3.1). Here the image and diffraction pattern are arranged as recorded in the microscope. In fig. 3.2(b) the image has been rotated so that it is in the same orientation as the out-of-focus image in the defocussed diffraction pattern. This involves rotating the image anticlockwise with respect to the diffraction pattern through an angle ϕ which is approximately equal to 206° (i.e. 180° + 26°). Figure 3.2(c) shows the image of, and the diffraction pattern from, a crystal of MoO_3 and the angle between the long edge of the image of the crystal and the direction of

---

* By decreasing the current in the intermediate lens relative to the setting corresponding to a focussed diffraction pattern, region BB can be imaged, whereas by increasing the current, region AA would be imaged.

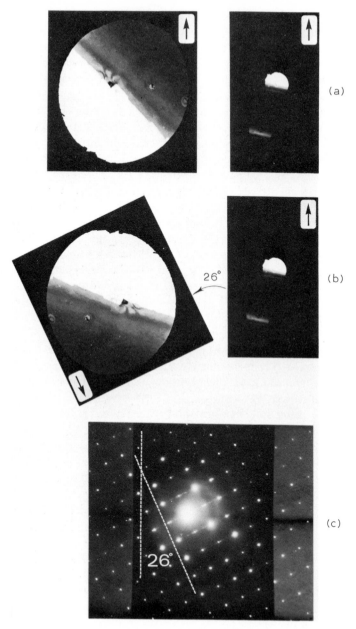

Fig. 3.2. An illustration of the use of a defocussed diffraction pattern and the image and diffraction pattern from a crystal of MoO_3 to determine the correct orientation between the image and the diffraction pattern for the Siemens microscope. The image and defocussed diffraction pattern are arranged as recorded (a), and in their approximately correct orientation (b). In (c) the correct acute angle for setting the image and diffraction pattern is determined.

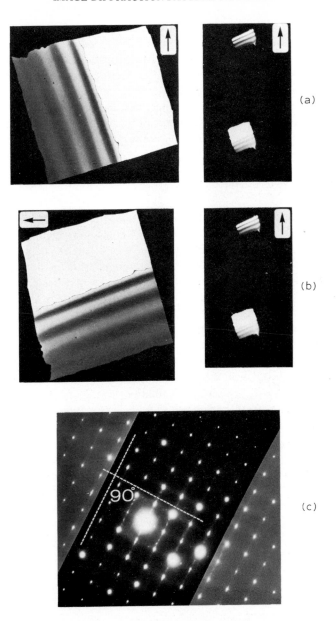

Fig. 3.3. An illustration of the use of a defocussed diffraction pattern and the image and diffraction pattern from a crystal of MoO_3 to determine the correct orientation between the image and the diffraction pattern for the Philips microscope. The image and defocussed diffraction pattern are arranged as recorded (a), and in their approximately correct orientation (b). In (c) the correct angle for setting the image and diffraction pattern is determined.

the larger spacing in the diffraction pattern has been measured as $26° ± 1°$. Therefore, the angle ϕ for the Siemens microscope is $206° ± 1°$.

In fig. 3.3 exactly the same procedure has been adopted for the Philips microscope where it is found that the image needs to be rotated anticlockwise with respect to the diffraction pattern by an angle $\phi = 90° ± 1°$.

Once the calibration described and illustrated in this section has been done for a particular microscope and operating conditions, the relation between images and diffraction patterns is known for future use.

3.3. Crystal tilting technique

When the electron microscope is used in conjunction with image computation to analyse defects in crystals, a systematic procedure which allows the necessary data to be determined should be followed. This procedure involves the recording of a set of images and their corresponding diffraction patterns for a series of different diffracting vectors in a number of different beam directions. To carry out this procedure it is necessary to be able to tilt the crystal about two orthogonal axes and to recognise the cross-grating and Kikuchi line patterns associated with low index crystallographic directions for the material under consideration.

For tilting experiments in the electron microscope, a specimen stage capable of large angles of tilt about two orthogonal axes, with a minimum of $±20°$ about each axis, is essential. In addition, an efficient anticontamination system is a considerable advantage as, with such a system, image quality may be maintained for a sufficient time to allow the setting up and recording of an adequate series of diffraction patterns and associated images.

The required crystal tilting technique may be described most simply with reference to a chosen set of cross-grating patterns for a particular crystal structure and as a simple example the face-centred cubic structure will be used. Figure 3.4(a) shows the relationship between the cross-grating patterns of prominent low index directions in the two neighbouring stereographic triangles [001], [011], [111] and [001], [101], [111]. As will be seen later, in order to specifically index each diffraction pattern, it is necesary to consider the spatial arrangement of the beam directions used. These two triangles have been chosen because for a cubic crystal they specify a minimal area of a standard stereographic projection which contains all possible non-equivalent beam directions. However, for other crystal systems, larger areas of the corresponding stereographic projections of crystal directions would be required.

When commencing a series of tilting experiments, a recognisable cross-grating pattern may not be visible, but on random tilting a low order reflection and its associated pair of Kikuchi lines will be readily found. By controlled

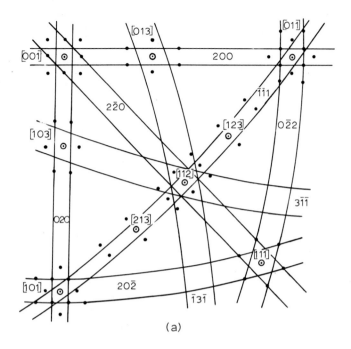

(a)

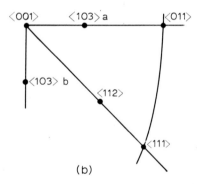

(b)

Fig. 3.4. (a) Kikuchi line map showing, for a face-centred cubic crystal, some low index Kikuchi line pairs and illustrating the relation between beam directions marked $[u\,v\,w]$ and their associated Kikuchi line pairs marked $h\,k\,l$. The Kikuchi line map and the diffraction patterns are not to scale and only part of the [213] and [123] diffraction patterns are included. The map corresponds to the minimal area of a standard stereographic projection for a cubic crystal (see text). (b) Orientation map as it may be initially recorded during operation of the microscope.

tilting, so as to keep the pair of low order Kikuchi lines passing approximately through the central spot and the operative diffraction spot (i.e. by tilting about the crystal direction normal to the reflecting planes), a low index cross-grating pattern is readily located. Consider that the [112] cross-grating pattern in fig. 3.4(a) has been reached in this way. After recording the images and diffraction patterns for appropriate diffracting vectors associated with this cross-grating pattern, several alternate paths may be followed. Rotation about the $\bar{1}\bar{1}1$ diffracting vector in one particular sense, for example, would change the orientation of the crystal so that the beam direction would approach [011] via [123]. Alternatively, if the crystal were rotated about $\bar{1}\bar{1}1$ in the opposite sense, the beam direction would approach [101] via [213]. Similarly, rotation about the $2\bar{2}0$ diffracting vector in [112] in opposite senses would result in the beam directions [001] and [111]. It can be seen from fig. 3.4(a) that other low index beam directions could be reached by similar rotations *.

It will be shown in §3.4 that to index diffraction patterns in such a way that the correct specific indices are given to the diffraction spots, it is necessary to have a record of the rotation of the crystal when it is tilted from one beam direction to another. There are several methods for obtaining this record, but the one adopted here is to note the direction of movement of Kikuchi line patterns on the fluorescent screen. Since Kikuchi lines may be regarded as being fixed to the crystal (§2.2), their movement provides a record which may be related to the actual rotation of the crystal. The direction of movement of the Kikuchi line patterns is recorded by an 'orientation map' of the type shown in fig. 3.4(b), indicating the relative positions of low index directions. For example, if a ⟨112⟩ diffraction pattern was the starting pattern for the tilting experiment, the map as drawn in fig. 3.4(b) means that the ⟨011⟩ diffraction pattern appeared on the fluorescent screen from a position equivalent to 2 o'clock, the ⟨111⟩ pattern from 4 o'clock and the ⟨001⟩ pattern from 10 o'clock. In fig. 3.4(b) two positions from which different ⟨103⟩ cross-grating patterns appeared on the fluorescent screen are recorded as ⟨103⟩(a) and ⟨103⟩(b). It will be seen in §§3.4 and 3.5 that the type of map recorded in fig. 3.4(b) enables the beam directions and the diffraction spots associated with the diffraction patterns to be indexed specifically.

To ensure that sufficient information is obtained, at least three non-coplanar beam directions should be used in establishing the orientation map.

---

* In representing such rotations of the crystal on a standard stereographic projection, it is convenient to consider that the crystal is stationary and that the electron beam moves from one crystal direction to another. However, it is clear that the real situation corresponds to bringing various crystallographic directions into coincidence with the electron beam direction.

Near each low index beam direction, images and diffraction patterns for several diffracting vectors should be photographed. For example, in a ⟨112⟩ pattern for a face-centred cubic crystal it would be usual to photograph images and diffraction patterns for the 111, 220 and 311 diffracting vectors. This procedure will ensure that the series contains three non-coplanar diffracting vectors so that all components of the displacement field of the defect will be sampled. For each image the diffraction conditions must be set by rotating the crystal slightly about the diffracting vector so that a good experimental approximation to two-beam diffraction is obtained. It will be found that in most cases this condition can only be fulfilled for beam directions which are at least a few degrees away from an exact low order cross-grating pattern *. For instance, for a beam direction such as ⟨101⟩ a rotation of approximately 5° is usually necessary. Since the actual beam directions may be several degrees away from low index directions, their approximate positions, relative to the low index directions, should be marked on the orientation map to facilitate their later identification.

The manner in which images, diffraction patterns and orientation maps are used to provide the data needed for computing images will be discussed in the remainder of this chapter.

3.4. Specific indexing of the orientation map and diffracting vectors

The crystallographic data used for computing images is required in specific index form (e.g. for the aluminium example in ch. 5, u = [523], g = 11$\bar{1}$, B = [156], F = [528]) and in order to obtain the data in this form it is first necessary to give specific indices to the low index directions on the orientation map and to the diffracting vectors in the diffraction patterns.

Two standard stereographic projections are used in assigning specific indices. The first, a standard stereographic projection of crystal directions, is used to index the orientation map with respect to the real lattice and the second, a standard stereographic projection of plane normals, is used to index the diffracting vectors with respect to the reciprocal lattice. The relations between the two different projections can be illustrated by considering how a fixed direction in space is represented on each. The fixed direction will be represented by a point in the same position on each projection but its indices will be different. The fixed direction may be considered to be the

---

* A further small rotation of the crystal is required to adjust the deviation from the Bragg condition. This rotation is made about an axis normal to the beam and to the diffracting vector.

normal to the set of planes $(h\,k\,l)$ or to be in the direction $[u\,v\,w]$ in the crystal *. Therefore, in the stereographic projection of plane normals the point will have the indices $h\,k\,l$ whereas in the stereographic projection of crystal directions it will have the indices $u\,v\,w$. In the special case of cubic crystals the normal to the plane $(h\,k\,l)$ is the crystal direction $[h\,k\,l]$ so that the two projections are identical **.

The procedure set out below is designed to obtain the correct relative orientation of the stereographic projections, the orientation map and the diffraction patterns, so that not only may the orientation map and diffracting vectors be given specific indices but also the geometry of the defect may be analysed. In this procedure the orientation of diffraction patterns as recorded in the microscope is taken as the fixed orientation relative to which all rotations are made.

Step 1. The orientation map is identified with a portion of a standard stereographic projection of crystal directions and given specific indices accordingly.

Step 2. The indexed map is rotated through $180°$ with respect to the diffraction patterns.

Step 3. The diffracting vectors and other diffraction spots in the patterns are indexed in accordance with a standard stereographic projection of plane normals placed in the same orientation as the indexed map.

In order to carry out stereographic analysis of defects, it is necessary to mark the directions of the diffracting vectors on the images. To do this an additional step is required.

Step 4. The images are rotated through the angle ϕ so that they are oriented correctly with respect to their diffraction patterns (§3.2). The directions of the diffracting vectors are transferred directly from the diffraction patterns to the images ***.

---

* The crystal direction $[u\,v\,w]$ normal to the plane $(h\,k\,l)$ is given by,

$$\begin{pmatrix} u \\ v \\ w \end{pmatrix} = \begin{pmatrix} a_1^*\!\cdot\!a_1^* & a_1^*\!\cdot\!a_2^* & a_1^*\!\cdot\!a_3^* \\ a_2^*\!\cdot\!a_1^* & a_2^*\!\cdot\!a_2^* & a_2^*\!\cdot\!a_3^* \\ a_3^*\!\cdot\!a_1^* & a_3^*\!\cdot\!a_2^* & a_3^*\!\cdot\!a_3^* \end{pmatrix} \begin{pmatrix} h \\ k \\ l \end{pmatrix},$$

where the reciprocal lattice base vectors a_1^*, a_2^*, a_3^* are given in terms of the real lattice base vectors a_1, a_2, a_3 and the volume V_c of the unit cell by $a_1^* = (a_2 \wedge a_3)/V_c$, $a_2^* = (a_3 \wedge a_1)/V_c$ and $a_3^* = (a_1 \wedge a_2)/V_c$.

** In general, standard projections of crystal directions are used to index u and B and standard projections of plane normals to index F. In the case of cubic crystals when the two projections are identical we have specified F as a crystal direction $[h\,k\,l]$ rather than the plane normal $(h\,k\,l)$.

*** In addition it is useful to mark on each image an approximate direction from the central spot to a weak diffraction spot (see §3.6).

The basis of steps 1−3 is discussed in the remainder of this section and examples illustrating the procedure are given in §3.4.1.

In explaining steps 1−3 we will be concerned with crystal directions, plane normals, beam directions and a direction for stereographic projection, and we must adopt a consistent convention for specifying the sense of these directions. We have already chosen the sense of the beam direction B to be opposite to the direction of the electron flow, i.e. upwards towards the electron gun. This same upwards sense will be used to specify crystal directions and plane normals and the direction of projection when these are represented on a stereographic projection. In the discussion, we will ignore electromagnetic rotations produced in the microscope between the crystal and its diffraction patterns on the fluorescent screen as it will be shown later that such rotations do not influence the conclusions.

Consider first the relationship between the orientation map and a standard projection representing beam directions as defined here. The orientation map may be regarded as mapping out the movement of downward drawn directions when the crystal is rotated so as to bring different crystal directions into coincidence with the beam direction. However, on a stereographic projection with an upward sense of projection, these same crystal rotations would be represented by a map of upward drawn directions. These two representations of the same crystal rotations are related by a rotation of $180°$ about an axis normal to the map. Since only a rotation is involved the relative positions of crystal directions in both representations will be the same so that the recorded orientation map can be identified with the standard stereographic projection of crystal directions. Because of the limitations of crystal tilt, the map will represent only a portion of the standard stereographic projection of crystal directions. This portion has to be recognised and the map located on it by suitably orienting the standard projection. When this is done the map can be labelled directly with specific indices.

In the case of crystals of the lowest symmetry, there is no choice in the assignment of the portion of the stereographic projection. However, in the case of crystals of higher symmetry, the map can be recognised as belonging to a minimal portion of the stereographic projection which contains all possible non-equivalent crystal directions; the orientation map can then be labelled accordingly. One such area of a stereographic projection for a face-centred cubic crystal would correspond to the two stereographic triangles indicated by fig. 3.4(a). Clearly, in the case of crystals of such high symmetry, the specific indices assigned to the orientation map will be determined by the particular minimal area of the projection selected. However, since all such areas are crystallographically equivalent, the choice of a different area would not influence the interpretation of the physical situation.

The bases for steps 2 and 3 will be considered together. The object of these steps is to assign specific indices to the diffracting vectors as represented on the diffraction patterns so that these indices are consistent with the specifically indexed orientation map. The relationship between the indexed orientation map and the diffracting vectors is readily seen by considering the relationship of each to the crystal.

Consider first the relationship between the diffracting vector as defined in the crystal and its representation in the diffraction pattern. The diffracting vector is defined in the crystal to be the normal to the diffracting planes in the direction in which the diffracted beam is displaced from the direct beam and is acute with *B*. Since the diffracting vector is acute with *B*, it can also be represented directly on a stereographic projection with an upward sense of projection. In the diffraction pattern the diffracting vector is represented by the displacement of the diffracted spot formed by the diffracted electrons, from the central spot formed by the transmitted electrons. Remembering that electromagnetic rotations are not being considered, there is no rotation between the direction of the diffracting vector in the crystal and its representation in the diffraction pattern (see fig. 3.1).

Thus the direction of the diffracting vector as recorded in the diffraction pattern is directly compatible with its direction in the crystal within the framework of the conventions adopted. However, we have already seen that the orientation map has to be rotated through 180° to make it compatible with upward drawn directions in the crystal. Therefore, the specifically indexed orientation map has to be rotated through 180° with respect to the diffraction patterns in order to make it compatible with the diffracting vectors as represented in the diffraction patterns and in the crystal (step 2). With the diffraction patterns and the indexed orientation map placed in this correct relative orientation, the diffraction spots in each pattern can be indexed with the specific indices given by the standard stereographic projection of plane normals placed in the same orientation as the map (step 3).

In this discussion we have ignored electromagnetic rotations which in a real situation are always produced in the microscope. However, electromagnetic rotations cannot change the relative positions of directions as recorded in the orientation map, so that the conclusion that the map can be labelled with specific indices from a standard stereographic projection of crystal directions remains valid. Further, the electromagnetic rotations which rotate the diffraction patterns, and therefore the diffracting vectors, relative to the specimen as they are magnified and projected onto the fluorescent screen, apply equally to the orientation map, which is of course determined from diffraction pattern movements. Therefore the relative rotation of 180° between the map and its associated diffracting vectors in the diffraction patterns is the only requirement that is necessary to keep them compatible.

The direction of the diffracting vector is used both in determining the

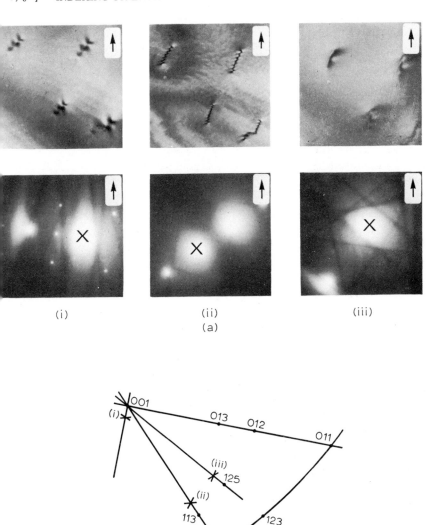

Fig. 3.5. (a) Three images and their corresponding diffraction patterns (i), (ii) and (iii) for a thin foil of rutile and an orientation map (b) as recorded in the Philips microscope. The central diffraction spot on each of the patterns is marked X and the approximate beam direction corresponding to each pattern is marked by a cross on the orientation map. Images × 20,000.

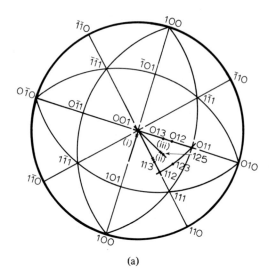

(a)

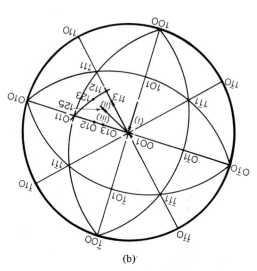

(b)

Fig. 3.6. Illustrating the procedure for indexing the orientation map and the diffracting vectors of fig. 3.5: (a) a suitably oriented standard projection of crystal directions with the map located on it (step 1); (b) specifically indexed orientation map and its associated projection rotated through 180° with respect to its as recorded orientation (step 2); (c) standard projection of plane normals placed in the same orientation as the rotated map in (b); (d) diffraction patterns in which the diffracting vectors have been specifically indexed in accordance with the projections in (b) and (c) (step 3); and (e) images oriented correctly relative to the diffraction patterns with the direction of the diffracting vectors transferred to them (step 4).

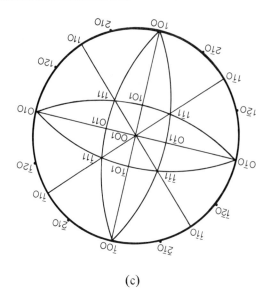

(c)

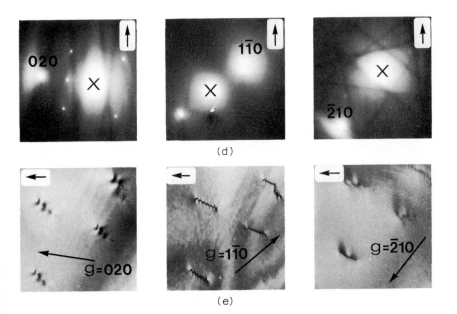

(d)

(e)

geometry of the specimen and in the diffraction theory. For the purposes
of diffraction theory, e.g. evaluating β' in eq. (2.30), the indices of the
diffracting vectors are required with respect to the reciprocal lattice and if
this were the sole requirement, then it would be necessary to rotate only the
stereographic projection of plane normals through $180°$ i.e. it would not be
necessary to rotate the orientation map. However, the direction of the diffracting vector in the real lattice is used for analysis of directions in the specimen and in this context it is necessary to rotate the orientation map through
$180°$ as described in step 2. The orientation map and its extension in the
form of a standard projection of crystal directions is then in the correct
orientation relative to the standard projection of plane normals for the direction of the diffracting vector to be represented by a point in the same position
on both projections.

3.4.1. EXPERIMENTAL EXAMPLES

Examples for a tetragonal crystal, rutile (c/a = 0.6439), and a face-
centred cubic crystal, aluminium, will be used to illustrate the recommended
procedure (steps 1–4 above) for determining the specific indices of the low
index beam directions in the orientation map and the specific indices of the
diffracting vectors, and for marking the directions of the diffracting vectors
on the corresponding images. For rutile, three diffracting vectors in three
beam directions from the series are indexed whilst for aluminium two diffracting vectors in two beam directions from the series are indexed. The
example for rutile was obtained using the Philips EM 200 microscope and
that for aluminium using the Siemens Elmiskop 1A.

(a) *Rutile* (TiO_2)

Figure 3.5(a), (i)–(iii), shows three images and their corresponding diffraction patterns for a specimen of rutile in the orientation in which they were
recorded in the Philips microscope. Figure 3.5(b) is an orientation map of
the low index beam directions visited in the experiment and has been
recorded as described in §3.3. The crosses on the map (i), (ii), (iii) indicate
the approximate positions of the beam directions corresponding to the
images and the diffraction patterns in fig. 3.5(a). In fig. 3.6(a) a standard
projection of crystal directions has been oriented so that the map can be
located directly on it thus enabling the map to be specifically indexed (step
1). The orientation map and its extension in the form of the stereographic
projection of crystal directions has been rotated through $180°$ in fig. 3.6(b)
(step 2). In fig. 3.6(c) the standard stereographic projection of plane
normals is arranged in the same orientation as the rotated map. For each
diffraction pattern the position of the diffracting vector is located by
inspection on the zone of plane normals perpendicular to the corresponding
beam direction and the diffracting vector is indexed accordingly (step 3). In

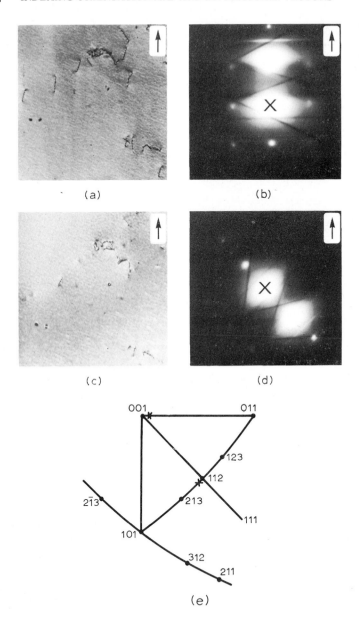

Fig. 3.7. Two images (a) and (c), corresponding diffraction patterns (b) and (d) and a specifically indexed orientation map (e) for a thin foil of aluminium in the orientation as recorded in a Siemens microscope. The central diffraction spot in each of the patterns (b) and (d) is marked X, and the approximate beam directions corresponding to (b) and (d) are indicated by crosses on the orientation map (e). Images X 20,000.

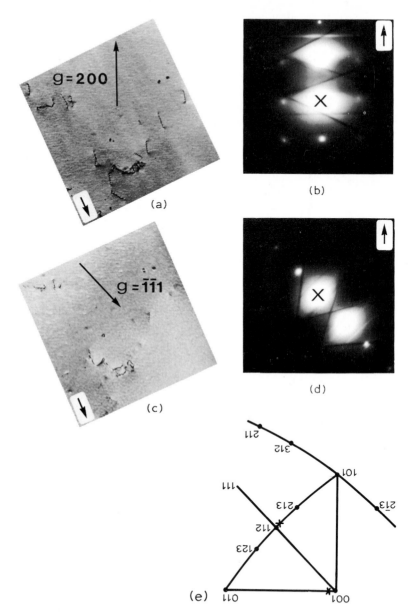

Fig. 3.8. The images, corresponding diffraction patterns and orientation map of fig. 3.7 arranged in their correct relative orientation for determining the indices of the operative diffracting vectors from the standard stereographic projection of plane normals (f). The central diffraction spot in each pattern is marked X and the diffracting vectors are marked on the images. Images × 20,000.

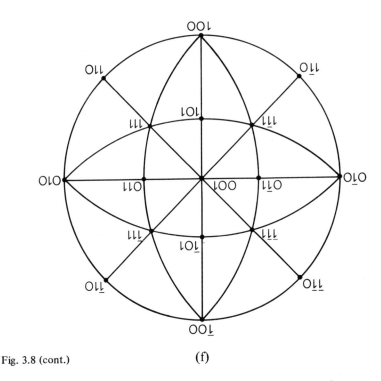

Fig. 3.8 (cont.)   (f)

fig. 3.6(e) the images have been rotated through the angle ϕ (90° anticlockwise) so that they are in their correct orientation relative to the diffraction patterns and the directions of the diffracting vectors have been transferred to them.(step 4).

(b) *Aluminium*

    Since aluminium is cubic, the stereographic projections of crystal directions and plane normals are identical so that the execution of the procedure is somewhat simplified. Figure 3.7(a)–(d) shows two images and corresponding diffraction patterns for a specimen of aluminium in the orientation in which they were recorded in the Siemens microscope. Figure 3.7(e) is an orientation map of the low index beam directions visited in the experiment and indexed according to the area of the stereographic projection shown in fig. 3.4(a) (step 1). The crosses on the orientation map indicate the approximate positions of the two different beam directions shown in fig. 3.7 in relation to the low index directions. Figures 3.7(a) and (b) are for the beam direction close to [001] and figs. 3.7(c) and (d) are for the beam direction close to [112]. In fig. 3.8(a)–(d) the images have been rotated through the angle $\phi = 206°$ anticlockwise with respect to the diffraction patterns (step 4), so that they are now in their correct relative orientation. In fig. 3.8(e) the orientation map has been rotated through 180° with respect to the diffraction pattern (step 2) and fig. 3.8(f) shows a standard stereographic projection of plane normals in the same orientation as the map. With the stereographic projection aligned in this way, specific indices can be given to the diffraction spot corresponding to the diffracting vector in each pattern (step 3), e.g. in fig. 3.8(b) the diffracting vector is 200 and in fig. 3.8(d) the diffracting vector is $\overline{1}\overline{1}1$. The directions of the diffracting vectors are marked on the images (step 4).

3.5. Determination of beam direction B

The attainment of two-beam conditions appropriate for image matching necessitates the use of beam directions which may be several degrees from those corresponding to prominent low-index cross-grating patterns. It will be seen in later chapters that the topology of an image is sometimes sensitive to the precise electron beam direction in the crystal. Further, a knowledge of the beam direction within $\pm\frac{1}{2}$° is important when determining crystallographic directions by stereographic analysis as will be discussed in §3.6. Beam directions can be readily determined with the required accuracy from the Kikuchi line patterns associated with each diffraction pattern.

In general the diffraction spots in a pattern cannot be used to determine accurate beam directions since tilting a crystal through small angles merely alters the intensity of the diffraction spots without altering their positions. Kikuchi lines, however, can be used for this purpose since they move as though they are rigidly fixed to the crystal and thus enable small tilts of the crystal to be readily detected. The excess and deficient Kikuchi lines which form a pair have an angular separation of twice the Bragg angle $2\theta_B$ and when the crystal is tilted through this angle, they move by a distance on the diffraction pattern equal to their spacing. Therefore, a linear measurement on the diffraction pattern can be related to an angle of tilt. Obviously, it is necessary to have a calibration which relates a given linear dimension on the diffraction pattern to the angle through which the crystal has been tilted. In practice this calibration is given directly by the relation between the distance separating diffraction spots for a particular g and their angular separation $2\theta_B$ calculated for that g.

From the record that has been kept on the orientation map of approximate positions of beam directions relative to low index directions (§3.3), it is a relatively simple matter to determine the true beam direction. The first step is to identify at least two intersecting pairs of Kikuchi lines on the diffraction pattern, one pair associated with the strongly diffracted beam (diffracting vector g), and the other associated with a weakly diffracted

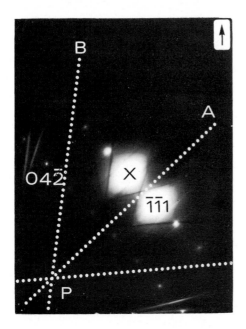

Fig. 3.9. Illustration of the determination of a true beam direction from construction lines drawn midway between, and parallel to, pairs of Kikuchi lines intersecting at P. P is the nearest low order direction [112].

beam (diffracting vector g'). Lines drawn parallel to and midway between each Kikuchi line pair are extended until they intersect. The point of intersection is then the crystallographic direction $g \wedge g'$ which will usually be the low index direction nearest to the approximate true beam direction previously marked on the orientation map *. The distance from this point of intersection to the systematic row of spots containing g is measured. From the previous calibration this distance gives the angle between the true beam direction and the direction $g \wedge g'$. The true beam direction is then calculated using the angular relationships between crystallographic directions (e.g. Barrett, 1952, p. 632) and the fact that the rotation is about the diffracting vector g in the sense recorded on the orientation map.

An example of the determination of a beam direction is illustrated in fig. 3.9. The approximate beam direction for the diffraction pattern in fig. 3.8(d) is shown on the orientation map in fig. 3.8(e) to be near [112], but displaced towards [213]. Figure 3.8(d) is reproduced in fig. 3.9 with lines drawn

* Since $g \wedge g' = -(g' \wedge g)$ the order of the vectors in the cross product must be chosen to give an upward drawn beam direction as defined previously.

parallel to and midway between three pairs of prominent Kikuchi lines and these lines intersect at point P. The pairs of Kikuchi lines indicated by the construction lines A and B are the $\bar{1}\bar{1}1$ and $04\bar{2}$ pairs for which $\boldsymbol{g} \wedge \boldsymbol{g}'$ gives the indices of the low index direction P as $[112]$. From the known lattice parameter of aluminium ($a = 4.0490$ Å) $2\theta_B$ for the $\bar{1}\bar{1}1$ reflection is $54.5'$ of arc for 100 kV electrons and from the diffraction pattern the spacing of the diffraction spots corresponding to $2\theta_B$ is 0.89 cm. Thus for the case considered a distance of 1 cm on the diffraction pattern can be taken as corresponding to an angle of $1°$. The distance from P to the $\bar{1}\bar{1}1$ row of systematic diffraction spots is 3.3 cm, so that the beam direction is $3.3°$ from $[112]$ towards $[213]$. This direction has been assigned the approximate indices $[549]$.

3.6. Determination of defect line direction u

In order to determine crystallographic directions such as the line direction $\boldsymbol{u}$ of the defect, it is necessary to record images of the defect in at least two beam directions. However, three beam directions should be considered as a minimum requirement to obtain a reliable result. The problem involved then is one of determining a direction in space from at least three projections of that direction. This problem is most simply solved using the technique of stereographic projection and is most conveniently described with reference to a specific example.

As an example of the determination of an unknown direction in a crystal, the $\boldsymbol{u}$ for a dislocation in the specimen of aluminium used as an example in §§3.4.1 and 3.5 will be determined. Four images of the dislocation labelled A are given in fig. 3.10(a)–(d). In each image the specific diffracting vector $\boldsymbol{g}$ is shown together with the sense of a direction to a weak diffraction spot obtained from the corresponding diffraction pattern *. For each image a line is also drawn parallel to the projection of $\boldsymbol{u}$ and the measured angle between $\boldsymbol{g}$ and the projection of $\boldsymbol{u}$ is marked on each image. At this stage we have four projected directions of $\boldsymbol{u}$ in known directions of projection, i.e. the true beam directions, and the angles between these projected directions and the operative diffracting vectors. The true crystallographic direction of $\boldsymbol{u}$ giving rise to these four projected directions can now be determined using a stereographic net.

* Since micrographs are generally taken in beam directions which are not low order, $\boldsymbol{g}$ is the only readily determined true direction in the plane of the micrograph. The weak diffraction spot does not give a true direction in the plane of the micrograph and is only used to obtain the sense of the angle from $\boldsymbol{g}$ to $\boldsymbol{u}$.

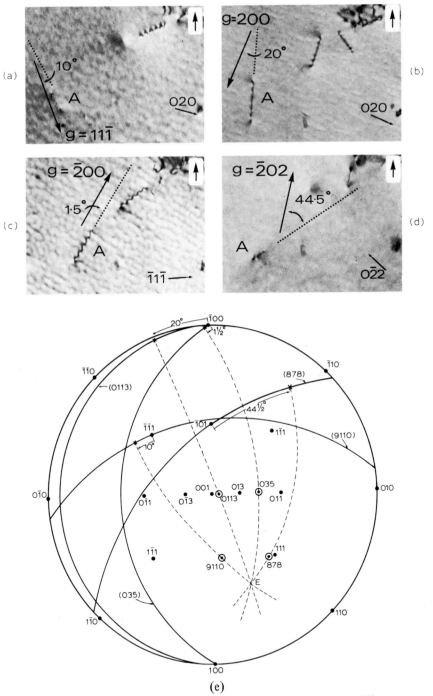

Fig. 3.10. Images of dislocations in a thin foil of aluminium viewed in four different beam directions: (a) B = [9 1 10]; (b) B = [0 1 13]; (c) B = [035]; and (d) B = [878]. The stereographic projection (e) illustrates the determination of u for dislocation A. Images × 18,000.

In the stereographic projection shown in fig. 3.10(e) the great circles corresponding to the planes of projection for each of the beam directions are labelled with their specific indices. For each plane of projection the projected direction of u is marked at the corresponding angle from the diffracting vector in a known sense. For example for the [878] beam direction in fig. 3.10(d) the projected direction of u is $44\frac{1}{2}°$ from the diffracting vector $\bar{2}02$ away from $0\bar{2}2$ and in fig. 3.10(e) this angle has been marked in the correct sense on the appropriate great circle.

The true direction of u must lie in the plane containing the beam direction and the projection of u in that beam direction. This plane is constructed for each beam direction by drawing the great circle containing the projected direction of u and the beam direction. These are shown in fig. 3.10(e) as dashed lines. The region of intersection E of these great circles defines the direction u of the dislocation and in this case the uncertainty defined by the points of intersection of the great circles is very small. In some cases the uncertainty is considerably larger than this and often it is not possible to determine u to a precision of better than about $3°$.

The indices of the direction at the centre of region E must now be determined. In general this can be done by measuring the angles between the region E and low index directions in the standard stereographic projection and then using the appropriate formula for angles between crystal directions. For the cubic crystal considered in this example the indices of the direction u correspond to its direction cosines, i.e. to the cosines of the angles between E and [100], [010] and [001]. These are approximately 0.81, 0.35 and 0.47 respectively. For the purposes of computation the direction corresponding to these direction cosines has been assigned the approximate indices [523].

3.7. Determination of foil normal F

The direction normal to the plane of the thin foil specimen is an essential piece of information required in the computer programs. The foil normal is important since it determines the entrance and exit boundaries for the electron beam passing through the foil, and will thus affect both the thickness of the foil in the beam direction and the orientation of image features relative to the line of the defect. Since the taper in a foil is generally very small, the plane of either of the foil surfaces or the mid-plane of the foil can be determined and used as F.

If the tilting stage has an accurate means of setting the specimen normal to the electron beam, the foil normal can be determined by solving the diffraction pattern corresponding to this setting. However, care should be taken in using this technique as the specimen may be buckled in the specimen holder and this could give rise to a spurious result.

Other methods of determining the foil normal all rely on stereographic analysis of traces in the specimen surfaces or of constructed traces. If surface traces are available from planes which are not readily identifiable, then images of these traces in a minimum of three different beam directions are required. The procedure discussed in the previous section is then used to determine the crystallographic direction of each trace. The plane defined by these directions is then the foil plane. The problem is greatly simplified if the traces come from planes of known type which can be specifically identified by tilting experiments, which is often the case if slip traces and stacking fault fringes are present. The simplification arises because only one image in a particular beam direction is required to define the crystallographic directions of the surface traces of the known planes.

If surface traces are not available, then effective surface traces can be constructed by joining the mid-points of widely spaced dislocations which run through the foil. Such traces define the mid-plane of the foil. In practice, we have found that this method of determining F is simpler than using dislocations to construct actual surface traces largely because of the difficulty of distinguishing between intersections with the top and bottom surfaces.

The same aluminium specimen used for the previous examples will again be taken to illustrate the determination of foil normal. Two of the previously mentioned techniques will be illustrated, namely a determination of the mid-plane of the foil and a determination of the foil surface plane from traces of known planes.

Method 1. Figure 3.11 shows three images of the same area of an aluminium foil and the diffracting vectors are indicated. Three dislocations, A, B and C have been selected. In the images in fig. 3.11 the centres of the images of the dislocations have been joined by the lines AB, BC and CA. These lines can be taken as the projections in each beam direction of imaginary lines ab, bc and ca joining the centres of these dislocations in the crystal. The directions of the lines ab, bc and ca may be determined in the manner described in §3.6 and this determination is illustrated in the present case by the stereographic projection in fig. 3.12. Any two of the directions ab, bc or ca will define the mid-plane of the foil. However, a more reliable result may be obtained by taking the great circle which gives the best fit to all three directions. In fig. 3.12 this great circle is labelled 'Foil Plane'. The pole of this plane, labelled 'Foil Normal' can now be indexed using a stereographic projection of plane normals. This example is for a cubic crystal for which the projections of plane normals and directions are identical so that either may be used. Using the projection of crystal directions and taking direction cosines

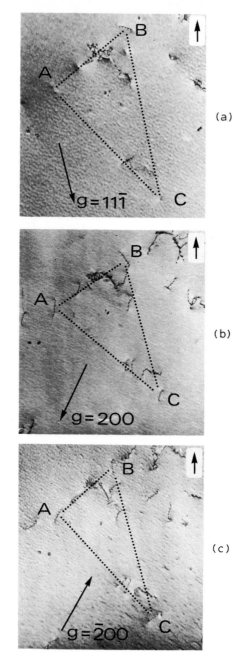

Fig. 3.11. Images of dislocations in a thin foil of aluminium viewed in three different beam directions: (a) B = [9 1 10] ; (b) B = [0 1 13] ; and (c) B = [035] . Construction lines joining the mid-points of dislocations A, B and C are used to determine the foil normal. Images × 20,000.

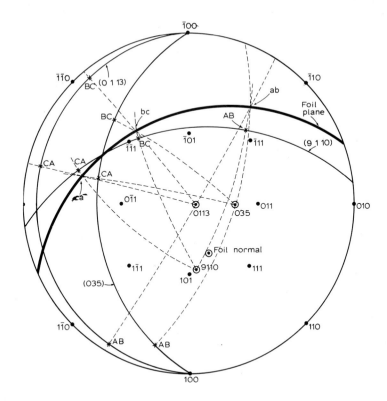

Fig. 3.12. Stereographic projection showing the manner in which the lines AB, BC and CA of fig. 3.11 are used to determine the foil normal. The points marked AB, BC and CA correspond to the measured projections of the mid-foil traces in the beam directions [9 1 10], [0 1 13] and [035] whereas ab, bc and ca are the directions of the mid-foil traces determined from these projections. The great circle passing through the points ab, bc and ca is the 'Foil Plane' and the pole of this great circle is denoted 'Foil Normal'.

as in §3.6, the cosines of the angles between the foil normal and [100], [010], [001] are approximately 0.53, 0.21 and 0.82 respectively. For the purpose of image computation, the foil normal corresponding to these direction cosines is assigned the approximate indices [528].

Method 2. Figure 3.13(a) shows the same area of the aluminium specimen as in fig. 3.11, but in this case for the [013] beam direction. The foil has been allowed to contaminate in the microscope to induce slip and the slip traces resulting from moving dislocations can be seen in the micrograph. The slip traces of three different sets of planes are clearly visible and it is assumed

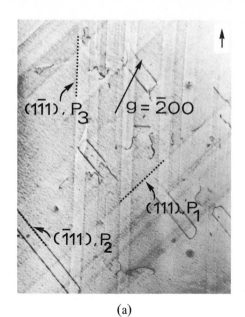

(a)

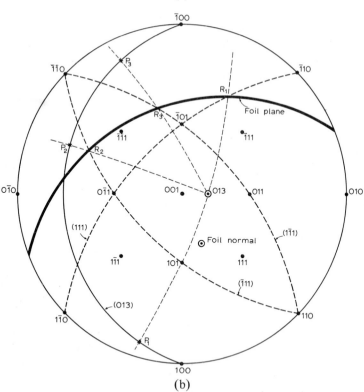

(b)

Fig. 3.13. Illustration of the use of slip traces to determine foil normal. (a) Image × 20,000 for **B** = [013] showing slip traces from planes (111), ($\bar{1}$11) and (1$\bar{1}$1) where the projected directions of these traces are designated P_1, P_2 and P_3 respectively. (b) Stereographic projection showing the determination of foil normal.

that these traces correspond to the intersection of {111} planes with the foil surfaces. For a given foil, the projected width of a slip plane, as indicated by a pair of slip traces, is a function of the beam direction. By noting the changes in projected widths of the {111} slip planes on rotating the crystal to different beam directions, the indices of the planes corresponding to the various slip traces can be readily determined. The indices of the planes giving the slip traces in fig. 3.13(a) have been determined in this manner and are indicated. The angles between the various slip traces and the diffracting vector are 18° clockwise and 68.5° and 26° anticlockwise for (111), $(\bar{1}11)$ and $(1\bar{1}1)$ respectively.

The projected directions of the surface traces are plotted on a stereographic projection in the manner described for previous examples. The projections of the surface traces of (111), $(\bar{1}11)$ and $(1\bar{1}1)$ are labelled P_1, P_2 and P_3 respectively in fig. 3.13(b). Clearly, the crystallographic direction corresponding to P_1, for example, must lie in (111) and in the plane defined by the beam direction and P_1. This is the point labelled R_1 in fig. 3.13(b), i.e. the intersection of the great circle corresponding to (111) and the great circle containing P_1 and the beam direction. Similarly, the crystallographic directions corresponding to P_2 and P_3 are the points R_2 and R_3. Any two of these crystallographic directions define the plane of the foil surface and the pole of the best fitting great circle to all three points, R_1, R_2 and R_3 gives the foil normal. This is indistinguishable from that determined by method 1, and is given the indices [528].

3.8. Extinction distance

When computing images, all dimensions are specified in units of extinction distance, and the deviation from the Bragg condition is expressed as the dimensionless parameter w which also involves extinction distance. It will be realised from the discussion in § § 2.5 and 2.6 that some value of extinction distance is needed as a starting point for image computation in order to specify the dimensionless parameter w and for this purpose the theoretical two-beam extinction distance ξ_g is used. Values of ξ_g for pure metals may be calculated from the atomic scattering amplitudes for electrons given by Smith and Burge (1962) and Doyle and Turner (1968) or from the crystal lattice potential calculations of Radi (1970). Table 3.1 gives values of ξ_g for some common metals. The values in table 3.1(a) have been calculated using the atomic scattering amplitudes of Smith and Burge, those in table 3.1(b) using atomic scattering amplitudes of Doyle and Turner and those in table 3.1(c) are based on the lattice potential calculations of Radi. It is clear from a comparison of tables 3.1(a), (b) and (c) that for the same material and the

TABLE 3.1
Extinction distances in Å for some common metals *

(a) Values based on atomic scattering amplitudes due to Smith and Burge (1962)

Reflection	Al	Cu	Ni	Ag	Pt	Au	Fe	Nb
110	–	–	–	–	–	–	270	261
111	556	242	236	224	147	159	–	–
200	673	281	275	255	166	179	395	367
211	–	–	–	–	–	–	503	457
220	1057	416	409	363	232	248	606	539
310	–	–	–	–	–	–	712	619
311	1300	505	499	433	274	292	–	–

	Mg	Co	Zn	Cd	Zr
0002	811	248	260	244	317
$\bar{1}101$	1001	306	351	324	379
$\bar{1}\bar{1}20$	1405	429	497	438	493
$\bar{1}100$	1509	467	553	519	594

(b) Values based on atomic scattering amplitudes due to Doyle and Turner (1968)

Reflection	Al	Cu	Ni	Ag	Pt	Au	Fe	Nb
110	–	–	–	–	–	–	282	262
111	556	292	263	238	154	179	–	–
200	673	325	302	265	182	197	399	365
211	–	–	–	–	–	–	500	460
220	1057	441	420	359	247	264	592	552
310	–	–	–	–	–	–	685	639
311	1300	523	499	422	293	310	–	–

	Mg	Co	Zn	Cd	Zr
0002	806	265	321	261	313
$\bar{1}101$	1071	342	446	361	396
$\bar{1}\bar{1}20$	1436	434	540	437	495
$\bar{1}100$	1502	499	673	557	575

same diffracting vector, there are differences of approximately 20% in the calculated values of ξ_g.

In the case of alloys, values of ξ_g will vary with alloy composition so that it is necessary to calculate ξ_g for the particular alloy of interest.

Two examples of the calculation of extinction distance will be given, the

TABLE 3.1 (continued)

(c) Values based on lattice potential calculations due to Radi (1970)

Reflection	Al	Cu	Ni	Ag	Pt	Au	Fe	Nb
110	–	–	–	–	–	–	304	281
111	598	316	384	257	175	191	–	–
200	713	351	321	283	193	209	423	388
211	–	–	–	–	–	–	527	485
220	1120	471	448	380	258	276	627	579
310	–	–	–	–	–	–	725	670
311	1381	555	533	449	304	324	–	–

	Mg	Co	Zn	Cd	Zr
0002	867	287	344	284	336
$\bar{1}101$	1072	349	453	369	403
$\bar{1}\bar{1}20$	1518	455	577	463	528
$\bar{1}100$	1620	543	728	599	624

* These values are the corrected values for 100 kV electrons but do not include the Debye–Waller correction for thermal diffuse scattering.

first for an ordered alloy (NiAl) and the second for a homogeneous solid solution (Cu + 11 at % Ni). In these calculations the values for atomic scattering amplitudes for electrons f given by Doyle and Turner (1968) will be used, and values of f for Al, Ni and Cu are plotted as a function of $(\sin \theta)/\lambda$ in fig. 3.14. The values of the thermal Debye parameters used are $B_{Ni} = 0.425$, $B_{Al} = 0.776$ and $B_{Cu} = 0.576$ at 293°K. All calculations are for 100 kV electrons with $\lambda = 0.0370$ Å and expressions (2.26), (2.28) and (2.25) of §2.6 are used.

1. NiAl

For the ordered alloy NiAl, the lattice parameter a is 2.887 Å giving a

TABLE 3.2

Diffracting vector	$\dfrac{\sin \theta}{\lambda}$	f_{Al}	Corrected * f_{Al}	f_{Ni}	Corrected * f_{Ni}	exp $(-M_g)$	
						Al	Ni
100	0.173	2.71	3.24	3.91	4.67	0.975	0.986
110	0.245	1.80	2.15	2.95	3.53	0.952	0.973
200	0.346	1.12	1.34	2.16	2.58	0.913	0.949

* The values for f are taken from fig. 3.14 and have been corrected by using the relativistic factor $(1 - v^2/c^2)^{-\frac{1}{2}} = 1.1957$ for 100 kV electrons.

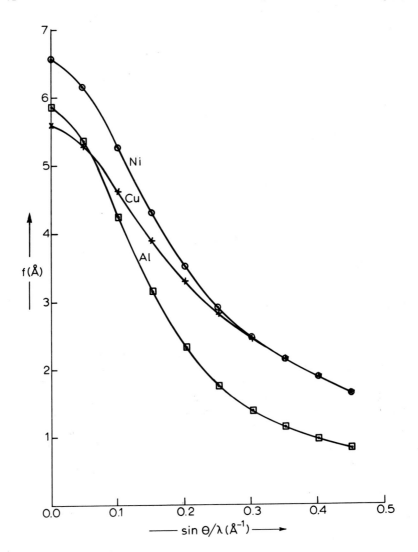

Fig. 3.14. Atomic scattering amplitudes for electrons f for Al, Cu and Ni as a function of $(\sin \theta)/\lambda$ from the results of Doyle and Turner (1968).

volume of the unit cell V_c of 24.062 Å^3. NiAl has the caesium chloride structure with two atoms per unit cell and the position coordinates of the Ni and Al atoms will be taken at 0, 0, 0 and $\frac{1}{2}, \frac{1}{2}, \frac{1}{2}$ respectively. Table 3.2 gives the data necessary for the calculation.

(i) *100 diffracting vector (superlattice reflection)*
From eq. (2.28),

$$F_{100} = f_{Ni} \exp(-M_{100})_{(Ni)} \cos 2\pi(0) + f_{Al} \exp(-M_{100})_{(Al)} \cos 2\pi(\tfrac{1}{2})$$

$$= 4.67 \times 0.986 \times 1 + 3.24 \times 0.975 \times (-1)$$

$$= 1.44 ,$$

and from eq. (2.26),

$$\xi_{100} = \frac{\pi V_c \cos \theta_B}{\lambda |F_{100}|}$$

$$= \frac{\pi \times 24.062 \times 1}{0.0370 \times 1.44}$$

$$= 1420 \text{ Å} .$$

(ii) *110 diffracting vector*

$$F_{110} = f_{Ni} \exp(-M_{110})_{(Ni)} \cos 2\pi(0) + f_{Al} \exp(-M_{110})_{(Al)} \cos 2\pi(\tfrac{1}{2} + \tfrac{1}{2})$$

$$= 3.53 \times 0.973 \times 1 + 2.15 \times 0.952 \times 1$$

$$= 5.49.$$

Therefore

$$\xi_{110} = \frac{\pi \times 24.062 \times 1}{0.0370 \times 5.49}$$

$$= 372 \text{ Å}.$$

(iii) *200 diffracting vector*

$$F_{200} = f_{Ni} \exp(-M_{200})_{(Ni)} \cos 2\pi(0) + f_{Al} \exp(-M_{200})_{(Al)} \cos 2\pi(1)$$

$$= 2.58 \times 0.949 \times 1 + 1.34 \times 0.913 \times 1$$

$$= 3.68.$$

Therefore

$$\xi_{200} = \frac{\pi \times 24.062 \times 1}{0.0370 \times 3.68}$$

$$= 555 \text{ Å}.$$

2. Cu + 11 at% Ni

In this example the alloy has a face-centred cubic structure with a random distribution of Cu and Ni atoms between the lattice sites with position coordinates 0, 0, 0; 0, $\frac{1}{2}$, $\frac{1}{2}$; $\frac{1}{2}$, 0, $\frac{1}{2}$ and $\frac{1}{2}$, $\frac{1}{2}$, 0. The lattice parameter a for this alloy is 3.596 Å, giving a V_c of 46.50 Å^3. Two different assumptions could be used as suitable approximations for calculating ξ_g in this case. First, it may be assumed that each lattice site is occupied by a species of atom which has an atomic scattering amplitude f which is made up of the atomic scattering amplitudes of Cu and Ni in the atomic proportions of these elements in the alloy. Second, it may be assumed that the alloy consists of a random mixture of unit cells containing atoms of only one species and that the F_g for the alloy is obtained by combining the F_g for the component species according to the atomic proportions of Cu and Ni in the alloy. These two assumptions lead to the same answer and the second assumption will be taken to illustrate the calculation. The calculation will only be done for the 111 diffracting vector and the necessary data is given in table 3.3.

$$F_{111(Ni)} = f_{Ni} \exp(-M_{111})_{(Ni)} \cos 2\pi(0) + 3\{f_{Ni} \exp(-M_{111})_{(Ni)} \cos 2\pi(1)\}$$

$$= 4f_{Ni} \exp(-M_{111})_{(Ni)}.$$

Similarly for a unit cell containing only Cu atoms,

$$F_{111(Cu)} = 4f_{Cu} \exp(-M_{111})_{(Cu)}.$$

TABLE 3.3

Diffracting vector	$\frac{\sin \theta}{\lambda}$	f_{Cu}	Corrected * f_{Cu}	f_{Ni}	Corrected * f_{Ni}	$\exp(-M_g)$	
						Cu	Ni
111	0.241	2.88	3.44	3.00	3.59	0.965	0.975

* The values of f are taken from fig. 3.14 and have been corrected by using the relativistic factor $(1 - v^2/c^2)^{-\frac{1}{2}} = 1.1957$ for 100 kV electrons.

Then for the Cu + 11 at % Ni alloy,

$$F_{111 \, (alloy)} = 4\{0.11 f_{Ni} \exp(-M_{111})_{(Ni)}\} + 4\{0.89 f_{Cu} \exp(-M_{111})_{(Cu)}\}$$

$$= 4(0.11 \times 3.59 \times 0.975) + 4(0.89 \times 3.44 \times 0.965)$$

$$= 13.37.$$

Therefore

$$\xi_{111 \, (alloy)} = \frac{\pi \times 46.50 \times 1}{0.0370 \times 13.37} = 296 \text{ Å}.$$

3.9. Determination of w

It has been seen in ch. 2 that the deviation from the Bragg condition is an important parameter involved in the equations describing the propagation of electron waves through a crystal. Obviously the deviation from the Bragg condition applying to a particular experimental image must be determined before corresponding theoretical images can be computed.

In the form of the Howie–Whelan equations we have used, the deviation from the Bragg condition is represented by the dimensionless parameter w, where $w = \xi_g s$. The parameter s is the distance in reciprocal space from the reciprocal lattice point corresponding to the operative diffracting vector to the Ewald sphere and, in evaluating w for use in the programs, s has to be determined.

Figure 3.15 represents a crystal that has been rotated through the angle $\Delta\theta_1$ from the exact Bragg condition for the diffracting vector $\mathbf{g} = \mathbf{OG_1}$ so that the reciprocal lattice point G_1 lies inside the Ewald sphere. This is defined as a diffraction condition for which s is positive. It is clear from fig. 3.15 that

$$s = |\mathbf{g}| \, \Delta\theta_1 , \tag{3.1}$$

as both θ_B and $\Delta\theta_1$ are very small angles.

A convenient parameter specifying s which can be measured directly from diffraction patterns is the distance between Kikuchi lines and diffraction spots as indicated in fig. 3.16. In fig. 3.16(a) the crystal is set so that, for the first order diffracting vector, $s = 0$ (the exact Bragg condition) in which case the first order excess Kikuchi line E_1 passes through the first order diffraction spot and the second order excess Kikuchi line E_2 passes

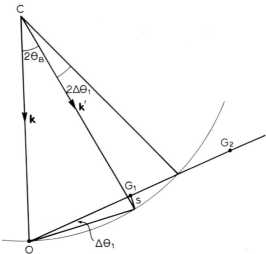

Fig. 3.15. Section of Ewald sphere, showing the deviation parameter s associated with a crystal rotation $\Delta\theta_1$.

mid-way between the first order and second order diffraction spots. When the crystal is rotated so that s is positive (fig. 3.16(b)) the first order excess Kikuchi line E_1 is displaced a distance Δx_1 on the diffraction pattern towards the second order diffraction spot, and the second order excess line E_2 is displaced by the same amount and is then at a distance Δx_2 from the second order diffraction spot. Clearly,

$$\Delta x_1 + \Delta x_2 = \tfrac{1}{2}x , \qquad (3.2)$$

where x is the measured distance between neighbouring diffraction spots in the systematic row on the diffraction pattern *. As discussed previously, the movement of Kikuchi lines records rotations of the crystal and in this case the rotations involved are about a direction normal to the operative diffracting vector, where a rotation of $2\theta_B$ would correspond to a movement of a particular Kikuchi line on the diffraction pattern through a distance x. Therefore the angle $\Delta\theta_1$ through which the crystal has been rotated to give a displacement Δx_1 of the Kikuchi lines is given by

$$\Delta\theta_1/2\theta_B = \Delta x_1/x . \qquad (3.3)$$

Combining eqs. (3.1) and (3.3) gives

$$s = 2|g|(\Delta x_1/x)\theta_B . \qquad (3.4)$$

* In practice, the central beam and diffracted beam give diffuse spots and to obtain an accurate value of x it is necessary to measure the distance between sharper spots (e.g. between $-g$ and $2g$ giving the value of $3x$).

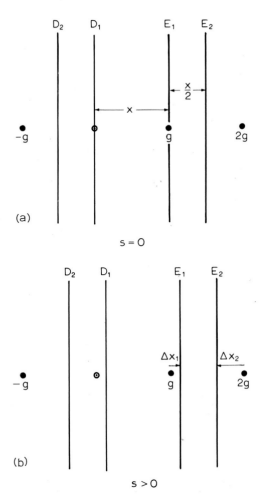

Fig. 3.16. Schematic illustration of the movement of the first order and second order excess (E_1, E_2) and deficient (D_1, D_2) Kikuchi lines relative to the diffraction spots. In (a) the crystal is set at the exact Bragg position and in (b) tilted so that s is positive for the diffracting vector g.

Since the first order excess Kikuchi line is usually diffuse, in practice it is more accurate to measure from the diffraction pattern the distance Δx_2 between the second order diffraction spot and its associated excess Kikuchi line. By combining eqs. (3.2) and (3.4) we obtain an expression for s in terms of Δx_2,

$$s = |g|\, \theta_B (1 - 2\Delta x_2/x) . \qquad (3.5)$$

Then

$$w = \xi_g |\boldsymbol{g}| \theta_B (1 - 2\Delta x_2/x) . \qquad (3.6)$$

Since w is a linear function of $\Delta x_2/x$, it is convenient to plot w against $\Delta x_2/x$ for a particular material and diffracting vector, using the two fixed values $\Delta x_2 = 0$ (i.e. when $w = \xi_g |\boldsymbol{g}| \theta_B$) and $\Delta x_2 = \frac{1}{2}x$ (i.e. when $w = 0$). Figure 3.17 shows the variation of w with $\Delta x_2/x$ for different diffracting vectors in aluminium using the two-beam extinction distances given in table 3.1(b) with the appropriate Debye–Waller correction.

As an example of the determination of w the diffraction pattern in fig. 3.8(b) will be used. Here the value of $\Delta x_2/x$ for the 200 diffraction spot is 0.35 ± 0.05 which from fig. 3.17 gives a value for w of 0.95 ± 0.1, where the error quoted on the value of w has been taken as the error in the measurement of $\Delta x_2/x$.

With most double tilting stages, the magnification of the diffraction pattern will alter with the angle of tilt and x will vary from one diffraction pattern to the next so that x as well as Δx_2 must be measured for each diffraction pattern.

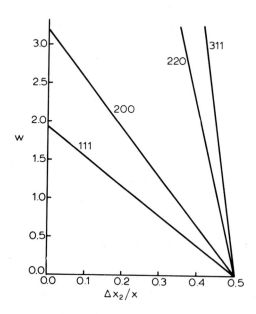

Fig. 3.17. Variations in w as a function of $\Delta x_2/x$ for 111, 200, 220 and 311 diffracting vectors in aluminium.

3.10. Determination of foil thickness

To compute theoretical images, an estimate of the foil thickness is required. There are many possible methods for determining the thickness of a foil (see for example Hirsch et al., 1965, p. 415) but only a few of these are directly applicable to thinned foils *in situ* in the electron microscope. Common methods used involve the measurement from micrographs of features which are projections of corresponding features·in the crystal.

The foil thickness can be readily calculated from a direct measurement on a single micrograph of the projected length of a straight defect which intersects the top and bottom surfaces of the foil. A defect which could be used for this purpose is a straight dislocation running completely through the foil. The method involves knowing the u of the dislocation (§3.6), the beam direction for the micrograph (§3.5) and the foil normal (§3.7). Consider a defect DS which runs from the bottom to the top of a tilted foil of thickness t and the projected length ℓ of this defect on the plane normal to the beam direction B, as illustrated in fig. 3.18. The relationship between t and ℓ can be seen by considering the relationship of each to the length DS. Thus, $t = \mathrm{DS}\cos\alpha$ and $\ell = \mathrm{DS}\sin\beta$ giving:

$$t = \frac{\ell \cos\alpha}{\sin\beta} \, , \tag{3.7}$$

where α is the angle between u and the foil normal and β is the angle between u and the beam direction. The angles α and β can readily be obtained from a stereographic projection.

Features other than dislocations such as traces of single or intersecting slip planes also provide a ready means of determining foil thickness. For example, if the intersection of a known slip plane with the foil surfaces is indicated by slip traces or fault fringes, then the projected width of this plane may be measured on the micrograph. The crystallographic direction of the line perpendicular to the traces in the micrograph can be determined from a stereographic projection, using the fact that it lies in the known slip plane. When this direction has been found the foil thickness may be obtained from eq. (3.7). If two known planes intersect, then the crystallographic direction of this intersection is known and the line of intersection may be used as the straight line feature.

All methods for determining foil thickness which use measurements on micrographs involve knowing the magnification of the particular micrograph. It should be noted that with many double tilt stages the magnification of images may vary by as much as ±10% between extremes of tilt.

The methods discussed so far give an absolute measurement of foil thick-

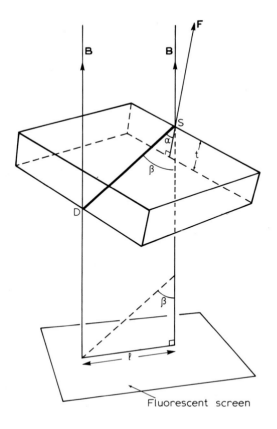

Fig. 3.18. Schematic illustration of the geometry of a tilted foil.

ness. For image computation foil thicknesses (and in fact all geometrical dimensions of defects) are required in units of extinction distance. However, as pointed out in ch. 2, the apparent value of extinction distance that is needed to relate an image computed on the two-beam approximation to an experimental image is likely to differ from the theoretical two-beam extinction distance ξ_g. For this reason the methods described above for determining foil thickness are not those most readily applicable to image computation. A more useful method for the purposes of image computation therefore is one which provides an estimate of the foil thickness directly in units of apparent extinction distance. A suitable method which satisfies this requirement uses the oscillatory character of the contrast of images of defects in crystals as a function of depth in the foil (e.g., fault fringes, grain-boundary fringes, and oscillations in the intensity of dislocation images). For the usual range of experimental foil thickness and for normal values of $\mathcal{A}$, the number of these

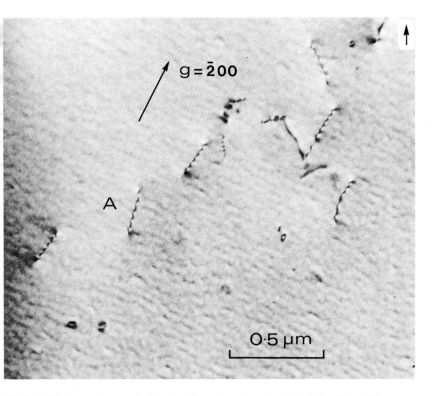

Fig. 3.19. Electron micrograph showing dislocations in a thin foil of aluminium. The beam direction B is [013] and the diffracting vector g is indicated.

oscillations along the length of a defect which intersects both surfaces of the foil, can be interpreted as a measure of the foil thickness in units of an effective extinction distance ξ_{ga}^{w}, for the operative diffracting vector g at the appropriate deviation w from the exact Bragg condition. This thickness can be readily expressed in terms of the apparent extinction distance ξ_{ga} at zero w by making use of the relation:

$$\xi_{ga}^{w} = \xi_{ga}(1 + w^2)^{-\frac{1}{2}} . \qquad (3.8)$$

The value obtained by this means is a measurement of the foil thickness in the beam direction t' and the true foil thickness t is subsequently obtained from the relation

$$t = t' \cos\delta , \qquad (3.9)$$

where δ is the angle between the beam direction and the foil normal.

The method of counting the number of contrast oscillations in an image gives an approximate value for the foil thickness but this estimate can be improved by averaging over several images. When these involve different diffracting vectors the values of foil thickness are scaled in the ratio of the relevant extinction distances *. It will be seen in ch. 5 that this approximate value of t can be refined very readily by image computation using the program DELUGE.

As an example of the method of using oscillations in contrast to determine foil thickness, the image of dislocation A in fig. 3.19 will be used. This has nearly six complete oscillations in contrast along its length. The value of w for this image determined in the manner shown in §3.9 is 0.50 ± 0.1 and the angle δ between the foil normal [528] and the beam direction [013] is $32°$. Assuming that the number of contrast oscillations is in fact six, i.e. $t' = 6\xi_{200a}^{w}$, then by combining eqs. (3.8) and (3.9), the foil thickness t is given by

$$ t = \frac{6 \cos 32°}{(1 + 0.5^2)^{\frac{1}{2}}} \xi_{200a} \, , $$

i.e.

$$ t = 4.6 \xi_{200a} \, . $$

As an example of a method for determining an absolute value of foil thickness, the projected length of dislocation A in fig. 3.19 will be used. This length is $0.24 \pm 0.02 \, \mu m$ and the angles α and β in eq. (3.7) are $25°$ and $54.5°$ respectively. Thus from eq. (3.7),

$$ t = \frac{0.24 \times 0.906}{0.814} \, \mu m \, , $$

i.e.

$$ t = 2670 \pm 250 \, \text{Å} \, . $$

An estimate for the apparent extinction distance ξ_{200a} in Ångströms can be obtained by dividing the value of t in Ångströms by the value t in units of ξ_{200a} and the resulting value of ξ_{200a} is 580 ± 55 Å. This value may be compared with the value of the theoretical Debye–Waller corrected two-beam extinction distance, $\xi_{200} = 702$ Å. A determination of apparent extinction distances using computed images will be illustrated in ch. 7.

* For this purpose the ratios of ξ_{ga} are taken to be the ratios of ξ_g.

3.11. Anomalous absorption coefficient

A value for the anomalous absorption coefficient $\mathcal{A}$ is required for image computation. Humphreys and Hirsch (1968) have shown that the traditional use of $\mathcal{A}$ = 0.1, independent of diffracting vector and material, may be inappropriate. Estimates of $\mathcal{A}$ for some materials and diffracting vectors can be made from the theoretical values of Humphreys and Hirsch (reproduced in fig. 3.20) or alternatively from the values of V_g and V'_g given by Radi (1970). The values shown in fig. 3.20 and those obtained from Radi's results are for the theoretical case of 'zero aperture' and in practice, where objective apertures with angular diameters of the order of the Bragg angle may be used, these values generally need to be increased (Metherell and Whelan, 1967). Image matching itself can be used to determine values of $\mathcal{A}$ applicable to particular images (see §8.5). Table 3.4 lists for several metals

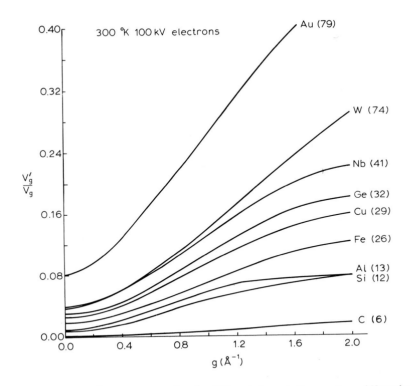

Fig. 3.20. $V'_g/V_g = \mathcal{A}$ as a function of $|g|$ for different elements (by courtesy of Humphreys and Hirsch , 1968).

TABLE 3.4
Experimental and theoretical values of $\mathscr{A}$

			Experimental				Radi		
Material	g	111	200	220	311	111	200	220	311
Al		0.06	0.07	0.09	0.11	0.031	0.034	0.043	0.051
Cu		0.07	0.08	0.1	0.1	0.075	0.079	0.091	0.099
Ni		0.07	0.08	0.1	0.12	0.056	0.061	0.073	0.080
Cu +15 at % Al		0.067	0.08	0.1	0.1				
Cu +8 at % Si		0.067	0.08	0.1	0.1				

and alloys values of $\mathscr{A}$ which we have found appropriate for an aperture angle of approximately 1° and included in this table are zero-aperture values of $\mathscr{A}$ for pure metals taken from Radi.

4 | PRINCIPLES OF ONEDIS

4.1. Introduction

By now it will be appreciated that, unlike the isotropic case, it is not possible to formulate general invisibility rules for anisotropic elasticity and each individual case must be computed numerically. It follows that for any identification technique based on anisotropic elasticity to be practicable, the computation of the image and its comparison with experiment must be quick and easy.

The major time-consuming step in computing a theoretical micrograph is the numerical integration of the differential equations. The computation of a halftone picture of the type used in this technique, consisting of about 8000 separate values of intensity, would normally require the integration of the Howie–Whelan equations (2.5) down this number of columns, the length of each being equal to the thickness of the foil. However, using one simplifying assumption, it may be shown that the displacements in the columns, and therefore the integrations, are not entirely independent. Using the relation between displacement fields in neighbouring columns of the crystal, and the fact that the Howie–Whelan equations are a pair of coupled *linear* differential equations, the effective number of integrations which have to be performed may be reduced from 8000 to 240.

This chapter deals with the details of how this reduction is achieved and how a halftone theoretical image may be obtained for single, isolated, linear defects. The crystal dislocation is, of course, the major example of such a defect, but in fact many of the principles described here apply to any linear defect. The name of the computer program which produces theoretical micrographs of a single dislocation in cubic crystals is ONEDIS.

It will be understood that there is not just one computer program which produces theoretical micrographs, but a whole family of them designed to deal with different types and configurations of defect. Since all of them employ the concepts embodied in ONEDIS we have chosen to describe the basic principles and common features in detail here. The other programs can be obtained by modifications of ONEDIS, usually to the main program (the geometry and organisation) and to the displacement function (DERIV).

4.2. The two basic principles

The geometry of the specimen and defect and their relation to the computed micrograph are shown in fig. 4.1. The figure represents a cuboid cut from a parallel sided specimen in such a way as to just include the defect which slopes from one surface of the foil to the other. The planes EFML, HGNO are parts of the original foil surfaces and the edges of the cuboid EH, FG, MN and LO are all parallel to the electron beam. The defect is represented by the straight line DS and it slopes through the foil such that it emerges at the bottom surface of the crystal at D and the top surface at S. The micrograph is formed by the electron beam passing through the crystal and recording an image on the photographic plate placed normal to it. The micrograph is represented by $H_2G_2N_2O_2$ in fig. 4.1 and it may be seen that it just

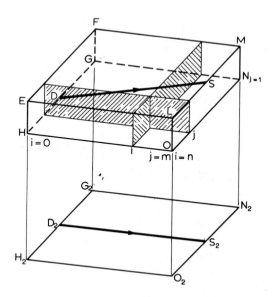

Fig. 4.1. The volume of an untilted foil EFMLHGNO, which just contains the linear defect DS, in relation to its electron micrograph $H_2G_2N_2O_2$.

accommodates the projected length of the defect D_2S_2. This is the standard way of framing the micrograph. As depicted in fig. 4.1, the crystal is untilted; that is, the foil normal is parallel to the beam direction. In §4.3, tilted foils, different ways of framing the micrograph and changes in magnification will be dealt with.

Integration of the Howie–Whelan equations down columns parallel to EH which are spaced over the area EFML will produce the information necessary for a theoretical micrograph. If columns are chosen in a plane crossing the defect, e.g. the shaded plane marked i in fig. 4.1, then intensities corresponding to a profile will be produced. However, the displacements from one column to another in this plane are generally not simply related. It is much more worthwhile to consider columns in planes parallel to the defect line, e.g. the shaded plane marked j. Integration of the equations down columns taken in this plane give intensities along a line parallel to the projection of the defect on the micrograph.

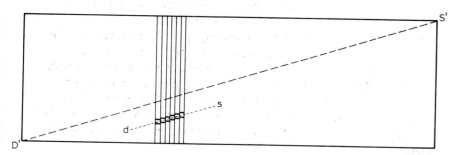

Fig. 4.2. Side elevation of an untilted foil illustrating that the displacements in neighbouring columns of the crystal are the same if they lie on a line such as ds which is parallel to the defect line (projection D'S') provided that the effects at the free surfaces are neglected.

In fig. 4.2, the plane j is redrawn in elevation looking along the direction ON of fig. 4.1. The dashed line D'S' represents the projection of the defect line DS onto the plane j, the line of the defect itself lying below the plane of the paper. At this stage, the simplifying assumption is made that only straight defects will be considered and that the displacements around the defect are those for an infinite defect in an infinite medium. That is, it is as if the piece of crystal EFML HGNO has been cut out of the infinite medium and tractions have been applied over the planes EFML and HGNO such that the state of strain which existed in the infinite crystal is maintained *. A common way

* The other planes, EFGH, FMNG, LMNO and ELOH which bound the cuboid in fig. 4.1 are merely to restrict the volume of crystal considered. As far as the elasticity problem, and in particular the displacement field, is concerned, the crystal is infinite beyond these planes.

of expressing this is to say that no relaxations are allowed at the free surfaces, but this can be misleading because it may be taken to imply that all stresses and all displacements are zero at a free surface. This, of course, is not the case. At a free surface, only those stresses which act across the surface must be zero; the other stresses and the displacements are in general non-zero and their values can be obtained by solving the ensuing elasticity problem. Thus, without detailed calculation, it is not possible to say how the displacements differ from those in the infinite crystal. The assumption that they do not change at all is obviously unphysical and the consequences of this will be discussed in ch. 9. The advantage in making this assumption is that it leads to the displacements due to a defect being constant along any line parallel to the defect. Consider neighbouring columns in the plane depicted in fig. 4.2. An element in one column will have the same displacements as an element in the neighbouring column if the two elements lie on a line parallel to the defect. That is, the displacements in the elements lying on the line ds in fig. 4.2 are all the same. It is readily seen that, except for small elements of material at the top and bottom of the columns, all of the elements in two neighbouring columns are related in this way. Thus the displacements which are encountered by electrons passing down the two columns are substantially the same. In integrating the Howie–Whelan equations to evaluate the intensities of neighbouring points on a row of the micrograph, the majority of the values of the function β' are the same. It is the elimination of this repetition from one column to the next which reduces the effective number of integrations through the thickness of the foil from 7740 to 240 per micrograph.

4.2.1. THE GENERALISED CROSS-SECTION

The first step in the elimination of wasteful integration is to re-define the elasticity problem so that it reduces from three dimensions to two. This may be done by projecting the displacement field in a direction parallel to the line of the defect onto a plane which intersects the defect. Since the direction of projection is also the direction of constant displacement, the displacements on this plane are unique and single valued. They are, however, still a complete description of the three-dimensional situation. The plane which is chosen may be any plane which intersects the defect, but for convenience it is chosen to include the electron beam direction B. In fact, the plane which is chosen is that which is normal to the vector $(u \wedge B) \wedge B$, where u is a vector along the line of the defect. This plane is parallel to the plane LMNO in fig. 4.1. The portion of the plane, which contains the displacements in the piece of crystal shown in fig. 4.1 necessary for the computation of the theoretical micrograph, is called the generalised cross-section for that piece of crystal. This is shown in fig. 4.3. The lines HG and LM in fig. 4.1 project into $H_1 G_1$ and

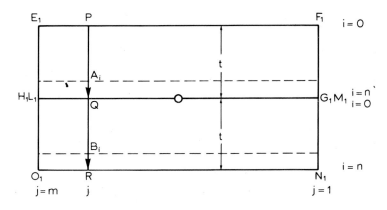

Fig. 4.3. Generalised cross-section for a single linear defect in an untilted parallel sided foil.

$L_1 M_1$ respectively in fig. 4.3 and these, of course, are coincident. The defect is marked by the small circle on this line; the defect line is coming out of the page, but is not perpendicular to it. The lines EF and ON in fig. 4.1 project into the lines $E_1 F_1$ and $O_1 N_1$ respectively in fig. 4.3. Note that, for the standard way of framing the micrograph, the height of the generalised cross-section $E_1 O_1$ is exactly twice the thickness t of the crystal (LO).

The displacements within the rectangle $E_1 F_1 N_1 O_1$ of fig. 4.3 represent all those found in the volume of crystal EFMLGHNO and thus are all that are necessary to produce the theoretical micrograph. This may be seen by considering two lines, a constant distance t apart, drawn across the generalised cross-section parallel to $E_1 F_1$. When the lines are at $E_1 F_1$ and $H_1 G_1$ respectively, they delineate that part of the displacement field found in the crystal when the defect is just at the bottom of the foil. The positions $L_1 M_1$ and $O_1 N_1$ delineate the portion of the displacement field in the crystal with the defect just leaving the top surface. Intermediate positions of the lines, such as those indicated by the dashed lines in fig. 4.3, delineate the displacement field found on the shaded plane i in fig. 4.1. Note that the positions of the top line occur only in the top half of the generalised cross-section and correspond to points on the top surface of the real crystal. Positions of the bottom line occur only in the bottom half and correspond to points on the bottom surface of the crystal. Integration of the Howie–Whelan equations down a column such as that marked j in the generalised cross-section corresponds to integration down all columns contained by the plane marked j in the piece of real crystal (fig. 4.1) and eventually gives the intensity of the image along a row parallel to the defect. Integration down successive columns in the generalised cross-section from $E_1 O_1$ to $F_1 N_1$ therefore provides all the intensity information for the computed micrograph.

4.2.2. LINEAR COMBINATIONS

Having established the concept of the generalised cross-section which completely specifies the displacement field and therefore the function β' (§ 2.7), it is now necessary to consider the interaction of the electrons with this displacement field. The basic fact which has to be recognised when dealing with this aspect of the problem is that the equations describing the diffraction phenomenon, eqs. (2.5), are a coupled pair of first-order linear differential equations in two unknowns, T and S. Because these equations are linear, their general solution can be written as a linear combination of independent particular solutions. The number of independent solutions for these equations is two, since they are a pair of first-order equations. So the solution corresponding to any particular boundary condition can be constructed by taking the appropriate linear combination of a pair of independent solutions. In outline, therefore, the procedure to obtain intensity values for a row of the micrograph is to perform two independent integrations of eqs. (2.5) down columns j in the generalised cross-section, so that the two independent solutions are available, and then to combine these linearly to satisfy the appropriate boundary conditions for each starting point. Since two independent integrations down a column of length $2t$ of the generalised cross-section (i.e. the equivalent of four integrations through the thickness of the foil t) provide all the information for 129 points of intensity along a row parallel to the defect in the computed micrograph, this represents a saving of 125 integrations compared with obtaining the same information in the conventional manner.

In detail, the procedure is as follows. Consider a representative column j in the generalised cross-section (fig. 4.3). This is divided into two equal parts; the first from P to Q (part A) and the second from Q to R (part B). Each of these is divided into n equal steps, where the integer n is related to the number of intensity values required in a row of the micrograph. Two independent 'experiments' are performed simultaneously down this column. Independence is assured by setting $T = 1$ and $S = 0$ as the initial values at P for one experiment and $T = 0$ and $S = 1$ for the other experiment. Equations (2.5), with the same values of the function β' and the other parameters, are used for both experiments and they are integrated down the column. The end of each of the n steps in the first part of the integration will represent a point on the top surface of the real crystal in the jth plane. Thus at the end of each step in the first part of the integration, the values of the amplitudes T and S from each experiment are combined linearly and in such a way that the resulting values of the amplitudes represent those of an electron beam in a vacuum about to enter the crystal, i.e. $T = 1, S = 0$. If the amplitudes for the first experiment at the position A_i in fig. 4.3 are $T_{A_i}^{(1)}$ and $S_{A_i}^{(1)}$ and those for the second experiment at the same position are $T_{A_i}^{(2)}$ and $S_{A_i}^{(2)}$, then the required condition is that:

$$a_i T_{A_i}^{(1)} + b_i T_{A_i}^{(2)} = 1 \, ,$$

and

$$a_i S_{A_i}^{(1)} + b_i S_{A_i}^{(2)} = 0 \, , \tag{4.1}$$

where a_i and b_i are constants to be determined. Thus, at the end of each stage of integration in the first part of the column, eqs. (4.1) are solved for the proportionality constants a_i and b_i and these are stored in the computer memory. It should be remembered that, since T and S are complex, a_i and b_i are also complex. However, in the programs themselves, for reasons of speed, complex arithmetic is not used but T, S, a_i and b_i are split up into their real and imaginary parts and the resulting four equations (corresponding to eqs. (4.1)) are used in the calculation. The amplitudes T and S appear in the program as subscripted variables Y. T and S for the first experiment are defined by:

$$T^{(1)} = \mathrm{Y}(1) + \sqrt{(-1)}\,\mathrm{Y}(2) \, ,$$

$$S^{(1)} = \mathrm{Y}(3) + \sqrt{(-1)}\,\mathrm{Y}(4) \, , \tag{4.2}$$

and for the second experiment:

$$T^{(2)} = \mathrm{Y}(5) + \sqrt{(-1)}\,\mathrm{Y}(6) \, ,$$

$$S^{(2)} = \mathrm{Y}(7) + \sqrt{(-1)}\,\mathrm{Y}(8) \, . \tag{4.3}$$

The constants a_i and b_i are the doubly subscripted variable FX and their definitions are:

$$a_i = \mathrm{FX}(i, 1) + \sqrt{(-1)}\mathrm{FX}(i, 2) \, ,$$

$$b_i = \mathrm{FX}(i, 3) + \sqrt{(-1)}\,\mathrm{FX}(i, 4) \, . \tag{4.4}$$

The integration of eqs. (2.5) is continued in the second part of the column and again the process is interrupted at the end of each of the n steps. This time, however, the final amplitudes required for the micrograph, T^F and S^F, are calculated from the current amplitudes. At a position B_i (fig. 4.3) in the second part of the integration (at depth t below A_i) T^F and S^F may be calculated from the amplitudes of the two experiments using the constants a_i

and b_i (evaluated at the level A_i) from the equations:

$$T_i^F = a_i T_{B_i}^{(1)} + b_i T_{B_i}^{(2)} ,$$

$$S_i^F = a_i S_{B_i}^{(1)} + b_i S_{B_i}^{(2)} . \qquad (4.5)$$

Squaring the modulus of T_i^F and of S_i^F gives the bright field and dark field intensities respectively of the $(i+1)$th point in the row of the micrograph corresponding to the jth plane. The bright and dark field intensities for the first point in the row are obtained simply by squaring the moduli of the amplitudes of the first experiment at the point Q. This may be done because the initial conditions at a distance t above this, i.e. at P, already conform to the conditions expressed in eqs. (4.1), namely $T^{(1)} = 1$ and $S^{(1)} = 0$.

Following the procedure described above, and allowing i to run from 1 to n for both parts of the integration, results in $n+1$ values of intensity along the jth row of the micrograph parallel to the defect. The intensity values are each divided by background intensity * and they are stored successively in the array TB until all $n+1$ values for a row have been accumulated. The intensities so normalised are then transmitted to the line printer where they are printed as one row of the micrograph. Running the index j from 1 to m scans the columns of the generalised cross-section and results in the m rows of the micrograph. The values of n and m were decided upon by considerations of the thickness of the foil, the diffraction conditions, the displacement field of the defect, the optimum speed of the integration routine, and the size of the paper used by the line printer.

The line printer of the computer was chosen as the means for printing the theoretical micrographs because it is a standard piece of equipment with most computer installations and, in our case at least, may be programmed by the user to print and overprint any of its characters. Thus it required the least intervention by the computer operator. It will be seen in §4.5 that 'photographically' this form of output has slight disadvantages, but nevertheless, it will be assumed for the present that the prospective user of the technique will also be employing this form of output.

The size of the line printer page is of the order of 130 characters by 60 lines. In the program, the projection of the defect line is arranged to be parallel to the lines of the printed page so that the rows of intensity values corresponding to planes j are in fact lines of characters in the printed micro-

---

* Background intensity is the intensity which is obtained from a perfect crystal under the same diffracting conditions. In the programs, its value is calculated by performing an integration of eqs. (2.5) through the thickness of the foil at a very large distance from the line of the defect.

graph. In order to produce as large a micrograph as possible, the number of rows of the picture, that is the value of m, was chosen to be 60. The projection of the defect is always exactly midway between the 30th and 31st rows. This ensures that the columns in the planes corresponding to these rows are at a maximum distance from the core of the defect where the displacement function β' is largest and changing most rapidly.

The number of intensities in a row was chosen to be 129, although the number of steps n in each half of the integration is only 64 the remaining intensities being obtained by interpolation. The reason for this lies in obtaining the optimum speed of the programs for the range of foil thickness usually considered. The integration routine used in the programs is the Runge–Kutta fourth order process incorporating a modification by Merson (Lance, 1960). This is called SUBROUTINE RKM in the programs. This routine is one which automatically adjusts the size of the integration step taken (the internal step) to meet a previously chosen error criterion. The criterion for the error in the amplitudes has been set at 0.0001/step and with this, for dislocations in foils of the order of five extinction distances thick with a value of the deviation parameter w of the order of 0.5, the natural (internal) step length is in the range $\frac{1}{35} t$ to $\frac{1}{60} t$ over most of the generalised cross-section. The step size becomes smaller than this within a few columns or a few steps of the dislocation line due to the magnitude or rate of change of β', but this of course is unavoidable. The choice of $n = 64$ means that each of the required steps of the integration down a column is $\frac{1}{64} t$ which is generally smaller than the natural step of the integration routine. Thus, the specified step is done in one internal integration step. If n were 32, then each specified step would be $\frac{1}{32} t$ and the routine would generally break this down into two internal steps. Compared with the situation for $n = 64$, therefore, virtually no time would be saved. On the other hand, if n were chosen to be 128, this would necessitate at least 128 calls of the integration routine, an increase of about a factor of 2 compared with $n = 64$. In short, the speed of the integration routine (and thus the speed of the programs) is optimised when the specified steps down a column of the generalised cross-section are just smaller than those which the routine would naturally take in the absence of such restrictions.

Factors such as the thickness of the foil and its degree of tilt affect the size of the specified step, and factors such as values of w, β' and the absorption coefficients (§2.4) affect the size of the internal step. With so many factors involved, it is not practical to endeavour to achieve optimum conditions in all circumstances. Another aspect to bear in mind is that of valid interpolation. For example, if the foil thickness is very small, the specified step may be much smaller than the internal step and it may be possible to increase the speed by computing every third or fourth value of intensity. However, the problem of valid interpolation between these values may now become insuperable. On the other hand, if the foil thickness is large, the specified step size may be much larger than that of the internal step, and although no improvement in speed can be made, every value of intensity in a row of the micrograph could be calculated. Our experience has been that calculation of every second value of intensity represents the best compromise between the speed of computation and the validity of the resulting micrograph.

With the value of n set at 64, 65 values of intensity are obtained. These are assigned to the odd numbers of the 129 intensity values in the array TB which will form a row of the micrograph, the other 64 even values being obtained by simple linear interpolation. In the majority of cases this produces a theoretical micrograph which is visually indistinguishable from one in which all the values of intensity are computed by integration ($n = 128$).

Since there are of the order of 100 steps down a column in the generalised cross-section (128 steps for $n = 64$ if each step is performed in one internal step), then for an error criterion of 0.0001/step, the amplitudes are accurate to about 1% and the final intensity values to about 2%.

From the foregoing description, it is apparent that eqs. (4.1) have to be solved at each step in the first part of the column in order to evaluate the proportionality constants a_i and b_i. Evaluation of eqs. (4.5) during the second part of the integration gives both the bright field amplitudes T and the dark field amplitudes S. Thus the modulus of either, or both, of these may be squared, normalised to the appropriate background intensity, and used to produce either the bright field or dark field micrograph (or both). However, the programs described in ch. 10 do not evaluate the equation for S in expressions (4.5) and only the bright field micrograph is produced. This emphasis on bright field microscopy of defects reflects, in part, the authors' interests, but nevertheless, there are several disadvantages in the technique of dark field microscopy. The main one stems from the fact that in order to minimise lens aberrations and to obtain high resolution images experimentally, the diffracted beam has to be made to pass down the optical axis of the microscope. Even with modern beam deflecting devices this is tedious, especially in a technique of this nature where many different diffracting vectors are used. From the point of view of the theoretical micrographs, dark field images have large deviations in contrast both above and below background intensity so that their reproduction presents serious difficulties. In any case, it has been shown theoretically (Head, 1969(b) and (c)) that bright and dark field images contain exactly the same information about the displacement field of a defect. Thus, in general, the use of bright field techniques for image matching is recommended.

Since the concepts of the generalised cross-section and the two independent solutions of the Howie—Whelan equations are of central importance in the production of theoretical micrographs, it is necessary that the reader and prospective user of the technique be fully conversant with them if he intends to write his own program or make large modifications to the programs given here. To this end, the following section contains several examples in detail of how the concepts are used to produce micrographs which cover most aspects of practical microscopy.

4.3. Modifications to the generalised cross-section to accommodate experimental situations

The previous section dealt with the principles of obtaining computed micrographs from untilted foils of constant thickness framed in such a way as to just include the extreme ends of the defect. In practice, the foils are nearly always tilted with respect to the electron beam direction, and frequently it is necessary to examine part of a defect image at greater magnification. In addition, for the purposes of image matching it is often useful to have computed images of the same defect for several different foil thicknesses. Occasionally it may be necessary to compute images for a tapered foil. All of these situations can be handled quickly and easily using the principles described in the previous section. However, modifications are required to the generalised cross-section or to the arrangement of steps down the columns of the cross-section.

4.3.1. TILTED FOILS

Consider first tilted foils. Figure 4.4 depicts a piece of tilted crystal HGNOEFML of uniform thickness which just contains a defect DS. The edges of the crystal HE, GF, NM and OL are parallel to the electron beam direction B. As for untilted foils, the generalised cross-section for this situation is obtained by projection along the direction of the line of the defect u (DS) onto a plane (LMNO) normal to the vector $(u \wedge B) \wedge B$. The generalised cross-section for micrographs which are framed in the standard way (i.e. to just contain the projection of the line of the defect) is shown in fig. 4.5. The height of the generalised cross-section $E_1 O_1$ is no longer $2t$ where t is the thickness of the foil, but $2t'$ where t' is the thickness of the foil measured in the beam direction. The program name for the variable t' is THBM and t' is given in terms of t by:

$$t' = t/\cos \delta , \tag{4.6}$$

where δ is the angle between the normal to the foil surface and the beam direction. The thickness t' (PQ and QR) rather than t is now divided into n equal steps.

The generalised cross-section for a tilted foil is a parallelogram compared

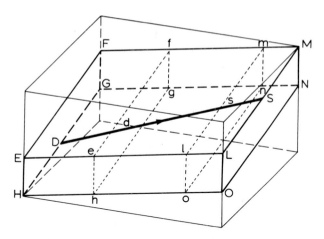

Fig. 4.4. A linear defect DS just contained in a volume EFMLHGNO of tilted crystal. The volume of crystal efmlhgno relates to the computation of a magnified image of the portion ds of the defect.

with a rectangle for untilted foils. This means that the integration of the equations is started on the line $E_1 F_1$ which is at an angle to the beam. The angle is determined by the component of tilt of the foil, with respect to the beam direction, in the generalised cross-section plane. The other component of tilt (in the plane containing the beam direction and the defect line) is automatically taken into account by this method of forming the micrograph so long as t' is used instead of t.

4.3.2. CHANGES IN THE MAGNIFICATION AND IN THE FRAMING OF COMPUTED MICROGRAPHS

Changing the framing of the theoretical micrograph is usually accompanied by a change in magnification and these two aspects of the production of theoretical micrographs may conveniently be treated together. Consider the case of a tilted foil with a defect running through it in the usual way. Suppose that it is required to magnify a section of the image corresponding to the length ds of the defect. The volume of crystal involved in this is bounded by the planes efgh, lmno in fig. 4.4.

The generalised cross-section for this case is probably best seen in the first instance by its relation to the generalised cross-section for the case where the micrograph is framed in the standard way. In fig. 4.5, $E_1 F_1 N_1 O_1$ is the generalised cross-section for the standard case: projection of the lines ef, hg, lm and on in fig. 4.4 gives the lines $e_1 f_1$, $h_1 g_1$, $l_1 m_1$, $o_1 n_1$ in fig. 4.5. A little thought will show that the portions of the displacement field needed for the magnified image range from the area selected by $e_1 f_1$ to $h_1 g_1$ (which

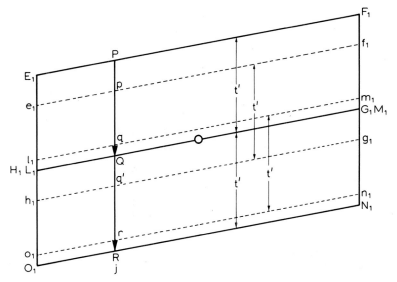

Fig. 4.5. Generalised cross-section for a single linear defect in a tilted, parallel sided foil. The dashed lines indicate the limited ranges of integration necessary to produce a magnified image of a portion of the defect.

are t' apart) to that selected by $l_1 m_1$ to $o_1 n_1$ (which are also t' apart). Thus, if the lengths pq and $q'r$ of the jth column of the generalised cross-section (fig. 4.5) are divided into n steps, then the two experiments may be started at p and the integrations carried through as before to provide the 129 intensity values in the micrograph. Since the 129 points now come from a restricted area of the generalised cross-section, but are spaced over the same area of line printer output, magnification has been achieved.

There are, however, two differences in the integration procedure which have to be noted when the micrograph is not framed in the standard way. As may be inferred by a comparison of the two generalised cross-sections shown in figs. 4.3 and 4.5, the integration of the two experiments is carried out from p to q to obtain the values of a_i and b_i and from q' to r to obtain the final amplitudes by linear combination. However, in the case of a magnified image, the integration of the two experiments must also be continued from q to q', although in this region no prescribed steps are imposed and the integration routine is allowed to go as fast as possible using its own natural step size. The other difference is that, since the points i in a row of intensities in the micrograph correspond to a smaller length in the real crystal, the spacing of the columns j in the generalised cross-section must be chosen in such a way that they are commensurate. This is done so that magnifications are the same in all directions on the micrograph and no distortions are produced. Thus, in the

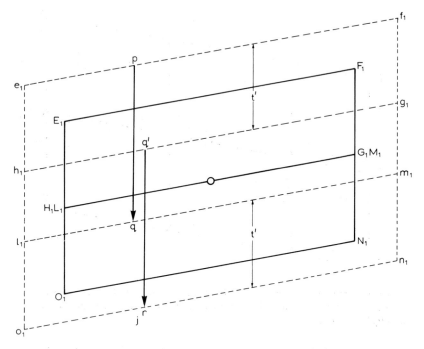

Fig. 4.6. Generalised cross-section for a single linear defect in a tilted, parallel sided foil. The cross-section enclosed by the full lines $E_1 F_1 N_1 O_1$ is that required to produce a standardly framed micrograph whilst the cross-section enclosed by the dashed lines $e_1 f_1 n_1 o_1$ is required to compute a demagnified image of the defect.

generalised cross-section, when the ranges of integration are restricted to pq and q'r, the width $e_1 f_1$ must also be restricted: this has not been done in fig. 4.5. It will be seen in the next section that the height of the micrograph (which corresponds to the width of the generalised cross-section) is defined in terms of its length, so that the variation of the spacing of columns j in the generalised cross-section in terms of the spacing of the steps down the column is automatically taken into account.

The generalised cross-section $e_1 f_1 n_1 o_1$ necessary to produce a demagnified image of a defect is shown in fig. 4.6 in relation to the standard cross-section $E_1 F_1 N_1 O_1$. The area $e_1 f_1 n_1 o_1$ contains the displacements necessary to compute the image of the piece of crystal efmlhgno shown in fig. 4.7. It will be noted from fig. 4.6 that the line $h_1 g_1$ is now above $l_1 m_1$ whereas it was below it for a magnified image (fig. 4.5). However, the lengths $e_1 h_1$ and $l_1 o_1$ are both equal to t' in each of the figures. The procedure for obtaining one row of intensity values parallel to the defect line is, as before, to divide each of pq and q'r in the jth column of the generalised cross-section into n equal steps.

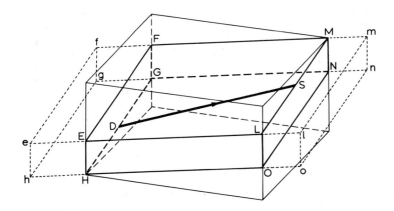

Fig. 4.7. A linear defect DS in a tilted crystal. The displacements contained in the volume efmlhgno correspond to those found in the generalised cross-section $e_1f_1n_1o_1$ in fig. 4.6.

In fig. 4.6, for the sake of clarity, pq and $q'r$ are not collinear, but it should be remembered that they both refer to the same jth column. As before, the integration of the two experiments down pq is stopped at the end of each step to calculate the constants of proportionality a_i and b_i, and the integration down $q'r$ is stopped at each step to combine the amplitudes of the two experiments in the ratios determined by a_i and b_i. However, the unusual feature in this case is that the two ranges of integration now overlap and this presents some problems in programming. It would be obviously wasteful to integrate from p to q, from q to q' and then from q' to r as we did in the case of a magnified image, because the integration would then pass up and down the piece qq' of the column three times. On the other hand, there are organisational difficulties if the procedures of the second part of the integration are carried out simultaneously with those of the first part over the length $q'q$. The compromise which has been adopted is that, before starting the first part of the integration, the position of the point q' is defined (SURFAC in the programs) and before performing each of the n steps in the first part of the integration, a test is made to see if the point q' occurs in the step. If or when it does, the integrations are interrupted at q' and the amplitudes stored in the memory (TEMPY in the programs). At the end of the first part of the integration, these amplitudes are recovered from the memory and used as the starting conditions for the second part of the integration from q' to r. This is carried out in the usual manner. This way of solving the problem involves integration down the part of the column $q'q$ twice, but, provided the integration routine does each of the n steps in one internal step, this is in fact as fast

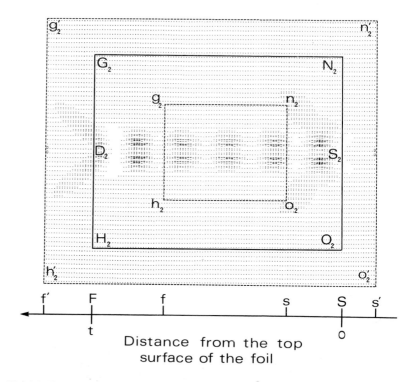

Distance from the top
surface of the foil

Fig. 4.8. The relationship between three ways of framing a theoretical micrograph, the corresponding values of START (S, s or s') and FINISH (F, f or f') to be used as data, and the positions which these values correspond to in a foil of thickness t .

as doing the first and second part procedures simultaneously down $q'q$ *.

The programs are written in such a way that all the options of non-standard framing and variable magnification are handled automatically. The variables which are needed as data to determine the options are START and FINISH. These represent distances measured in units of the extinction distance in a direction antiparallel to the normal to the foil surface, the origin being taken at the point where the defect line meets the top surface of the foil. Thus, START = 0, FINISH = t, will frame the micrograph in the standard way; FINISH−START > t produces demagnified micrographs and FINISH−START < t produces magnified images of part of the defect.

* This is because in general q' will not occur at one of the boundaries between the n steps, so that each step will be broken down into two; at the end of one, constants a_i and b_i are calculated, and at the end of the other, amplitudes are combined. Since the step is broken down into two, this takes about twice as long as one normal step.

Another way of considering the influence of the variables START and FINISH is illustrated in fig. 4.8. In this figure the rectangle $H_2G_2N_2O_2$ represents the micrograph framed around the defect in the standard way so that S_2 represents a point on the top surface of the foil and D_2 a point on the bottom surface. Thus the length of the picture H_2O_2 may be taken to represent the thickness t of the foil * and the point O_2 is equivalent to a value of START = 0 and the point H_2 to a value of FINISH = t; these are indicated on the scale by the points S and F. If it is wished to magnify the area $h_2g_2n_2o_2$ to the size of a full computed micrograph by restricting the range of integration, then START corresponds to s and FINISH to f. Similarly the area $h_2'g_2'n_2'o_2'$ will be computed for START corresponding to s' (which will be a negative number) and FINISH to f'.

Magnified images are necessary for a variety of reasons. The main one concerns resolution in the micrograph. The maximum resolution available on the theoretical micrographs is determined by the inter-character and inter-row spacing of the line printer output and since this is constant, increasing the magnification also increases the resolution. This is illustrated in fig. 4.9, where the defect and diffracting conditions are the same for each of the micrographs (a) and (b), but because of the increased magnification and resolution in (b), the narrow black line feature becomes visible.

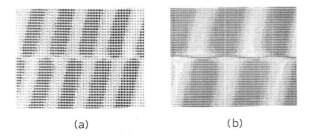

(a)   (b)

Fig. 4.9. Theoretical micrographs computed for the same defect (a complex loop, see §8.11) under the same diffracting conditions, illustrating the increased resolution available in computed images at increased magnification.

The need for computing images over a range which is greater in extent than the projection of the line of the defect on the micrograph may not be so obvious. However, it should be remembered that the displacement field of a defect extends throughout the crystal, and it is often of appreciable strength outside the volume of crystal which just contains the defect, i.e. the volume

* Note that H_2O_2 represents the actual foil thickness t and not the thickness of the foil in the beam direction t'.

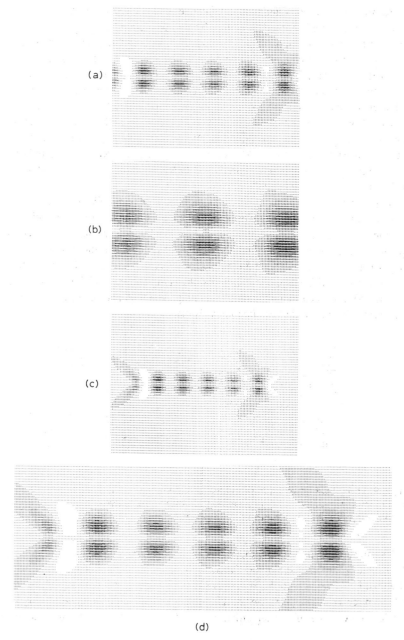

Fig. 4.10. Illustrating four possible ways of producing the computed image of a defect: (a) standard framing, (b) magnification of a portion of the image, (c) demagnification of the whole of the image, and (d) a magnified image of the whole defect using two adjoining computed micrographs.

selected in a normally framed micrograph. Thus, the images of defects nearly always extend beyond the ends of the projection of the actual line of the defect on the micrograph and in many cases it is useful to include this part of the image on the micrograph.

If regions at both ends of the defect are included on the micrograph, this can lead to an unacceptable demagnification and loss of resolution of the image and a method commonly employed to overcome this is to compute an image in two parts, each part on a separate micrograph. A convenient way of doing this is to put START < 0 and FINISH $= \frac{1}{2}t$ for one micrograph and START $= \frac{1}{2}t$ and FINISH $> t$ for the second *. When images are made up from multiple micrographs in this way and START for one is the same as FINISH for another, the left-hand column of the micrograph for the upper part of the defect is identical with the right-hand column of the micrograph of the lower part. Thus the micrographs may be easily oriented and joined. Figure 4.10 illustrates the four basic variations in methods of framing computed micrographs. The example is that of a $[\bar{1}11]$ screw dislocation in a foil of β-brass $5\xi_{110}$ thick imaged with the $\bar{1}10$ diffracting vector. Figure 4.10(a) shows the standard framing, START = 0.0, FINISH = 5.0; fig. 4.10(b) illustrates a magnified portion of the image, START = 1.2, FINISH = 3.4; fig. 4.10(c) is a demagnified image on one micrograph, START = -1.0, FINISH = 6.0; fig. 4.10(d) is a composite of two micrographs, START = -0.5, FINISH = 2.5 for the right-hand half of the image, and START = 2.5, FINISH = 5.5 for the left-hand half.

4.3.3. VARIABLE FOIL THICKNESS

It will be appreciated from the discussion in §§ 2.6 and 3.10 that foil thickness is one of the least well-known parameters required for micrograph computation. Thus in the initial stages of image matching it is very con-venient to be able to quickly compute several micrographs of the same defect in foils of different thickness. The program modification which does this is called DELUGE (§ 10.8), and the principles underlying this program are as follows. Figure 4.11(a) shows the generalised cross-section for a defect in an untilted foil of thickness t, where for the purposes of illustration the jth column has been divided up into two lots of nine equal steps. The boundaries of these steps are marked 0 to 9 in the figure and, because the cross-section corresponds to a standard framing of the micrograph, boundary 9 of the first part of the integration coincides with boundary 0 of the second part. The two independent experiments are integrated down the first part of the column and the proportionality constants a_i and b_i calculated from expressions (4.1) at

---

* For the magnification of both computed images to be the same, the difference (FINISH−START) must be the same in each.

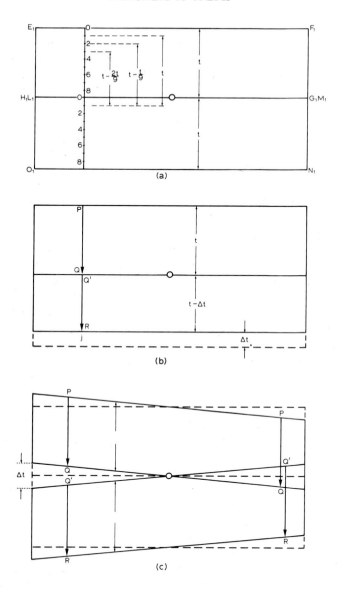

Fig. 4.11. Generalised cross-sections for single linear defects in foils of varying thickness. (a) Illustrating the 'mis-combinations' principle to obtain images of the same defect in a series of parallel sided foils with thicknesses less than t at the expense of very little extra computing time. This is the basis of program DELUGE. (b) The generalised cross-section for a single linear defect in a foil tapered uniformly in a plane containing the defect line. (c) The generalised cross-section for a single linear defect in a foil tapered uniformly in a plane normal to the defect line.

the end of each step in the usual way. Continuing the integrations through the second part of the column and using a_i and b_i at the appropriate boundaries according to expressions (4.5) gives T^F and S^F. Since the length of each half of the column is t and since each is divided into the same number of equal steps, then using a_1 and b_1 in eqs. (4.5) at boundary 1 in the second part, a_2 and b_2 at boundary 2 and so on, results in final amplitudes which correspond to a foil thickness t. However, it will be apparent that it is also possible to use the constants a_1 and b_1 for boundary 0 in the second part, a_2 and b_2 for boundary 1 and so on, to a_9 and b_9 for boundary 8, and thus obtain values of T^F and S^F for a foil thickness of $t - \frac{1}{9}t$. Moreover, a whole series of similar 'mis-combinations' can be used to obtain values of T^F and S^F for foils which have thicknesses decreasing in steps of $\frac{1}{9}t$. For actual micrographs the number of steps n in each part of the integration is much greater than 9 (n = 64 in the programs given in ch. 10). Thus, if not only the constants a_i and b_i, but also the amplitudes of the two experiments for the second part of the integration are stored, then there is sufficient information to compute micrographs of the same defect in foils decreasing from a thickness t to zero in steps of t/n without the necessity for further integration. Hence extra computed micrographs come at very little extra cost. Note that if the first micrograph in the series, the one for which foil thickness is t, is framed in the standard way then each of the successive images will also be standardly framed and will contain successively one less value of intensity per row of the micrograph if interpolation is not being used, and two less if interpolation between neighbouring intensities is being used.

The constructions of the generalised cross-sections have so far all been described in terms of a foil which has a constant thickness. In fact, the areas of the specimen one tends to select in practice have essentially a constant thickness with perhaps only a slight amount of taper. Because the topology of the images is usually insensitive to the amount of taper which is encountered, in practice programs for tapered foils are rarely needed. However, they are considered here for the sake of completeness.

The generalised cross-section for a single defect in a tapered but untilted foil is shown in figs. 4.11(b) and 4.11(c). In these figures, the generalised cross-section for a foil of constant thickness is shown in dashed lines. Figure 4.11(b) shows the generalised cross-section for a foil which is uniformly tapered in a plane containing the defect line. The two ranges of integration for a representative column j are PQ and Q'R, where PQ = t and Q'R = $t - \Delta t$, and these are each divided into n steps. Since PQ $\neq$ Q'R, the step size is no longer equal in the two parts of the integration. A little thought will reveal that combining the results of the integrations at the end of corresponding steps will produce intensities appropriate to a foil which tapers uniformly from a thickness t, when the defect is at the bottom of the foil, to a thickness $t - \Delta t$

when it is at the top of the foil. That is, in the micrograph the thickness is t on the left and $t - \Delta t$ on the right. For example, in fig. 4.1 the thickness would be t along the line H_2G_2 and $t - \Delta t$ along O_2N_2.

Figure 4.11(c) shows the generalised cross-section for a single defect in an untilted foil which is uniformly tapered in a plane normal to the defect line. In this case, the ranges of integration PQ and $Q'R$ are both equal to t and are each divided into n equal steps. However, the ranges are separated by an amount Δt at the extreme left of the cross-section and overlap by this amount at the extreme right. Combining the results at the end of corresponding steps in each part of the integration produces a theoretical micrograph which corresponds to a foil thickness $t - \Delta t$ at the top, t in the middle and $t + \Delta t$ at the bottom of the micrograph, i.e. in fig. 4.1, $t - \Delta t$ along G_2N_2, t along D_2S_2 and $t + \Delta t$ along H_2O_2.

Programs for tapered foils are not given in ch. 10, but certain difficulties associated with their use are discussed in §9.5.

4.4. Program geometry

So far, only the principles of the programs have been discussed and although the programs themselves are presented and discussed in ch. 10, it is convenient to give more detailed information here, particularly about the geometry concerned, in order that the prospective user will make the transition from principles to actual programs as smoothly as possible.

There are four distinct axis systems which are used in the programs. The first of these is the crystal axis system. The crystallographic data, b, u, g, B and F are denoted by indices with respect to this axis system with g and F being referred to the reciprocal lattice. For this data, the magnitudes of b and g are important whereas those of u, B and F are not. The crystal axis system reflects the symmetry of the crystal whereas the other three axis systems are all cartesian systems.

The first of these to occur in the programs is the one used for specifying the elastic constants c_{mn} (§2.7.2). For crystals of cubic symmetry, this axis system and the crystal axis system are coincident and so in the program ONEDIS given in ch. 10, only three axis systems may be discerned. For crystals of non-cubic symmetry, it is convenient to change the experimental data from its index form characteristic of the crystal system to a floating point number form in the elastic constants axis system soon after it is read into the program. This is the reason for working with floating point variables even in the cubic case (e.g. CU(J) rather than LU(J) for the components of the defect line direction u) and the reader should compare conversions of the type LU to CU for cubic crystals with those for hexagonal or tetragonal crystals (§10.6).

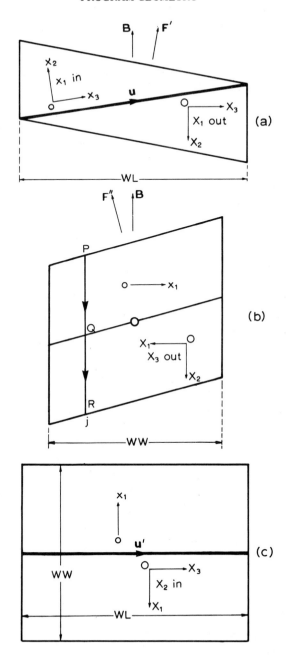

Fig. 4.12. Three views of the geometry concerned in producing a standardly framed theoretical micrograph of a single linear defect in a tilted, parallel sided foil: (a) side elevation of the foil, (b) the generalised cross-section and (c) the micrograph.

The remaining two axis systems depend on the specific geometry of the micrograph being computed. One is based on the defect line and the beam direction and is referred to as the defect axis system and the other is based on the generalised cross-section and is called the generalised cross-section axis system. The defect axes are related to the elastic constant axes by direction cosines, called in the program $DC(1, J)$, $DC(2, J)$ and $DC(3, J)$, J running from 1 to 3; the generalised cross-section axes have direction cosines $DCX(1, J)$, $DCX(2, J)$ and $DCX(3, J)$ with respect to the elastic constants axes. Figure 4.12 shows a side view of the foil (a), the generalised cross-section (b), and the micrograph (c) on which the defect axes ox_1, ox_2, ox_3 and the generalised cross-section axes OX_1, OX_2, OX_3 are marked.

Figure 4.12(a) shows a section through the defect line which contains the beam direction B. The positive direction of the defect line u is by convention always taken to be acute with the foil normal F, and the axis ox_3 is oriented along this positive direction. The axis ox_1 is taken to be normal to the plane containing B and u and has its positive sense along $B \wedge u$. The axis ox_2 is taken as $ox_3 \wedge ox_1$ to complete the right-handed set and of course lies in the plane containing B and u (the section of fig. 4.12(a)). The generalised cross-section axis system may be obtained from the defect axis system by a rotation of the latter about ox_1 until ox_2 lies in the plane of the generalised cross-section, followed by a rotation about ox_3 of $180°$. Thus $OX_1 = -ox_1$, $OX_2 = -B$ and OX_3 is chosen to complete a right-handed set.

In the programs, vectors and directions resolved with respect to the elastic constants axis system have the prefix C in their variable name, and variables given in terms of the generalised cross-section axis system have the letter X as the last letter in their name. For example, the foil normal F has the integer variable name LFN in crystal axes, CFN in elastic constants axes, FN in defect axes and FNX in generalised cross-section axes. All the directions and axes marked in fig. 4.12(a), (b) and (c) are either in the plane of the page or perpendicular to it. Thus in fig. 4.12(a), F' is the projection of F in the plane containing B and u, in fig. 4.12(b), F'' is the projection of F in the generalised cross-section and in fig. 4.12(c), u' is the projection of u onto the plane of the micrograph.

The programs are arranged so that the projection of the defect line direction runs from left to right in the micrograph. The defect is at the bottom of the foil at the left-hand side of the micrograph and at the top on the right-hand side. The length of the micrograph in a direction parallel to u' is called WL in the programs and the standard value of this (corresponding to standard framing of the micrograph) is obtained by projecting the length of the defect line onto a plane normal to the beam direction (i.e., the micrograph plane). The calculation of WL is fundamental to the program since from it the height of the micrograph (WW) and the spacing of the rows of intensity values (spacing of columns j in fig. 4.3) are determined.

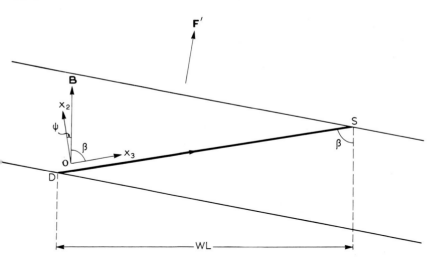

Fig. 4.13. Side elevation of a single linear defect in a tilted foil illustrating the geometry for obtaining the length of the computed micrograph WL for the case of standard framing.

The way in which WL is calculated may be seen by referring to figs. 3.18 and 4.13; fig. 4.13 is a similar section to that shown in fig. 4.12(a). It is apparent from fig. 4.13 that the length WL is just the projected length ℓ of the defect line in the micrograph and a relationship between ℓ and t (THICK), the thickness of the foil, has already been given in §3.10:

$$t = \frac{\ell \cos \alpha}{\sin \beta} \ , \qquad\qquad\qquad [(3.7)]$$

where α is the angle between the defect line direction u and the foil normal F and β is the angle between u and the beam direction B. We have therefore

$$WL = \frac{THICK \sin \beta}{\cos \alpha} \ . \qquad\qquad\qquad (4.7)$$

In the programs, both the foil normal F and the beam direction B are resolved with respect to the defect axis system and they are normalised so that each constitutes a unit vector. That is, their components are the direction cosines of F and B relative to ox_1, ox_2, ox_3. Since ox_3 is along u it follows that $\cos \alpha$ in expression (4.7) is given by the third component of F resolved in this way:

$$\cos \alpha = FN(3) \ . \qquad\qquad\qquad (4.8)$$

The beam direction lies in the ox_2-ox_3 plane (see fig. 4.13) so that its first component is identically zero and the other components are:

$$BM(2) = \cos \psi , \tag{4.9}$$

$$BM(3) = \cos \beta . \tag{4.10}$$

However, since B is in the plane of the section shown in fig. 4.13 we have:

$$\sin \beta = \cos \psi = BM(2) , \tag{4.11}$$

so that in terms of the notation used in the program, the length of the micrograph WL is given by:

$$WL = \frac{THICK * BM(2)}{FN(3)} . \tag{4.12}$$

In the case of non-standard framing, the variables START and FINISH are used to define the fraction f (FRACTN) of the foil thickness over which the micrograph is to be computed. FRACTN is simply defined as:

$$FRACTN = \frac{FINISH - START}{THICK} \tag{4.13}$$

and the corresponding length of the micrograph is given by:

$$WL = THICK * FRACTN * BM(2)/FN(3) \tag{4.14}$$

The height of the micrograph (WW) is determined from WL and from the specifications of the line printer output. If $2n + 1$ is the number of characters in one row of the micrograph and m is the number of rows, then the number of intercharacter spacings in a row is $2n$ and in a column, $m - 1$. If S_1 is the number of characters per unit length of a row and S_2 is the number of characters per unit length in a column, then the height of the micrograph is given by:

$$WW = WL \frac{m-1}{2n} \frac{S_1}{S_2} . \tag{4.15}$$

For the micrographs we have computed, $m = 60$ and $n = 64$ and for our line printer, $S_1 = 10$ characters/inch and $S_2 = 6$ characters/inch, thus WW = 59.0 * 10.0 * WL/(6.0 * 128.0). The quantities START, FINISH, THICK, WL and WW are all measured in units of the extinction distance.

The inter-column spacing in the generalised cross-section (DELW) is obtained by dividing WW by $(m-1)$. However, since the unit of length of the Howie—Whelan equations (2.5) is extinction distance divided by π, DELW is defined as:

$$\text{DELW} = \frac{\pi \text{WW}}{m-1} \; . \tag{4.16}$$

The length of step down a column in the generalised cross-section (DELT) is also in units of extinction distance divided by π, but is defined directly in terms of the thickness of the foil in the beam direction t' (THBM), the fraction f (FRACTN) of the thickness over which the micrograph is being computed and the number of steps n in each part of the integration:

$$\text{DELT} = \frac{f \pi t'}{n} \; . \tag{4.17}$$

DELW and DELT are the fundamental intervals of measurement in directions parallel to OX_1 and OX_2 in the generalised cross-section plane. The origin O is taken at the point at which the defect line intersects the generalised cross-section. The general variable along the OX_1 axis (CN(15)) is defined in terms of integer multiples of DELW. There is no equivalent general variable down a column in the generalised cross-section, but the integration routine, within each required step, starts at a point X and proceeds to a point X1 (a distance DELT deeper in the foil) up-dating the value of X as it goes. The slope of the lines which bound the upper and lower parts of the generalised cross-section ($E_1 F_1$ and $O_1 N_1$ in fig. 4.5) are defined in terms of CN(15) and the components of the foil normal resolved along OX_1 and OX_2. Thus the upper boundary of the generalised cross-section and the staring point p (the first set value of X) for the first part of the integration in terms of the program notation is:

$$X = \frac{-\text{PY} * \text{FINISH}}{\text{FNBM}} - \frac{\text{CN}(15) * \text{FNX}(1)}{\text{FNX}(2)} \; , \tag{4.18}$$

where PY is π and FNBM is the cosine of the angle between the foil normal F and the electron beam direction B. The point q' (SURFAC) where the second part of the integration starts is obtained simply by adding $\pi t'$ (TBP) to the value given by eq. (4.18).

Up to this point, we have established the geometry of the micrograph itself (its length and height) and the geometry of the generalised cross-section which is necessary for the organisation of the integration. It only remains to establish the relation between the displacements around the defect, evaluated in defect

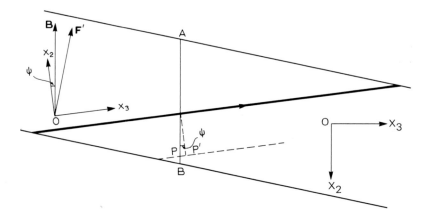

Fig. 4.14. Side elevation of a single linear defect in a tilted, parallel sided foil illustrating the relation between the point P in generalised cross-section coordinates (X_1, X_2) and P′ in defect coordinates (x_1, x_2).

axes, and the geometry of the generalised cross-section. Consider a section through the foil which contains both the defect direction and the beam direction but which does not necessarily pass through the actual line of the defect. This is shown in fig. 4.14. Integration is carried out down columns in the generalised cross-section in the OX_2 direction. This is the Z coordinate of eqs. (2.5). However, the displacements are calculated with respect to ox_2 and ox_1; note that apart from a change of sign, the axes ox_1 and OX_1 are coincident. Thus, the main correlation which is needed is between ox_2 and OX_2.

Consider an arbitrary column in the generalised cross-section which projects into the line AB in the section shown in fig. 4.14. Let a point P in this column have coordinates (X_1, X_2) with respect to the generalised cross-section axes. Now consider a point P′ which is chosen such that PP′ is parallel to the defect and P′ lies on the line parallel to ox_2 passing through the point of intersection of AB with the defect line. Let the coordinates of P′ be (x_1, x_2) with respect to the defect axes. Because no surface relaxations are allowed, the displacements at P are exactly the same as those at P′ and so far as the displacements are concerned, the coordinates (X_1, X_2) are related to (x_1, x_2) by:

$$x_1 = -X_1 ,$$

$$x_2 = -X_2 \cos \psi , \tag{4.19}$$

where ψ is the angle between ox_2 and $-OX_2$.

It is now necessary to introduce the specific form of the displacements and what follows applies only to dislocations. The latter part of expression (2.42) gives the derivative with respect to ρx_2 of the scalar product of the diffracting vector with the displacements at the point P' due to a dislocation as:

$$\frac{d}{dx_2}(g_k u_k) = \sum_\alpha \frac{P_\alpha x_1 + Q_\alpha x_2}{(x_1 + R_\alpha x_2)^2 + (S_\alpha x_2)^2} \, ,\qquad (4.20)$$

where $\alpha = 1, 2, 3$ and $P_\alpha, Q_\alpha, R_\alpha$ and S_α are constants (CN(1) to CN(12)) determined from the solution to the elasticity problem. To carry out the integration of the Howie–Whelan equations (2.5) in the generalised cross-section, we need to evaluate the function β' at the point P. This is given by the first part of expression (2.42) which is, replacing Z by X_2:

$$\beta' = \frac{d}{dX_2}(g\cdot R) \, . \qquad (4.21)$$

Substituting for x_1 and x_2 from eq. (4.19) in expression (4.20) we obtain

$$-\frac{1}{\cos\psi}\frac{d}{dX_2}(g_k u_k) = \sum_\alpha \frac{-P_\alpha X_1 - Q_\alpha X_2 \cos\psi}{(-X_1 - R_\alpha X_2 \cos\psi)^2 + (-S_\alpha X_2 \cos\psi)^2}$$

$$(4.22)$$

and thus

$$\beta' = \cos\psi \sum_\alpha \frac{P_\alpha X_1 + Q_\alpha X_2 \cos\psi}{(X_1 + R_\alpha X_2 \cos\psi)^2 + (S_\alpha X_2 \cos\psi)^2} \, . \qquad (4.23)$$

The speed of the program depends to a large extent on the evaluation of β' since this has to be calculated four times in each internal integration step. Therefore, it is worthwhile to look for forms of eq. (4.23) which can be evaluated efficiently. Expression (4.23) may be rearranged to give:

$$\beta' = \sum_\alpha \frac{P_\alpha X_1 / \cos\psi + Q_\alpha X_2}{(X_1 / \cos\psi + R_\alpha X_2)^2 + (S_\alpha X_2)^2} \, , \qquad (4.24)$$

and it is apparent from this expression that if, instead of X_1, a new variable $X_1 / \cos\psi$ is defined before the evaluation of β', many arithmetic operations can be saved. This is done in the programs. Instead of the X_1 coordinate (CN(15)) being transmitted to the subroutine DERIV where the evaluation of β' is carried out, the quantity CN(29) serves this purpose, where:

$$CN(29) = CN(15)/BM(2) , \tag{4.25}$$

since BM(2) = cos ψ from eq. (4.9). The expression for β' is even further simplified by dividing numerator and denominator by X_2^2 giving

$$\beta' = \frac{1}{X_2} \sum_\alpha \frac{P_\alpha \rho + Q_\alpha}{(\rho + R_\alpha)^2 + S_\alpha^2} . \tag{4.26}$$

The new variable ρ (R in DERIV) is given by

$$\rho = \frac{X_1}{X_2 \cos \psi} , \tag{4.27}$$

but it is evaluated within subroutine DERIV rather than in the main program as was the case for CN(29).

In eq. (4.24) only the coordinate X_1 is divided by cos ψ. It should be noted that this property depends on the specific form of the displacement function β' for a *dislocation*. Such is not the case for other displacement functions, e.g. for a line of dilation (§8.4). Hirsch et al. (1960) were the first to note that this implied that, for dislocations at different angles to the beam direction, columns at a distance $X_1/\cos \psi$ contained the same displacements. They gave this the physical interpretation that the images of dislocations at different angles to the beam direction would differ only in width and not in character. Such an interpretation is only applicable in the framework of isotropic elasticity. It is invalid in the case of anisotropic elasticity because dislocations at different angles to the beam direction must necessarily run in different crystallographic directions and therefore have different displacement fields and images. Thus, it is useful to think of the change of coordinate between the main program and subroutine DERIV (expression (4.25)) merely as a mathematical expediency and attribute no physical meaning to it whatsoever. This is also true for the coordinate change (expression (4.27)) which takes place subsequently.

The main points of this section may be summarised as follows. There are four axis systems which are used in the programs: the crystal axis system, the elastic constants axis system, the defect (dislocation) axis system and the generalised cross-section axis system. For crystals of cubic symmetry, the first two axis systems are coincident. The positions of the origins for the first two axis systems are immaterial; the origin for the defect axis system is taken anywhere on the defect line; the origin for the generalised cross-section axis system is taken at the point in the generalised cross-section where the defect intersects it. The dimensions of the micrograph are measured in units of the extinction distance; the dimensions of the generalised cross-section are measured in units of extinction distance divided by π; the units used for the evaluation of β' are extinction distance divided by π for the X_2 coordinate and extinction distance times $\cos \psi$ divided by π for X_1. The fundamental measures of length are the length of the micrograph WL and the thickness of the foil t; these are measured in extinction distances. The fundamental quantities which determine orientation are the defect line direction $\boldsymbol{u}$, the electron beam direction $\boldsymbol{B}$ and the foil normal $\boldsymbol{F}$.

4.5. The grey scale and printing the micrograph

The previous sections in this chapter have dealt with the principles of the calculation and its practical organisation in the computer program ONEDIS. This section concerns the presentation of the calculated intensity values in the form of a halftone picture to simulate as nearly as possible the experimental micrograph. The method we have employed, and the one which will be described in detail here, is that of using a line printer. Line printer output is the usual means of retrieving information from a computing system. It requires little operator intervention, it is quick (of the order of 1000 lines/minute), and the quality of the output is reasonably constant over long periods of time (years) so that once standardised, it does not have to be recalibrated. Providing that the micrographs are pictorially acceptable, therefore, the line printer affords a quick, cheap, standard way of producing them. Maher et al. (1971) have used special display equipment and optical techniques and have shown that, if sufficient care is taken in standardising their use, computed micrographs can be produced which are virtually indistinguishable in their texture and shading from the experimental ones. However, this degree of sophistication is not usually necessary and image matching and defect identification can be made more quickly and efficiently using the line printer.

In a halftone reproduction, the lights and shades of the original are represented by small or large dots. This is the method used to reproduce experimental micrographs in printed journals and it is this method, with the dots replaced by line printer characters, which is used to transform the calculated intensities into a theoretical micrograph. The set of letters and numbers usually available on a line printer are, by themselves, not very suitable for forming a graded set of grey dots or symbols, since it is a characteristic of good type face that there are no large differences in density between one character and

TABLE 4.1

Grey scale symbols based on characters available on our line printer

Shade	1	2	3	4	5	6	7	8	9	10	11
First print		.	:	'	=	"	"	H	"	H	B
Over print				,	.	•	_	I	10	Z	%
Symbol		.	:	!	=	!!	!!	Ħ	!!	฿	฿

another. Thus, in order to obtain symbols which have a large density difference, we have made use of punctuation marks etc. at the light end of the scale
and overprinting of characters at the dark end.

The choice of symbols to constitute a grey scale will depend on a number
of factors. Obviously, it will depend not only on the character set available
on each particular line printer, but also on whether it is possible to obtain
access to the characters and the facilities (e.g. overprinting) of the line printer
through normal FORTRAN programming. The symbols which we have used
for all our micrographs are shown in table 4.1. It will be seen that we have
used just one overprint and we have chosen ten symbols which, together with
blank paper, constitute the grey scale. It will be seen from table 4.1 that many
of the characters are punctuation marks and other special symbols which may
not be generally available. Because of this we have devised another set of symbols which are made up from only the characters used in FORTRAN. Moreover,
the subroutine HALFTN has been rewritten (from the version we commonly
use) so that it is written in simple FORTRAN and does not use internal codes
to access the characters. This grey scale which consists of eight characters
(including blank paper) and also employs one overprint is listed in table 4.2.
The scale in table 4.1 is regarded as probably the best which could be
obtained from our line printer and that in table 4.2 is presented as a scale
which should be generally available on all line printers. However, because of
differences in type face and character spacing, the FORTRAN grey scale,
table 4.2, may not be suitable for other line printers. In any case the user
will usually be able to establish a better scale.

Overprinting has been employed to achieve two aims: to produce darker
shades than is possible with single printing (e.g. symbols 10 and 11 in table
4.1 and symbols 7 and 8 in table 4.2) and to distribute density in the space
available (e.g. symbols 6 and 7 in table 4.1). It will be appreciated that even
though a symbol itself may be quite black (e.g. symbol 11), the overall

TABLE 4.2

Symbols of the grey scale in the program listing (§10.5) based on the characters used in FORTRAN

Shade	1	2	3	4	5	6	7	8
First print		.	+	*	+	*	0	G
Over print					/	/	+	*
Symbol		.	+	*	⨍	⨍	❶	❶

effect will be modified in a micrograph by the margin of white paper around each symbol arising from the spacing between rows and characters on the line printer. This leads to a reduced photographic range compared with experimental micrographs and is one of the disadvantages of this method of producing theoretical micrographs. In the grey scale we have used, an attempt has been made to produce symbols in which the density is spread as much as possible and the structure of a symbol is reduced to a minimum. Symbols 6 to 11 in table 4.1 are good examples of this, but symbol 5 (=) does not fulfil these requirements. As a consequence, regions of the image where areas of symbol 5 occur, tend to be outstanding, even though reflectivity measurements indicate that symbol 5 has the correct shade of grey.

The line printer produces a theoretical micrograph which is 129 symbols by 60 symbols and measures about 13 in. by 10 in. At this size the individual symbols are, of course, clearly distinguishable, but for the purposes of journal reproduction, the original output is usually reduced by about a factor of 10. Although this is a substantial factor, the resulting density of symbols (about 30/cm) is still less than the density (about 60/cm) used for halftone reproduction of the experimental micrographs. This, together with the inability to join symbols together as the shades get darker, gives the theoretical micrographs a characteristic 'grainy' appearance.

The single defect in program ONEDIS is situated between rows 30 and 31 of the printed output. These rows are marked with the letter D in the left-hand margin. Underneath the micrograph is printed a three row legend which gives details of the data used in the calculation and some of the results obtained (other than the intensities which are printed as symbols in the micrograph). One of the quantities contained in the legend is the value of background intensity. This is the intensity calculated when the equations are integrated through the thickness of the foil at a distance of some 1000 units (ξ_g/π) away from the defect and is thus essentially the intensity which would be transmitted by a perfect crystal under the same diffracting conditions. All the intensity values calculated for the micrograph are divided by the value of background intensity before being allocated a symbol in the grey scale and printed.

Before considering the central problem of the choice of symbols for the grey scale and their allocation to intensity values, we must consider the photographic characteristics of the experimental and theoretical micrographs. Comparison between theory and experiment is usually made between a positive print which has been obtained from the original experimental plate and the actual line printer output. In allocating grey scale symbols to particular intensity ranges, therefore, account should be taken of the two photographic processes involved in obtaining the experimental images. The sum total of both processes is difficult to assess, depending as it does on such factors as exposure times, the response of the plates to different numbers of electrons and of the paper to the intensity of light, the type of plates and paper used and the developers and developing techniques. It is extremely difficult to standardise all these factors in order to deduce the relation between the exposure (number of electrons) and the blackness (or the reflectivity) of the final print. In the absence of detailed knowledge of the photographic processes, we have assumed one of the empirical laws which often hold in photography. The usual form in which this law is expressed is:

$$D = \gamma \log_{10} E \,, \tag{4.28}$$

where D is the photographic density, E is the exposure and γ is a measure of the degree of the contrast. The density D is equal to the logarithm of the reciprocal of the transmission (for a negative), or the logarithm of the reflectivity R (for a positive print). The exposure E is defined as the product of intensity and time. Thus, an expression which has the form of eq. (4.28) describing the overall process involved in obtaining the experimental micrograph may be written:

$$\log_{10}(I/I_0) = \gamma^{-1} \log_{10}(R/\tau) \,, \tag{4.29}$$

where I is the intensity of the electrons incident on the plate, I_0 is the background intensity, R is the reflectivity of the positive print, γ is the contrast of the combined photographic process and τ $(= (\text{exposure time})^\gamma)$ is a measure of exposure. It will be appreciated that expression (4.29) will not be valid over the whole range of density of the plate, or the whole range of reflectivity of the print, but our experience of its use over a number of years leads us to believe it is quite adequate for the purposes of image matching.

Most of the detail in bright field micrographs is in areas which are darker than background intensity, so that when a grey scale was chosen, only one shade, blank paper, was allocated to those areas which are above background intensity. The situation is not the same for dark field micrographs. For these, there is appreciable detail in the areas both above and below background intensity, so that it would probably be necessary to scan all the computed values of intensity which make up the theoretical dark field micrograph, in order to allocate the symbols of the grey scale in the best possible way. This, of course, entails storing all the computed intensity values rather than just those in one line of the micrograph, and also a different allocation may have to be made for each micrograph. As stated earlier in this chapter, our main concern is with bright field micrographs, and the remarks which follow are specifically related to the production of a grey scale suitable for the representation of these.

Because of differences in style of the type face and characters available on a particular line printer, the establishment of the grey scale is one area in which the user will almost certainly be involved in making photometric measurements and program modifications. Thus, the following description refers to the establishment of the grey scale used in our micrographs.

The first step in choosing the symbols and the grey scale was to obtain examples of each of the 64 symbols available on our line printer overprinted with each of the others, including itself and blank paper. By inspection, it was apparent that the two lightest symbols were blank paper and full stop and the darkest symbol was a B overprinted with %. For bright field micrographs it was thought that the most usual choice of grey scale would involve only one shade of grey above background intensity. Therefore the lightest symbol (blank paper) was allocated to this and the next symbol (full stop) necessarily was allocated to background intensity. From the remaining block of 64 X 64 possible symbols, several were chosen by inspection to fill in the region between full stop and B overprinted by %, and full pages of each from the chosen set were produced so that the reflectivities of these could be measured. Measurements were taken using a constant, even illumination (four reading lamps, one at each edge of the sheet) and care was taken that the photometric device 'saw' only the characters on the printed output (not the margin or surrounds) and did not receive any stray reflections from the room or the observer. Symbols were chosen such that the differences between the reflectivities of successive symbols were roughly the same when expressed on a logarithmic scale. To the human eye, the symbols then form a grey scale with roughly equal steps in reflectivity. It was found difficult to choose symbols to fulfil this criterion because of the limited number of characters, especially at the light end of the scale. However, in the light of our experience in matching images, it does appear to be important that the difference in $\log_{10}R$ between full stop and the next symbol down should not be greater than the difference in $\log_{10}R$ between blank paper and full stop. This is because these three symbols determine the visibility limits of the image above and below background intensity and the visibility limit for details below background is invariably less than that for detail above background. Further, the symbol below background intensity largely determines the outline of the image and this is an important feature of the topology for image matching. In addition to choosing symbols which were at suitable intervals in reflectivity, an attempt was made to choose symbols in which the ink was spread over the available symbol area as evenly and as fully as possible. This was done so that the symbols would blend into one another smoothly and the eye would not pick up changes in symbol rather then changes in reflectivity. As mentioned earlier, the fifth symbol on our grey scale (= table 4.1) does not meet this condition, but it was not possible to find another character having suitable reflectivity which did.

Having found suitable symbols for the grey scale, a graph was drawn with $\log_{10}$ (reflectivity of symbols) as abscissa, in arbitrary units, and $\log_{10}$ (calculated intensity normalised to background intensity I_0) as ordinate. This is

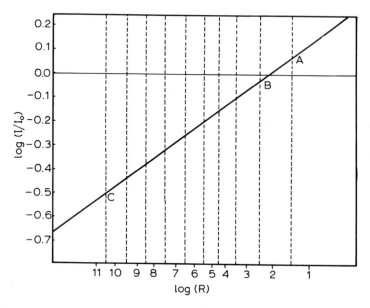

Fig. 4.15. Graph of $\log_{10}$ (calculated intensity I normalised to background intensity I_0) as a function of $\log_{10}$ (reflectivity R of grey scale symbols) for the grey scale we have used. The numbers on the abscissa represent the symbol numbers in table 4.1.

shown in fig. 4.15, where the specific value of $\log_{10}R$ for each of the grey
scale symbols is indicated by its shade number in table 4.1. The vertical
dashed lines in fig. 4.15 mid-way between each specific value of $\log_{10}R$
represent the values of $\log_{10}R$ at which one symbol changes to the next.
Using expression (4.29), the allocation of the grey scale symbols to the calculated intensities I/I_0 is determined by a straight line ABC on the graph having
slope $1/\gamma$. Choosing symbol 2 to represent background intensity, such a line
must pass through the zero value of $\log_{10}(I/I_0)$ within the interval defined
by the two vertical dashed lines on either side of symbol 2. The precise position of the line was determined by assuming values for the visibility limits.
Visibility limits are values of intensity above and below background which
denote the threshold at which contrast may be detected. Their actual values
depend on factors such as the structure of the image, its overall faintness or its
photographic range and experimental details such as the fog level of the plate
or the degree of mottle often left on the surface of the specimen by the elec-
tropolishing process. Our experience has shown that for images such as those
of dislocations in which the contrast covers an appreciable fraction of the
photographic range, suitable visibility limits are 15% above background
intensity and 7% below background intensity. Referred to fig. 4.15, this
means that the straight line must cut the dashed line between symbols 1 and
2 at a value of $\log_{10}(I/I_0)$ of 0.061 and the dashed line between symbols 2
and 3 at a value of $\log_{10}(I/I_0)$ of -0.032. These points are denoted A and
B on fig. 4.15.

Clearly, other choices may be made for the visibility limits and this will
affect the slope of the line, i.e. the contrast of the process. Maintaining the
same slope (contrast) of the line, but moving it parallel to itself, perhaps into
regions where symbol 3 or symbol 1 correspond to background intensity,
corresponds to different exposures τ. In the programs, provision is made for
nine allocations of the symbols, corresponding to nine different lines on a
graph such as fig. 4.15. However, it should be mentioned that the line which
corresponds to visibility limits of 15% above and 7% below background
intensity has been used almost exclusively and the other eight hardly at all.
On some occasions, a line parallel to this but which passes through symbol
3 (:) at background has been used and, for viewing objects which are everywhere weak (see §8.13), another scale has been used. This has visibility
limits of 2% below and 5% above background intensity.

In the programs, the whole of the allocation of the symbols is handled
algebraically by subroutine HALFTN. The position of the line, however, is
determined not from the visibility limits A and B (as in the description given
here), but from the points A and C at which the lightest and darkest symbols
become operative. These points are named WHITE and BLACK in the programs.
The values of BLACK and WHITE are printed in the legend to each computed

micrograph, and the allocation of the symbols together with the intensities (referred to background intensity) at which one symbol changes to the next, is produced in tabular form on the line printer page preceeding the micrograph. Subroutine HALFTN also has the facility for allocations of the symbols such that the negative plate may be simulated rather than the positive print. However, this facility has never been employed in image matching.

The values of BLACK and WHITE given for grey scale 1 in the program listing (§ 10.2.9) correspond to visibility limits of 15% above and 11% below background intensity for the FORTRAN grey scale table 4.2, although they give 15% above and 7% below for our original grey scale. The other values of BLACK and WHITE in the programs corresponding to the eight other choices of grey scale have also been left at our original values. These may be overwritten as the user develops his own set of symbols or as his matching needs dictate.

This method of using the line printer to produce halftone micrographs has proved to be entirely suitable. There has been only one occasion on which the grey scale was found to be inadequate. This occurred when trying to image the boundary between two crystals in a polycrystalline aggregate where one crystal was set close to the Bragg diffracting position and the other was non-diffracting. It was found in this case that the dark end of the grey scale was not sufficiently black to cover the photographic range of the experimental print.

There are two sorts of fault which occur from time to time in the output from our line printer and users of other line printers may experience other faults. The most common faults were minor 'phasing errors' and uneven inking of the paper from left to right of the micrograph. Phasing errors are errors in the timing of the hammers which push the paper onto the ribbon and the character drum. The result is that the characters are unevenly or lightly printed and in most cases this fault is accompanied by adjacent characters on the drum being also lightly printed underneath or above the intended character. This produces a smudged column on the micrograph. Uneven inking of the paper refers to the fact that usually the characters on the left-hand side of the print-out are lighter than those on the right-hand side. This occurs because most line printer output is left-justified and the characters and particularly the ink ribbon wear most quickly on that side. This defect in printing is most irksome when a composite image is being made up from two or more micrographs, since in this case the jump in reflectivity across the join is immediately obvious. These defects in printing are not important in the ordinary everyday use of the technique, and with the co-operation of the computer operator, they may be eliminated or reduced sufficiently to produce good output when it is needed for reproduction in scientific journals.

In connection with the publication of theoretical micrographs in books
and journals, it should be noted that the micrographs should be treated by
the printer as line diagrams and not as photographs. If they are treated as
ordinary photographs and a halftone screen is interposed in the block making
process, it is probable that artifacts in the form of moiré fringes will appear
due to the interaction of the screen and the grid of dots in the theoretical
micrograph. It has been our experience that if the micrographs are treated
as line drawings and they are supplied to the printer at two or three times
the size finally required for publication, the resulting illustration seems to
suffer no visual deterioration.

5 | MATCHING WITH ONEDIS

5.1. Introduction

In this chapter the program ONEDIS will be used to illustrate the technique for determining the Burgers vector of a dislocation by matching computed images to electron micrographs. The two examples that will be treated are a dislocation in a nearly elastically isotropic crystal (aluminium) and a dislocation in a highly elastically anisotropic crystal (β-brass) *. Although at this stage the computer program only allows a single dislocation to be treated, the examples taken will illustrate a general procedure that may be applied for identifying not only single dislocations but also more complex defects for which other computer programs will be developed later.

The Burgers vectors of single dislocations in crystals which are close to being elastically isotropic have usually been identified using the $g \cdot b$ invisibility criteria. Clearly aluminium is a case where the invisibility criteria might well be expected to provide an adequate identification of the Burgers vector of the dislocation. A dislocation in aluminium therefore forms an interesting first example since it allows a comparison to be made between invisibility criteria and image matching techniques. It will be seen that in this case the most likely Burgers vector of the dislocation obtained from invisibility criteria agrees with that found by image matching. However, it will become clear that much more confidence can be placed in the result when the image matching technique is used.

For the example involving the highly elastically anisotropic crystal (β-brass)

---

* Although ordered alloys with the CsCl structure are normally denoted 'β'-phases' the prime notation will be omitted since in this book β' is used for the derivative of the displacement field produced by a particular defect.

it will be seen that the situation is very different. In this case it is impossible
to apply invisibility criteria since all the experimental images show strong
contrast. Here the technique of matching computed images to experimental
micrographs is essential for the identification of the Burgers vector.

5.2. Aluminium

The determination of the Burgers vector of the dislocation marked A in the
aluminium specimen used throughout ch. 3 (see for example fig. 3.19) will
now be used as an example to illustrate the technique of defect identification
by image matching. It will have been realised from the discussion in ch. 4 that
the technique of image computation is strictly applicable only to straight
defects. Although the image of dislocation A in fig. 3.19 suggests that it is
straight, images in other beam directions show that this defect has some
curvature near one end. However, since dislocations usually display some
curvature, dislocation A will be taken to illustrate the point that in practice
the technique can still be applied with considerable confidence provided the
departure from linearity is not too great.

   In ch. 3 the crystallographic information required for computing an image
of dislocation A was determined. The vector along the dislocation line u was
determined as [523] (§3.6), the foil normal F as [528] (§3.7) and the foil
thickness t in the region of dislocation A as approximately 4.6 ξ_{200a} (§3.10)
where ξ_{200a} is the apparent extinction distance for the 200 diffracting vector.
For different diffracting vectors this value of t was scaled in the ratio of the
theoretical two-beam extinction distances.

   The first step in determining a Burgers vector by image computation
involves choosing a set of experimental images of the dislocation from the
available electron micrographs. In selecting this set of images it should be
noted that the matching process will be greatly facilitated if the images have
distinctly differing topologies arising from distinguishing features of contrast.
Moreover, as mentioned previously, the chosen set should contain three non-
coplanar diffracting vectors in order to sample all components of the displacement field of the defect.

   A set of micrographs for dislocation A which have been selected in this
way are shown in fig. 5.1 and labelled (a)–(g). The diffracting vectors g,
beam directions B and values of the deviation from the Bragg condition w,
corresponding to each micrograph have been determined in the manner
described in ch. 3 and are listed in table 5.1, together with appropriate
values of theoretical two-beam extinction distances ξ_g and values of apparent
anomalous absorption coefficient $\mathscr{A}$. The elastic constants used are c_{11} =
10.82, c_{12} = 6.13 and c_{44} = 2.85 dyne cm^{-2}×10^{11} (Huntington, 1958).

TABLE 5.1

Parameters used in computing the theoretical micrographs shown in fig. 5.1

Micro-graph	Diffracting vector g	Beam direction B	Extinction distance * ξ_g (Å)	Deviation from the Bragg con-dition ** $w = s\xi_g$	Apparent anomalous absorption coefficient *** $\mathcal{A}$
(a)	$\bar{2}00$	[013]	702	0.50 ± 0.1	0.07
(b)	020	[103]	702	0.52 ± 0.1	0.07
(c)	$\bar{1}11$	[10 1 11]	580	0.36 ± 0.1	0.06
(d)	$11\bar{1}$	[156]	580	0.27 ± 0.1	0.06
(e)	$\bar{2}02$	[8$\bar{1}$8]	1192	0.15 ± 0.3	0.09
(f)	$2\bar{2}0$	[118]	1192	0.00 ± 0.3	0.09
(g)	$\bar{3}\bar{1}1$	[6 $\bar{1}$ 17]	1478	0.90 ± 0.3	0.11

* The values of ξ_g are based on the atomic scattering amplitudes of Doyle and Turner (1968) and include the Debye–Waller correction appropriate to 293°K.
** The quoted errors in w are due to the uncertainties in the measurements of s.
*** The values of $\mathcal{A}$ are approximately twice those for zero aperture given by Radi (1970). Preliminary image computations showed that the Radi values had to be increased by a factor of approximately 2 to take account of the aperture size used.

Before proceeding to the computation of images, an assessment of the most likely Burgers vectors for the dislocation is made. Dislocation A was observed to slip when the foil was finally allowed to contaminate and the slip plane as determined from the slip traces was ($\bar{1}$11) which is compatible with the determined u of [523]. Since slip in aluminium results from the movement of dislocations with Burgers vectors of the type $\frac{1}{2}\langle 110 \rangle$ there are only six possible Burgers vectors that a glissile dislocation, such as dislocation A, slipping on ($\bar{1}$11) can have, namely: $\frac{1}{2}[110]$, $\frac{1}{2}[\bar{1}\bar{1}0]$, $\frac{1}{2}[101]$, $\frac{1}{2}[\bar{1}0\bar{1}]$, $\frac{1}{2}[0\bar{1}1]$ and $\frac{1}{2}[01\bar{1}]$. Therefore, in the first instance, we will restrict ourselves to considering just these six possibilities and to determining whether any of these six give computed images which match the electron micrographs.

The six possibilities consist of three pairs of equal but opposite Burgers vectors. Of these six only three Burgers vectors need to be computed since, for fixed diffraction conditions, isolated dislocations with Burgers vectors $+b$ and $-b$ have bright field images which are related by a 180° rotation around the beam direction (see Appendix). Of course, the computed images may have to be rotated through 180° to match the experimental images, and if this is the case, the Burgers vector of the dislocation will be equal but opposite to that used in the computed images *. For example, if an image

* It should be noted that if *any* computed image for a particular Burgers vector is rotated through 180° to produce a match, then *all* the computed images for that Burgers vector must be similarly rotated when making comparisons with their corresponding experimental images.

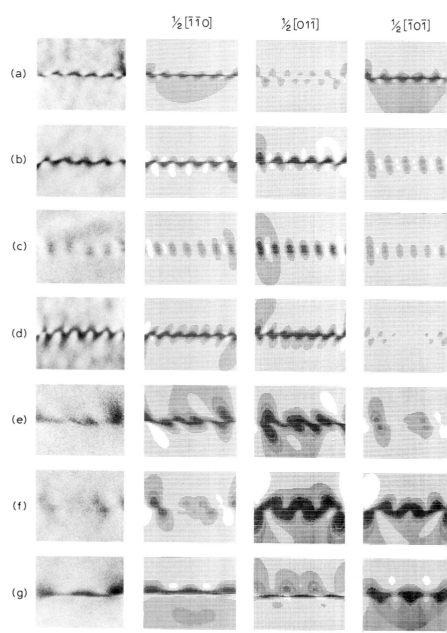

Fig. 5.1. A set of experimental images (a)–(g) of dislocation A (see text) in a lightly deformed specimen of aluminium, taken with the diffraction conditions given in table 5.1, and three sets of computed images for the same diffraction conditions corresponding to the Burgers vectors $\frac{1}{2}[1\bar{1}0]$, $\frac{1}{2}[01\bar{1}]$ and $\frac{1}{2}[\bar{1}0\bar{1}]$.

TABLE 5.2

Values of $\mathbf{g} \cdot \mathbf{b}$ for dislocation A

Micro-graph	Diffracting vector	$\mathbf{g} \cdot \mathbf{b}$		
		$\pm\frac{1}{2}[\bar{1}\bar{1}0]$	$\pm\frac{1}{2}[01\bar{1}]$	$\pm\frac{1}{2}[\bar{1}0\bar{1}]$
(a)	$\bar{2}00$	±1	0	±1
(b)	020	∓1	±1	0
(c)	$\bar{1}11$	0	0	0
(d)	$11\bar{1}$	∓1	±1	0
(e)	$\bar{2}02$	±1	∓1	0
(f)	$2\bar{2}0$	0	∓1	∓1
(g)	$3\bar{1}1$	±2	∓1	±1

computed for a Burgers vector of $+\mathbf{b}$ has to be rotated through $180°$ to match the experimental image, the Burgers vector of the dislocation in the experimental image is $-\mathbf{b}$.

Figure 5.1 represents the first step in the identification of the Burgers vector of dislocation A. In this figure, in addition to the set of seven experimental images, three sets of computed images are presented. These images have been computed for the diffraction conditions specified by the values given in table 5.1 and as indicated in the figure, correspond to three of the six possible Burgers vectors *.

The theoretical images have been computed so that they are standardly framed, i.e. include only the length of dislocation joining its intersections with the top and bottom surfaces of the foil. The objective is to select the set of computed images that is in best visual agreement with the experimental set. It can be seen from fig. 5.1 that the set of images corresponding to the Burgers vector $\frac{1}{2}[\bar{1}\bar{1}0]$ provides without a $180°$ rotation the best visual match to the experimental set. For instance, starting with images (a) and (b), the computed image for the Burgers vector $\frac{1}{2}[01\bar{1}]$ is not in agreement with the experimental image (a) and the computed image for the Burgers vector $\frac{1}{2}[\bar{1}0\bar{1}]$ is not in agreement with image (b). On these grounds therefore, the Burgers vector of dislocation A is unlikely to be either of these possibilities and a further comparison of the remaining computed and experimental images confirms this conclusion.

At this stage, it can be seen that the selected set only gives agreement with respect to major topological features in the experimental images. A more

---

* If the dislocation had not been positively identified as a glissile one, it would have been necessary to increase the number of possible Burgers vectors and compute their corresponding sets of images.

detailed match cannot necessarily be expected mainly because of inaccuracies in the determination of w and t. However, it can be seen from fig. 5.1 that the visual agreement is sufficient to conclude that the most likely Burgers vector of dislocation A is $\frac{1}{2}[\bar{1}\bar{1}0]$.

For the majority of cases the procedure as it has been described so far is adequate for the identification of the Burgers vector of a single dislocation. If, however, the choice of experimental images had been more restricted than that shown in fig. 5.1, the decision between the various possibilities may not have been so clear cut. Then in order to obtain increased confidence in the identification it would be necessary to test for an improvement in the degree of agreement between images by an adjustment of the variables w and t for the computed images within the limits of the estimated experimental errors. In the case of defects which are more complicated than a single dislocation, this type of refinement is usually an essential part of the complete identification of the defect as will be seen in ch. 7. However, to illustrate the procedure adopted to achieve improved agreement between experimental and computed images, we will continue to use the simple case of the single dislocation A.

The process of investigating small variations in w and t does not involve as much computing time as might first be imagined. The reason for this is that the program modification DELUGE can be used to sample a wide range of foil thickness t in a very economical way (§4.3.3). The most convenient way to proceed is to choose a single experimental image and then to use the program DELUGE to scan image topology over a range of specimen thickness for a chosen set of values of w.

The experimental image chosen for this purpose is image (a) of fig. 5.1 for which the diffracting vector g is $\bar{2}00$ and the measured value of w is 0.5. This image is reproduced in fig. 5.2 together with three sets of computed images for values of w equal to 0.45, 0.50 and 0.55. Computed images in each set have been selected from one run of DELUGE and they show a range of foil thickness t from $5.00\xi_{200a}$ to $3.94\xi_{200a}$ which is an adequate range about the approximate experimental value of $4.6\,\xi_{200a}$ found in §3.10. An examination of the computed images shows that for values of $t > 4.70\,\xi_{200a}$ the images at the three values of w contain too many oscillations in contrast and for values of $t < 4.06\,\xi_{200a}$ the images contain too few. A more detailed comparison between the experimental and computed images, where particular attention is paid to the *shape* of features including those above background level, shows that the best match lies between values of t/ξ_{200a} of 4.53–4.38, 4.38–4.22 and 4.38–4.22 at values of w of 0.45, 0.50 and 0.55 respectively. The computed images in fig. 5.2 represent only a portion of the range of w investigated and the computed images shown have been selected from a larger set in which the incremental change in t was finer ($\cong 0.08\,\xi_{200a}$). In fact, from the complete set of computed images, those for the lower values

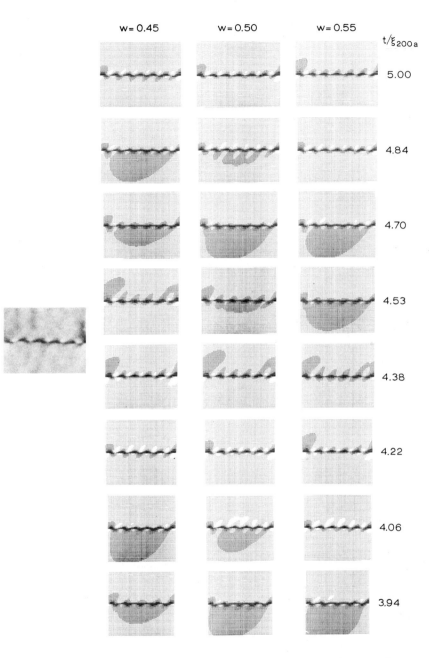

Fig. 5.2. The experimental image (a) of fig. 5.1 together with three sets of computed images for the Burgers vector $\frac{1}{2}[1\bar{1}0]$ at different values of w and t as indicated.

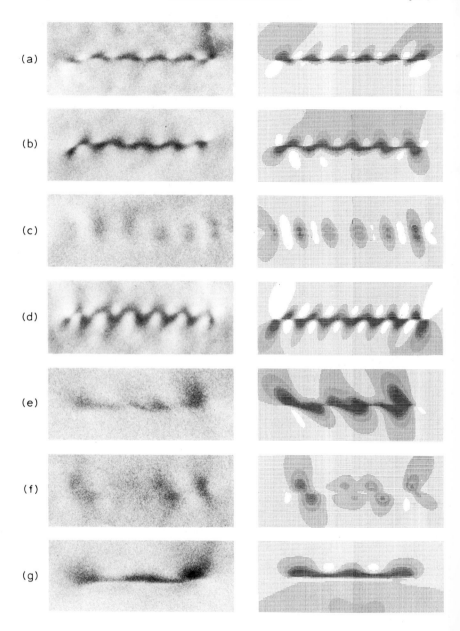

Fig. 5.3. The same set of experimental images of fig. 5.1 at a higher magnification, together with matching computed images for the Burgers vector $\frac{1}{2}[\bar{1}\bar{1}0]$. The value of t is 4.45 ξ_{200a} and the values of w for each image are: (a) 0.45, (b) 0.50, (c) 0.20, (d) 0.15, (e) 0.33, (f) 0.29 and (g) 0.97.

of w gave the best matches to the light features of the experimental image and the image for $t = 4.45\,\xi_{200a}$ and $w = 0.45$ was taken as the best match to the experimental image although the images for the two neighbouring values of t were also good matches. Figure 5.3(a) shows a comparison between the experimental and matching computed image for $t = 4.45\,\xi_{200a}$ and $w = 0.45$.

Having used this image to establish a value of foil thickness, this value can now be used for the refinement of the computed images corresponding to the remaining six experimental images. Where experimental images correspond to other diffracting vectors, i.e. images (c)–(g) in fig. 5.1, the determined foil thickness is scaled in the ratio of the extinction distances in table 5.1 (§2.6.2). Therefore, the refinement will now only involve testing over a range of w for these six images. The final matching images are shown in fig. 5.3 and in this case the computed images have been framed so as to give approximately twice the magnification of those in fig. 5.1 and to include a region outside the intersection of the dislocation with the foil surfaces (§4.3.2). It is clear that refining the values of w for the refined value of t results in a considerable improvement in image matching from that shown in fig. 5.1.

It is of general interest to apply the refined values of t and w to the other Burgers vectors that were initially considered as possibilities for dislocation A in fig. 5.1. The experimental images and computed images using the refined values are shown in fig. 5.4 where clearly the sets of computed images for Burgers vectors of $\frac{1}{2}[01\bar{1}]$ and $\frac{1}{2}[\bar{1}0\bar{1}]$ bear no relation to the set of experimental images. Therefore the determination of the Burgers vector of dislocation A as $\frac{1}{2}[\bar{1}\bar{1}0]$ is confirmed.

Dislocation A can now be described in detail since its Burgers vector ($\frac{1}{2}[\bar{1}\bar{1}0]$) has been determined in relation to a vector along its line ([523]). Therefore the dislocation is a $\frac{1}{2}[\bar{1}\bar{1}0](\bar{1}11)$ glissile dislocation which is approximately $37°$ towards [101] from left-handed screw orientation.

Having determined the Burgers vector of dislocation A by image computation using the program ONEDIS, it is of interest to compare this result with the conclusion that would be reached using the conventional method of applying invisibility criteria. An inspection of the experimental images (a)–(g) shows that contrast is obtained for all the diffracting vectors. However, images (c) and (f) are weaker than the others and might tentatively be described as images for which $\mathbf{g}\cdot\mathbf{b} = 0$. In table 5.2 the values of $\mathbf{g}\cdot\mathbf{b}$ are listed for the six Burgers vectors $\pm\frac{1}{2}[\bar{1}\bar{1}0]$, $\pm\frac{1}{2}[01\bar{1}]$ and $\pm\frac{1}{2}[\bar{1}0\bar{1}]$. It can be seen from this table that only the Burgers vectors $\pm\frac{1}{2}[\bar{1}\bar{1}0]$ have values of $\mathbf{g}\cdot\mathbf{b} = 0$ for both image (c) and image (f).

The conclusion from assigning $\mathbf{g}\cdot\mathbf{b} = 0$ to images (c) and (f) is that the Burgers vector of dislocation A is $\pm\frac{1}{2}[\bar{1}\bar{1}0]$. Clearly this identification lacks the degree of certainty provided by the image matching technique and in addition cannot distinguish between the two possible signs for the Burgers vector.

$\frac{1}{2}[\bar{1}\bar{1}0]$ $\qquad$ $\frac{1}{2}[01\bar{1}]$ $\qquad$ $\frac{1}{2}[\bar{1}0\bar{1}]$

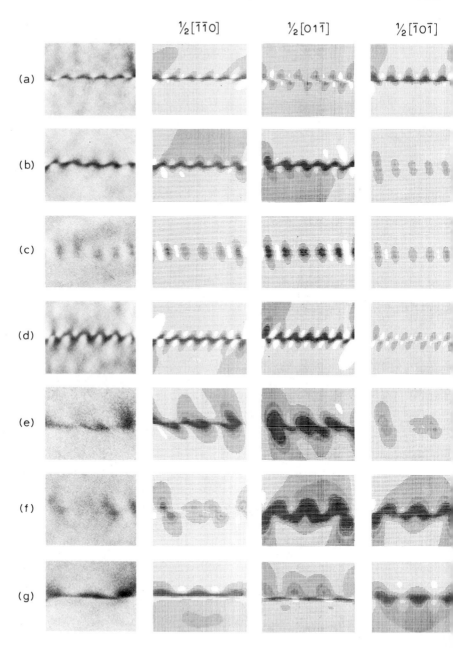

Fig. 5.4. Experimental and the corresponding computed images obtained with refined values of w and t (see text).

The technique of image matching makes use not only of the visibility of an image but also, as has already been pointed out, the distribution of distinctive features of contrast which makes up an image's overall topology. Thus images with characteristic topology should be chosen for image matching. For a given diffracting vector the topology of an image is different for different values of w and B. This is illustrated in figs. 5.5 and 5.6 and fig. 5.6 shows that, for a given B, the user has a degree of control over the topology of an image by adjusting the deviation from the Bragg condition.

Figure 5.5 shows three experimental images of dislocation A and their matching computed images for the same $11\bar{1}$ diffracting vector in different beam directions and for different values of w. Clearly the topologies of the three experimental images differ considerably and each has been matched by computed images for the Burgers vector $\frac{1}{2}[\bar{1}\bar{1}0]$ at values of w close to the measured values. The fact that dislocation A is not straight, is apparent in experimental image (b) of fig. 5.5, but this does not seriously impair the use of image matching in this case. Similarly, the curvature of the dislocation has little significant influence on the quality of the agreement between experimental and computed images for the other two cases in fig. 5.5.

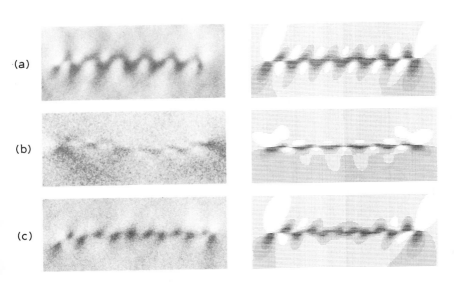

(a)

(b)

(c)

Fig. 5.5. Three experimental images (a), (b) and (c) and their corresponding computed images for the same diffracting vector $11\bar{1}$ and for the beam directions and values of w of (a) [156], 0.15; (b) [819], 0.28 and (c) [123], −0.02.

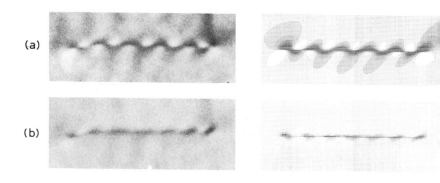

Fig. 5.6. Two experimental micrographs (a) and (b) and their corresponding computed images for the same beam direction [013] and diffracting vector 200 at values of w of: (a) 0.25 and (b) 0.96.

Figure 5.6 shows two experimental images and their matching computed images for the same values of g and B but for different values of w; w is 0.25 and 0.96 in images (a) and (b) respectively. It can be seen that the image (a) for the smaller value of w has a more characteristic topology than image (b) for the larger value of w and is therefore to be preferred. In general, it has been found that images taken at large deviations from the Bragg condition are not the most suitable for image matching.

The assingment of a Burgers vector by the technique of image matching rather than by the use of invisibility criteria has been demonstrated in this section. It has been shown that image matching has been able to take account of the details in all the experimental images for a wide range of diffracting conditions. It is this which gives added confidence compared with the use of invisibility criteria for which the images presented here could only be described either as being 'weak' or 'in-contrast'.

5.3. β-brass

An electron micrograph of a lightly deformed specimen of β-brass is shown in fig. 5.7. The dislocation marked B will be used as an example of the application of the image matching technique for the determination of Burgers vectors in highly elastically anisotropic crystals. The procedure to be followed is the same as that described previously for aluminium. The crystallographic information required for computing images of dislocation B was determined

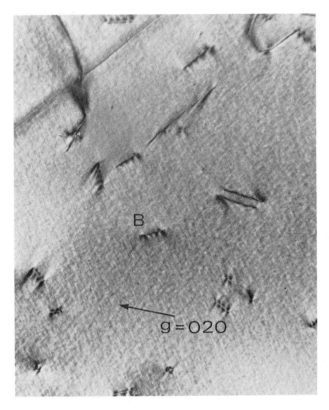

Fig. 5.7. Electron micrograph of a thin foil of lightly deformed β-brass. The diffracting vector is indicated.. × 90,000.

in the manner described in ch. 3. The vector along the line of the dislocation u was found to be $[5\bar{4}5]$, the foil normal F $[213]$ and the foil thickness t approximately $5.0\,\xi_{110a}$, where ξ_{110a} is the apparent extinction distance for the 110 diffracting vector.

Following the general procedure already developed, six electron micrographs were chosen covering an adequate range of image character and diffracting vectors and these are numbered (a)–(f) in fig. 5.8. The diffracting vectors g, beam directions B and values of the deviation from the Bragg condition w corresponding to each micrograph have been determined and are listed in table 5.3 together with appropriate values of the theoretical two-beam extinction distance ξ_g and apparent anomalous absorption coefficient $\mathcal{A}$.

Although images for all possible Burgers vectors could be computed, the determined u of dislocation B in the deformed specimen is $[5\bar{4}5]$, consistent with slip on the $(\bar{1}01)$ plane, and therefore only glissile dislocations on this

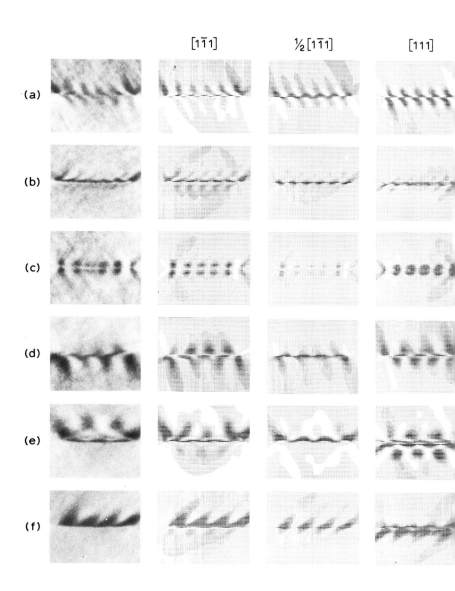

Fig. 5.8. A set of experimental images (a)–(f) of dislocation B of fig. 5.7, taken with the diffraction conditions given in table 5.3 and six sets of computed images for the same diffraction conditions corresponding to the Burgers vectors $[1\bar{1}1]$, $\frac{1}{2}[1\bar{1}1]$, $[111]$, $\frac{1}{2}[111]$, $[010]$ and $[101]$.

½ [111]   [010]   [101]

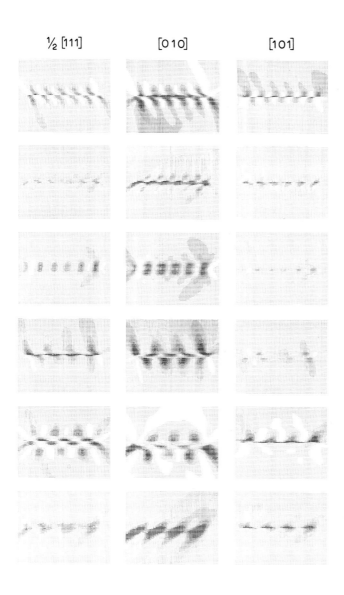

Fig. 5.8 (continued).

TABLE 5.3

Parameters used in computing the theoretical micrographs in fig. 5.8

Micro-graph	Diffracting vector g	Beam direction B	Extinction distance * ξ_g (Å)	Deviation from the Bragg condition ** $w = s\xi_g$	Apparent anomalous absorption $\mathscr{A}$
(a)	$0\bar{1}1$	[233]	324	0.15 ± 0.1	0.07
(b)	$1\bar{1}0$	[334]	324	0.57 ± 0.1	0.07
(c)	$10\bar{1}$	[535]	324	0.15 ± 0.1	0.07
(d)	020	[407]	446	0.30 ± 0.1	0.08
(e)	$1\bar{2}1$	[678]	576	0.60 ± 0.3	0.10
(f)	$2\bar{1}\bar{1}$	[657]	576	0.90 ± 0.3	0.10

* These values of ξ_g for the alloy were calculated from the atomic scattering amplitudes of Doyle and Turner (1968) for copper and zinc (§ 3.8) and include the Debye–Waller correction appropriate to 293°K.

** The quoted errors in w are due to the uncertainties in the measurements of s.

plane will be considered to reduce the number of possibilities for computation. For a glissile dislocation on $(\bar{1}01)$ the likely Burgers vectors are: $\pm[1\bar{1}1]$, $\pm\frac{1}{2}[1\bar{1}1]$, $\pm[111]$, $\pm\frac{1}{2}[111]$, $\pm[010]$ and $\pm[101]$. Therefore, in the first instance, we will consider only these Burgers vectors, remembering that only the six positive values of the twelve possible Burgers vectors need to be computed. Six sets of computed images for these six Burgers vectors ($[1\bar{1}1]$, $\frac{1}{2}[1\bar{1}1]$, $[111]$, $\frac{1}{2}[111]$, $[010]$, $[101]$) are given in fig. 5.8 and these images have been computed using the experimentally determined diffraction conditions given in table 5.3, a value of t equivalent to $5.0\xi_{110a}$ and the elastic constants $c_{11} = 12.91$, $c_{12} = 10.97$ and $c_{44} = 8.24$ dyne cm$^{-2} \times 10^{11}$ (Lazarus, 1948, 1949).

When using the group of experimental and computed images in fig. 5.8 to determine the Burgers vector of dislocation B, a convenient method is to make a series of comparisons of the set of experimental images with each set of computed images for the six different Burgers vectors. For example, in the case of the $[1\bar{1}1]$ Burgers vector, all the computed images are in general agreement with the experimental images except for the absence of dark features below the centre line in the computed image for (a). For the $\frac{1}{2}[1\bar{1}1]$ Burgers vector, the computed image for (c) is too weak and that for (f) too discontinuous and the overall match is not as good as for $[1\bar{1}1]$. In the case of the $[111]$ and $[010]$ Burgers vectors, the general match of all images is improved by rotating the computed images through 180° *, but even when this is done, the topology of

* When this is done, the Burgers vectors corresponding to the rotated images are $[\bar{1}\bar{1}\bar{1}]$ and $[0\bar{1}0]$ respectively.

the images in (e) and (f) does not match the topology in the experimental images and these possibilities are therefore unlikely. Neither of the sets of images for Burgers vectors $\frac{1}{2}[111]$ or $[101]$ provide an adequate match to the experimental set since many of the images are either too weak or too discontinuous. Clearly, therefore, the set that must be selected to be in best visual agreement with the experimental images is that corresponding to the $[1\bar{1}1]$ Burgers vector, but at this stage the sets for Burgers vectors $[\bar{1}\bar{1}\bar{1}]$ and $[0\bar{1}0]$ cannot be completely eliminated.

In order to confirm the assignment of the $[1\bar{1}1]$ Burgers vector to dislocation B, we will look for improved agreement between computed and experimental images by refining the values of w and t within the limits of experimental error. A refined value of $t = 4.8\,\xi_{110a}$ was obtained for image (c) by using the program DELUGE. This refined value of t was then used for all other images, scaled where required in the ratio of theoretical two-beam extinction distances, and the match between individual experimental and computed images was improved by varying w, i.e. the procedure was identical with that used previously for the aluminium example. The final set of experimental and matching computed images is shown in fig. 5.9. The detailed agreement between experimental and computed images in fig. 5.9 could not be obtained with either of the two other likely Burgers vectors $[\bar{1}\bar{1}\bar{1}]$ and $[0\bar{1}0]$. Thus, we have identified dislocation B as being a $[1\bar{1}1](\bar{1}01)$ dislocation approximately $6°$ towards $[101]$ from a right-handed screw orientation.

Unlike the case of aluminium, all the experimental images in fig. 5.8 show almost equally strong contrast, so that it is not possible to make even a tentative choice of images for which $g \cdot b$ could be given the value zero (e.g. with the determined b of $[1\bar{1}1]$, image (c) corresponds to $g \cdot b = 0$). It is this behaviour which makes the application of invisibility criteria to the determination of Burgers vectors in elastically anisotropic crystals such as β-brass virtually impossible. On this point the necessity for image computation is clear. Furthermore, image computation has the added advantage that not only can the sense of the Burgers vector be determined, but also its magnitude since, for example, it is clear from fig. 5.8 that a distinction can be made between the Burgers vectors $[1\bar{1}1]$ and $\frac{1}{2}[1\bar{1}1]$ and only the former may be assigned to dislocation B.

In this chapter, the general procedure developed for image matching has made use of the fact that for the same diffraction conditions the bright field images of dislocations with the same u, but with Burgers vectors $+b$ and $-b$ are simply related by a rotation of $180°$. Although this can be formally proved from the results of Howie and Whelan (1961) (see Appendix) it is difficult to demonstrate experimentally. However, an equivalent statement is that for a single dislocation, images taken with diffracting vectors of $+g$ and $-g$ are also related by a rotation of $180°$, provided the other diffracting condi-

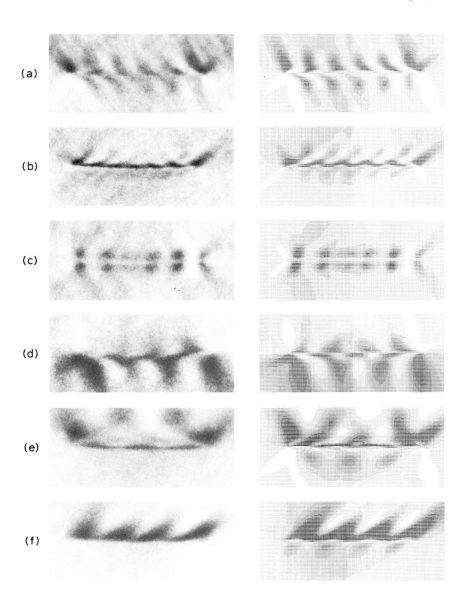

Fig. 5.9. The same set of experimental images of fig. 5.8 at a higher magnification, together with matching computed images for the Burgers vector $[1\bar{1}1]$. The value of t is 4.8 ξ_{110a} and the values of w for each image are: (a) 0.12, (b) 0.57, (c) 0.20, (d) 0.18, (e) 0.60 and (f) 0.90.

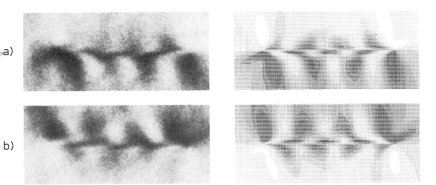

Fig. 5.10. Experimental and computed images for dislocation B for the diffracting vectors 020 in (a) and 0$\bar{2}$0 in (b). The values of w are 0.20 in (a) and 0.18 in (b).

tions (such as B and w) are identical. This equivalent statement can be readily demonstrated experimentally. Figure 5.10 illustrates this relation between images taken with +g and −g for dislocation B using the 020 and 0$\bar{2}$0 diffracting vectors. Although the values of w differ slightly for the two images, it can be seen that they are approximately related by a rotation of 180°.

6 PRINCIPLES OF TWODIS

6.1. Introduction

A program which computes the contrast from two dislocations and three stacking faults, TWODIS, was developed directly from the program ONEDIS described in ch. 4. Although it was originally created to fulfil a specific need[*], TWODIS has proved to be useful in such a large number of other cases that it is now regarded as a standard program. Moreover, the principles and techniques of calculation embodied in it have been made as general as possible so that it may be used as a basis for formulating programs which compute the contrast from configurations containing many dislocations and stacking faults.

Although the programs ONEDIS and TWODIS are written in a fairly general way, they were developed for specific uses. One instance of this specialisation is that both are oriented towards their authors' interests in cubic crystals. In ONEDIS, this is reflected in two main areas. One of these occurs where data is inserted into the program in terms of cubic crystallographic indices and the other concerns the structure of the initial part of the subroutine ANCALC. In TWODIS, an additional specialised area arises. This concerns the conventions and their attendant checking procedures for the representation of the translation of one part of a crystal with respect to another caused by a stacking fault. In this respect, TWODIS is specific to crystals which are specified by a three axis system, and the interpretation of the checking procedure has to be carried out by the program user on the basis of this axis system.

---

[*] TWODIS was developed to compute the contrast from stepped faulted loops (§ 8.11).

6.2. The two basic principles

The structure and large parts of the program TWODIS are the same
as ONEDIS and the only modifications, which are mainly additions, occur in
the main program and subroutine DERIV. In the main program, the modifications concern:

(i) the establishment of the geometry of the configuration of two dislocations and three fault planes;

(ii) the calculation and the sorting of the heights of the fault planes in the
generalised cross-section so that the electrons interact with them at the correct
positions and in the correct order;

(iii) the more complex procedure for integrating down a column in the
generalised cross-section to allow for the increased number of possible interactions between the electrons and the discontinuities; and

(iv) ensuring that the columns of integration do not pass too close to the
core of either dislocation.

Also in the main program, the calculation of a new set of constants P_α, Q_α,
R_α and S_α (see expression (4.20)) arising from the inclusion of a second dislocation is carried out. The only modifications to subroutine DERIV are the
inclusion of an extra term of the form of expression (4.20) corresponding to
the displacement function β' for the second dislocation and ensuring that the
function β' for each dislocation is evaluated with that dislocation as origin.

These changes represent technical complications rather than modifications
of principle, and the two basic principles used in micrograph computation for
one dislocation, those of the establishment of a generalised cross-section and
of the use of linear combinations of two known solutions to the electron
beam amplitudes, are retained.

6.2.1. THE GENERALISED CROSS-SECTION

The assumption which had to be made in ch. 4 in order to define the
generalised cross-section for a single dislocation was that no relaxation of the
stresses or strains was allowed at the surfaces of the foil. Using this assumption, the displacement field of the dislocation is the same at all points along
any line drawn parallel to the dislocation line and is just the displacement field
obtained for a long straight dislocation in an infinite medium. The generalised
cross-section for this situation may be obtained by projecting the displacement
field along the direction parallel to the dislocation line onto a plane which
intersects the dislocation line and contains the electron beam direction.

It is apparent that, using the same assumption, a generalised cross-section
may be defined in the same way for any number of defects, providing they are
all parallel. Thus, the conditions for the existence of a generalised cross-section

are that all the dislocations are parallel and all the stacking faults must be on
planes* which contain a direction parallel to the dislocation lines. When these
conditions are fulfilled, the displacement fields of the dislocations** may be
projected onto the generalised cross-section such that the displacement values
on this plane are unique and single valued. Each of the fault planes* projects
as a single line on the generalised cross-section and there is a unique relationship
between the displacement fields on each side of the lines due to the fault translation vectors R. In effect therefore, the conditions under which a generalised
cross-section may be defined are just those which enable the displacement field
of the configuration to be reduced from three dimensions to two, and the
generalised cross-section provides a convenient plane on which to specify
uniquely the two-dimensional displacement fields.

The two dislocations and the central fault plane in a parallel-sided tilted
crystal of uniform thickness t are shown in fig. 6.1 in relation to their computed
micrograph. For the sake of clarity in this figure, the other two fault planes
have been omitted. The two parallel dislocations $D_1 S_1$ and $D_2 S_2$ run from the
bottom of the foil to the top and the portion of crystal illustrated in fig. 6.1
depicts that volume which just contains the extremities of both dislocations
(cf. fig. 4.4 for a single dislocation). Projection of this volume in the direction
of travel of electrons LO, leads to the 'standardly framed' micrograph shown
in the lower part of fig. 6.1. The lines $S_1 S_2$ and $D_1 D_2$ are lines in the top and
bottom surfaces of the crystal respectively, where the central stacking fault
emerges from the crystal. Since the surfaces are parallel, $S_1 S_2$ and $D_1 D_2$ are
parallel and in the micrograph their projections $S_1'' S_2''$ and $D_1'' D_2''$, and any fringes
which may be produced by the stacking fault, are all parallel. The projections
of the dislocation lines in the micrograph lie at equal distances from the centre
line (between rows 30 and 31) of the micrograph, and the central fault plane
lies between them. Each of the other two fault planes runs from one of the
dislocations until it meets the edge of the micrograph.

For the geometry shown in fig. 6.1, the generalised cross-section is obtained
by projection along the direction $D_1 S_1$ onto a plane parallel to LMNO. The
generalised cross-section is illustrated in fig. 6.2 where all three fault planes
(p_1, p_2 and p_3) are indicated in addition to both dislocations. Of course, the
planes project as lines and the dislocations as points. The areas EFGH and

---

* Here the word 'plane' is used in the geometric sense and is of infinite extent. The term
'fault plane' is used to describe that portion of a plane which is restricted by the geometry of the program. The fault plane may be faulted or unfaulted depending on the
value of the fault translation vector R assigned to it. A fault plane is specified by its
normal and by the geometry written into the program.
** Since linear elasticity is being used, the displacement at a given point in the crystal
due to the presence of several dislocations is simply the linear (vector) sum of the displacement due to each of them.

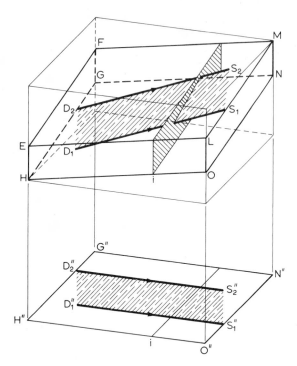

Fig. 6.1. Volume of a parallel-sided tilted foil EFMLHGNO which just contains two dislocations $D_1 S_1$ and $D_2 S_2$ and a connecting stacking fault. The resulting micrograph is
illustrated schematically as $H''G''N''O''$.

LMNO in fig. 6.1 project into the areas $E'F'G'H'$ and $L'M'N'O'$ respectively in
fig. 6.2. From the discussion of the generalised cross-section in ch. 4 (§ 4.2.1)
it will be appreciated that the displacements contained in the area $E'F'G'H'$ of
fig. 6.2 correspond to the situation where dislocation $D_2 S_2$ (S_2' in fig. 6.2) is
just at the bottom of the foil ($D_1 S_1$ (S_1') is not yet in the foil) and that these
displacements give rise to intensity values along the column $H''G''$ in the
micrograph in fig. 6.1. Similarly, the area $L'M'N'O'$ of the generalised cross-
section, fig. 6.2, contains the displacements corresponding to the column
$N''O''$ of the micrograph, fig. 6.1, where the dislocation $D_1 S_1$ is just emerging
from the top surface of the foil and $D_2 S_2$ is no longer in it. Intermediate areas
on the generalised cross-section, for example, that between the dashed lines
in fig. 6.2, correspond to the plane marked i in fig. 6.1 and the column marked
i on the computed micrograph.

Compared with the generalised cross-section for one dislocation (fig. 4.5),
the generalised cross-section for two dislocations contains an extra region
$H'G'M'L'$. This region is necessary if the micrograph is to be framed to include

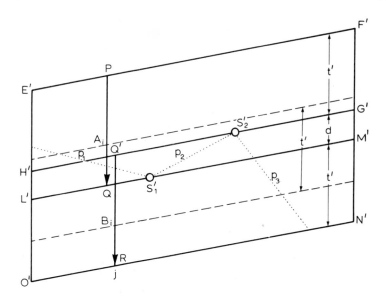

Fig. 6.2. Generalised cross-section for computing a standardly framed micrograph of two dislocations (S_1' and S_2') and three stacking faults (p_1, p_2 and p_3) in a parallel-sided tilted foil.

the extremities of *both* dislocations. Whereas the heights $F'G'$ and $M'N'$ are equal to t', the thickness of the foil in the beam direction, and are independent of the geometry of the defect configuration, the height of the extra area, $G'M' = d$ is entirely dependent on this geometry. The calculation of d, along with the evaluation of the other geometry necessary for the program, will be discussed further in § 6.4.

It can be seen from fig. 6.1 that the positive direction of the dislocations is taken in the sense from the bottom of the foil to the top, and the projections of these directions have the sense which runs from the left-hand side of the micrograph $H''G''$ to the right-hand side $N''O''$. The top and bottom of the micrograph are defined by $G''N''$ and $H''O''$ respectively: the legend appears below the line $H''O''$. The generalised cross-section follows the convention established for ONEDIS in that it is oriented so that the positive sense of the dislocations, S_1' and S_2', is out of the paper in fig. 6.2, although, of course, not perpendicular to it. Program TWODIS is written so that the planes p_1 and p_2 always meet at dislocation 1 (S_1') and planes p_2 and p_3 always meet at dislocation 2 (S_2'). In order to obtain the required configurations, the planes and their faults are evaluated only over restricted regions of the generalised cross-section. Thus, fault plane p_2 is restricted to the region between the two dislocations, p_1 occurs only to the left of dislocation S_1' and p_3 only to the right of dislocation S_2'. If, as is usually the case, the dislocation lines are located within the area of the computed micrograph, the fault plane p_1 always extends from dislocation 1 ($D_1''S_1''$) towards the bottom of the micrograph and p_3 always extends from dislocation 2 ($D_2''S_2''$) towards the top. However, the relative positions of the dislocations is not fixed. That is, dislocation 1 may be to the left of dislocation 2 (this is the case shown in figs. 6.1 and 6.2) or 2 may be to the left of 1. This latter arrangement leads to an overlapping fault configuration in between the two dislocations and in this region the electron beam traverses all three fault planes and not just p_2 as shown in figs. 6.1 and 6.2. Some of the various configurations which it is possible to consider with TWODIS and their relation to cases of physical interest are discussed further in § 6.3.

6.2.2. LINEAR COMBINATIONS

The generalised cross-section defining the displacement field of the dislocations and stacking faults is used in a similar way to that described for a single dislocation. Two independent integrations of the Howie–Whelan equations are performed down columns in the generalised cross-section and the resulting two independent solutions are combined linearly to obtain the amplitudes T and S of the electron waves at points corresponding to the top and bottom surfaces of the foil.

Consider a representative column j in the generalised cross-section for a standardly framed micrograph, fig. 6.2. As in the case of single dislocations, the integration down this column is divided into two equal parts: the first from P to Q and the second from Q' to R. Unlike the standardly framed single dislocation case (but like the demagnified case, see fig. 4.6), these ranges of integration overlap and for the sake of clarity, in fig. 6.2 they have been represented separately. However, it should be emphasised that, in fact, they both refer to the same column j. Both PQ and Q'R are subdivided into n equal steps and two simultaneous, but independent, 'experiments' or integrations of the Howie–Whelan differential equations (eqs. (2.5)) are carried out down the column. In the first part of the integration PQ, the two experiments are combined linearly to give the boundary conditions equivalent to an electron beam entering the top surface of the foil, i.e. $T = 1$, $S = 0$. Thus at the end of each of the n steps in the first part of the integration, e.g. A_j, the constants of proportionality a_i and b_i, necessary to satisfy these boundary conditions, are calculated using expression (4.1). In the second part of the integration the solutions to the two experiments are again combined. At the end of each of the corresponding steps in the second part of the integration, e.g. at B_j, the constants a_i and b_i are used to calculate the final amplitudes (expression (4.5)). These are representative of the bottom surface of the foil because the positions B_i are each at a distance t' from their corresponding positions A_i in the first part of the integration.

In principle therefore, this procedure is exactly the same as for a single dislocation where the integration columns in the generalised cross-section have been arranged to give a demagnified micrograph (cf. fig. 4.6). Indeed, as in that case, when performing the first part of the integration, a search has to be made for the point Q' (SURFAC) at which the second part of the integration starts. It will be recalled that when the integrations reach this point, the amplitudes are stored (in TEMPY) and the integrations are then continued step by step to the point Q. The amplitudes TEMPY are used as the starting amplitudes for the second part of the integration. In a similar way, when dealing with configurations containing planar defects (stacking faults), the column has to be searched for the occurrence of these in each particular step. If a stacking fault occurs in an integration step, the integrations are stopped at the fault, the wave amplitudes are adjusted in phase and the integrations continued to the end of the step.

The way in which the amplitudes are adjusted was discussed in § 2.7.1. If R is the translation vector of the part of the crystal which the electrons are about to enter with respect to the part of the crystal they are just leaving, then a phase angle α may be defined:

$$\alpha = 2\pi g \cdot R. \qquad [(2.29)]$$

If T and S are the transmitted and diffracted amplitudes just before the interface between the two parts of the crystal, then the amplitudes T_{new} and S_{new} just after the interface are given by $T_{new} = T$ and $S_{new} = S \exp(i\alpha)$. As in program ONEDIS, complex arithmetic is not used and T and S appear in the program as the subscripted real variables Y. T and S for the first experiment are defined by:

$$T^{(1)} = Y(1) + \sqrt{(-1)}Y(2),$$
$$\qquad\qquad [(4.2)]$$
$$S^{(1)} = Y(3) + \sqrt{(-1)}Y(4),$$

and for the second experiment by:

$$T^{(2)} = Y(5) + \sqrt{(-1)}Y(6),$$
$$\qquad\qquad [(4.3)]$$
$$S^{(2)} = Y(7) + \sqrt{(-1)}Y(8).$$

On traversing the fault, $T^{(1)}$ and $T^{(2)}$ remain unchanged, but $S^{(1)}$ and $S^{(2)}$ become:

$$S^{(1)} = Y(3) \cos \alpha - Y(4) \sin \alpha + \sqrt{(-1)}[Y(4) \cos \alpha + Y(3) \sin \alpha], \qquad (6.1)$$

$$S^{(2)} = Y(7) \cos \alpha - Y(8) \sin \alpha + \sqrt{(-1)}[Y(8) \cos \alpha + Y(7) \sin \alpha]. \qquad (6.2)$$

Within the integration procedures the provision is made that the three faults and SURFAC may all be encountered within the same specified integration step. After the electron beam traverses a fault plane, the height of that plane is set to an artificial large negative value so that effectively it is never subsequently considered in that column of integration. The details of this and of other calculation procedures are the subject of § 6.4.

As in program ONEDIS, each part of the integration is divided into n equal steps where n is 64. This leads to 65 directly calculated intensity values along a line parallel to the dislocations. The other 64 intensity values needed to complete the row of intensity in the micrograph are obtained by linear interpolation of the directly calculated intensities. However, since program TWODIS deals with more complex situations than ONEDIS, there is the increased possibility that the procedure of obtaining half of the intensities by linear interpolation will not lead to a valid picture. For instance, fault fringes which may be shown to be symmetrical analytically, may be depicted as being slightly asymmetrical. Depending upon the level of refinement at which the final micrograph is examined, this may or may not be important. If it is decided to be important in a particular instance, then n may be increased to 128 and all 129 intensity values in a row of the micrograph computed. Out of many thousands of micrographs computed by the authors, this has been considered necessary in only a few cases.

6.3. The operation of the program

From the previous section it will be appreciated that program TWODIS uses exactly the same principles as those employed in program ONEDIS, although the execution of these principles is somewhat more complicated. Before discussing the mechanics of the calculation in detail, it is advantageous to have a better idea of the configurations which program TWODIS can handle, the extra data needed to run it, and some of the problems involved. With this knowledge, the arrangement of the actual calculations will be more readily appreciated.

6.3.1. EXAMPLES OF THE CASES WHICH MAY BE COMPUTED WITH TWODIS

Program TWODIS is designed to compute the contrast from a defect configuration consisting of up to two dislocations and up to three stacking faults.

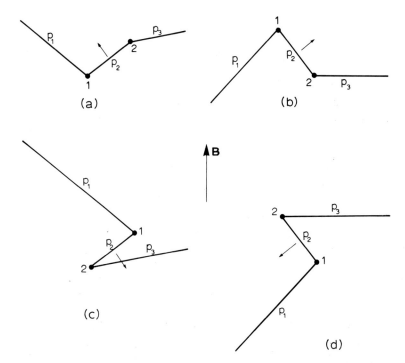

Fig. 6.3. Illustrating the four types of two dislocation–three stacking fault configurations it is possible to consider with program TWODIS. Note that overlapping fault configurations ((c) and (d)) are obtained by using the sense of the normal to fault plane p_2 which is downward with respect to **B**.

The limitations on the geometry of the faults and dislocations which are necessary in order for a generalised cross-section to be defined were discussed in the previous section, but there are many possible configurations within these limitations. The most complex configurations which the existing form of program TWODIS will allow, may be described as steps (e.g. fig. 6.3(a) and (b)) or Z or S shapes (e.g. fig. 6.3(c) and (d)). These may also be termed non-overlapping or overlapping configurations[*], referring to the relative arrangement of the fault planes in the region between the two dislocations. In fig. 6.3 the view is as it was for the generalised cross-section, that is, with the dislocations coming out of the paper and the electron beam direction **B** upwards[**]. The dislocations are marked 1 and 2 and the three planes, p_1, p_2 and p_3.

[*]   In overlapping cases such as fig. 6.3(c) and (d), it is possible that fault planes p_1 and p_3 intersect. The program will compute these cases, but will not take into account any defect formed at the intersection.

[**]   It will be recalled (§ 2.2) that B is defined in the sense of the direction towards the electron gun; the direction of travel of electrons is the reverse of this.

Cases shown in figs. 6.3(a) and (b) represent non-overlapping configurations, whereas those in figs. 6.3(c) and (d) represent overlapping configurations. It will be noted, however, that the slopes of planes p_1, p_2 and p_3 in (a) are the same as those of the corresponding planes in (c) and a similar relation holds for the slopes of the planes in (b) and (d). Figure 6.3 has been deliberately arranged in this manner to illustrate the specific difference between non-overlapping and overlapping cases. In figs. 6.3(a) and (b) the normal to the second fault plane p_2 (indicated by the small arrow) has been specified as upward, that is, acute with B and in figs. 6.3(c) and (d), it is downward. This is the means used in the program for obtaining overlapping or non-overlapping configurations. It will be recalled from the previous section that the geometry of the dislocations is specified such that dislocation 1 is always at the intersection of p_1 and p_2 and dislocation 2 at the intersection of p_2 and p_3. This specification requires that dislocation 2 is to the right of dislocation 1 in non-overlapping cases (a) and (b), but to the left of dislocation 1 in overlapping cases (c) and (d).

Compared with ONEDIS, the extra data needed for program TWODIS is: the Burgers vector of the second dislocation (LB2/LD2); the distance between the two dislocation lines in units of the extinction distance (SEP); the normals to each of the faulted planes (LFP)[*]; and the translation vector R (often a shear) of the lower part of the crystal with respect to the upper part across each plane (LS1/LQ(1), LS2/LQ(2), LS3/LQ(3)). This additional data is all specified on a separate (third) data card, and any or all of these quantities may be left blank. In this event, their values are generally taken to be zero except for the divisors, LD2, LQ(1), LQ(2) and LQ(3) since zero values in these cases would cause difficulties in calculation. Thus, LD2, LQ(1), LQ(2) and LQ(3) are all set to unity if they appear to be zero on the data card.

As discussed above, the sense of the normal to the central plane LFP(1,2) is important since it is this which determines whether the case in an overlapping or non-overlapping one, but the sense of the normals to the other fault planes is immaterial. The distance between the two dislocations SEP may be any positive number, including zero. It is measured in units of the extinction distance, in the direction normal to the dislocation lines, in the plane joining the two dislocations.

Because some of the translation vectors and/or Burgers vectors may be omitted and because the separation of the two dislocations may be zero, many

---

[*] In the program, the normals to each of the fault planes are contained in the doubly subscripted array LFP. In the generalised cross-section axis system, they are used as the singly subscripted arrays FP1X, FP2X and FP3X equivalenced to the doubly subscripted array FPX. In the dislocation axis system, only the normal to the second fault plane is used and this appears as the singly subscripted array FP.

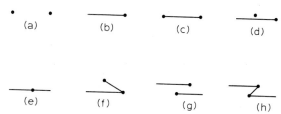

Fig. 6.4. Some of the configurations which can be considered by program TWODIS. For example, the illustrations can represent: (a) a dislocation dipole; (b) a stacking fault with one bounding partial dislocation; (c) a glide dislocation dissociated into partials; (d) the interaction between an undissociated glide dislocation and part of a dissociated one; (e) a Shockley partial dislocation separating areas of intrinsic and extrinsic stacking fault; (f) the dissociation of a Frank dislocation at the edge of a loop to form a stair-rod dislocation, with a Shockley dislocation and stacking fault on an intersecting plane; (g) areas of stacking fault on parallel planes bounded by Shockley or Frank dislocations, and (h) a faulted step bounded by stair-rod dislocations.

defect configurations other than those shown in fig. 6.3 are possible. Some of the more commonly occurring physical examples of dislocation–stacking fault configurations which can be handled by program TWODIS, are depicted schematically in fig. 6.4. In these sketches, the electron beam may be thought of as being incident in any direction, so that fig. 6.4(b), for example, re-presents the cases where a fault is terminated by a partial dislocation either on the left or on the right, and fig. 6.4(h) is representative of non-overlapping faults as well as overlapping ones. Descriptions of the physical situations relating to the configurations depicted in the sketches are noted in the legend to the figure; these will give the reader an indication of the versatility of the program and its usefulness to him.

6.3.2. CHECK SUMS AND CONVENTIONS

With the possibility of being able to compute the contrast from such a large number of different configurations and with the increased possibility of errors in data preparation which this brings, it was considered necessary to in-corporate into the program as many checks as possible. This has been done not only for computing reasons (e.g. to ensure that all divisors are non-zero) but also to ensure that only physically real cases are considered. The major check of this latter kind in program TWODIS consists of two check sums in-volving the Burgers vectors of the dislocations and the translation vectors of the faults. The check sums add up the Burgers vector and the translation vectors (with appropriate signs) around a circuit taken about each dislocation line. If crystallinity is to be preserved, the answers to these sums should be zero, or a proper translation vector of the lattice. The results of these sums for dislocations 1 and 2 are respectively the subscripted variables VEC1 and VEC2. They are printed out at the end of the first and second rows of the legend as two groups of three floating point numbers followed by the identification V1 and V2.

Since the answers to these sums should be lattice vectors, the type of answer which is acceptable in a particular case depends on the crystal structure of the specimen for that case and only the fractional parts need be considered[*]. For example, for a primitive structure, the fractional parts of the three floating point numbers should all be zero; for a body-centred structure the fractional parts should all be zero or all ± 0.5; and for a face-centred structure, they should all be zero or two of the three should be ± 0.5 and the other one zero.

Caution should be exercised when computing cases where the variable SEP is zero, there is only one dislocation present, and the planes p_1 and p_3 are joined (see, for example, fig. 6.4 (e)). In such cases, the check sums may not be lattice vectors. However, if the configuration is crystallographically possible, the algebraic sum of the corresponding components of the two check sums will give values which are components of a lattice vector.

Whilst the check sums are intended to be the ultimate means of ensuring that no mistakes have been made, they are only available after a micrograph has been computed. In preparing the data, the program user will usually have followed some sort of convention in order that the fault translation vectors and the Burgers vectors are compatible. It was explained in § 2.7.2 that the Burgers vectors of whole dislocations, and hence their associated displacement fields, are defined using the convention designated FS/RH where the closure failure of the circuit around the dislocation line is in the good crystal. This convention may also be applied to define the Burgers vectors of partial dislocations provided that the circuit starts at the faulted plane. This condition is necessary so that the circuit does not pass through 'bad' crystal, but of course, the Burgers vector so defined is completely dependent upon the translation vector of the fault. This is what is meant when it is stated that the Burgers vector and the translation vector must be compatible.

Another way of considering this dependency or compatibility is in terms of the stacking disorder left behind on the slip plane when a partial dislocation passes over it, and for this it is necessary to have a convention, compatible with the FS/RH rule, which defines the direction of positive motion of the partial dislocation. Thompson (1953) has given such a rule as follows. Consider an observer to be situated in either of the semi-infinite crystals separated by the slip (fault) plane and to be looking towards this plane. The observer

---

[*] The integer parts can of course be ignored since they represent lattice vectors for *all* crystal structures.

makes a rotation of $90°$ in a clockwise sense from the positive direction of the dislocation line and the direction in which he is now facing defines the positive direction of motion. When the dislocation passes across the slip plane in this positive direction of motion, the half of the crystal towards which the observer is looking will move relative to the half in which he is situated by an amount equal to, and in the direction of, the Burgers vector of the dislocation.

In the program, however, the translation vector R across the fault is always defined as the movement of the part of the crystal which the electrons are about to enter with respect to the part of the crystal they are just leaving[*] (§ 2.7.1). Thus, when applying the rule for the positive direction of motion of the dislocation in the context of the programs, the observer must always be situated in the upper part of the crystal (nearest to the electron source) looking across the fault towards the lower part.

These two rules together are all that is necessary to obtain Burgers vectors and fault translation vectors which are compatible. However, there are several factors which can lead to mistakes when these rules are used to prepare data for the program.

One factor is that the positive direction of the dislocation line is always taken to be out of the generalised cross-section, i.e. from left to right in the micrograph. This applies to both dislocations, so that if the dislocations constitute the opposite sides of a closed dislocation loop, for example, the Burgers vector of one of the dislocations will be the reverse of the Burgers vector of the other.

Another factor is that stacking faults may arise from mechanisms other than slip (the aggregation of vacancies, for example) and in such cases the convention for the positive direction of motion is applicable, although such motion is climb rather than glide.

A third factor can arise when a fault plane is close to the vertical position. Tilting of the specimen (to obtain different diffracting vectors, for example) may cause the plane to pass through the vertical position. It follows directly from the definition of R that in computing the set of matching micrographs it will be necessary to use a translation vector R when the fault is on one side of the vertical, but $-R$ when it is on the other side, even though the fault itself remains the same physical entity.

A fourth factor concerns the terminology of intrinsic and extrinsic faults. Frank (1951) differentiated between an intrinsic fault, in which the lattice in each half of the crystal extends undisturbed up to the fault plane, and an extrinsic fault, which contains at least one atomic plane which belongs to neither lattice. In the face-centred cubic structure an extrinsic fault is two

---

[*] Note that this definition of R depends on the direction of flow of electrons in the crystal which is opposite to the direction B.

intrinsic faults separated by one plane of atoms. Since an intrinsic fault is specified by a single translation vector, an extrinsic fault may be specified by two such vectors one atom plane apart. If the separation between the two faults is neglected, then the vectors may be combined to form a single resultant which will represent the translation vector of an extrinsic fault. In face-centred cubic materials this resultant vector is equivalent to a vector equal in magnitude but opposite in direction to the vector used to specify an intrinsic fault*. In image computation, this approximate representation of an extrinsic fault by a single translation vector is almost universally adopted, but it means that extra caution has to be exercised in determining the correct sense of a fault translation vector.

By far the most common materials in which stacking faults have been studied are those with the face-centred cubic structure and for this structure Thompson (1953) has given a notation and a crystallographic aid (a tetrahedron representing the {111} planes in the structure) which may be used to obtain compatible sets of Burgers vectors and fault translation vectors. The authors have found this to be the best method for preparing data on dislocation–stacking fault configurations in face-centred cubic materials. However, the disadvantage of such a system (and that of any similar system devised for other structures) is that it assumes a definite position for the observer (e.g. outside the tetrahedron). This position may or may not coincide with that used in image computations, namely, an observer above the faulted plane looking downwards in the direction of flow of the electrons. Thus considerable care has to be used in transferring from the purely crystallographic system to one in which the electron beam is an additional and overriding consideration.

For several reasons, therefore, it is possible to accidentally compute theoretical micrographs which are not those intended, and perhaps not even physically possible. The calculation of the micrograph is not aborted in these cases, but the lattice vector check sums will give a reliable indication of whether or not a physical case has been considered. Since apparently genuine micrographs can be computed unintentionally, it cannot be emphasised too strongly that the program user should read and check the data and the lattice vector sums which appear in the legend to each micrograph before accepting it.

6.4. Program geometry and arrangement of the calculation

The axis systems and the units of measurement used in TWODIS are exactly

---

* This equivalence arises because a lattice vector may be added to a fault translation vector without affecting the diffraction situation. For example, $\frac{1}{6}[11\bar{2}] + \frac{1}{6}[11\bar{2}] + \frac{1}{2}[\bar{1}\bar{1}2] = \frac{1}{6}[\bar{1}\bar{1}2]$.

the same as those used in ONEDIS. However, since there are now two dislocations rather than one, it is no longer possible to position the dislocation axis system with $\text{o}x_3$ along *the* dislocation, nor to centre the origin of the generalised cross-section axis system at the point in the generalised cross-section plane where *the* dislocation emerges. In program TWODIS, both the dislocation axis system and the generalised cross-section axis system are still positioned so that the projection of $\text{o}x_3$ and OX_3 on the micrograph are along the middle of the micrograph, between rows 30 and 31. Dimensions in the dislocation axis system and in the micrograph are measured in units of the extinction distance and dimensions in the generalised cross-section axis system are measured in units of extinction distance divided by π. The origin of the generalised cross-section axis system is still taken to be in the centre of the generalised cross-section, and the geometry is arranged such that the middle fault plane p_2 passes through the origin and the dislocations are in p_2, symmetrically disposed about the origin. The coordinates of the dislocations are calculated as follows.

Figure 6.5 shows an end-on view of the two dislocations 1 and 2 in which $\text{o}x_3$ is directly out of the paper and where the distances between the dislocations measured parallel to $\text{o}x_1$ and $\text{o}x_2$ are PT′ and SL′ respectively. The shortest distance between the two dislocations is, of course, the program variable SEP, and the normal to p_2, FP, lies in the $\text{o}x_1 - \text{o}x_2$ plane. Let us define a vector normal to 1 and 2 and in the sense from 2 to 1 by taking the vector product $\text{o}x_3 \wedge \text{FP}$ and make this of unit magnitude by normalisation. The components of such a unit vector are $-\text{FP}(2)/Z$ along $\text{o}x_1$ and $\text{FP}(1)/Z$ along $\text{o}x_2$ where $Z = \sqrt{(\text{FP}(1)^2 + \text{FP}(2)^2)}$. Thus it follows that, in the $\text{o}x_1$, $\text{o}x_2$, $\text{o}x_3$ coordinate system:

$$\text{PT}' = -\text{SEP} * \text{FP}(2)/Z, \tag{6.3}$$

and

$$\text{SL}' = \text{SEP} * \text{FP}(1)/Z. \tag{6.4}$$

Consider now a similar geometry, fig. 6.6, in the generalised cross-section,

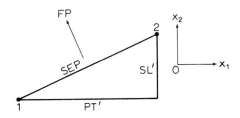

Fig. 6.5. Geometry for the separations PT′ and SL′ of dislocations 1 and 2 in the dislocation axis system.

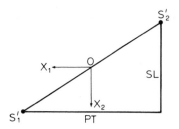

Fig. 6.6. Geometry for the separations PT and SL of dislocations 1 and 2 in the generalised cross-section.

in which the equivalent quantities to PT$'$ and SL$'$ are PT and SL. The relationship between the dislocation axes and the generalised cross-section axes was derived in ch. 4 and is given by expression (4.19):

$$x_1 = -X_1,$$

$$x_2 = -X_2 \cos \psi, \qquad\qquad [(4.19)]$$

where ψ is the angle between ox_2 and $-OX_2$ (i.e. between ox_2 and the beam direction B). The beam direction referred to the dislocation axes becomes the subscripted variable BM which is normalised to be a unit vector in the ox_2-ox_3 plane. Thus, from eq. (4.9), $\cos \psi = $ BM(2) and

$$PT = SEP * FP(2)/Z, \qquad\qquad (6.5)$$

and

$$SL = -SEP * FP(1)/(Z * BM(2)). \qquad\qquad (6.6)$$

Although PT and SL have been defined in generalised cross-section axes, it should be noted that they do not contain the factor π expected for the units in those axes. In fact, PT and SL appear in the program exactly as shown in expressions (6.5) and (6.6) since they are later used in establishing micrograph geometry where the units system does not require the factor π.

The program variables CN(16) and CN(17) are used to denote the coordinates of the first dislocation S_1' with respect to the axes OX_1 and OX_2, and since the dislocations are symmetric about the origin, it follows that the coordinates of the second dislocation S_2' are $-$CN(16) and $-$CN(17). From fig. 6.6 and expressions (6.5) and (6.6), it can easily be seen that:

$$CN(16) = PY * PT/2.0, \qquad\qquad (6.7)$$

$$CN(17) = PY * SL/2.0, \qquad\qquad (6.8)$$

where $\bar{P}Y = \pi$ and the coordinates, therefore, have their correct units.

It was explained in § 4.4 that in the case of crystal dislocations, much arithmetic manipulation can be saved if the variable along the OX_1 axis in the expression for the displacement function β' is changed from X_1 to $X_1/\cos\psi$. Thus, for transmission to, and use in, subroutine DERIV, the coordinate CN(16) is redefined as:

$$CN(30) = CN(16)/BM(2) \tag{6.9}$$

(compare this with the redefinition of CN(15) as CN(29) in expression (4.25)). Indeed, it was found that the most efficient form of the displacement function for a dislocation was:

$$\beta' = \frac{1}{X_2} \sum_\alpha \frac{P_\alpha \rho + Q_\alpha}{(\rho + R_\alpha)^2 + (S_\alpha)^2} \qquad [(4.26)]$$

where P_α, Q_α, R_α, S_α are constants (CN(1) to CN(12)) determined from the solution to the anisotropic elasticity problem and ρ (R in ONEDIS DERIV) is given in terms of the variables along OX_1 and OX_2 by

$$\rho = \frac{X_1}{X_2 \cos\psi}, \qquad [(4.27)]$$

or

$$R = CN(29)/X, \tag{6.10}$$

in DERIV where X is the program variable along OX_2.

In the case of two dislocations, DERIV contains a sum of two expressions of the form of eq. (4.26) each with its own definition of ρ (R1 and R2). However, expression (4.26) refers to the displacement function evaluated with the dislocation at the origin and so in calculating each of R1 and R2 the origin of coordinates has to be moved to centre on each dislocation in turn. Thus:

$$R1 = (CN(29) - CN(30))/(X - CN(17)), \tag{6.11}$$

and

$$R2 = (CN(29) + CN(30))/(X + CN(17)). \tag{6.12}$$

Although it takes twelve constants P_α, Q_α, R_α and S_α (CN(1) to CN(12)) to define the expression (4.26) for a single dislocation, it should be noted that only six of them, CN(1) to CN(6) are dependent upon the Burgers vector, the other six depending only upon the dislocation line direction, the diffracting vector etc.. Thus, in computing β' for two dislocations, only six new constants are required (CN(21) to CN(26)) and in the second expression of the form of eq. (4.26) in DERIV for TWODIS these replace CN(1) to CN(6). All the constants required for evaluating β' are calculated in the main program, being transmitted to DERIV through COMMON/RKMDRV in the usual way.

On examination of subroutine DERIV, it will be noticed that the denominators in the expression (6.10) (DERIV for ONEDIS) or in expressions (6.11) and (6.12) (DERIV for TWODIS) are tested to ensure that they are non-zero before the expressions are evaluated. This, of course, is common programming practice. In addition, however, the numerators of expressions (6.10), (6.11) and (6.12) must also be non-zero. If the numerators are zero, this corresponds physically to the column of integration passing exactly through the core of the dislocation and when this happens the integration routine RKM tends to stall, taking shorter and shorter intervals in an endeavour to follow the large and discontinuous displacement function. This situation can never arise for ONEDIS because the dislocation is always positioned exactly between two columns of integration. In TWODIS, however, unless precautions are taken, situations of this sort would be quite possible. It is for this reason that in the main program the variable along OX_1 (CN(15)) is compared with the coordinates of the dislocation in this direction ($\pm$CN(16)) to see if the integration column is within a prescribed distance (SHIFT) of either of the dislocation cores. If this is the case, then the integration column is moved to be SHIFT away from the dislocation line. Usually, SHIFT is set to the constant value 0.01 in units of ξ_g/π, but if this is larger than half the spacing between columns this latter value is taken for SHIFT. Care is taken that, when the column is moved, the sense of its relation to the dislocation line is not altered. That is to say, if a column is to the left of a dislocation, but within a distance SHIFT of it, the column is moved further to the left until it is just SHIFT away.

Of course, since the spacing of the rows of intensity in the micrograph is determined by the mechanism of the line printer, when a column of integration is moved in this way the intensities corresponding to it are not. Because this procedure could be misleading, when a column has to be moved, a flag (MOVE) is set and this flag is subsequently recognised at the stage at which intensities are printed and the letter M is printed in the left-hand margin of the micrograph alongside the appropriate row. In passing, it may be noted that since the dislocations are symmetrically disposed about the origin, the moving procedure occurs either at both dislocations or neither of them.

Before leaving the topic of the proximity of the integration column to the dislocation core, it should be stated that the procedure contained in TWODIS only ensures that the column will not actually pass through the centre of the dislocation core, and that the integration routine is not asked to calculate

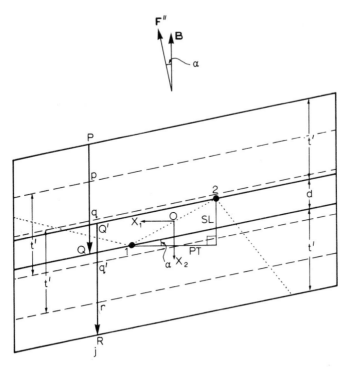

Fig. 6.7. A combination of figs. 6.2 and 6.6 showing the relationship between SL, PT and d in the generalised cross-section for two dislocations.

something it is unable to. Even though no column comes within SHIFT of the line, because SHIFT is small it is still quite possible (in large magnification micrographs, or in micrographs where the dislocation line makes only a small angle with the beam direction, for example) for integration columns to pass through regions of the crystal where the displacement function, although not discontinuous, is large and changing rapidly. This will inevitably result in a greater time for computation, since the integration routine will be forced to take a very large number of very small steps through these regions in order to compute each step to the prescribed accuracy. The increase in computation time will usually be obvious, but what may not be so apparent is the decreased accuracy of the overall computation due to the increased number of steps. This inaccuracy may also occur, of course, in ordinary micrographs for the columns which have been moved. In these cases, however, the other columns will usually be far from the core and the intensity values in the rows corresponding to these columns will have their usual accuracy. This is an additional reason for caution in interpreting the rows of intensity in the micrograph marked with an M in the margin.

Now let us turn to considerations of how the micrograph is framed and how the integration calculation is arranged in the program. Consider the view of the generalised cross-section shown in fig. 6.7. This is really a combination of figs. 6.2 and 6.6 and it shows the relationship between SL and PT, the defect geometry, the generalised cross-section and its axes, and the dimensions t' and d.

The quantity marked d in fig. 6.7 (denoted as EXTRA in the program) is a fundamental one. It can be seen immediately from fig. 6.7 that d is given by:

$$d = \text{SL} - \text{PT} \tan \alpha, \tag{6.13}$$

where PT and SL are given by expressions (6.5) and (6.6) and α is the angle between OX_1 and the projection of the foil surface in the generalised cross-section plane. Or alternatively, α is the angle between the projection of the foil normal in the generalised cross-section plane and $-OX_2$. From this latter definition:

$$\tan \alpha = \text{FNX(1)}/(-\text{FNX(2)}), \tag{6.14}$$

where FNX(1) and FNX(2) are the components of the foil normal resolved along OX_1 and OX_2 respectively. Since the dimension d must be positive for all geometries, it is defined in the program as:

$$\text{EXTRA} = \text{ABS(SL} + \text{PT} * \text{FNX(1)/FNX(2))}. \tag{6.15}$$

As explained earlier in § 6.2, the two ranges of integration for a representative column j are PQ and Q'R and each of these is divided into n equal steps. The step length (DELT) involves both t' (THBM), the thickness of the foil in the beam direction, and d (EXTRA). By direct analogy with the corresponding definition given in ONEDIS (expression (4.17)), the value of DELT is given by:

$$\text{DELT} = \text{PY} * \text{FRACTN} * (\text{THBM} + \text{EXTRA})/64.0, \tag{6.16}$$

where the quantity FRACTN (expression (4.13)) is included to allow for variable magnification of the micrograph and the factor PY (π) is included to obtain the correct units (ξ_g/π).

Consider now the point at which the integrations for the two 'experiments' start. For a standardly framed micrograph this is the point P; for a non-standard micrograph, the point p (fig. 6.7). For a standardly framed TWODIS micrograph the first part of the integration starts at P and finishes at Q and the second part starts at Q' and finishes at R. For other ways of framing the micrograph, the ranges of integration are represented by lower case letters: p, q, q' and r. How-

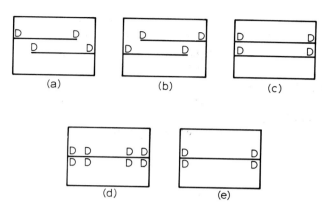

Fig. 6.9. Schematic illustration for a standardly framed micrograph of the five possible cases for the positions of the D's which mark the emergence of the dislocations from the surfaces of the foil.

planes resolved in the generalised cross-section plane and since the normal to p_2 can be upward or downward drawn with respect to the beam direction, whereas the foil normal is always upward drawn, the sign of the normal to p_2 has to be tested also. The case depicted in fig. 6.9(c) occurs when p_2 and the foil surface have the same slopes in the generalised cross-section; that in fig. 6.9(d) when p_2 is vertical, i.e. parallel to the beam direction; and that in fig. 6.9(e) when the value of SEP is zero. In the last two cases, two 'D's are usually put in at each point in neighbouring rows of the micrograph. This is because DELL includes a constant (0.00000001) to allow for any rounding-off errors in the computations.

In addition to 'D's marked in the micrograph, 'D's (or 'M's if the integration column has been moved and the flag, MOVE, has been set) are printed in the left-hand margin alongside the row of intensity closest to the dislocation line.

In the case of non-standardly framed micrographs, the 'D's in the micrograph do not necessarily mark the points of emergence of the dislocation lines from the surfaces of the foil. They will do so at the left-hand side of the micrograph only if FINISH = t and at the right-hand side only if START = 0. If these conditions are not fulfilled the 'D's are still inserted into the row of intensity closest to the dislocation line, but in such a way that the 'D's at any one side of the micrograph indicate only a line parallel to the trace of plane p_2 in the surface of the foil and not the actual trace.

The only major topic concerning TWODIS which remains to be discussed is how the program handles the planes and stacking faults. The planes on which the stacking faults occur appear as lines on the generalised cross-section, fig. 6.2, and the geometry of these is determined by defining a point through which they pass and then using their slopes in the generalised cross-section plane. The slopes are specified by the components of the plane normals projected into the generalised cross-section (FP1X(1),FP1X(2) for p_1, etc.). The second fault plane p_2 passes through the origin of the generalised cross-section axes and the first and third planes p_1 and p_3 pass through the points in the generalised cross-section representing dislocations 1 and 2 respectively. These points are specified by their coordinates: CN(16),CN(17) for dislocation 1, $-$CN(16), $-$CN(17) for dislocation 2. Thus, for a particular integration column (i.e. for a particular value of CN(15)), the positions at which the column may cross a fault plane are given, in units of ξ_g/π, by:

$$POS(1, 1) = CN(17) - (CN(15) - CN(16)) * FP1X(1)/FP1X(2), \qquad (6.26)$$

$$POS(1, 2) = -CN(15) * FP2X(1)/FP2X(2), \qquad (6.27)$$

$$POS(1, 3) = -CN(17) - (CN(15) + CN(16)) * FP3X(1)/FP3X(2), \qquad (6.28)$$

for planes p_1, p_2 and p_3 respectively.

The surface in the generalised cross-section where the second part of the integration starts, q' (SURFAC), is treated in much the same way as a fault plane, and is defined as being $\pi t'$ below the line STARTA. Therefore, the point at which this line intersects an integration column is given by:

$$POS(1, 4) = STARTA + TBP. \qquad (6.29)$$

Coupled with each of the planes and SURFAC is an integer (ITYPE) which is used to recognise the type of operation which is to be performed when a particular 'event' occurs in an integration step. That is, when a value of POS(1,i) is found to occur in the integration step being performed, ITYPE is used to determine the particular phase angle adjustment for that stacking fault (in the case of faults) or to store the amplitudes in TEMPY (in the case of SURFAC).

Of course, the expressions (6.26), (6.27), (6.28) are defined everywhere in the generalised cross-section plane, and the limitation of the geometry to the cases shown schematically in fig. 6.3 is done in the following way. For each particular column of integration, the variables XXX and YYY are defined:

$$XXX = CN(15) + CN(16), \qquad (6.30)$$

$$YYY = CN(15) - CN(16), \qquad (6.31)$$

and these are used to test whether the column is to the left of dislocation 1 (YYY positive), to the right of dislocation 2 (XXX negative) or in between the two dislocations (XXX * YYY negative). In the first case, eq. (6.26) is evaluated, in the second, eq. (6.28) is evaluated, and in the third, eq. (6.27) is evaluated. For non-overlapping cases, e.g. fig. 6.3(a) and (b), this leads to only one fault plane being considered in each region, but for overlapping cases, e.g. fig. 6.3(c) and (d), all three fault planes are considered for columns which pass between the two dislocations. If, for any reason, a particular plane or stacking fault is not encountered (e.g. its normal or its translation vector is not present on the data card, or the column passes through a region for which the appropriate expression is not evaluated) then a false, large, negative value (-10000.0) is loaded into the appropriate POS(1,i). Thus, all three fault planes and SURFAC are defined for every column in the generalised cross-section, although some of the planes may be falsely defined. The values of POS(1,i) are sorted so that they are of increasing magnitude with respect to the integration direction OX_2, their corresponding values of ITYPE being sorted with them.

The integration down a column is done in two main parts (each divided into n steps), p to q and q′ to r with a possible joining integration between q and q′, if q′ is below q. The point q′ (SURFAC) may be found within the first part; it constitutes the actual finishing point of the joining integration and the starting point of the second part. Thus only those fault planes which occur below q′ (i.e. which have values of POS(1,i) greater than SURFAC) may appear in the second part of the integration. The values of POS(1,i) are therefore used in the first part of the integration and in the joining integration (if any) and those values of POS(1,i) which are greater than SURFAC are transferred to another array POS(2,i) which is used in the second part of the integration. Values of POS(1,i) which are less than SURFAC are loaded into POS(2,i) as a large negative number (-10050.0) so that once again all the fault planes are defined.

The part of the program which handles the fault planes and SURFAC and their attendant integration requirements is in the nature of an internal subroutine situated at the end of the main program. It is linked to the three integration regions (which are DO LOOPS from p to q and from q′ to r, to obtain the n steps, and a single step from q to q′) by the identifying integer LINK. LINK is 1 for the first part of the integration, 2 for the second and 3 for the joining part. The internal subroutine operates on the premise that all possible events are present in an integration region (although, of course, some or all of them may be falsely present) and that they are listed in the order in which the electron beam encouters them.

A counter KOUNTF is used in the internal subroutine and this is tested immediately upon entry to see if there are any events left to be considered in this column of the integration. If there are not, control passes straight back to the appropriate part of the main program (through LINK) where a simple call of the integration routine RKM is made to effect the integration of that step. If the check on KOUNTF shows that there are more events to come, this test is followed by another to see if the next event on the list occurs in this particular step. If it does not, control is again returned to the appropriate part of the main program. If an event is to occur in this step, integration is carried out down to the position of the event and the necessary manipulations of the amplitudes performed (according to expressions (6.1) and (6.2) for stacking faults or storing the amplitudes in TEMPY if the event is SURFAC). If the event is a fault, after manipulation its position is effectively cancelled by loading a large negative value (-9000.0) into the appropriate POS. If and when the position of SURFAC is found in the first part of the integration, a flag is set (IFLAG = 1) which is tested at the end of the first part of the integration to see if the joining integration, q to q', is necessary. After manipulation at an event, KOUNTF is incremented by one and the internal subroutine traversed again to search for another event in the remaining part of the step. If none is found, control is returned to the appropriate part of the main program to complete the integration in the remainder of the step. These operations are repeated until the test of KOUNTF indicates that all the events have occurred and, in this case, the call to the internal subroutine becomes redundant since control is immediately transferred back to the main program.

At the end of each step in the first part of the integration, the constants of proportionality FX are determined, and at the end of each corresponding step in the second part, the final amplitudes TT are calculated. These operations are exactly the same as those described for ONEDIS.

6.5. Extension of the program to more complex configurations

From what has been said in the previous sections of this chapter and in ch. 4, it will be apparent that the technique of micrograph computation can be extended to any dislocation—stacking fault configuration, provided that all the dislocations are parallel and the stacking faults contain a direction parallel to the dislocation line. These represent the only limitations in principle, although there may be other effective limitations due, for example, to the complexity of the geometry of the configuration, or to the excessive time for computation because of the increased complexity of the displacement function in DERIV. Moreover, there are likely to be complications of detail which will be different from case to case. These effective limitations and complications are likely to be resolved on the basis of specific requirements in particular cases and what the user (programmer) finds most convenient. However, some of the problems likely to be encountered in extending TWODIS will be outlined briefly.

From the description just given, it may be readily seen how the internal sub-routine may be extended to handle any number of fault planes and how extra terms may be added to DERIV to accommodate more dislocations. Of course, the ancillary geometry (calculation of fault heights and dislocation coordinates, movement of integration columns from the proximity of the core) and calculations (establishment of phase angles, sorting of the POS values and the evaluation of the six extra constants for each dislocation displacement function) have to be worked out as well.

However, considerations which are likely to be more troublesome will probably arise in establishing the geometrical configuration itself, in framing the micrograph or even in marking the 'D's at the ends of the dislocation lines. In the case of TWODIS, the geometry of the configuration was obtained using a combination of generally defined coordinates (for the dislocations) and lines (representing the planes) and subsequently limiting the extent of the planes using the variables XXX and YYY. For other geometries, other methods will almost certainly be more convenient. The framing of the micrograph would seem to represent the most awkward part of extending the program. Indeed, in the case of a FOURDIS program we have written, it was found most convenient to retain the standard TWODIS framing, using START and FINISH to include the extremities of the other two dislocations as necessary. Further, in the case of FOURDIS it was considered not to be worth the effort involved to mark 'D's in the micrograph, although the row of the micrograph closest to the dislocation line is marked with a 'D' (or 'M') in the margin.

In short, therefore, within the limitations of being able to define a generalised cross-section, the micrograph programs may be extended indefinitely. Whether it is worth the programming effort involved depends, amongst other things, upon the complexity of the configuration and the amount of information likely to be obtained by using the program to match experimental images and identify the configuration. The user will have to decide his own attitude to these considerations for each specific case.

7 | MATCHING WITH TWODIS

7.1. Introduction

In this chapter the use of program TWODIS will be illustrated by its application to defects which involve partial dislocations bordering stacking faults. Two examples of this type of defect will be considered in the face-centred cubic alloy Cu + 15.6 at % Al. These examples are both contained in fig. 7.1 which is an electron micrograph of a lightly deformed specimen of this alloy whose foil normal has been determined as [945].

The first example, defect A in fig. 7.1, was chosen as it appeared to be a simple case of partial dislocations bordering an extensive region of fault. In this defect the partials are sufficiently separated for them to be treated individually so that if diffracting vectors for which $g \cdot R$ is integral are used (fault out of contrast) the usual invisibility criteria for dislocations can be applied to make a preliminary identification of the partial dislocations. In this simple example, therefore, the identification of the Burgers vectors of the partials will be carried out initially using invisibility criteria and computed images will be used to confirm this result.

The second example, defect B in fig. 7.1, is a much narrower defect and shows contrast on all diffracting vectors. In this case invisibility criteria cannot be used and it is necessary to use image computation to identify the defect.

7.2. Example 1, defect A

The crystallography and geometry of defect A have been determined in the manner described in ch. 3. The dislocations intersect the top of the foil at 2 and 4 and the bottom of the foil at 1 and 3 (fig. 7.2). The dislocations are

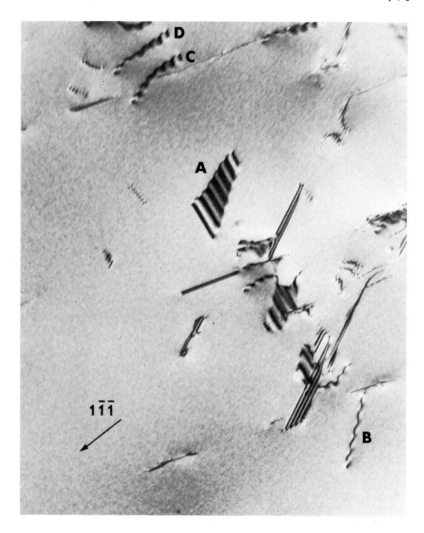

Fig. 7.1. An electron micrograph of a thin foil of lightly deformed Cu + 15.6 at % Al alloy. The beam direction is close to [101] and *g* is indicated. × 44,000.

not straight and the vectors along the dislocation lines were taken as the lines joining the points of intersection $1 \to 2$, $3 \to 4$ and determined as $[5\bar{2}3]$ for dislocation *a* and $[10\bar{1}]$ for dislocation *b*. These vectors define the plane of the defect as (111) which is compatible with the observed change in projected width of this slip plane in different beam directions.

The first step in making an identification of this defect is to determine the displacement vector R^* associated with the stacking fault, since this vector defines the nature of the fault, i.e. whether it is intrinsic or extrinsic. Following Hashimoto et al. (1962)[**], the nature of the fault can be determined from the contrast of the outermost fault fringes in the bright field image of fig. 7.2(a). Here the outermost fringes are white, so that $g \cdot R = +\frac{1}{3}$. Since g is $\bar{1}11$, R must be $\frac{1}{3}[111]$ and therefore since R is acute with the beam direction $[514]$ the fault is intrinsic.

Since the fault is intrinsic, defect A has most likely arisen from a $\frac{1}{2}\langle 110\rangle$ dislocation dissociating into Shockley partial dislocations during slip on (111). The next step therefore is to determine the Burgers vectors of the partial dislocations bordering the fault. In the first instance, this is done using the $g \cdot b$ invisibility criteria on the assumption that the material is elastically isotropic. Under this assumption the criteria are only applicable to partial dislocations when they are sufficiently separated to be treated individually and when diffraction conditions are such that there is no contribution to the contrast from the fault, i.e. for diffraction conditions such that $g \cdot R$ is an integer. For diffraction conditions where $g \cdot R$ is non-integral, contrast near a partial dislocation results from a combination of contrast from the displacement field of the dislocation and the shear of the fault. An empirical set of $g \cdot b$ rules has been proposed for situations where $g \cdot R$ is non-integral (Howie and Whelan, 1962; Silcock and Tunstall, 1964; Clarebrough, 1971), but care must be taken in using these rules as will be pointed out in § 8.9 and in this example they will be avoided.

Figure 7.2(b), (c) and (d) shows three images of defect A where the diffracting vectors are such that $g \cdot R$ is an integer and fault contrast is absent. The possible Burgers vectors for the Shockley dislocations on (111) are $\pm\frac{1}{6}[2\bar{1}\bar{1}]$, $\pm\frac{1}{6}[\bar{1}2\bar{1}]$ and $\pm\frac{1}{6}[\bar{1}\bar{1}2]$. It can be seen from fig. 7.2(b), (c) and (d) that dislocation a is in contrast for the diffracting vectors 202 and 131 and shows very little contrast for the diffracting vector $13\bar{1}$. Clearly therefore the Burgers vectors $\pm\frac{1}{6}[\bar{2}11]$ satisfy this contrast behaviour, i.e. have $g \cdot b = 0$ for the $13\bar{1}$ diffracting vector. Similarly, dislocation b shows very little contrast for the $1\bar{3}\bar{1}$ diffracting vector and this can be assigned the Burgers vectors

---

[*] In the face-centred cubic system the displacement vector R can be expressed as a shear vector in the plane of the fault (of the type $\frac{1}{6}\langle 112\rangle$) or by an equivalent displacement vector normal to the fault plane (of the type $\frac{1}{3}\langle 111\rangle$) by the addition of a lattice vector to the shear vector (Art et al., 1963). For the conventions adopted (§ 6.3.2) and, for this latter way of specifying R, a displacement vector acute with the beam direction B corresponds to an intrinsic fault, whereas a displacement vector obtuse with B corresponds to an extrinsic fault.

[**] The rule given by Hashimoto et al. (1962) for determining R is applicable to nearly all experimental conditions likely to be encountered in practice. However, there are certain circumstances where it breaks down and these will be discussed in § 8.6.

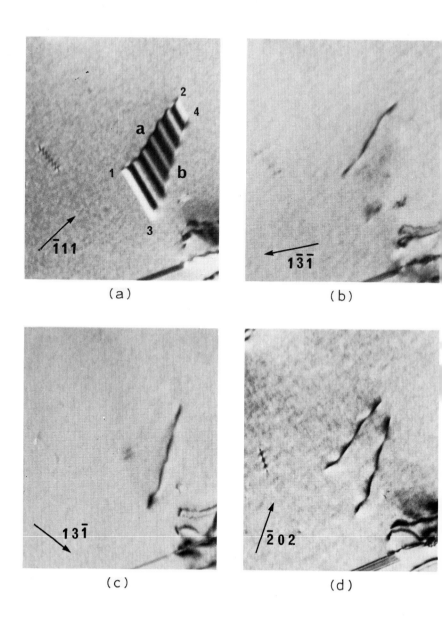

Fig. 7.2. Electron micrographs of the defect marked A in fig. 7.1 taken using the following diffracting vectors and approximate beam directions: (a) $\bar{1}11$, [101]; (b) $1\bar{3}\bar{1}$, [101]; (c) $13\bar{1}$, [101] and (d) $\bar{2}02$, [111]. × 60,000.

$\pm\frac{1}{6}[\bar{1}\bar{1}2]$. With the defined sense of u for dislocations a and b only the Burgers vector $\frac{1}{6}[\bar{2}11]$ for dislocation a and $\frac{1}{6}[\bar{1}\bar{1}2]$ for dislocation b are compatible with the intrinsic fault (Thompson, 1953). This preliminary identification indicates that defect A is an intrinsic fault bordered by Shockley partial dislocations resulting from the dissociation reaction,

$$\tfrac{1}{2}[\bar{1}01] = \tfrac{1}{6}[\bar{1}\bar{1}2] + \tfrac{1}{6}[\bar{2}11].$$

Having used conventional methods, the image matching technique will now be applied to dislocation a and its associated stacking fault. In contrast to the use of invisibility criteria, there is no need to confine the image matching technique to cases where $g \cdot R$ is integral, as this technique takes account of the contributions to the overall image contrast from both the displacement field of the dislocation and the shear of the fault. In fact, in the examples of image computation to be considered, attention will be confined solely to images with non-integral values of $g \cdot R$ so that fault fringes will be present. From the point of view of image matching, such images have the advantage that they possess striking character. In this example, the additional information contained in these images gives confirmation of the preliminary result already obtained using invisibility criteria for images with integral values of $g \cdot R$.

Figure 7.3 shows three experimental images (a), (b) and (c) of dislocation a for the diffracting conditions listed in table 7.1, together with three sets of computed images for the three possible Shockley partial dislocations ($\frac{1}{6}[\bar{2}11]$, $\frac{1}{6}[1\bar{2}1]$ and $\frac{1}{6}[11\bar{2}]$) on (111) that could border the intrinsic fault along

TABLE 7.1
Diffraction conditions for the experimental images of defect A in fig. 7.3

Micrograph	Diffracting vector g	Beam direction B	Extinction distance[*] $\xi_g(\text{Å})$	Deviation from the Bragg condition[**] $w = s\,\xi_g$	Apparent anomalous absorption coefficient $\mathscr{A}$
(a)	$\bar{1}11$	[514]	326	-0.20 ± 0.1	0.065
(b)	$\bar{1}\bar{1}1$	[516]	326	0.55 ± 0.1	0.065
(c)	$0\bar{2}0$	[705]	386	0.30 ± 0.1	0.080

[*] The values of ξ_g for the alloy are based on the atomic scattering amplitudes for copper and aluminium of Doyle and Turner (1968) and include the Debye–Waller correction appropriate to 293° K.

[**] The quoted errors in w are due to the uncertainties in the measurements of s.

$$\tfrac{1}{6}[\bar{2}11]$$

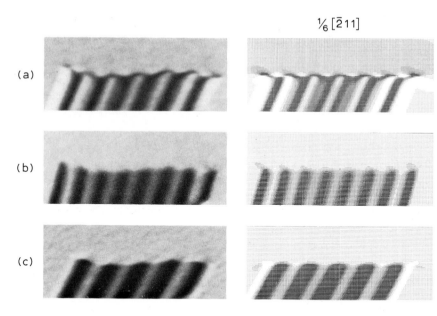

Fig. 7.3. A set of three experimental images (a), (b) and (c) taken with the diffraction conditions given in table 7.1 and three sets of computed images for an intrinsic fault on (111) bordered by the Shockley partial dislocations $\tfrac{1}{6}[\bar{2}11]$, $\tfrac{1}{6}[1\bar{2}1]$ and $\tfrac{1}{6}[11\bar{2}]$. For the computed images the values of t and w are: 5.90 ξ_{111a}, -0.21 in (a); 5.90 ξ_{111a}, 0.62 in (b); and 4.98 ξ_{020a}, 0.29 in (c).

$1 \to 2$. Refined values of t and w for the computed images were obtained by use of the program DELUGE in the manner described in ch. 5. These refined values are given in the legend to the figure. The elastic constants for the Cu + 15.6 at% Al alloy were not known and in all computations the values $c_{11} = 15.95$, $c_{12} = 11.76$ and $c_{44} = 7.66$ dyne cm$^{-2} \times 10^{11}$ for a Cu + 10 at% Al alloy were used (Hearmon, 1956).

Despite the fact that dislocation a is not straight and despite possible inaccuracy in the elastic constants used, it can be seen from the first column of computed images that the measure of agreement between the detail in the experimental and computed images is very satisfactory, whereas the other two columns of computed images do not match the experimental images. Thus the Burgers vector of dislocation a is $\tfrac{1}{6}[\bar{2}11]$, in agreement with the preliminary identification.

Defect A was deliberately chosen as a simple example which could be identified with reasonable certainty either by the use of invisibility criteria or image matching. However, for the identification of the other defect (defect B) chosen from the general area in fig. 7.1, image computation is essential.

$\frac{1}{6}[1\bar{2}1]$ $\frac{1}{6}[11\bar{2}]$

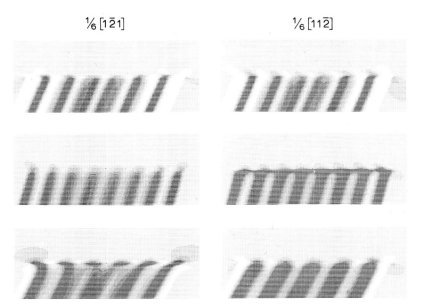

7.3. Example 2, defect B

All the experimental images of defect B taken over a wide range of diffracting conditions showed strong contrast and nine images representative of the range of contrast shown by the defect, and taken for the diffraction conditions listed in table 7.2, are shown in fig. 7.4 (a)–(i). Since the copper–aluminium alloy is not highly elastically anisotropic, and since $g \cdot b$ would have been zero for all Burgers vectors of the type $\frac{1}{2}\langle 110 \rangle$ for at least one of the diffracting vectors used, this suggests that defect B is not simply an isolated dislocation with a Burgers vector of this type. However, since the alloy has a low stacking-fault energy, it is possible that the defect consists of a $\frac{1}{2}\langle 110 \rangle$ dislocation which has dissociated into its component Shockley partial dislocations separated by a narrow region of stacking fault.

The vector u along the line of defect B was determined as $[10\bar{1}]$. Defect B thus lies along the intersection of the two slip planes (111) and $(1\bar{1}1)$ and could have resulted from a $\frac{1}{2}\langle 110 \rangle$ dislocation dissociating on either of these two planes. The normal method of distinguishing between dissociation on these two planes would be to examine the change in width of the image in different beam directions. However, the partial dislocations in defect B are separated by a distance comparable with their image widths so that they cannot be individually resolved, and such a rotation experiment was inconclusive. Therefore, when computing images to identify defect B, it is necessary to consider all the possible combinations of Shockley partial dislocations on

TABLE 7.2

Diffraction conditions for the experimental images of defect B in figs. 7.4, 7.5 and 7.6

Micrograph	Diffracting vector g	Beam direction B	Extinction distance[*] ξ_g(Å)	Deviation from the Bragg condition[**] $w = s\,\xi_g$	Apparent anomalous absorption coefficient $\mathcal{A}$
(a)	$1\bar{1}\bar{1}$	[514]	326	-0.15 ± 0.1	0.065
(b)	$\bar{1}11$	[11 2 9]	326	1.00 ± 0.1	0.065
(c)	$11\bar{1}$	[516]	326	0.25 ± 0.1	0.065
(d)	020	[301]	386	0.27 ± 0.1	0.08
(e)	$20\bar{2}$	[616]	540	0.00 ± 0.3	0.10
(f)	$\bar{2}02$	[15 17 15]	540	1.80 ± 0.3	0.10
(g)	$2\bar{2}0$	[9 9 10]	540	0.23 ± 0.3	0.10
(h)	$\bar{2}20$	[9 9 10]	540	0.60 ± 0.3	0.10
(i)	$13\bar{1}$	[15 $\bar{1}$ 12]	652	0.30 ± 0.3	0.12

[*] The values of ξ_g for the alloy are based on the atomic scattering amplitudes for copper and aluminium of Doyle and Turner (1968) and include the Debye–Waller correction appropriate to 293° K.

[**] The quoted errors in w are due to the uncertainties in the measurements of s.

(111) and ($1\bar{1}\bar{1}$) (both for intrinsic and extrinsic faulting) that could give rise to a defect lying along [$10\bar{1}$], and then to determine which of these matches the set of experimental images.

Table 7.3 illustrates the 24 possible dissociation reactions for $\frac{1}{2}\langle 110\rangle$ dislocations generating combinations of Shockley partial dislocations on (111) and ($1\bar{1}1$) which could constitute defect B. The dissociation reactions for these $\frac{1}{2}\langle 110\rangle$ dislocations are listed in two sets of neighbouring columns 1, 2 and 3, 4. Columns 1 and 2 list the dissociations for intrinsic faults and columns 3 and 4 for extrinsic faults. It can be seen that each dissociation in columns 1 and 3 has an adjacent neighbour in columns 2 and 4 which is the dissociation for the Burgers vector of opposite sign resulting in the same type of fault. It will be recalled from ch. 5 that the bright field images of undissociated $\frac{1}{2}\langle 110\rangle$ dislocations of opposite sign taken with the same diffracting conditions are related to one another simply by a rotation of 180°. Similarly partial dislocations resulting from the dissociation of these $\frac{1}{2}\langle 110\rangle$ dislocations of opposite sign give, for the same diffracting conditions, bright field images which are also related by a simple rotation of 180°, provided they border faults of the same type (see Appendix). Hence when computing the various combinations required to match defect B, only those combinations in columns

TABLE 7.3

Possible combinations of Burgers vectors of Shockley partial dislocations for defect B with $u = [10\bar{1}]$ *

1	2	3	4

Defect B on (111)

Intrinsic dissociation		Extrinsic dissociation	
(i) $\frac{1}{2}[\bar{1}01] \to$ $\frac{1}{6}[\bar{2}11]$ $\frac{1}{6}[\bar{1}\bar{1}2]$	$\frac{1}{2}[10\bar{1}] \to$ $\frac{1}{6}[11\bar{2}]$ $\frac{1}{6}[2\bar{1}\bar{1}]$	(i) $\frac{1}{2}[\bar{1}01] \to$ $\frac{1}{6}[\bar{1}\bar{1}2]$ $\frac{1}{6}[\bar{2}11]$	$\frac{1}{2}[10\bar{1}] \to$ $\frac{1}{6}[2\bar{1}\bar{1}]$ $\frac{1}{6}[11\bar{2}]$
(ii) $\frac{1}{2}[1\bar{1}0] \to$ $\frac{1}{6}[1\bar{2}1]$ $\frac{1}{6}[2\bar{1}\bar{1}]$	$\frac{1}{2}[\bar{1}10] \to$ $\frac{1}{6}[\bar{2}11]$ $\frac{1}{6}[\bar{1}2\bar{1}]$	(ii) $\frac{1}{2}[1\bar{1}0] \to$ $\frac{1}{6}[2\bar{1}\bar{1}]$ $\frac{1}{6}[1\bar{2}1]$	$\frac{1}{2}[\bar{1}10] \to$ $\frac{1}{6}[\bar{1}2\bar{1}]$ $\frac{1}{6}[\bar{2}11]$
(iii) $\frac{1}{2}[01\bar{1}] \to$ $\frac{1}{6}[11\bar{2}]$ $\frac{1}{6}[\bar{1}2\bar{1}]$	$\frac{1}{2}[0\bar{1}1] \to$ $\frac{1}{6}[1\bar{2}1]$ $\frac{1}{6}[\bar{1}\bar{1}2]$	(iii) $\frac{1}{2}[01\bar{1}] \to$ $\frac{1}{6}[\bar{1}2\bar{1}]$ $\frac{1}{6}[11\bar{2}]$	$\frac{1}{2}[0\bar{1}1] \to$ $\frac{1}{6}[\bar{1}\bar{1}2]$ $\frac{1}{6}[1\bar{2}1]$

Defect B on (1$\bar{1}$1)

Intrinsic dissociation		Extrinsic dissociation	
(iv) $\frac{1}{2}[\bar{1}01] \to$ $\frac{1}{6}[\bar{2}\bar{1}1]$ $\frac{1}{6}[\bar{1}12]$	$\frac{1}{2}[10\bar{1}] \to$ $\frac{1}{6}[11\bar{2}1]$ $\frac{1}{6}[2\bar{1}\bar{1}]$	(iv) $\frac{1}{2}[\bar{1}01] \to$ $\frac{1}{6}[\bar{1}12]$ $\frac{1}{6}[\bar{2}\bar{1}1]$	$\frac{1}{2}[10\bar{1}] \to$ $\frac{1}{6}[21\bar{1}]$ $\frac{1}{6}[1\bar{1}\bar{2}]$
(v) $\frac{1}{2}[0\bar{1}\bar{1}] \to$ $\frac{1}{6}[1\bar{1}\bar{2}]$ $\frac{1}{6}[\bar{1}2\bar{1}]$	$\frac{1}{2}[011] \to$ $\frac{1}{6}[121]$ $\frac{1}{6}[\bar{1}\bar{1}2]$	(v) $\frac{1}{2}[0\bar{1}\bar{1}] \to$ $\frac{1}{6}[\bar{1}\bar{2}\bar{1}]$ $\frac{1}{6}[1\bar{1}\bar{2}]$	$\frac{1}{2}[011] \to$ $\frac{1}{6}[\bar{1}12]$ $\frac{1}{6}[121]$
(vi) $\frac{1}{2}[110] \to$ $\frac{1}{6}[121]$ $\frac{1}{6}[21\bar{1}]$	$\frac{1}{2}[\bar{1}\bar{1}0] \to$ $\frac{1}{6}[\bar{2}\bar{1}1]$ $\frac{1}{6}[\bar{1}\bar{2}\bar{1}]$	(vi) $\frac{1}{2}[110] \to$ $\frac{1}{6}[21\bar{1}]$ $\frac{1}{6}[121]$	$\frac{1}{2}[\bar{1}\bar{1}0] \to$ $\frac{1}{6}[\bar{1}\bar{2}\bar{1}]$ $\frac{1}{6}[\bar{2}\bar{1}1]$

* This sense of u is from left to right in the diagrams.

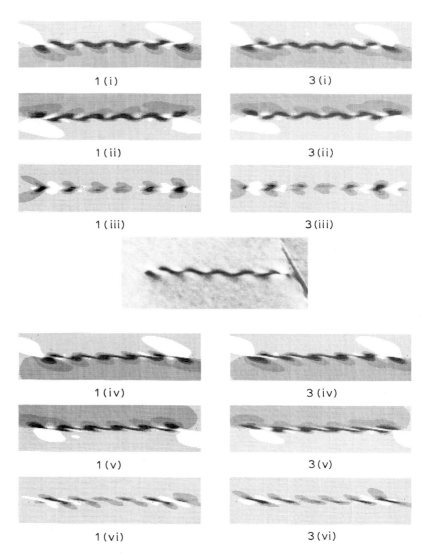

1 (i)   3 (i)

1 (ii)   3 (ii)

1 (iii)   3 (iii)

1 (iv)   3 (iv)

1 (v)   3 (v)

1 (vi)   3 (vi)

Fig. 7.4. (a) Comparison of an experimental image for the diffracting vector $1\bar{1}\bar{1}$, w = −0.15 and B = [514] with computed images for combinations of Shockley partial Burgers vectors and stacking faults as given in table 7.3.

1 and 3 of table 7.3 need to be considered, since the images for combinations in columns 2 and 4 are related to those in 1 and 3 by a rotation of 180°. Of course, when comparing experimental and computed images, it must be remembered that a rotation of 180° may be necessary in order to obtain a match. If a

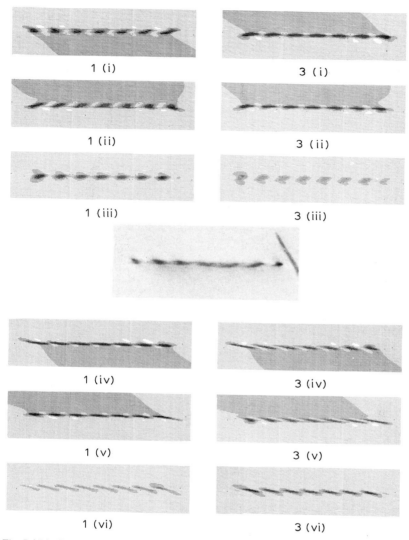

1 (i)

3 (i)

1 (ii)

3 (ii)

1 (iii)

3 (iii)

1 (iv)

3 (iv)

1 (v)

3 (v)

1 (vi)

3 (vi)

Fig. 7.4(b). Comparison of an experimental image for the diffracting vector $\bar{1}11$, $w = 1.0$ and $\boldsymbol{B} = [11\ 2\ 9]$ with computed images for combinations of Shockley partial Burgers vectors and stacking faults as given in table 7.3.

180° rotation were required, it would be the dissociation reaction for the $\frac{1}{2}\langle 110\rangle$ dislocation of the opposite sign from that used in the computed image which would described the defect. For example, if an image for a combination in column 1 is found to match an experimental image after a rotation of 180°,

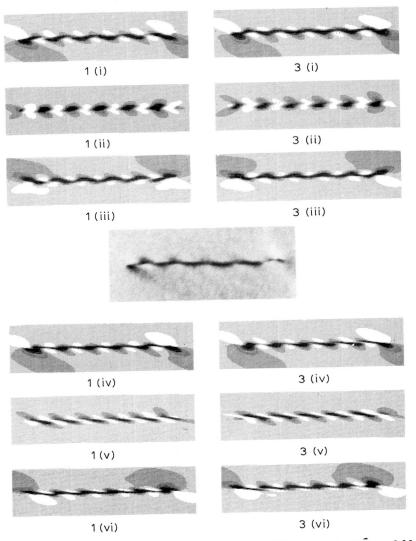

Fig. 7.4(c). Comparison of an experimental image for the diffracting vector $11\bar{1}$, $w = 0.25$ and $B = [516]$ with computed images for combinations of Shockley partial Burgers vectors and stacking faults as given in table 7.3.

then the combination of Burgers vectors specifying the defect would be that of the adjacent reaction in column 2.

Figure 7.4 is divided into nine parts (a)–(i). Each of these parts shows an experimental image for one diffracting vector, together with twelve computed

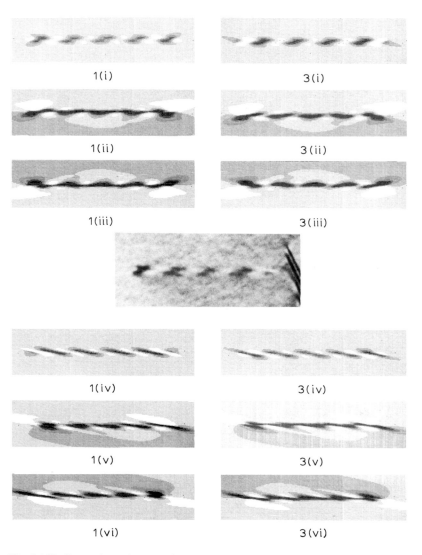

1(i)   3(i)

1(ii)   3(ii)

1(iii)   3(iii)

1(iv)   3(iv)

1(v)   3(v)

1(vi)   3(vi)

Fig. 7.4(d). Comparison of an experimental image for the diffracting vector 020, $w = 0.27$ and $B = [301]$ with computed images for combinations of Shockley partial Burgers vectors and stacking faults as given in table 7.3.

images covering intrinsic and extrinsic dissociation on (111) and intrinsic and extrinsic dissociation on (1$\bar{1}$1) for three of the possible six $\frac{1}{2}\langle 110 \rangle$ Burgers vectors on each of these planes. In parts (a)–(i) of fig. 7.4, the combinations of Burgers vectors correspond to columns 1 and 3 of table 7.3 and the com-

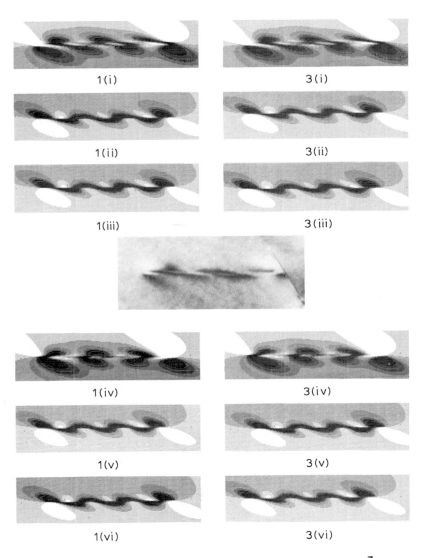

Fig. 7.4(e). Comparison of an experimental image for the diffracting vector $20\bar{2}$, $w = 0.0$ and $\boldsymbol{B} = [616]$ with computed images for combinations of Shockley partial Burgers vectors and stacking faults as given in table 7.3.

puted images are appropriately marked to relate them to the blocks in the table. For example, the computed image labelled 3(vi) on each part of fig. 7.4 corresponds to block (vi) in column 3 of table 7.3, i.e. the extrinsic dissociation of $\frac{1}{2}[110]$ on $(1\bar{1}1)$. The value of foil thickness t used, as estimated ap-

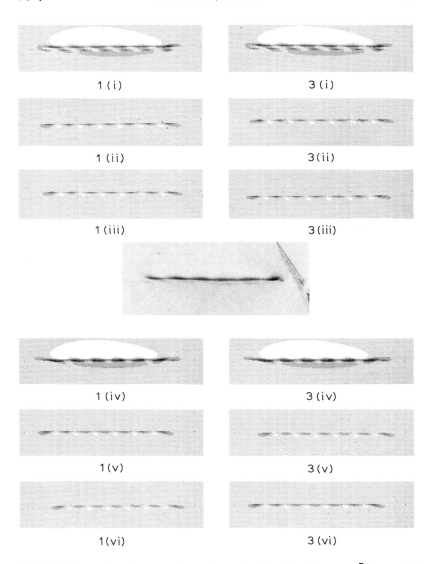

Fig. 7.4(f). Comparison of an experimental image for the diffracting vector $\bar{2}02$, $w = 1.80$ and $B = [15\ 17\ 15]$ with computed images for combinations of Shockley partial Burgers vectors and stacking faults as given in table 7.3.

proximately from the number of oscillations in contrast in various images (§ 3.10), was $4.9\ \xi_{111a}$. The separation of the partial dislocations S_p on the two possible slip planes has been estimated from the experimental micrographs to be in the range 100–200 Å and a value of 150 Å has been used in all the

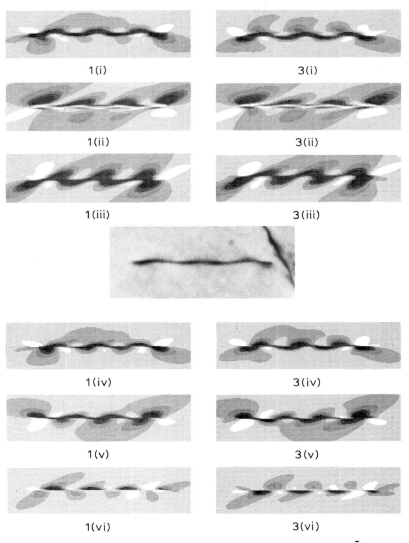

Fig. 7.4(g). Comparison of an experimental image for the diffracting vector $2\bar{2}0$, $w = 0.23$ and $B = [9\ 9\ 10]$ with computed images for combinations of Shockley partial Burgers vectors and stacking faults as given in table 7.3.

computed images. The values of t and S_p are scaled, in the usual way, for images with different diffracting vectors in the ratio of the appropriate values of two-beam extinction distances ξ_g listed in table 7.2.

The contrast of defect B at the position where it intersects the top of the

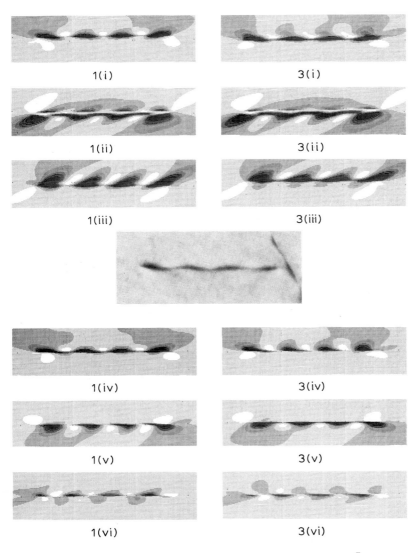

1(i)   3(i)

1(ii)   3(ii)

1(iii)   3(iii)

1(iv)   3(iv)

1(v)   3(v)

1(vi)   3(vi)

Fig. 7.4(h). Comparison of an experimental image for the diffracting vector $\bar{2}20$, $w = 0.6$ and $\boldsymbol{B}$ = [9 9 10] with computed images for combinations of Shockley partial Burgers vectors and stacking faults as given in table 7.3.

foil is influenced in some micrographs by the presence of a stacking fault on an inclined plane (see fig. 7.1). When comparing experimental and computed images, it must be realised that the computed images do not take any account of this effect.

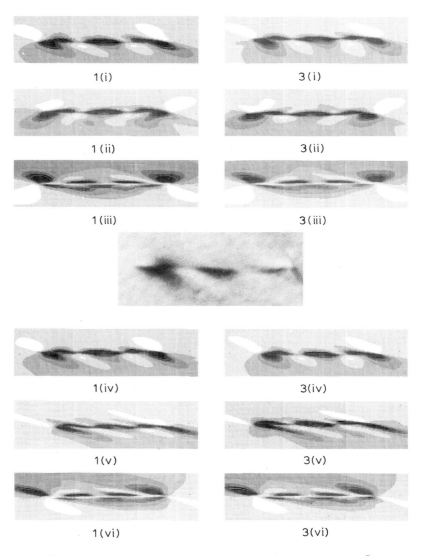

1(i)   3(i)

1(ii)   3(ii)

1(iii)   3(iii)

1(iv)   3(iv)

1(v)   3(v)

1(vi)   3(vi)

Fig. 7.4(i). Comparison of an experimental image for the diffracting vector $1\bar{3}\bar{1}$, $w = 0.30$ and $B = [15\ \bar{1}\ 12]$ with computed images for combinations of Shockley partial Burgers vectors and stacking faults as given in table 7.3.

The procedure to follow now, as in the example of the single dislocation in ch. 5, is to select from fig. 7.4 that set of nine computed images which gives the best approximate match to the experimental set, remembering that all the images in any computed set can be rotated through $180°$ to give the required agreement.

From a comparison of the experimental and computed images in fig. 7.4 for the nine diffracting vectors, it can be seen that no combination of Burgers vectors from 1(ii) to 1(vi) or from 3(ii) to 3(vi) gives satisfactory agreement with all the experimental images with or without a rotation of $180°$. A closer examination of the combinations 1(i) and 3(i) (intrinsic and extrinsic dissociation respectively of $\frac{1}{2}[\bar{1}01]$ on (111)) shows that the images for 1(i) are a much better fit to the experimental images than those for 3(i). In particular, the images for 1(i) in fig. 7.4(b) and (d) are a much better match than those for 3(i). In fig. 7.4(b) the shapes of the discrete blobs of contrast below background intensity near to the dislocations in 1(i) closely resemble the shapes of the corresponding regions of the experimental image, whereas those in 3(i) do not. In fig. 7.4(d), image 1(i) has five features with strong contrast below background level and the main contrast close to the surface intersections is below background, whereas image 3(i) has only four regions of strong contrast below background and the main contrast close to the surface intersections is above background. It is concluded, therefore, that the defect is specified by the reaction (i) in column 1 of table 7.3, i.e. defect B has arisen from the intrinsic dissociation of the left-handed screw dislocation $\frac{1}{2}[\bar{1}01]$ on (111) according to the reaction

$$\tfrac{1}{2}[\bar{1}01] = \tfrac{1}{6}[\bar{2}11] + \tfrac{1}{6}[\bar{1}\bar{1}2].$$

It is of interest to note that if the defect were the undissociated $\frac{1}{2}[\bar{1}01]$ dislocation, it would be completely out of contrast for the 020 diffracting vector (image 7.4(d)) independent of the degree of elastic anisotropy.

For some purposes this analysis of the defect may be adequate. However, it may be desired to determine the separation of the partial dislocations with more accuracy, as would be the case, for example, if a comparison were required between the experimental separation and that predicted by equilibrium calculations. The general procedure to be followed is to select several characteristic images and to find the ranges of S_p for which satisfactory agreement is obtained between the experimental and computed images. A comparison of these ranges should then indicate a narrower range of values of S_p common to all images and this narrower range will specify the separation of the partial dislocations. This procedure may be done in two ways. The first method imposes the usual assumption that all dimensions of the defect expressed in units of apparent extinction distance ξ_{ga} are related for different diffracting vectors by the ratios of the theoretical two-beam extinction distances ξ_g. The second method, which involves more computing time, does not rely on this assumption. Each of these methods will be outlined in turn and their final results compared.

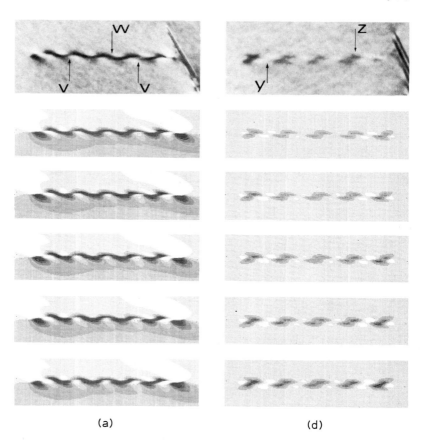

(a)　　　　　　　　　　　　　　　　　(d)

Fig. 7.5. Four experimental and corresponding computed images for five different values of S_p. In each column of images the values of S_p increase from top to bottom and are given opposite:

Method 1. An experimental image showing characteristic contrast is chosen and then the program DELUGE is used to vary t for a series of values of w over the ranges of experimental error for various separations of the partial dislocations. Image (d) of fig. 7.4 was chosen initially as a suitable image for this purpose. By use of the program DELUGE this image could be adequately matched for values of t in the range 4.10–4.24 ξ_{020a}, for values of w in the range 0.24–0.30 and for values of S_p in the range 0.26–0.36 ξ_{020a}. From these results a mean value for t of 4.17 ξ_{020a} was chosen as the best estimate of the foil thickness for the mean value for w of 0.27. A number of other experimental images in the series (images (a), (e) and (f) in fig. 7.4) were matched at this value of foil thickness by varying S_p for variations of w about the

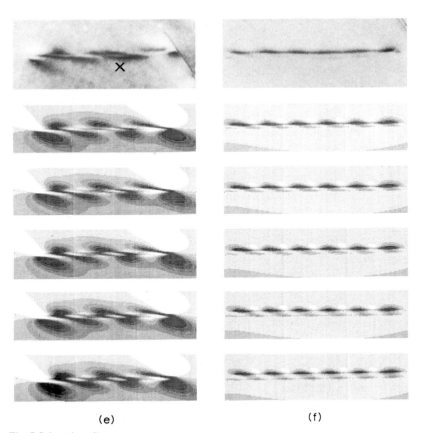

(e)   (f)

Fig. 7.5 (continued).

S_p in units of ξ_{020a}

Image (a)	Image (d)	Image (e)	Image (f)
0.21	0.21	0.31	0.26
0.26	0.26	0.36	0.31
0.31	0.31	0.41	0.36
0.36	0.36	0.47	0.41
0.42	0.42	0.52	0.47

measured values. The values of foil thickness appropriate to the different diffracting vectors were obtained by scaling the value of 4.17 ξ_{020a} in the ratio
of the theoretical two-beam extinction distances and the final values of w used
were: −0.16 for image (a), 0.0 for image (e), and 1.65 for image (f). Figure
7.5 shows the four experimental images (a), (d), (e) and (f), together with
computed images which cover a range of values of S_p. In fig. 7.5, the images

were computed for values of S_p in units of ξ_{ga}. However, in order to compare the four ranges of S_p, values of S_p need to be converted to a common unit. For convenience, ξ_{020a} was chosen as the common unit and the appropriate ratios of the theoretical two-beam extinction distance were taken as conversion factors.

It can be seen for each diffracting vector in fig. 7.5 that the three central images in the range of S_p are reasonably acceptable matches to the corresponding experimental image, whereas the two remaining computed images which bound the range are unacceptable matches. For example, for the lower bound of S_p, i.e. the top computed image in each column: Image (a) does not show breaks in the strong contrast at positions v where breaks occur in the experimental image; image (d) is too weak; the central region x of image (e) is not sufficiently enclosed by dark contrast on both sides of the inner lighter region, and image (f) does not show adequate separation between the weak and strong regions of the double image. For the upper bound of S_p, i.e. the bottom image in each column: The shape of image (a) in regions such as w, shows too great a departure from the shape in the experimental image; image (d) does not show sufficient resolution in the regions at y and at z above and below background level; image (e) shows contrast joining the central region x with the left-hand region and image (f) is too wide with the portion showing strong contrast not sufficiently continuous.

Disregarding the two bounding values of S_p in fig. 7.5, the ranges of values of S_p in units of ξ_{020a} which satisfy the images are: 0.26–0.36 for image (a); 0.26–0.36 for image (d); 0.36–0.47 for image (e), and 0.31–0.41 for image (f). These ranges only overlap at the common value of S_p of 0.36 ξ_{020a} which is thus taken to be the best estimate of the separation of the Shockley partial dislocations in defect B. To convert this value of S_p into Ångstroms, it is necessary to relate a dimension in Ångstroms on an experimental image to the same dimension in units of ξ_{020a} obtained from the best-fitting computed image. A suitable dimension for this purpose is the length of the image of defect B. A comparison is then made between this dimension as determined in Ångstroms from the known magnification of the experimental image (d) and the same dimension as represented by the appropriate fraction of the length of the computed image WL expressed in units of ξ_{020a}. Such a comparison gives the relation $\xi_{020a} = 323$ Å with an estimated error of ± 10% due to uncertainty in magnification of the experimental image. Therefore the separation of the partial dislocations in defect B is determined by this method as 113 ± 11 Å.

Method 2. In this method the four images (a), (d), (e) and (f) are treated individually using the program DELUGE so that the constraint of scaling t for different diffracting vectors in the ratio of theoretical two-beam extinction distances is removed. In other words, all four images are treated as for the case of the single image (d) described in method 1, acceptable matching images being obtained over a range of values of S_p at optimum values of t and w for each. The optimum values of t and w were found to be: $t = 5.04 \, \xi_{1\bar{1}\bar{1}a}$, $w = -0.1$ for image (a); $t = 4.17 \, \xi_{020a}$, $w = 0.27$ for image (d); $t = 2.88 \, \xi_{20\bar{2}a}$, $w = 0$ for image (e) and $t = 2.98 \, \xi_{\bar{2}02a}$, $w = 1.65$ for image (f). Figure 7.6 shows the four experimental images (a), (d), (e) and (f) together with computed images for a range of values of S_p where for each diffracting vector the outermost images of the range are unacceptable matches to the experimental images, whilst the central images cover a range of values of S_p giving acceptable matches. In order to compare the ranges of S_p for the four images, they must be expressed in common units by determining the apparent extinction distance in Ångstroms pertaining to each image. This is done in the same way as for image (d) in method 1 by comparing for each image a dimension in Ångstroms on the experimental image with the same dimension in units of apparent extinction distance on the corresponding best-fitting computed image. The following values of apparent extinction distance were found:

$$\xi_{1\bar{1}\bar{1}a} = 270 \pm 27 \text{ Å for image (a)},$$
$$\xi_{020a} = 323 \pm 32 \text{ Å for image (d)},$$
$$\xi_{20\bar{2}a} = 434 \pm 43 \text{ Å for image (e)}.$$
$$\xi_{\bar{2}02a} = 431 \pm 43 \text{ Å for image (f)};$$

the error arising from an estimated 10% error in magnification. Using these values of apparent extinction distance and disregarding the two bounding values of S_p, the range of values of S_p corresponding to acceptable matches between experimental and computed images in fig. 7.6 are: 99–132 Å for image (a); 84–117 Å for image (d); 112–144 Å for image (e), and 96–127 Å for image (f). Allowing for the estimated 10% error in the values of ξ_{ga}, the commom range of S_p is 101 Å to 129 Å, and thus the separation of the partial dislocations in defect B as determined by this method lies within this range.

Since the determination of S_p relies on the use of the experimentally determined values of apparent extinction distance, some check on the values of ξ_{ga} is needed. If the values of ξ_{ga} are consistent in representing the dimensions of the defect, then they should give, within the limits of experimental error, a constant value for foil thickness when the four values of t in units of ξ_{ga} are converted into Ångstroms. The values of t obtained in this way are: 1360 ± 136 Å for image (a); 1350 ± 135 Å for image (d); 1250 ± 125 Å for image (e) and 1285 ± 129 Å for image (f). These values of foil thickness are in agreement within the limits of experimental error.

Some check on the consistency of methods 1 and 2 may be obtained by

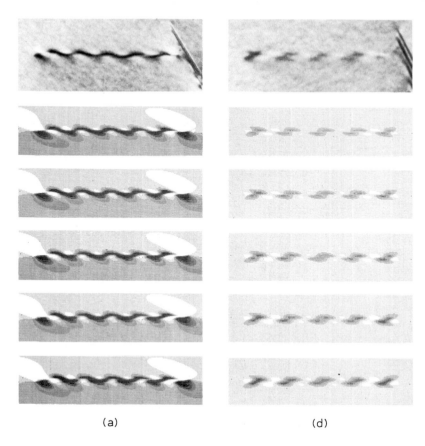

(a)   (d)

Fig. 7.6. Four experimental and corresponding computed images for five different values of S_p. In each column of images the values of S_p increase from top to bottom and are given opposite:

comparing for each image the experimentally measured value of the deviation parameter s with the value of s that applies to the corresponding best matching computed image. The latter value is obtained from the values of w and the apparent extinction distance determined from image matching. Table 7.4 lists the experimental values of s for each image, together with the values of s obtained in the above way for method 1 and method 2. It can be seen from this table that the values of s pertaining to methods 1 and 2 are in agreement with the measured values since they all lie within the limits of the experimental errors.

Having outlined the two methods of determining the separation of the partial dislocations in defect B, the relative advantages and disadvantages of

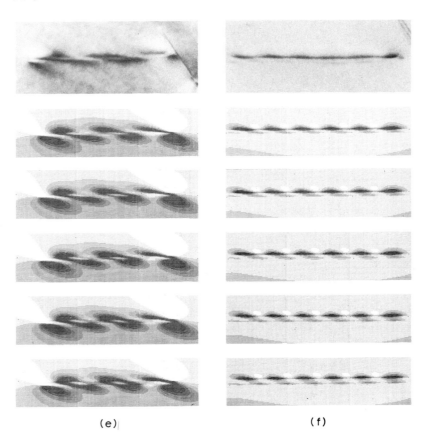

(e)   (f)

Fig. 7.6 (continued).

S_p in units of ξ_{ga}

Image (a) ($\xi_{1\bar{1}\bar{1}a}$)	Image (d) (ξ_{020a})	Image (e) ($\xi_{20\bar{2}a}$)	Image (f) ($\xi_{\bar{2}02a}$)
0.307	0.207	0.222	0.185
0.368	0.259	0.259	0.222
0.429	0.311	0.296	0.259
0.491	0.363	0.333	0.296
0.552	0.414	0.370	0.333

these two methods will be considered. Method 1 involves an artificial constraint in that the apparent extinction distances for the different diffracting
vectors are assumed to be related in the ratio of their theoretical two-beam
extinction distances. The effects of this constraint can be seen in fig. 7.5
where the best matches between computed and experimental images for the

TABLE 7.4

Comparison of experimental and matching values of s

Image	s (A^{-1})		
	Experimental	Method 1[*]	Method 2[*]
(a)	$4.6 \pm 3 \times 10^{-4}$	5.8×10^{-4}	3.7×10^{-4}
(d)	$7.0 \pm 3 \times 10^{-4}$	8.4×10^{-4}	8.4×10^{-4}
(e)	$0.0 \pm 6 \times 10^{-4}$	0.0	0.0
(f)	$32.3 \pm 6 \times 10^{-4}$	36.5×10^{-4}	38.3×10^{-4}

[*] These values are uncertain by ± 10% due to uncertainties in magnification involved in determining ξ_{ga}.

different diffracting vectors do not always occur at the final value of S_p that is common to all ranges. In method 2 this constraint is relaxed and it can be seen from fig. 7.6 that now the common range of S_p coincides better with the best matching images for the different diffracting vectors. However, the final value of S_p obtained in this example by method 2 is not significantly different from that given by method 1.

In summary, for problems of the type illustrated here where the overall displacement field results from more than one dislocation, and involves variables such as S_p which relate to the dimensions of the defect, a considerable amount of computing may be required for their complete solution. The amount of computing actually done will be governed by the type of information required. For example, the identification to the stage where the Burgers vectors of the dislocations are known is a relatively simple and quick process. However, if variables such as S_p need to be known in order to specify physical properties (such as stacking fault energy), it is clear that such variables need to be determined with as much accuracy as the technique affords.

8 | APPLICATIONS OF THE TECHNIQUE

8.1. Introduction

In earlier chapters the computer programs have been illustrated with examples that were not specifically related to any particular physical problem of immediate interest. These examples were deliberately chosen to be ones involving simple defects so that the kind of results obtainable with the different programs and the methods involved in their use could be demonstrated. In this chapter the emphasis will be changed to show how the computer programs have been used to obtain a better understanding of several physical problems which, in some cases, the authors had found to be intractable before the availability of this new technique. The range of physical problems to which the image matching technique has been applied is by no means exhaustive. The examples treated have been of particular interest to the authors, but there are many other examples for which the technique would find similar application.

The topics to be discussed here are essentially of two main types. Topics of the first type are of a general nature which are not necessarily related directly to the analysis of specific experimental observations, but use computed images to carry out surveys of significant contrast phenomena. These can be helpful for indicating which parameters may be critical in specific experimental situations. Topics of the second type are similar to the examples given already and deal with different kinds of defects in crystals. They serve to illustrate further how the programs are used to analyse and interpret experimental observations.

8.2. Influence of elastic anisotropy on the invisibility of dislocations

The contrast behaviour of dislocations in crystals of high elastic anisotropy has been illustrated in ch. 5 using β-brass as an example. It was shown in this example that images with strong contrast occurred for all the diffracting vectors used, thus demonstrating experimentally that invisibility criteria are generally inapplicable in elastically anisotropic materials. However, in particular cases dislocations can be made invisible even in highly elastically anisotropic materials and it is of interest to examine theoretically the specific conditions which give rise to such invisibility.

Some discussion of this topic has already been given in § 2.7.2, where it was shown that a condition for complete invisibility of a dislocation is that β' is zero. This corresponds to the operative diffracting vector g being normal to a set of crystallographic planes which remain flat in the presence of the displacement field of the dislocation. Since a plane cannot be flat if the closure failure of the Burgers circuit does not lie in it, the Burgers vector can have no component out of the flat plane. Hence, a necessary condition for complete invisibility of a dislocation is that $g \cdot b = 0$.

It has been mentioned in § 2.7.2(ii) that for an elastically anisotropic crystal, there are particular planes that remain flat when the line of the dislocation is normal to an elastic mirror plane. Then the expression for β' given in eq. (2.42) is separable into two components (one for the screw component of the Burgers vector and one for the edge component) either of which can be made identically zero by the familiar invisibility rules, $g \cdot b = 0$ for the screw component, and both $g \cdot b = 0$ and $g \cdot b \wedge u = 0$ for the edge component. In addition to this special case which is dependent upon a relationship between the dislocation direction u and the symmetry of the crystal, it has been shown that it is possible in anisotropic crystals for other situations to arise where sets of planes are flat, i.e. when β' (eq. (2.42)) becomes identically zero. Such cases can arise whenever the sextic equation (eq. (2.40)) has repeated roots (Head, 1969a). A survey of the occurrence of repeated roots in eq. (2.40), when applied to eq. (2.42) was made by Head (1969a) from which he was able to make the following statement: "For each anisotropic cubic crystal there is a direction of dislocation line in the {110} plane for which the sextic equation has double roots. For this direction there are two different Burgers vectors which have the property of leaving sets of planes flat. The Burgers vectors and the normals to the flat planes (which must of course be perpendicular to the Burgers vectors) lie in the same {110} plane as the dislocation line".

An example of invisibility of dislocations in a cubic crystal due to the sextic equation having double roots is shown in fig. 8.1. The curve marked u is a

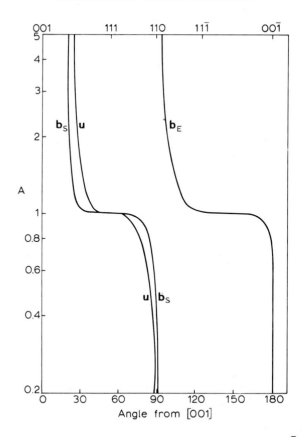

Fig. 8.1. Special conditions for invisibility of mixed dislocations on the $(1\bar{1}0)$ plane of a cubic crystal as a function of the elastic anisotropy ratio A for the value of the ratio $B = 4$. The curve marked u gives the direction of the dislocation line as an angle from [001], and those marked b_S and b_E give the two possible Burgers vectors for which a set of planes remains flat.

plot for different values of A^* (with $B = 4$) of those directions in the (110) plane for which dislocations with Burgers vectors in that plane can be made invisible. The values of A range on either side of isotropy $(A = 1)$ and the directions u are specified as angles from [001]. Included in fig. 8.1 are

---

* The atomic displacements around a dislocation in a cubic crystal depend on two independent ratios of the elastic constants and two convenient ratios are: $A = 2c_{44}/(c_{11} - c_{12})$, and $B = (c_{11} + 2c_{12})/c_{44}$. It has been found that the invisibility of dislocations depends mainly on ratio A and to a small extent on B.

two additional curves b_S and b_E (corresponding to near screw and near edge orientation respectively). These curves specify the directions of the Burgers vectors for those dislocations which would be invisible when they have, for each value of A, line directions given by the curve $\dot{u}$. Although the curves b_S and b_E are continuous, it is clear that Burgers vectors are only physically possible at discrete points on the b_S and b_E curves corresponding to low index crystallographic directions. When these low index crystallographic directions, e.g. $[00\bar{1}]$, $[11\bar{1}]$ and $[110]$ are considered, it can be seen from fig. 8.1 that for values of $A \neq 1$, complete invisibility can be obtained when the dislocations are neither pure screw nor pure edge. These cases satisfy the necessary condition $\mathbf{g} \cdot \mathbf{b} = 0$ but in general both $\mathbf{g} \cdot \mathbf{b}_e$ and $\mathbf{g} \cdot \mathbf{b} \wedge \mathbf{u}$ are not zero.

An interesting case of invisibility when $\mathbf{g} \cdot \mathbf{b} \neq 0$ arises in the limit of infinite elastic anisotropy ($A = \infty$) (Head, 1969a). For a screw dislocation parallel to a $\langle 111 \rangle$ direction in a cubic crystal, the component of the displacements in the direction of the dislocation line is given by:

$$R_z = \frac{b}{6\pi} \tan^{-1} (c \tan 3\theta), \tag{8.1}$$

where

$$c = \left[\frac{(2A + 1)(AB + A + 2B + 11)}{9(AB + 3A + 1)} \right]^{\frac{1}{2}} \tag{8.2}$$

For $A = 1$, this reduces to

$$R_z = \frac{b\theta}{2\pi}. \tag{8.3}$$

Equation 8.3 describes the well-known result for a screw dislocation in isotropy that the planes perpendicular to the dislocation line form a spiral ramp which rises by b for each revolution around the dislocation line. When A becomes greater than unity, eq. (8.1) shows that the spiral ramp becomes distorted and as $A \rightarrow \infty$ the ramp becomes a spiral staircase with six discrete steps per revolution of height $\frac{1}{6} b$ where the tread of each step tends to become flat. If an electron micrograph of this screw dislocation were taken with a diffracting vector $\mathbf{g}$ parallel to its line, then the flat treads of the steps would contribute no contrast and furthermore, the risers would give no contrast if $\frac{1}{6} \mathbf{g} \cdot \mathbf{b}$ were an integer. Thus this screw dislocation would be invisible for a diffracting vector parallel to its line for which $\mathbf{g} \cdot \mathbf{b} = 6$. This behaviour of a screw dislocation for infinite anisotropy makes an interesting

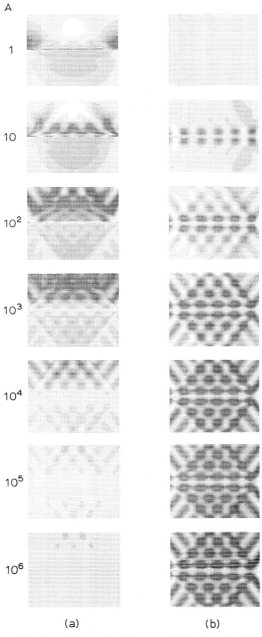

(a)	(b)

Fig. 8.2. Computed electron micrographs of a screw dislocation, b = [111], in a cubic crystal for increasing elastic anisotropy specified by the ratio A when B = 4. The images in (a) have $g \cdot b$ = 6 (g = 222) and those in (b) have $g \cdot b$ = 0 (g = $\bar{1}$10).

comparison with the contrast of an edge dislocation in isotropy, where invisibility results with a diffracting vector which is also parallel to the line of the dislocation but where $g \cdot b = 0$.

This theoretically predicted contrast behaviour of a screw dislocation can be demonstrated using computed images as shown in fig. 8.2(a). In this figure the contrast from a $[111]$ screw dislocation for a diffracting vector 222 $(g \cdot b = 6)$ is shown for increasing values of A from $1-10^6$ in equal powers of 10 with $B = 4$. Clearly at large values of A the images are approaching invisibility, but would only reach complete invisibility in the limiting case when A becomes infinite. In fig. 8.2(b) the computed images for the same dislocation and the same range of A with the diffracting vector $\bar{1}10$ $(g \cdot b = 0)$ are given. In this case invisibility occurs at $A = 1$ and the image contrast develops with increasing values of A.

8.3. Effective invisibility of images due to large values of w

In the previous section, the discussion was confined to the case of exact invisibility where the contribution from the displacement field of a dislocation to the diffraction contrast was zero. In practice, however, it is not only exact invisibility that is important, but also the more subjective case of experimental invisibility where an image is judged to be invisible. Such a judgment may be made when the contribution from the displacement field of a dislocation to the diffraction contrast is visually indistinguishable from background, although the case is not one where β' is zero. Examples involving this behaviour have been studied by France and Loretto (1968) in iron and by Loretto and France (1969) in copper. By making use of the program ONEDIS they were able to show for large diffracting vectors that images from dislocations which showed strong contrast at small and intermediate values of w became progressively weaker as w was increased, and at large values of w became indistinguishable from background and would be judged to be invisible. As they point out, the use of large diffracting vectors at large values of w can, and has, caused errors in the determination of Burgers vectors when the conventional invisibility criteria are used in this situation.

8.4. Diffraction contrast from lines of dilation

Most of the discussion in this book is concerned with the identification of defects which involve dislocations and stacking faults either singly of in various combinations. However, another type of linear defect with an associated displacement field which may be observed by electron microscopy is a line of dilation. Lines of dilation are of considerable practical interest since they may be generated in crystals by irradiation or rapid quenching. A detailed knowledge of the contrast behaviour of lines of dilation is valuable since it assists in the detection and positive identification of such defects. Moreover, it shows how a distinction can be made between lines of expansion and lines of contraction.

Blank and Amelinckx (1963) demonstrated that the contrast from fission tracks in irradiated uranium dioxide could be interpreted in terms of lines of dilation. In particular, they found that the contrast of these defects was very weak for diffracting vectors approximately parallel to the fission tracks. The diffraction contrast from lines of dilation in irradiated crystals was studied further by Chadderton (1964) who computed intensity profiles which demonstrated some of the properties of their images.

Following Blank and Amelinckx and Chadderton, computed images were used to examine the contrast from lines of dilation in elastically isotropic crystals (Humble, 1969). For this purpose the displacement field used in the computer program is that given by Coker and Filon (1957) where the displacements around a hollow circular cylinder in an infinite solid are radial and their magnitude u_r at a distance r from the centre line of the cylinder is given by:

$$u_r = \epsilon \Delta \epsilon / r, \tag{8.4}$$

where ϵ is the radius of the cylinder and $\Delta \epsilon$ is the displacement at $r = \epsilon$. Expansion and contraction correspond to positive and negative values of $\Delta \epsilon$ respectively. It can be seen from the derivative of eq. (8.4) that the strain field associated with a dilation varies as $1/r^2$, as opposed to that for a dislocation which varies as $1/r$. It is expected therefore that the images of lines of dilation will be narrower than those of dislocations, when it is assumed that similar displacements exist at the cores[*] of both types of defect. This property is readily demonstrated with computed images.

Computed images for a variety of different diffraction conditions have shown that, apart from the general feature of narrow and faint contrast, images of lines of dilation have three main properties which enable them to be identified, namely:

(1) images possess a centre of inversion;
(2) images taken with diffracting vectors $+g$ and $-g$ are in general unrelated;

---

[*] The term core is used in connection with lines of dilation with the same meaning and for similar reasons to the way it is used in dislocation theory.

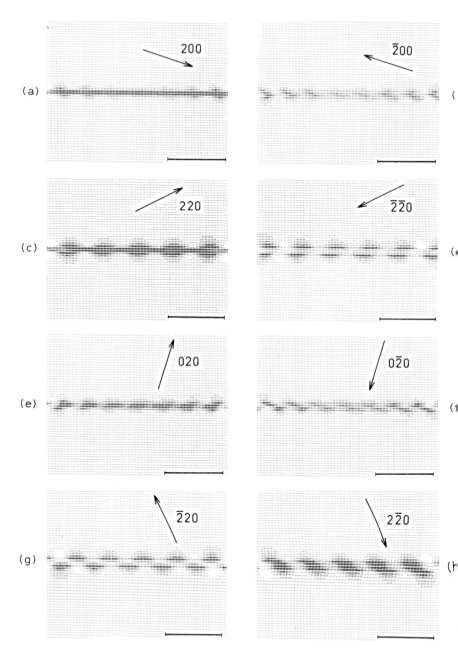

Fig. 8.3. Computed images for a line of expansion for low order diffracting vectors in a face-centred cubic crystal. B is [001], u is [314], F is [$\bar{1}$15] and w is 0.6. The length of the marker is 500 A.

(3) images are invisible when the diffracting vector is parallel to the line of the defect.

Figure 8.3 shows a series of computed images for an elastically isotropic face-centred cubic crystal with different diffracting vectors $+g$ and $-g$ contained in the [001] beam direction. For these images the line of dilation is along [314], the foil normal is [$\bar{1}$15] and the deviation from the Bragg condition w is 0.6. In order to show the properties of image contrast from lines of dilation it is advantageous to use artificially large displacement fields and for the examples in fig. 8.3 the values of $\Delta\epsilon$ and ϵ are made equal to three atomic distances. It can be seen that the images in fig. 8.3 illustrate properties (1) and (2) above, in that they have a centre of inversion at their mid-points, and that images for the diffracting vectors $+g$ and $-g$ bear no obvious relation to one another.

There is one exception to the property that images for $+g$ and $-g$ are unrelated, and this occurs when the line of dilation, the beam direction and the diffracting vectors are mutually perpendicular. In this case images for $+g$ and $-g$ are related by a reflection operation involving a mirror plane defined by the line of the image and the normal to the micrograph. An example of this relation is given in fig. 8.4 for the three mutually perpendicular directions defined by the line of dilation along [$0\bar{1}$1], the beam direction [011] and the diffracting vectors 200 (a) and $\bar{2}$00 (b).

Another symmetry property of the contrast from lines of dilation occurs for the special situation when the foil normal, the line of dilation and the beam direction are all coplanar. Under these conditions, identical images are obtained when the defect is imaged in turn with two diffracting vectors which are of the same type and are inclined at the same angle to the line of dilation.

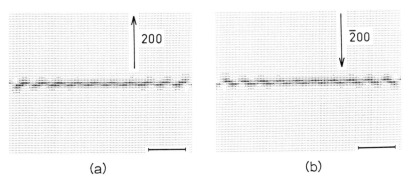

(a)   (b)

Fig. 8.4. Computed images for a line of expansion illustrating the relation between images for $+g$, 200, and $-g$, $\bar{2}$00, when u ([$0\bar{1}$1]), B ([011]) and g are mutually perpendicular. F is [001] and w is 0.6. The length of the marker is 500 Å.

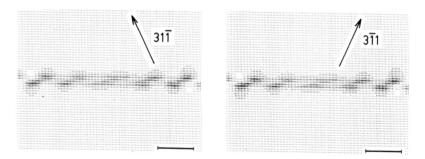

Fig. 8.5. Computed images for a line of expansion illustrating the relation between images for two diffracting vectors of the same type, $31\bar{1}$ and $3\bar{1}1$, which are equally inclined to u when u ($[0\bar{1}1]$), B ($[011]$) and F ($[001]$) are co-planar. w is 0.6 and the length of the marker is 500 Å.

This effect is illustrated in fig. 8.5 for the $31\bar{1}$ and $3\bar{1}1$ diffracting vectors, with the line of dilation along $[0\bar{1}1]$ which is co-planar with the $[011]$ beam direction and the $[001]$ foil normal.

The images used here to illustrate the contrast properties of lines of dilation have been computed for artificially large displacements. In practice, the displacements are likely to be approximately an order of magnitude smaller, so that the images to be expected will be much weaker than those given in figs. 8.3, 8.4 and 8.5. In order to obtain some idea of the intensity to be expected in experimental images, computations have been made for displacements $\Delta\epsilon$ equal to $\frac{1}{10}\epsilon$ at a radius ϵ equal to three atomic distances. An observer viewing weak images will normally adopt more sensitive visibility limits than those

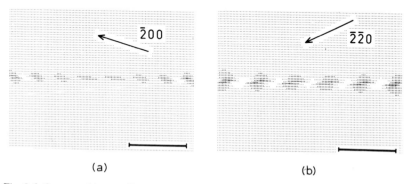

(a)   (b)

Fig. 8.6. Computed images illustrating the image intensity that might be expected for a physically reasonable displacement associated with a line of expansion. Images (a) and (b) correspond to images (b) and (d) respectively in fig. 8.3. The length of the marker is 500 Å. A more sensitive grey scale has been used for these images (see text).

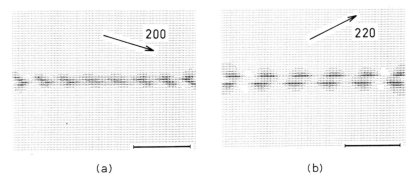

Fig. 8.7. Computed images (a) and (b) illustrating the contrast from lines of contraction for the same diffracting conditions as for the line of expansion shown in (a) and (c) of fig. 8.3. The length of the marker is 500Å.

applicable to stronger images. It has been found that suitable limits for weak images are approximately 5% above and 2% below background intensity. Using a grey scale based on these more sensitive visibility limits, images for the smaller displacements are shown in fig. 8.6. The diffraction conditions for these images are the same as those in fig. 8.3(b) and (d).

In this discussion of contrast from lines of dilation, only expansions in a crystal have been treated. For dilations involving contractions in a crystal, the images obtained with diffracting vectors $+g$ will be exactly the same as those obtained for an equal expansion with diffracting vectors $-g$. This point is illustrated by a comparison of fig. 8.3(b) and (d) with fig. 8.7(a) and (b) where the dilations are of the same magnitude but of opposite signs. Clearly, therefore, image computation can readily distinguish between lines of expansion and contraction in a crystal.

8.5. Apparent anomalous absorption

The distinguishing topological features of contrast contained in images of defects are necessary for the technique of image matching to be used to its best advantage. It has been found from computed images that such features can be particularly sensitive to the value chosen for the anomalous absorption coefficient $\mathcal{A}$. For example, it is well-known for dislocations that increasing anomalous absorption reduces oscillating contrast effects near the centre of the foil (Howie and Whelan, 1962) and for stacking faults tends to suppress subsidiary fringes and the main fringes near the centre of the foil (Hashimoto et al., 1960, 1962; Humphreys et al., 1967). Although, as discussed in ch. 3, calculated values for anomalous absorption are available, these values apply

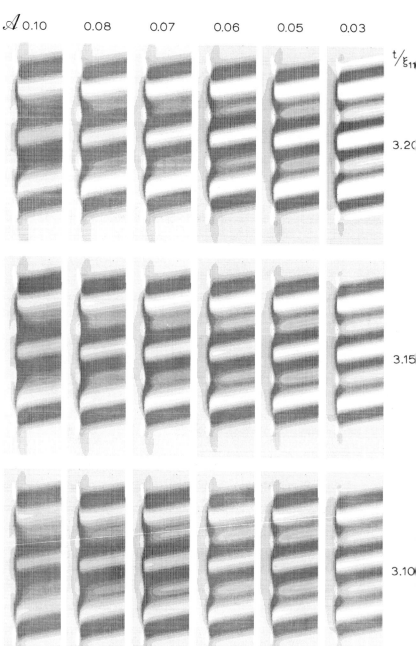

Fig. 8.8(a).

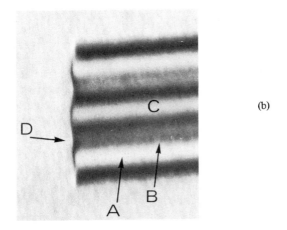

Fig. 8.8. Experimental image (b) (× 125,000) and computed images (a) for a Shockley partial dislocation and its intrinsic stacking fault on (111) in a Cu + 8 at % Si alloy. b is $\frac{1}{6}[11\bar{2}]$, u is $[\bar{2}\bar{1}3]$, B is $[347]$, F is $[9\ 9\ 14]$, g is $\bar{1}\bar{1}1$ and w is 0.15. Values of t and $\mathscr{A}$ used for the computed images are indicated.

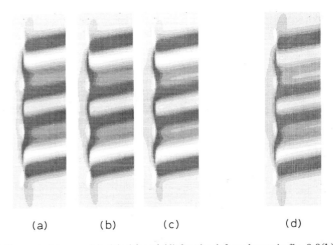

(a)   (b)   (c)   (d)

Fig. 8.9. Computed images (a), (b), (c) and (d) for the defect shown in fig. 8.8(b). The values of $\mathscr{A}$ and w are: 0.067, 0.10 in (a); 0.067, 0.15 in (b); 0.065, 0.20 in (c) and 0.067, 0.15 in (d). The image (d) has been computed for a tapered foil where the thickness of the foil is 3.10 ξ_{111a} at the top and 3.15 ξ_{111a} at the bottom of the micrograph.

to zero aperture and must be increased considerably to take account of the finite objective aperture size used in the experiment. The influence of objective aperture size on anomalous absorption has been measured (e.g. Metherell and Whelan, 1967) but the measurements cover a restricted range of aperture sizes and considerable extrapolation of the results is needed to take account of aperture sizes in the region of $2\theta_B$ which is about the size we have commonly used. In addition, contamination of the specimen surfaces in the microscope may result in the apparent anomalous absorption being higher than the theoretical value (Metherell, 1967). The uncertainty in the correction to be applied to the theoretical values of anomalous absorption may be overcome by making use of the influence that anomalous absorption has on topological features of images. One way of doing this is to use image matching to estimate the value of anomalous absorption appropriate to a particular set of experimental conditions (Clarebrough, 1969).

An example of the use of image matching to determine an effective two-beam value of $\mathscr{A}$ for a Cu + 8 at % Si alloy is shown in fig. 8.8(a) and (b). Figure 8.8(b) is an electron micrograph ($w = 0.15$) showing a Shockley partial dislocation ($u = [\bar{2}1\bar{3}]$ and $b = \frac{1}{6}[11\bar{2}]$) bordering an intrinsic fault. Figure 8.8(a) shows computed images for a range of values of foil thickness t from $3.10\,\xi_{111a} - 3.20\,\xi_{111a}$ and for a range of values of $\mathscr{A}$ from 0.03–0.10. Initially, additional images were computed for a range of w values from 0.10–0.20, but the influence of varying w in this range was small, and a value of $w = 0.15$ was used for the comparison between the experimental image and the computed images. The experimental image in fig. 8.8(b) is asymmetric about mid-foil in that the main light fringe near the bottom of the micrograph is above background intensity, whereas that near the top of the micrograph is at, or close to, background intensity. This asymmetry in the image is due to a very small taper in the foil (the foil thickness increasing from the top to the bottom of the micrograph) and not to any influence from the strain field of the dislocation. In making a comparison between the experimental micrograph and computed images, it should be remembered that the computed images apply to constant foil thickness. Therefore, to reduce the effect of foil taper in the experimental image, attention will be confined to the lower half of the experimental micrograph. In this portion of the micrograph the main features of the image which will be used in image matching are as follows: the main light fringe A is above background intensity; the subsidiary dark fringe B is resolved; the central light fringe C is close to background intensity and the image of the partial dislocation at D is narrow and just resolvable from the subsidiary light fringe. A careful inspection of fig. 8.8(a) reveals that these characteristics are approximately satisfied by values of $\mathscr{A}$ of 0.06 and 0.07 for $t = 3.15\,\xi_{111a}$. Further computations show that the best match between the experimental and computed images occurs at a value of $\mathscr{A}$ of 0.067. The

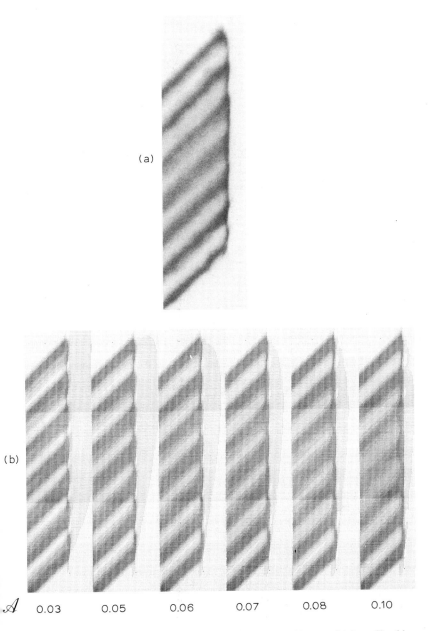

Fig. 8.10. Experimental image (a) (× 100,000) and computed images (b) for a Shockley partial dislocation and its intrinsic stacking fault on (111) in a Cu + 8 at % Si alloy. b is $\frac{1}{6}[11\bar{2}]$, u is $[0\bar{1}1]$, B is $[213]$, F is $[14\ 7\ 12]$, g is $\bar{1}\bar{1}1$, t is 5.95 ξ_{111a} and w is 0.57. The values of $\mathscr{A}$ are indicated.

computed image corresponding to this best fitting case is shown in fig. 8.9(b) together with the computed images (a) and (c) which are the best fit for values of w of 0.1 and 0.2 respectively. The value of $\mathcal{A}$ had to be reduced to 0.065 to produce a matching image for $w = 0.2$, but the value of 0.067 applies equally well for $w = 0.1$ and $w = 0.15$.

Throughout this example, image matching has been confined to the lower half of the experimental image in fig. 8.8(b). However, if instead the top half of the experimental image is used then the conclusions concerning the value of $\mathcal{A}$ are unaltered, but the matching image is obtained for a different foil thickness $t = 3.10\ \xi_{111a}$. Thus the taper of the foil in a direction approximately normal to the line of the fault fringes can be described as a change in foil thickness from 3.10 to 3.15 ξ_{111a} (i.e. approximately 12 Å) across the fault. Figure 8.9(d) shows the computed image for a foil tapered by this amount for $w = 0.15$ and $\mathcal{A} = 0.067$ and it can be seen that the agreement with the experimental image is good everywhere.

The results in fig. 8.8 show that images in thin foils are sensitive to small changes in $\mathcal{A}$. It is of interest to see whether a similar sensitivity exists for thicker foils. Figure 8.10(a) is an electron micrograph of a Shockley partial dislocation in the same alloy ($u = [0\bar{1}1]$, $b = \frac{1}{6}[11\bar{2}]$) bounding a region of intrinsic fault in a foil approximately 6 ξ_{111a} thick. The beam direction is [213] the diffracting vector is $\bar{1}1\bar{1}$ and $w = 0.57$. It can be seen from fig. 8.10(b), which is a series of computed images for various values of $\mathcal{A}$ at $t/\xi_{111a} = 5.95$, that at a value of $\mathcal{A} = 0.07$, a good match is obtained to the experimental image, but almost equally good matches result for values of $\mathcal{A}$ in the range 0.10–0.05. This illustrates a general result that as a foil gets thicker, images become less sensitive to $\mathcal{A}$.

8.6. Nature of stacking faults

In ch. 7, the nature of the stacking fault associated with a partial dislocation in a face-centred cubic crystal was determined using the rule of Hashimoto et al. (1962). This rule states that if g is the diffracting vector and R the displacement vector associated with the fault, then for sufficiently thick crystals at small values of w, the outermost fringe of a bright field image of a stacking fault on a positive print is above background intensity if $g \cdot R = +\frac{1}{3}$ and below background intensity if $g \cdot R = -\frac{1}{3}$.

Although this rule has proved to be invaluable for rapid and simple identification of the nature of stacking faults, there are combinations of t, w and $\mathcal{A}$ where the rule is not applicable (Head, 1969d). For example, the top right-hand image in fig. 8.8(a) shows a case for an intrinsic fault with $R = \frac{1}{3}[111]$ and $g = \bar{1}1\bar{1}$ where the rule breaks down. In this instance, the foil thickness is

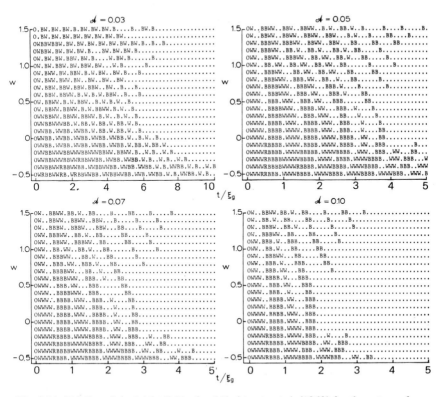

Fig. 8.11. Validity of the bright field rule of Hashimoto et al. (1962) for the nature of the outermost fringe of a stacking fault tested for a range of t, w and $\mathscr{A}$.

·   Bright field rule correct.

B   Outer fringe black for both $g \cdot R = +\frac{1}{3}$ and $g \cdot R = -\frac{1}{3}$.

W   Outer fringe white for both $g \cdot R = +\frac{1}{3}$ and $g \cdot R = -\frac{1}{3}$.

R   Bright field rule reversed.

Note that the abscissa has a different scale for $\mathscr{A} = 0.03$.

3.2 ξ_{111a}, the value of $\mathscr{A}$ is 0.03, the value of w is 0.15 and the outermost fringe is above background intensity, whereas the rule states that (for $g \cdot R = -\frac{1}{3}$) this fringe should be below background intensity. Clearly, there is a need to specify the region of validity of the rule for determining the nature of stacking faults in face-centred cubic crystals and Head (1969d) has done this for a wide range of t, $\mathscr{A}$ and w. The results for bright field images are given in fig. 8.11 where a dot indicates that the rule is applicable whilst a letter indicates that it is inapplicable. It is clear from this figure that the rule should be used with caution particularly for cases involving thin foils, low values of anomalous absorption and negative or large positive values of w.

8.7. Identification of bent dislocations

In elastically anisotropic crystals the minimum energy configuration of a
single dislocation is not always the minimum line length between two fixed
points (de Wit and Koehler, 1959). For some cases the energy is minimised
when the dislocation adopts a zig-zag configuration where each segment of the
dislocation avoids high energy directions in the crystal. Thus forbidden zones
for dislocation directions can exist and these zones will depend upon the
elastic constants of the crystal and the Burgers vector of the dislocation. Head
(1967b) has shown that for a dislocation in a cubic crystal the forbidden zones
depend on the two independent ratios of elastic constants:

$$A = 2c_{44}/(c_{11} - c_{12}) \qquad (8.5)$$

and

$$B = (c_{11} + 2c_{12})/c_{44} \qquad (8.6)$$

An example of an elastically anisotropic crystal for which the values of A
and B are such that the minimum energy configuration of a dislocation can
depart from one of minimum line length is β-brass (Head, 1967b). In a Cu
+ 48.6 at % Zn alloy, bent dislocations are frequently observed and experimental
determinations of the Burgers vectors, line directions and planes of a number
of these bent dislocations (Head et al., 1967) showed that the segments of the
bends lay at the extremities of forbidden zones as predicted by Head[*].

As pointed out by Head, the experimental determination of the boundaries
of forbidden zones using bent dislocations of known Burgers vectors provides
a method for measuring the elastic constant ratios (A and B) of a crystal. This
method enables the elastic constants of the small localised volume of crystal
containing the bent dislocation to be determined. Thus the method has an
advantage over the more conventional techniques which measure the elastic
properties of bulk specimens. For example, in the case of a two phase alloy,
the method using bent dislocations could give results for either phase, whereas
conventional methods would give a composite result to which the properties
of both phases contribute.

The method using bent dislocations to measure elastic constant ratios was
applied by Morton and Head (1970) to an example where an interesting comparison could be made with earlier measurements. McManus (1963) using conventional methods found a marked decrease in the elastic anisotropy of β-brass
as the zinc content increased beyond 48 %. However, alloys containing more

---

[*] The elastic constants used in these calculations were for a Cu + 48 at % Zn alloy (Lazarus,
1948, 1949).

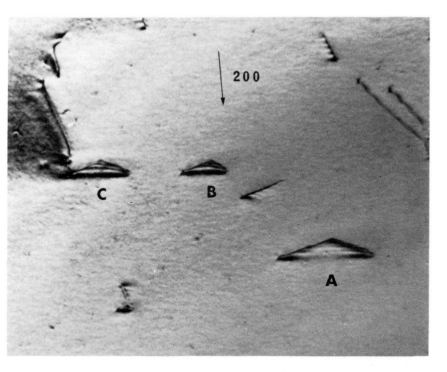

Fig. 8.12. Electron micrograph of bent dislocations at A, B and C in a specimen of Cu + 50.35 at % Zn. *B* is [013] and the diffracting vector is indicated. × 80,000.

than 48 % Zn can consist of both β and γ phases (e.g. Yoon and Bienenstock, 1968) so that the observed decrease in elastic anisotropy may have resulted from the presence of γ phase.

An essential step in using bent dislocations to determine the elastic constant ratios is to assign correctly Burgers vectors to the dislocations selected for the measurement of bend angles. For crystals as elastically anisotropic as β-brass, it has been seen in ch. 5 that image computation is a most convenient method of making this assignment. Figure 8.12 shows bent dislocations at A, B and C in a specimen of β-brass, containing 50.35 at % Zn, which has been quenched from 650° C so that at room temperature the alloy consists of homogeneous β-phase. The dislocations are markedly bent and do not extend completely through the foil, but both segments of each dislocation intersect the same surface. Because two distinctly different directions are needed to specify the dislocation, it is not possible to use the program ONEDIS to match the entire image of the dislocation in one operation. However, ONEDIS can be used in an attempt to match each individual segment of the dislocation by

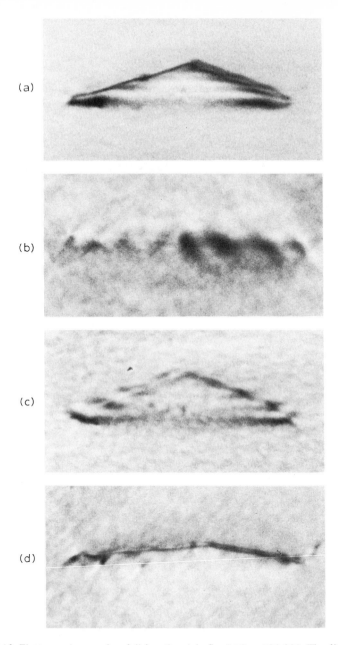

Fig. 8.13. Electron micrographs of dislocation A in fig. 8.12. × 180,000. The diffraction conditions are:

	B	g	w
(a)	[013]	200	1.0
(b)	[$\bar{1}$18]	110	0.5
(c)	[6$\bar{1}$6]	$\bar{1}$01	0.05
(d)	[335]	1$\bar{1}$0	0.60

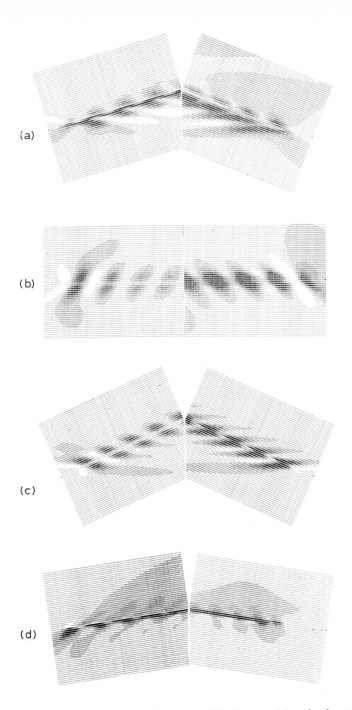

(a)

(b)

(c)

(d)

Fig. 8.14. Computed images corresponding to the diffraction conditions for the experimental micrographs (a)–(d) in fig. 8.13.

framing the computed images for each segment so that they include that portion of the crystal from the surface intersection to the depth in the crystal at
which the bend occurs. The image of each segment is computed for a common
Burgers vector, but with the separate values of u (determined in the manner
described in ch. 3) appropriate to each segment. When such pairs of computed
images are arranged at the bend angles observed in the experimental micrographs, then they are in a suitable orientation to display the overall topology
of the images. It must be realised that arranging computed micrographs in this
way is only displaying the computed segments of the whole dislocation to best
advantage and should not be taken to imply that these computed images take
account of the displacement field of a bent dislocation. However, it has been
found that, apart from a region close to the bend itself, the computed images
for individual segments match the experimented images sufficiently well to
allow the identification of the Burgers vector. An example of this is shown in fig
8.13 and 8.14 for images of dislocation A of fig. 8.12 taken under four different
diffracting conditions. The matching set of computed images in fig. 8.14 was obtained by the general procedure of eliminating similar sets of images for other
Burgers vectors, as discussed in chs. 5 and 7. In this way, the Burgers vector of
dislocation A was positively identified as $[1\bar{1}1]$.

A determination of the Burgers vectors and bend angles of a number of
bent dislocations showed that two forbidden zones of directions existed for
this alloy, and that these zones agreed with the results obtained previously for
a Cu + 48.6 at % Zn alloy (Head et al., 1967). It was deduced that the ratios of
elastic constants for the alloy used were in the range $A = 8.0-8.4$, $B = 4.0-$
4.4, rather than the values found by McManus of $A = 5.15$ and $B = 4.40$.

This result indicates that there is no marked change in elastic anisotropy
on increasing the zinc content of β-brass from 48.6 % to 50.35 %. Furthermore, if the values reported by McManus were correct, only one forbidden
zone for dislocation directions should have been observed, whereas two were
found.

Observations of bent dislocations in the β phase of a duplex structure of
β + γ obtained by slowly cooling a sample of the 50.35 % Zn alloy gave the
same results obtained for the quenched single phase alloy.

8.8. A dissociation reaction in β-brass

Recently there has been considerable activity in the identification of
Burgers vectors for dislocations in body-centred cubic crystals. In particular,
there has been some discussion as to the frequency of occurrence of dislocations with Burgers vectors of the type ⟨110⟩ in α-iron (e.g. Dingley and Hale,
1966; France and Loretto, 1968). It now appears that apart from the presence

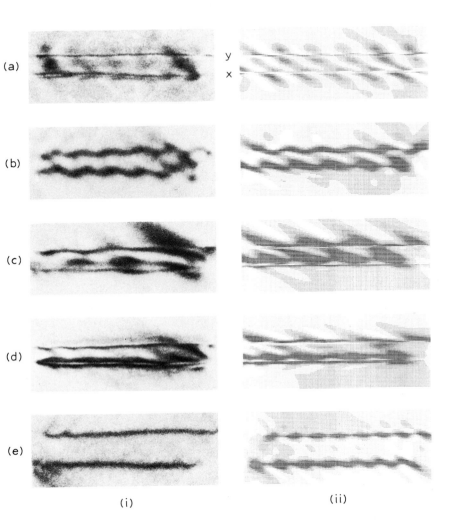

Fig. 8.15. Experimental images (i) and the corresponding computed images (ii) of a dislocation pair in β-brass. *u* for the pair is [111] and *F* is [319]. Dislocation *x* has *b* = [10$\bar{1}$] and *y* has *b* = [0$\bar{1}$0]. The diffraction conditions are:

	B	*g*	*w*
(a)	[001]	$\bar{1}\bar{1}0$	0.40
(b)	[001]	$1\bar{1}0$	0.37
(c)	[001]	$0\bar{2}0$	0.65
(d)	[$\bar{1}$02]	$0\bar{2}0$	0.75
(e)	[113]	$\bar{1}10$	0.75

of segments with $b = \langle 110 \rangle$ which result from dislocation interactions, such as those involved in the formation of dislocation networks, the occurrence of isolated dislocations with $b = \langle 110 \rangle$ is rare. This conclusion is in agreement with energy calculations which indicate that dislocations with Burgers vectors $b = \langle 110 \rangle$ are energetically unfavourable (Head, 1967b; France et al., 1967).

Recently Broom and Humble (1969) used image matching to identify a dislocation in β-brass with $b = \langle 110 \rangle$ which did not occur in a network, but which had resulted from a dissociation reaction of the type:

$$[1\bar{1}\bar{1}] = [0\bar{1}0] + [10\bar{1}].$$

Five experimental images of such an isolated dislocation pair are shown in fig. 8.15(i) and the line of these dislocations, determined in the usual way, was $[111]$. The results of Head (1967b) show that a dissociation reaction of the type given above for a glide dislocation along $[111]$ is only likely to occur for 70° dislocations, i.e. dislocations with Burgers vectors of $[\bar{1}11]$, $[1\bar{1}1]$ and $[11\bar{1}]$. For the screw orientation, i.e. the Burgers vector $[111]$, such a dissociation is energetically unfavourable. The possible dissociation reactions involving the above three Burgers vectors are:

$$[\bar{1}11]_{on\ (0\bar{1}1)} = [\bar{1}00]_{on\ (0\bar{1}1)} + [011]_{on\ (0\bar{1}1)} \qquad \text{A}$$

$$[\bar{1}11]_{on\ (0\bar{1}1)} = [001]_{on\ (1\bar{1}0)} + [\bar{1}10]_{on\ (11\bar{2})} \qquad \text{B}$$

$$[\bar{1}11]_{on\ (0\bar{1}1)} = [010]_{on\ (\bar{1}01)} + [\bar{1}01]_{on\ (1\bar{2}1)} \qquad \text{C}$$

$$[1\bar{1}1]_{on\ (\bar{1}01)} = [0\bar{1}0]_{on\ (\bar{1}01)} + [101]_{on\ (\bar{1}01)} \qquad \text{D}$$

$$[1\bar{1}1]_{on\ (\bar{1}01)} = [100]_{on\ (0\bar{1}1)} + [0\bar{1}1]_{on\ (\bar{2}11)} \qquad \text{E}$$

$$[1\bar{1}1]_{on\ (\bar{1}01)} = [001]_{on\ (1\bar{1}0)} + [1\bar{1}0]_{on\ (11\bar{2})} \qquad \text{F}$$

$$[\bar{1}\bar{1}1]_{on\ (1\bar{1}0)} = [001]_{on\ (1\bar{1}0)} + [\bar{1}\bar{1}0]_{on\ (1\bar{1}0)} \qquad \text{G}$$

$$[\bar{1}\bar{1}1]_{on\ (1\bar{1}0)} = [0\bar{1}0]_{on\ (\bar{1}01)} + [\bar{1}01]_{on\ (1\bar{2}1)} \qquad \text{H}$$

$$[\bar{1}\bar{1}1]_{on\ (1\bar{1}0)} = [\bar{1}00]_{on\ (0\bar{1}1)} + [0\bar{1}1]_{on\ (\bar{2}11)} \qquad \text{I}$$

From an examination of the dislocation pair for the beam directions given in fig. 8.15(i) and for a number of other beam directions, the plane of the defect was determined by stereographic analysis to be close to $(\bar{1}01)$. In the first instance it was assumed that the only glide plane involved in the dissociation reaction was $(\bar{1}01)$ and on this basis only the dissociation reactions C, D and H are possibilities.

Images were computed for the resultant dislocations of the three reactions C, D and H, taking into account all possible combinations of the sign of the Burgers vectors and the relative positions of the dislocations on the $(\bar{1}01)$ plane, i.e. with the $\langle 110 \rangle$ dislocation on the left of the pair and on the right. Of these, the computed images for the reaction minus C, namely

$$[1\overline{1}\overline{1}]_{on\ (0\overline{1}1)} = [0\overline{1}0]_{on\ (\overline{1}01)} + [10\overline{1}]_{on\ (1\overline{2}1)},$$

gave the best agreement with the experimental images and are shown in fig. 8.15(ii). As a final check of this result, all combinations of the resultant dislocations from the remaining six reactions (A, B, E, F, G and I) were computed and these results confirmed the previous conclusion.

The theoretical images in fig. 8.15(ii) were computed without any refinement of the experimentally determined parameters. When fine detail is considered, the degree of agreement between experimental and computed images in fig. 8.15 is not high. However, the agreement shown was better than that obtained for any other possible combination of Burgers vectors and thus was adequate for the purpose of this experiment, namely the positive identification of the Burgers vectors of the dislocation pair. This is an example of the use of the experimentally determined parameters, without any refinement, in order to solve a particular problem.

Of the three possible dissociation reactions on $(\overline{1}01)$, namely reactions C, D and H, only reaction D involves a decrease in energy, whereas reactions C and H are energetically neutral. Clearly the energetically favourable dissociation would be the most likely one to occur, but the products of such a reaction would be difficult to recognise as a pair since the repulsion between the product dislocations would result in them being widely separated. It is understandable therefore that the dislocation pair observed is associated with a neutral reaction.

8.9. Contrast from partial dislocations

8.9.1. PARTIAL DISLOCATIONS BORDERING A SINGLE STACKING FAULT

Earlier in ch. 7 an example of a Shockley partial dislocation ($b = \frac{1}{6}\langle 112 \rangle$) bounding an extensive region of stacking fault was considered, and it was mentioned in connection with this example that a set of empirical $g \cdot b$ rules for the contrast from partial dislocations involving non-integral values of $g \cdot R$ had been formulated. The rules for the contrast from partial dislocations were originally formulated by Howie and Whelan (1962) and later, in greater detail, by Silcock and Tunstall (1964). Their results have been summarized as follows (Hirsch, 1965; Hirsch et al., 1965, p. 269):
(a) $g \cdot b = \pm \frac{1}{3}$ gives invisibility for both small and large values of w;
(b) $g \cdot b = \pm \frac{2}{3}$; for $g \cdot b = +\frac{2}{3}$ partial dislocations are visible at small and

large values of w; for $\mathbf{g} \cdot \mathbf{b} = -\frac{2}{3}$ partial dislocations are visible at small values of w and invisible at large values of w (i.e. $w \gtrsim 0.7$)[*].

There appears to be no physical basis for these rules which have been formulated for isotropic elasticity from two-beam profile calculations for specific cases. The profiles corresponded to depths in the foil such that they crossed the dislocation line at the centres of the light fringes arising from the stacking fault. It has been commonly assumed that such profiles are characteristic of the whole image of the partial dislocation throughout the entire depth of the foil. This has led to the concept of an 'in contrast' (visible) dislocation image as being one where a dark line or band crosses all the light fringes along the line of the dislocation and an 'out of contrast' (invisible) image as one where such a line or band is absent. The topology of an image from a partial dislocation for non-integral values of $\mathbf{g} \cdot \mathbf{R}$ involves contrast from both the stacking fault and the displacement field of the dislocation and is usually more complex than merely the presence or absence of a dark line or band crossing the light fringes. For instance, it would be difficult to apply such a description to the images of the partial dislocations bounding the faults A, C and D in fig. 7.1. In order to give an adequate sample of the topology of partial dislocations, a large number of profiles would be required and computed micrographs are ideal for this purpose. Of course, the use of computed micrographs removes the main necessity for empirical rules such as those given above. We consider, therefore, that the contrast from, and identification of, partial dislocations is best treated by image matching in each individual case.

Theoretical micrographs may be computed over a range of conditions for a particular case of interest and such a survey for a copper–aluminium alloy[**] has been used to investigate the contrast behaviour of Shockley partial dislocations for the cases $\mathbf{g} \cdot \mathbf{b} = \pm \frac{1}{3}$ and $\mathbf{g} \cdot \mathbf{b} = \pm \frac{2}{3}$ for a range of orientations from edge to screw and for a range of values of w and foil thickness (Clarebrough, 1971). The contrast behaviour of Frank partials ($\mathbf{b} = \frac{1}{3}\langle 111 \rangle$) has also been investigated in this way for the same alloy, but in somewhat less detail (Clarebrough and Morton, 1969a; Clarebrough, 1971). Within the range of variables examined, several instances in which the above rules were inapplicable occurred. However, it should be pointed out that since it is only possible to

---

[*] In taking $\mathbf{g} \cdot \mathbf{b} = +\frac{2}{3}$ as the in contrast image and $\mathbf{g} \cdot \mathbf{b} = -\frac{2}{3}$ as the out of contrast image, it should be noted that this applies only when the fault is on the left looking along the u assigned to the dislocation. When the fault is on the right, the in contrast image would correspond to $\mathbf{g} \cdot \mathbf{b} = -\frac{2}{3}$, and the out of contrast image to $+\frac{2}{3}$ (see Appendix).

[**] The elastic constants used in computing the theoretical micrographs are those for a Cu + 10 at % Al alloy, $c_{11} = 15.95$, $c_{12} = 11.76$ and $c_{44} = 7.66$ dyne $cm^{-2} \times 10^{11}$ (Hearmon, 1956).

Fig. 8.16. An experimental ($\times$ 120,000) and matching computed image of a Shockley partial dislocation bordering an intrinsic fault on (111). b is $\frac{1}{6}[\bar{2}11]$, u is $[\bar{1}01]$, B is [167], F is [259], t is 5.07 ξ_{111a}, w is 0.4, g is $\bar{1}\bar{1}1$ and $g \cdot b = +\frac{1}{3}$.

compute specific cases, any 'empirical rules' drawn from a survey can only apply within the range of the survey and should not be taken as being universally applicable.

In discussing the results of this survey, comparisons are made with the above $g \cdot b$ rules and the cases $g \cdot b = \pm \frac{1}{3}$ and $g \cdot b = \pm \frac{2}{3}$ are treated in turn.

(i) $g \cdot b = \pm \frac{1}{3}$.

If the occurrence of a dark band crossing the light fault fringes at the position of the dislocation is taken to be the criterion of an in contrast image then, in general, the survey confirmed the previous profile calculations (Howie and Whelan, 1962; Silcock and Tunstall, 1964) that Shockley and Frank partials do not show contrast for $g \cdot b = \pm \frac{1}{3}$. However, for both types of partial dislocation there were weak contrast effects which were characteristic features of these images. An example of these for a Shockley partial dislocation is shown in fig. 8.16. These characteristic features of contrast occur at the dislocation and extend away from the fault fringes and consist of regions of contrast above background at depths in the foil corresponding to the light fringes and flares of contrast below background intensity emanating from the ends of the dark fringes. The occurrence of both these contrast effects is sensitive to w and foil thickness.

In the case of Frank partial dislocations, one exception has been found to the rule for $g \cdot b = \pm \frac{1}{3}$ (Clarebrough and Morton, 1969a). This exception is illustrated in fig. 8.17 where it can be seen that a dark band of contrast crosses

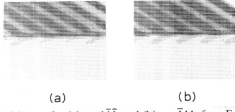

(a)   (b)

Fig. 8.17. Computed images for (a) $+g$, $1\bar{1}\bar{1}$, and (b) $-g$, $\bar{1}11$, for a Frank partial dislocation bordering an intrinsic fault on (111). b is $\frac{1}{3}[111]$, u is $[10\bar{1}]$, B is $[12\bar{1}]$, F is [110], t is 6 ξ_{111}, w is 0.3 and $g \cdot b = \pm \frac{1}{3}$.

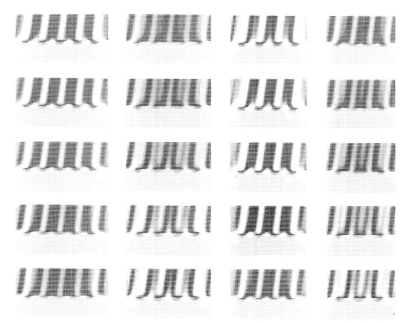

(a)

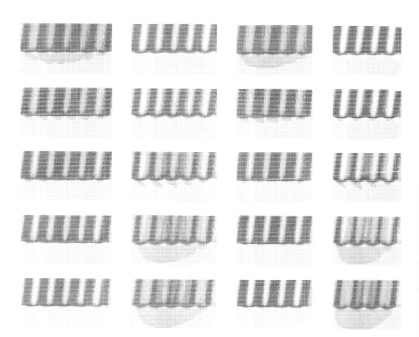

(b)

Fig. 8.18(a,b).

the light fringes for $g \cdot b = +\frac{1}{3}$ and $-\frac{1}{3}$. The geometry of the Frank partial and diffraction conditions are given in the legend to fig. 8.17 and the breakdown of the rule only applies for a narrow range of beam directions close to that indicated and is sensitive to foil thickness. Although this behaviour has not been observed for a Shockley partial dislocation, the possibility that a similar situation exists cannot be disregarded.

(ii) $g \cdot b = \pm \frac{2}{3}$.

The survey of images for $g \cdot b = \pm \frac{2}{3}$ indicated that the usual criterion for in contrast and out of contrast images involving the presence or absence of a dark band or line terminating the light fringes is too restrictive. However, if as before, this criterion is in fact adopted, then the rule (b) given above concerning images for $g \cdot b = \pm \frac{2}{3}$ needs some modification for the particular cases we have examined. It may be expressed as follows:

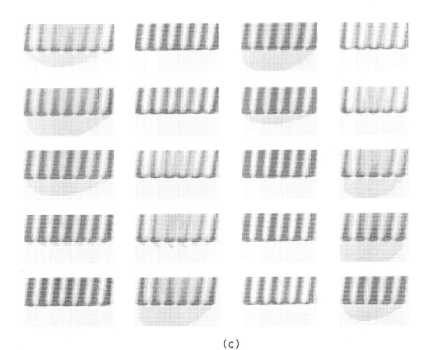

(c)

Fig. 8.18. Computed images showing the influence of t and w on the contrast of a Shockley partial dislocation bordering an intrinsic fault on (111) in a Cu–Al alloy when $g \cdot b = +\frac{2}{3}$, b is $\frac{1}{6}[1\bar{1}2]$, u is $[\bar{8}19]$, g is $\bar{1}\bar{1}1$, B is $[167]$, F is $[259]$, t decreases in equal increments down the columns in (a), (b) and (c) from 5.30 ξ_{111} (top left) to 3.67 ξ_{111} (bottom right), and w is -0.10 in (a), 0.50 in (b) and 0.90 in (c). The elastic constants used were for a Cu + 10 at % Al alloy.

g $\overline{1}\overline{1}1$ $\overline{1}\overline{1}1$

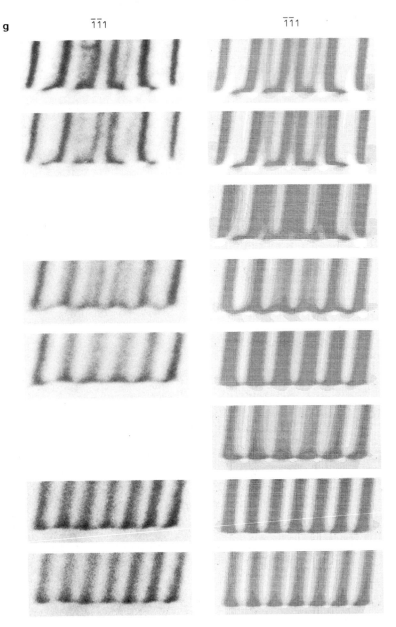

Fig. 8.19. Comparison of experimental (× 180,000) and computed images showing the influence of w on the contrast of a Shockley partial dislocation in $+g$, $\overline{1}\overline{1}1$, and $-g$, $11\overline{1}$. b is $\frac{1}{6}[\overline{1}\overline{1}2]$, u is $[\overline{8}\overline{1}9]$, B is $[167]$, F is $[259]$ and $t = 4.7\ \xi_{111}a$. The values of w are indicated.

$11\bar{1}$ $11\bar{1}$

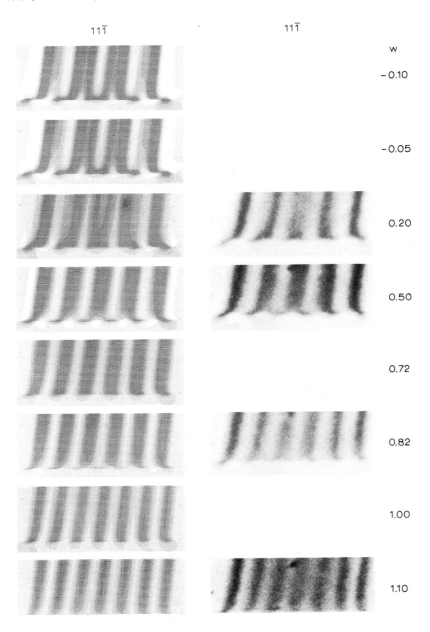

w

-0.10

-0.05

0.20

0.50

0.72

0.82

1.00

1.10

Fig. 8.19 (continued).

For $g \cdot b = +\frac{2}{3}$:

At values of w near zero ($-0.1 \lesssim w \lesssim 0.1$) images can be either in or out of contrast depending on foil thickness;

at intermediate values of w (≈ 0.5) images are in contrast independent of foil thickness;

at large values of w (≈ 1) images are weak or out of contrast depending on foil thickness.

For $g \cdot b = -\frac{2}{3}$:

Over a wide range of w ($-0.1 \lesssim w \lesssim 0.7$) images can be in or out of contrast depending on foil thickness;

at values of $w \lesssim 0.7$, images are out of contrast.

Specific illustrations covering a portion of the range of the amended rules for the case $g \cdot b = +\frac{2}{3}$ can be seen in figs. 8.18(a), (b) and (c) which show a selected set of computed images from the survey, for three values of w ($w = 0.1$, fig. 8.18(a); $w = 0.5$, fig. 8.18(b); $w = 0.9$, fig. 8.18(c)). They illustrate the influence of varying foil thickness within the range $5.30 \, \xi_{111}$ to $3.67 \, \xi_{111}$ on the contrast of a Shockley partial dislocation. These images also illustrate the limitations of describing in and out of contrast images in terms of the presence or absence of a dark band crossing the light fringes. Similar sets of images, not shown here, were used to investigate the contrast behaviour for $g \cdot b = -\frac{2}{3}$.

In fig. 8.19, experimental and matching computed images are used to show some of the features of contrast from a Shockley partial dislocation for a foil whose thickness is $4.7 \, \xi_{111a}$ (i.e. approximately midway in the range of thickness considered in fig. 8.18) and the defect in fig. 8.19 is identical with that used for the computations in fig. 8.18. The rules (a) and (b) as originally stated, imply that a Shockley partial dislocation will show a reversal of contrast between $+g$ and $-g$ provided that $w \lesssim 0.7$. However, the experimental and computed images in fig. 8.19 indicate that such a reversal can occur at values of w as low as 0.2 and that a failure of the reversal can occur at values of $w > 0.7$ such as that shown for $w = 1.1$. In fig. 8.20 it can be seen that for a thinner foil of the same alloy ($t = 3.24 \, \xi_{111a}$) the breakdown in the rules for images with $g \cdot b = \pm \frac{2}{3}$ is very apparent. Here there is an almost equivalent lack of contrast for $g \cdot b = +\frac{2}{3}$ (fig. 8.20(b)) as there is for $g \cdot b = -\frac{2}{3}$ (fig. 8.20(c)).

Although the computations on the contrast behaviour of Frank partial dislocations were less detailed than those for Shockley partial dislocations, they showed for the same range that the amended rules could also be applied to the contrast behaviour of Frank partial dislocations.

The survey was confined solely to partial dislocations bordering intrinsic faults, but identical conclusions will of course apply to extrinsic faults (see Appendix, fig. A.7).

The use of computed images has enabled the contrast behaviour of partial dislocations to be examined in considerable detail and the resultant reappraisal

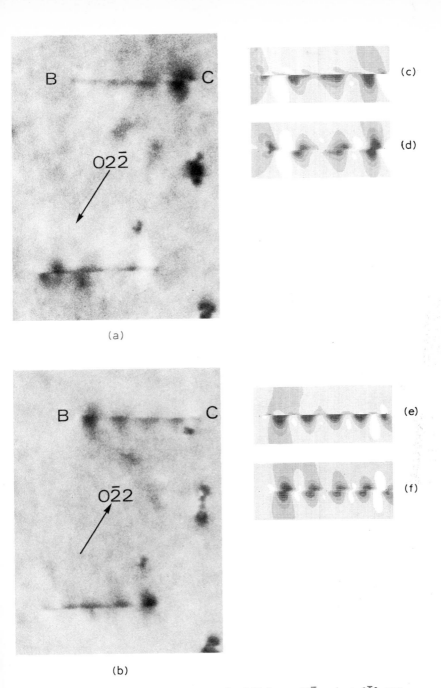

Fig. 8.24. Experimental images of the loop in fig. 8.23 for $+g$, $02\bar{2}$, and $-g$, $0\bar{2}2$, compared with computed images for the edge BC. The computed images are for an undissociated Frank dislocation ((d) and (f)) and for a dissociated Frank dislocation ((c) and (e)) with a separation of the stair-rod and Shockley partial dislocations of 60 Å, using $\xi_{220a} = 415$ Å. u is $[\bar{1}01]$, B is $[\bar{1}88]$, F is $[012]$ and w is 0.0 for (c) and (d) and 0.55 for (e) and (f).

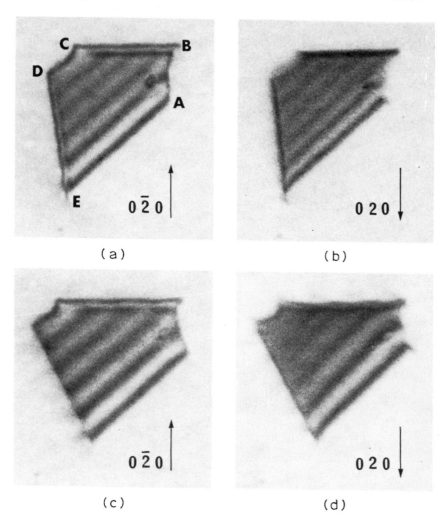

Fig. 8.25. Four micrographs of a Frank dislocation loop ABCDE on $(1\bar{1}1)$ in a Cu + 15.6 at % Al alloy. *B* is close to [001] in (a) and (b) and [102] in (c) and (d) and the diffracting vectors are indicated. × 200,000.

sociated and the optimum match between experimental and computed images was obtained for a dissociation of 60 Å (see fig. 8.24).

Features of the contrast from dissociated Frank dislocations using 020 diffracting vectors will be illustrated for a Frank loop in a Cu + 15.6 at % Al alloy, an alloy with a lower stacking fault energy than that of the Cu + 9.4 at % Al alloy. Figures 8.25 (a)–(d) show images of a Frank loop in a quenched

$S_p(\text{Å})$

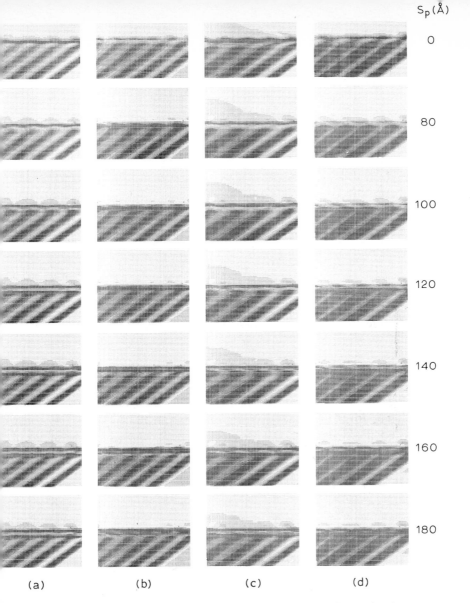

0

80

100

120

140

160

180

(a)   (b)   (c)   (d)

Fig. 8.26. Four sets of computed images (a), (b), (c) and (d) corresponding to the edge CB of the loop in fig. 8.25 (a), (b), (c) and (d). The top image in each set corresponds to an undissociated Frank dislocation with $b = \frac{1}{3}[1\bar{1}1]$ and the remaining images correspond to a dissociated Frank dislocation with the stair-rod dislocation, $b = \frac{1}{6}[101]$, and the Shockley partial dislocation, $b = \frac{1}{6}[1\bar{2}1]$. The indicated separations, S_p (Å), correspond to a value of $\xi_{020a} = 280$ Å. u is $[\bar{1}01]$, t is 6.5 ξ_{020a} and B, g and w are indicated below:

	B	g	w
(a)	[001]	$0\bar{2}0$	0.52
(b)	[001]	020	0.70
(c)	[102]	$0\bar{2}0$	0.36
(d)	[102]	020	0.34

specimen where the loop intersects the top surface of the foil along AE (fig. 8.25(a)). The edges CB and DE of the loop lie along ⟨110⟩ directions whilst the edges DC and AB do not lie along any simple direction. A comparison of fig. 8.25(a) with fig. 8.25(b) shows that the edges CB and DE show strong contrast in both the 0$\bar{2}$0 and 020 diffracting vectors whilst the edges DC and AB show contrast in 0$\bar{2}$0 and an absence of contrast in 020. From conclusion (c) above and from the survey of the contrast of undissociated Frank dislocations in this type of alloy (§ 8.9), the observed behaviour suggests that the segments of the Frank dislocation along CB and DE are dissociated whilst those along DC and AB are undissociated. This is to be expected since CB and DE lie along ⟨110⟩ directions (the required directions for the dissociation reaction to occur), whereas the other segments do not.

In making a comparison between the experimental and computed images in figs. 8.25 and 8.26, attention will be confined to the segment CB of the loop. It is clear that the computed images for the undissociated Frank dislocation do not agree with the experimental ones. It can be seen from the computed images for separations in the range 80 Å to 100 Å that a white band is present between the fault fringes and the edge of the loop for the 0$\bar{2}$0 diffracting vector (figs. 8.26(a) and (c)), in agreement with conclusion (c) above. As the separation increases, an additional dark band appears in the 0$\bar{2}$0 computed images and there is no reversal of contrast between 0$\bar{2}$0 and 020 in that a dark band of contrast terminates the fault fringes in both cases. The best agreement between the experimental and computed images is obtained for a separation of the Shockley and stair-rod dislocations in the range 140 Å to 160 Å.

The ability to determine the separation of the partial dislocations of a dissociated Frank dislocation provides a means for determining the stacking fault energy γ of the material. Since the partial dislocations that make up a dissociated Frank dislocation are in edge orientation, their equilibrium separation, r is given for elastic isotropy by (Read, 1953):

$$r = \frac{Gb^2(2+\nu)}{36\,\pi\gamma(1-\nu)} \tag{8.7}$$

where G is the shear modulus, b is the closest distance of approach of the atoms and ν is Poisson's ratio. If the separations obtained by image matching are assumed to be those corresponding to equilibrium conditions, then the values of $\gamma/(Gb)$ for the two copper–aluminium alloys can be obtained from eq. (8.7) (Clarebrough and Morton, 1969b). The results are in reasonable agreement with the values obtained from measurements on extended nodes in the same materials (Howie and Swann, 1961).

8.11. Growth of Frank loops by fault climb

The annihilation of vacancies by the climb of the dislocation bounding a faulted loop is more difficult when the dislocation is dissociated, since constriction of the partial dislocations is necessary to provide sites on the loop for the addition of vacancies. However, climb of a dissociated dislocation can occur without constriction by the mechanism of fault climb, i.e. where vacancies are incorporated in the stacking fault so as to cause a localised change in the level of the faulted plane (Barnes, 1954; Escaig, 1963; Schapink and de Jong, 1964).

Frank dislocation loops containing steps in the stacking fault ('complex loops') have been observed in quenched metals and alloys with stacking fault energies sufficiently low to allow significant dissociation of the Frank dislocation (Clarebrough et al., 1966). An important application of the image matching technique has been the identification of dislocation and stacking fault configurations at these steps and this identification provided strong evidence that fault climb is indeed an operative mechanism in the formation of these defects (Morton and Clarebrough, 1969).

The steps in these complex loops always lie along ⟨110⟩ directions and in some cases, where the step height is large, suitable rotations of the specimen enable the two levels of the loop on parallel {111} planes to be resolved and the face of the step to be identified as an inclined {111} plane (see, for example, fig. 8.27). In most cases the step height is smaller than that shown in fig. 8.27 and the steps can only be observed by some change in contrast occurring along a ⟨110⟩ direction within the loop, e.g. by a fringe displacement and often by a change in intensity. The contrast at the steps is in general more complex than the dark contrast for 111 reflections and the light contrast for 020 reflections which has been shown by Tunstall and Goodhew (1966) to be characteristic of overlapping Frank dislocation loops. For example, fig. 8.28 shows a complex loop in a Cu + 9.4 at % Al alloy where the contrast behaviour is opposite to that found by Tunstall and Goodhew in that the step shows dark contrast for the $0\bar{2}0$ diffracting vector and light contrast for the $\bar{1}\bar{1}1$ diffracting vector. Two characteristic configurations found for complex loops are those where steps form a triangular region (fig. 8.29) and those where the steps extend completely across the loops (fig. 8.28). In the case of complex loops showing a triangular region, one edge of the triangle is always coincident with one edge of the main loop; this is contrary to observations on double Frank loops where the smaller triangular loop is displaced from the edges of the larger loop (e.g. Tunstall and Goodhew, 1966).

A comparison of experimental and computed images of steps in complex loops in silver and copper—aluminium alloys has led to the following results:

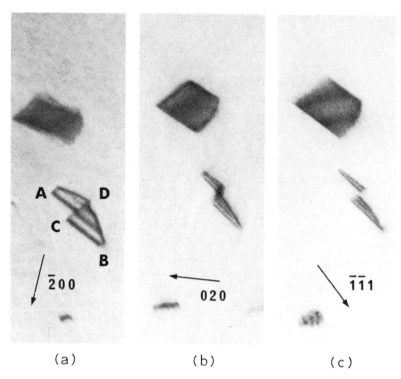

(a)   (b)   (c)

Fig. 8.27. Micrographs in three different beam directions [057] (a), [103] (b), and [213] (c), showing a large step CD on (11$\bar{1}$) in a Frank loop on ($\bar{1}$11) in a quenched Cu + 9.4 at % Al alloy. The loop intersects the bottom surface of the foil along ACB. The diffracting vectors are indicated. × 120,000.

(a) steps involving an acute bend in the stacking fault are the ones most frequently observed and these steps are faulted and bounded along their edges by pairs of stair-rod dislocations of opposite sign with Burgers vectors of the type $\pm \frac{1}{6}\langle 110 \rangle^*$;

(b) occasionally steps involving an obtuse bend are observed; in these cases the steps are unfaulted and bounded along their edges by Shockley partial dislocations of opposite sign, i.e. with Burgers vectors of the type $\pm \frac{1}{6}\langle 112 \rangle$;

(c) where steps are observed to enclose triangular regions, both steps involve acute bends in the stacking fault and are bounded by stair-rod dislocations of opposite sign with Burgers vectors of the type $\pm \frac{1}{6}\langle 110 \rangle$.

* Throughout this section, the symbol $\pm$ denotes + and −, rather than + or −.

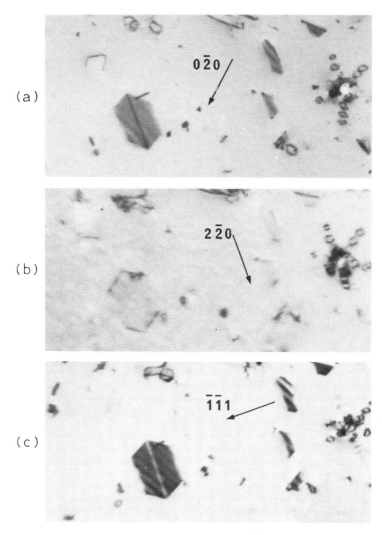

Fig. 8.28. Micrographs in beam directions close to [103] (a), [112] (b), and [213] (c), showing the contrast from a step parallel to [1$\bar{1}$0] in a Frank loop on (111) in a quenched Cu + 9.4 at % Al alloy. The diffracting vectors are indicated. × 60,000.

These results were obtained from an analysis of a total of thirteen examples of complex loops in silver and in a Cu + 9.4 at % Al alloy and some of these will be selected in this section to illustrate the results (a), (b) and (c).

Before these examples are discussed, it should be realised that there are a large number of possibilities for the configuration of dislocations and stacking

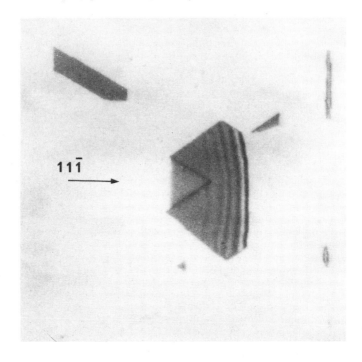

Fig. 8.29. Micrograph of a complex Frank loop in quenched silver. The beam direction is close to [112] and the diffracting vector is indicated. × 60,000.

faults at a step in a complex loop. For instance, the step may be unfaulted or intrinsically or extrinsically faulted, and the bends in the fault may be either acute or obtuse*; the type of dislocation bordering the step edges will, of course, depend on the particular combination of faults and bend angle**. In some cases the number of possibilities can be reduced by using the stacking fault fringe displacement at the step to determine whether the bend is acute or obtuse, and by using a diffracting vector parallel to the $\langle \bar{1}10 \rangle$ direction of the step edges to determine whether or not the bordering dislocations are edge***. However, even when this information is available, there are still a

---

* The possibility that the original Frank loop could be extrinsically faulted is not con-sidered since the defects form by the clustering of vacancies following a quench from near the melting point. However, this argument does not apply to the type of fault on the step, since this will depend on the details of the fault climb mechanism.

** Very high energy stair-rod dislocations with Burgers vectors greater than $\frac{1}{6}\langle 301 \rangle$ have not been considered.

*** For an edge dislocation along $\langle 110 \rangle$ there will be no contrast using a diffracting vector parallel to the same $\langle 110 \rangle$, independent of elastic anisotropy (§ 2.7.2(ii)).

large number of possible configurations remaining and image computation is necessary to decide between these and to determine the height of the step.

The first example of a complex loop to be analyzed is given in fig. 8.30 (a)–(h) which shows eight experimental images of a complex loop in a quenched Cu + 9.4 at% Al alloy. The loop is on (111), with the step AB (fig. 8.30(a)) along $[\bar{1}01]$ and the corners B and A are close to the top and bottom surfaces of the foil respectively. The fringe shift across the step suggests either a step height of approximately 0.75 ξ_{111a} for an acute bend or 0.25 ξ_{111a} for an obtuse bend. Furthermore, the set of images does not contain a diffracting vector that is parallel to $[\bar{1}01]$. In this case therefore, it is not known whether the step is acute or obtuse nor whether the dislocations at the edges of the step are edge dislocations. For these reasons all possible Burgers vectors for acute and obtuse bends need to be considered.

For an obtuse bend at a step height of 0.25 ξ_{111a}, all possible Burgers vectors for a faulted or unfaulted step were tested for two diffracting vectors and in no case was agreement obtained with the experimental images.

An acute bend with extrinsic fault in the step would be bordered by high energy stair-rod dislocations and these possibilities were computed, but in no case was agreement obtained with the experimental images. Those cases for which some agreement was obtained between experimental and computed images were:

(i) an acute bend with intrinsic fault in the step where the dislocations bordering the step were $\pm\frac{1}{6}[101]$ or $\pm\frac{1}{3}[101]$;

(ii) an unfaulted acute bend where the dislocations bordering the step were $\pm\frac{1}{6}[1\bar{2}1]$ or $\pm\frac{1}{6}[11\bar{2}]$ or $\pm\frac{1}{6}[\bar{2}11]$;

(iii) the case of two Frank loops (with $b = \pm\frac{1}{3}[111]$) slightly overlapping along AB.

Computed images for each of the six cases in (i), (ii) and (iii) for a step height of 0.75 ξ_{111a} are given in fig. 8.30 for each of the eight diffracting vectors. From a comparison between the experimental and computed images, it is possible to eliminate all but two possibilities; a faulted step bordered by low energy stair-rod dislocations ($\pm\frac{1}{6}[101]$), and overlapping Frank loops. It can be seen from fig. 8.30(f) that neither of the computed images for these two cases matches the fine detail of this experimental image. The main characteristic feature of the experimental image is a continuous dark line (approximately 30 Å wide) which passes through both the light and dark fringes. The line resolution in the computed images of fig. 8.30(f) is 50 Å which is insufficient to resolve this fine detail. In fig. 8.31 the magnification of the computed images has been increased to give a line resolution of 20 Å and it can now be seen that the image of the low energy stair-rod dipole ($\pm\frac{1}{6}[101]$) reproduces adequately the detail of the experimental image, where-

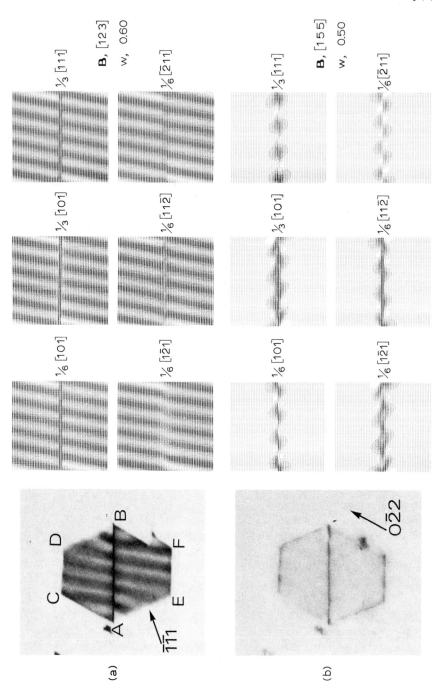

Fig. 8.30. Comparison of eight experimental images (a)–(h) (× 90,000) and the computed images for different combinations of dislocation

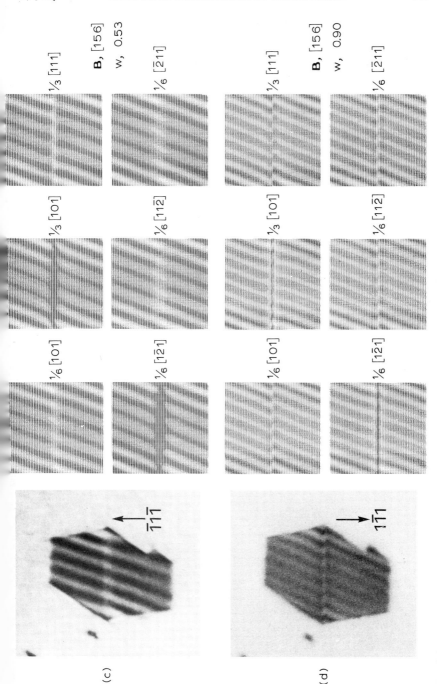

Fig. 8.30 (continued).

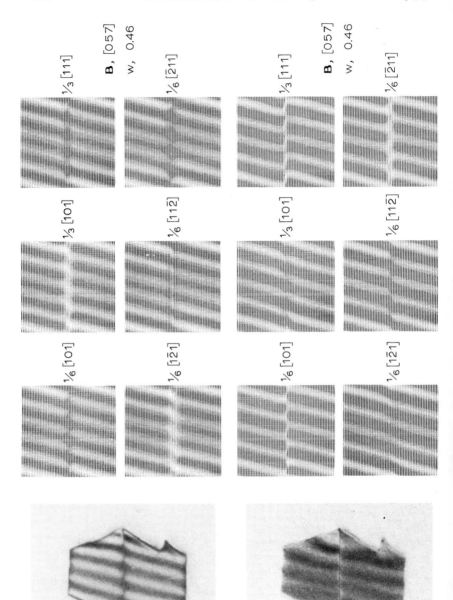

(e)

(f)

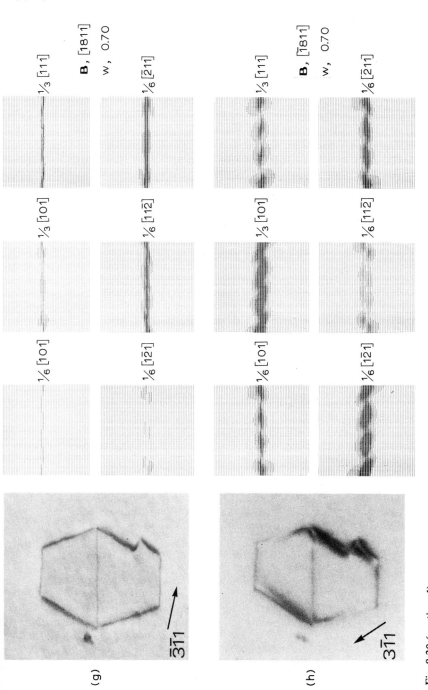

Fig. 8.30 (continued).

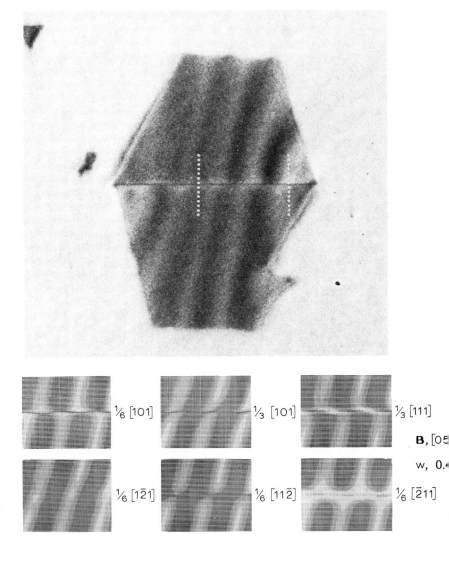

Fig. 8.31. Comparison of the marked portion of experimental image ((f) of fig. 8.30) with high magnification computed images for the six combinations of Burgers vectors tested in fig. 8.30. × 200,000.

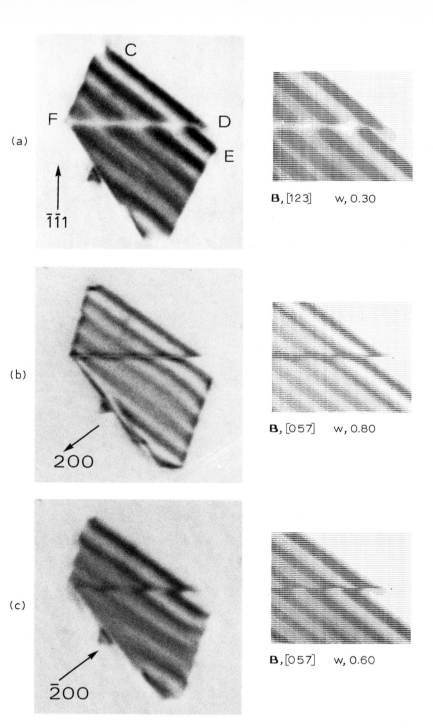

(a)

$\bar{1}\bar{1}1$

B, [123]   w, 0.30

(b)

200

B, [057]   w, 0.80

(c)

$\bar{2}00$

B, [057]   w, 0.60

Fig. 8.32. Comparison of experimental (× 147,000) and computed images for a complex Frank loop on (111) with a step along $[\bar{1}10]$ in a quenched Cu + 9.4 at % Al alloy. The combination of Burgers vectors at the step are $\pm \frac{1}{6}[110]$ separated by 0.5 ξ_{111a}. F is [157] and t is 6 ξ_{111a}. B, g and w are indicated.

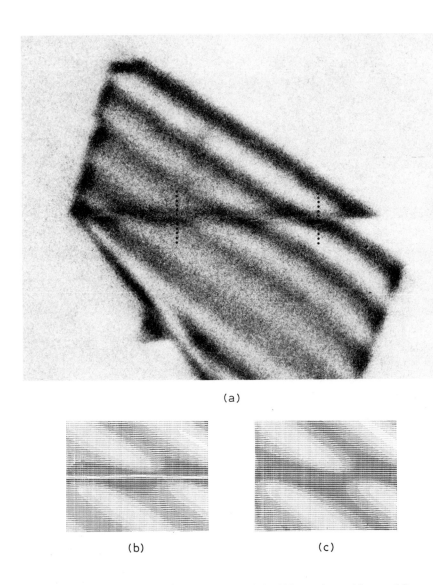

(a)

(b)   (c)

Fig. 8.33. Comparison at a higher magnification of the 200 experimental image of fig. 8.32 with computed images. Image (b) has been computed with $B = [057]$ and image (c) with $B = [011]$. The computed images should be compared with the marked portion of the experimental image. × 270,000.

as this is not so for the case of overlapping Frank loops or any of the other possibilities.

Another example in a Cu + 9.4 at % Al alloy involving low energy stair-rod dislocations is shown in fig. 8.32 where the fringe shift in fig. 8.32(a) at the surface intersection CDE indicates an acute step with a step height of approximately 0.5 ξ_{111a}. The loop is on (111) and the step FD is along $[\bar{1}10]$ so that the plane of the step is $(11\bar{1})$. As before, the configurations involving extrinsic fault and high energy stair-rod dislocations were considered and found to be in disagreement with the experimental images in all cases. The possible Burgers vectors for the dislocations bordering the step are: $\pm\frac{1}{6}[110]$ or $\pm\frac{1}{3}[110]$ for an intrinsically faulted bend; $\pm\frac{1}{6}[2\bar{1}\bar{1}]$ or $\pm\frac{1}{6}[\bar{1}2\bar{1}]$ or $\pm\frac{1}{6}[\bar{1}\bar{1}2]$ for an unfaulted bend; and $\frac{1}{3}[111]$ if the defect consists of two Frank dislocation loops slightly overlapping along FD. Of these Burgers vectors only the $\pm\frac{1}{6}[110]$ gave computed images which matched the experimental ones and these matching images for a step height of 0.5 ξ_{111a} are shown in fig. 8.32. The magnification of the computed image (line resolution 30 Å) in fig. 8.32(b) is not sufficient to resolve the fine detail of the 200 image, and this experimental image and a computed image at a higher magnification (line resolution 11 Å) are given in fig. 8.33(a) and (b) respectively. From these figures it can be seen that the characteristic features of the experimental image along the step, namely a light band bordered by two darker bands of contrast crossing the light fringes and accentuated dark contrast at the positions of the darker bands in the dark fringes, are adequately reproduced in the computed image. This is an example where the character of the image is particularly sensitive to the beam direction. For instance, if the approximate beam direction of [011] is used, then the computed image (fig. 8.33(c)) is in disagreement with the experimental image. This type of behaviour is to be expected in cases of defects involving a complex array of dislocations and stacking faults since the aspect of the defect when viewed in the beam direction (i.e. the displacements encountered in a column) can be markedly changed by a small rotation of the specimen.

So far only complex loops where the configuration at the step consists of intrinsically faulted acute bends bordered by low energy stair-rod dislocations (edge dislocations) have been considered. Figure 8.34 is an example of a complex loop where the step AB is bordered by non-edge dislocations as can be seen from the strong contrast for the $02\bar{2}$ diffracting vector in fig. 8.34(b). In this loop two parallel steps occur along $[0\bar{1}1]$ i.e. AB and CD. The loop is on $(\bar{1}11)$ and intersects the bottom of the foil along the line containing D. From the fringe shift at the surface intersection the step CD is obtuse and by fringe matching across the step AB this step is also found to be obtuse with a step height of approximately 0.25 ξ_{111a}. The possible Burgers vectors for the dislocation dipole at the step AB are: $\pm\frac{1}{6}[\bar{1}30]$ or $\pm\frac{1}{6}[103]$ or $\pm\frac{1}{6}[130]$ or $\pm\frac{1}{6}[10\bar{3}]$ for an intrinsically faulted step, and $\pm\frac{1}{6}[12\bar{1}]$ or $\pm\frac{1}{6}[11\bar{2}]$ for an

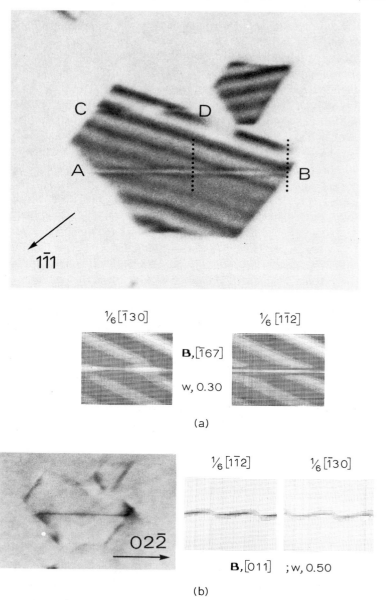

Fig. 8.34. Comparison of experimental images and computed images for a complex Frank loop on ($\bar{1}$11) in a quenched Cu + 9.4 at % Al alloy. The steps AB and CD along [0$\bar{1}$1] involve obtuse bends. Images for two combinations of Burgers vectors are shown for the step AB, namely $\pm\frac{1}{6}[1\bar{1}2]$ and $\pm\frac{1}{6}[\bar{1}30]$. Experimental image (a) × 200,000 and (b) × 90,000. F is [123], t is 7 ξ_{111a} and the separation of the dislocations at the step is 0.25 ξ_{111a}. The values of B, g, w and b are indicated.

unfaulted step. The cases of extrinsic faulting in the step and overlapping Frank dislocations need not be considered here since these would involve edge dislocations. Image matching indicated that $\pm \frac{1}{6}[\bar{1}30]$ and $\pm \frac{1}{6}[1\bar{1}2]$ were the only likely Burgers vectors, and a decision was made between them from a comparison of experimental and computed images for seven diffracting vectors. The most striking difference between the computed images for these two Burgers vectors was obtained for the $1\bar{1}1$ image (fig. 8.34(a)). Experimental and computed images of comparable resolution, fig. 8.34(a), show that only the dislocations $\pm \frac{1}{6}[112]$ bordering an unfaulted obtuse step match the characteristic detail of the experimental image, reproducing the two dark lines bordering the white band crossing all fringes.

As shown earlier, a characteristic configuration for complex loops is a triangular region within the main loop with one edge of the triangular region along one edge of the main loop. The example of this type of defect in quenched silver shown in fig. 8.35 has been analysed and will now be used to illustrate the result (c) given above.

The loop is on (111) and the $1\bar{3}\bar{1}$ image (fig. 8.35(f)) shows that it does not intersect either surface of the foil. The triangular region EFG (fig. 8.35(f)) is bounded by $[10\bar{1}]$ (EF), $[0\bar{1}1]$ (FG) and $[\bar{1}10]$ (GE). The protrusion outside the main loop of the projection of the triangular region in figs. 8.35(b) and (d) indicates a large separation between the triangular region and the main loop. Furthermore, the geometry of the triangular region and the above protrusion requires that faulted steps along FG and GE must involve acute bends in the fault. Discussion will be confined here to the edges GE and FE. The dislocations along GE and FE are edge because they are out of contrast on $2\bar{2}0$ and $20\bar{2}$ respectively and since the bend along GE is acute the only possibilities for the Burgers vectors of dislocations along GE are $\pm \frac{1}{6}[110]$ or $\pm \frac{1}{3}[110]$ if GE is a faulted step, $\pm \frac{1}{6}[11\bar{2}]$ if GE is an unfaulted step, or $\frac{1}{3}[111]$ if the contrast along GE is due to a triangular Frank dislocation overlapping a larger hexagonal loop. The contrast along FE is the same as that along BC for all diffracting vectors so that the defect at FE is unlikely to be two overlapping Frank dislocations, but is more likely to be either a dissociated or an undissociated Frank dislocation. This would suggest that the defect does not consist of a triangular Frank dislocation loop overlapping a hexagonal loop, but this possibility will not be dismissed at this stage.

Computations for the $\pm \frac{1}{6}[110]$ and $\frac{1}{3}[111]$ Burgers vectors showed that the separation of the triangular region from the main loop was approximately $0.7\ \xi_{020a}$. Computations were made for the four possible Burgers vectors along GE at a separation of $0.7\ \xi_{020a}$ for eight diffracting vectors. Obvious discrepancies between the experimental and computed images, e.g. dark instead of light contrast in the $\bar{1}11$ image, dismissed the $\pm \frac{1}{3}[110]$ and $\pm \frac{1}{6}[11\bar{2}]$ Burgers vectors, leaving a decision to be made between $\pm \frac{1}{6}[110]$ and $\frac{1}{3}[111]$. The

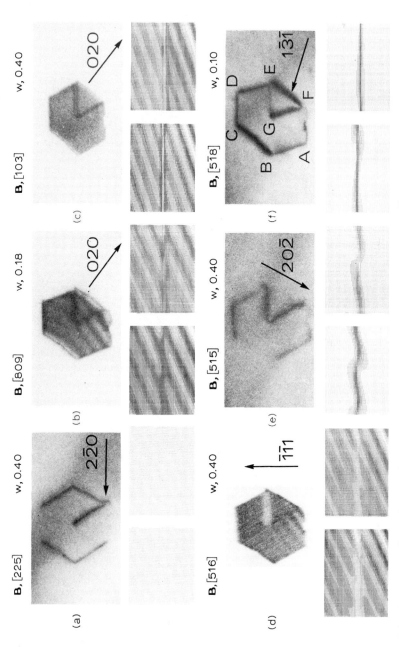

Fig. 8.35. Comparison of experimental ($\times$ 90,000) and computed images for the edge GE along [$\bar{1}$10] of a complex Frank loop on (111) in quenched silver. The Burgers vectors for the two computed images corresponding to each experimental image are $\pm\frac{1}{6}$[110] on the left and $\frac{1}{3}$[111] on the right as indicated in (a). In all computed images the step height is 0.7 ξ_{020a}. F is [418], t is 9 ξ_{111a} and $\mathbf{g}$, $\mathbf{B}$ and w are

computed images for these two Burgers vectors are compared with the experimental images in fig. 8.35. This comparison indicates that the defect along GE is a faulted step bordered by $\pm \frac{1}{6}[110]$ dislocations at a separation of $0.7\ \xi_{020a}$ for the following reasons:

(i) on rotation about the 020 diffracting vector from the beam direction [809] (fig. 8.35(b)) to the beam direction [103] (fig. 8.35(c)), the contrast along GE changes from an unresolved dark band to resolved dark lines approximately 100 Å apart. This change in contrast is in better agreement with the computed images for $\pm \frac{1}{6}[110]$ than for $\frac{1}{3}[111]$;

(ii) the broad light band in the $\bar{1}\bar{1}1$ image (fig. 8.35(d)) is similar in both computed images, but the width of the band is better matched by $\pm \frac{1}{6}[110]$;

(iii) the $20\bar{2}$ image (fig. 8.35(e)) is continuous and thus a better match with $\pm \frac{1}{6}[110]$.

Computed images for the edge GF similarly favour low energy stair-rod dislocations, in this case with Burgers vectors of $\pm \frac{1}{6}[011]$. For the remaining edge FE of the triangular region, image matching shows that it consists of a dissociated Frank dislocation with a separation of the Shockley and stair-rod dislocations of approximately $0.25\ \xi_{020a}$.

The complex loop in fig. 8.35 thus consists of a triangular region bordered by $\pm \frac{1}{6}\langle 110 \rangle$ stair-rod dislocations along the steps GE and GF making up acute bends in an intrinsic fault, and a dissociated Frank dislocation along FE.

In all the cases examined it has been found that the observed contrast was due to steps in the Frank dislocation loops. There are two mechanisms by which steps in Frank loops can form: (i) by the union of two edges of neighbouring loops by dissociation of these edges on a common {111} plane; or (ii) by climb of the stacking fault (Escaig, 1963). The union mechanism requires that the dissociation be coplanar which should be a relatively rare event, and would be considered unlikely to account for the observed density of complex loops in quenched silver and copper–aluminium alloys, which can be greater than 25 % of the loop population. Furthermore, the results (b) and (c) listed above are only compatible with the mechanism of fault climb (Morton and Clarebrough, 1969), whereas only result (a) is compatible with both mechanisms.

The use of the image matching technique to identify the dislocations bordering steps in faulted loops has provided direct evidence for the process of fault climb as a mechanism for the growth of Frank loops in low stacking fault energy metals and alloys. This mechanism is likely to be favoured in all materials where Frank dislocations are dissociated. The nucleation of climbed regions in the fault is favoured near the edges of the loop (Escaig, 1963). For edges which are dissociated below the plane of the loop, the nucleation of climbed regions will be favoured above the plane of the loop, and the reverse applies to edges which are dissociated above the plane of the loop. The formation of regions of climb above and below the loop-plane and the subsequent growth and union of these regions produces a step across the loop and leaves the dissociated edges of the loop in their original state. Once this step has been generated, it is unlikely that it will be annihilated by a step of the opposite sense since continued nucleation and growth of climbed regions would tend to follow the same sequence as before and increase the height of the step across the loop. This mechanism is discussed by Morton and Clarebrough (1969).

8.12. Dislocation dipoles in nickel

A dislocation dipole consists of two parallel dislocations with opposite Burgers vectors. These dislocations interact and if they are constrained to move on their respective slip planes they take up a stable equilibrium configuration of minimum energy at a particular value of the angle ϕ between the slip planes of the dislocations and the plane containing them, as shown schematically in fig. 8.36.

The image matching technique has been used to identify the Burgers vectors of some dislocation dipoles in nickel and to specify within close limits the geometrical configuration of these defects. The formation of dipoles involves one of the simplest forms of dislocation interaction which gives rise to a stable defect during the plastic deformation of a crystal, and the study of these defects has enabled some of the factors governing the interaction of dislocations to be investigated. For example, the importance of elastic anisotropy and stacking fault energy as they affect the equilibrium configuration of dipoles has been demonstrated (Forwood and Humble, 1970).

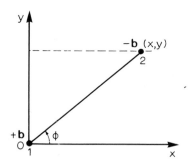

Fig. 8.36. Schematic diagram of a dislocation dipole. Dislocations 1 and 2 are parallel to Oz and slip on planes normal to Oy.

Although dipoles consist of two dislocations, it is not always possible to resolve the component dislocations in electron microscope images, and frequently a dipole image appears as a single entity. Thus it is necessary to know the features of contrast arising from dipoles which enable them to be distinguished from other defects. For example, in centro-symmetric crystals, the main feature of images of dipoles which distinguishes them from single dislocations is that they possess a centre of inversion. Such symmetry may easily be deduced for a dipole from the properties of the bright field images of isolated dislocations (see Appendix). This property is amply demonstrated by the experimental and computed images shown in this section.

The fact that images have a centre of inversion is true for any degree of elastic anisotropy and, in addition, the arguments hold if the dislocations are dissociated into partial dislocations provided that the configuration of separations, Burgers vectors and type of fault are symmetrically disposed. Although in the Appendix the derivation of the symmetry properties of images of dipoles is based on the two-beam theory of electron diffraction, it also applies for bright field images involving many-beam diffraction conditions. A centre of inversion will not be present in images if the component dislocations are not parallel (e.g., defect C in fig. 8.39).

Another property of bright field images of dislocation dipoles is that, in general, the image formed with a diffracting vector g bears no obvious relation

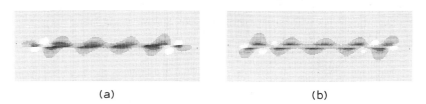

(a)   (b)

Fig. 8.37. Computed images of a narrowly separated dislocation dipole in nickel for $+g$, $\bar{1}\bar{1}1$ (a) and $-g$, $11\bar{1}$ (b). The separation of the dislocations is $0.15\ \xi_{111}$. b is $\pm\frac{1}{2}[\bar{1}01]$, u is $[\bar{1}\bar{1}2]$, ϕ is $60°$, B is $[819]$, F is $[419]$, t is $4.2\ \xi_{111}$ and $w = 0.4$.

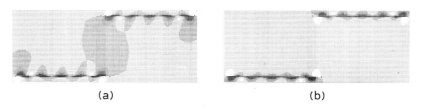

(a)   (b)

Fig. 8.38. Computed images of a widely separated dislocation dipole in nickel for $+g$, $\bar{1}\bar{1}1$ (a), and $-g$, $11\bar{1}$ (b). The separation of the dislocations is $6\ \xi_{111}$. b, u, ϕ, B, F, t and w are as in fig. 8.37.

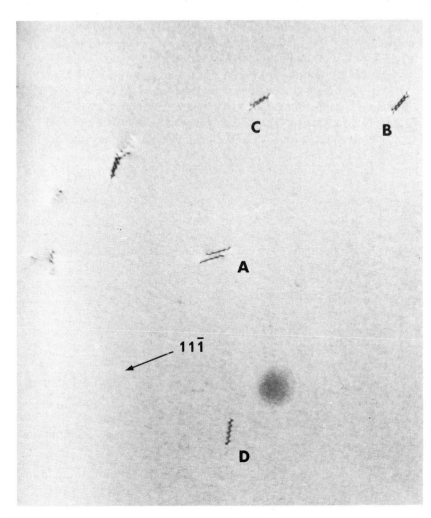

Fig. 8.39. Micrograph of a thin foil of nickel (× 42,000) showing dislocation dipoles at A, B and D. **B** is [213], **F** is [419] and **g** is indicated.

to that formed with a diffracting vector −**g**. This is obviously not the case for large separations where the displacement fields of the two dislocations do not overlap appreciably, since then the images are essentially those of isolated dislocations where the usual relation between images for +**g** and −**g**, namely a 180° rotation, applies. These points are illustrated in figs. 8.37 and 8.38. In figs. 8.37(a) and (b) the separation of the dislocations is 0.15 ξ₁₁₁ and there is no obvious relation between images for +**g** and −**g**, whereas in figs. 8.38(a) and (b) the separation of the same component dislocations has been increased to 6.0 ξ_{111} and it can be seen that the images of the component dislocations are approximately related by a 180° rotation.

Figure 8.39 is an electron micrograph of a thin foil of nickel containing three dipoles A, B and D which can be recognised as such by their centre of inversion symmetry. The defect at C consists of two dislocations with opposite Burgers vectors but since the dislocations are not parallel, this defect will not be considered here. The separation of the component dislocations differs between the three dipoles since it can be seen from the micrograph that the component dislocations in dipole A are clearly resolved, those in dipole B are just resolved and those in dipole D are unresolved. Image matching has been used to identify the Burgers vectors and relative geometry of the component dislocations in these three dipoles.

The u of the dislocations for dipole A is $[\bar{1}\bar{1}2]$ and the Burgers vectors of the component dislocations were determined by image matching to be $\pm\frac{1}{2}[10\bar{1}]$ so that dipole A consists of dislocations which are 30° from screw orientation. The program ONEDIS was used to determine these Burgers vectors since the component dislocations in most of the images were sufficiently well separated so that each dislocation could be identified individually.

Isotropic elasticity would predict that the equilibrium positions of the dislocations in dipole A would be such that the angle ϕ in fig. 8.36 is 90°, i.e. the dislocations should be aligned normal to their slip planes (Cottrell, 1953). To compute images of the defect as a whole, the program TWODIS was used and in fig. 8.40 an experimental image of dipole A for the $\bar{2}02$ diffracting vector is compared with an image computed for the same diffracting conditions on the assumption that the component dislocations are aligned according to isotropic elasticity. Clearly there is no agreement between the experimental and computed images. It can be concluded therefore that the dipole is not an equilibrium configuration as defined by isotropic elasticity. Although nickel is only slightly elastically anisotropic, when this was taken into account, the equilibrium configuration of the component dislocations differed markedly from that predicted by isotropic elasticity.

Fig. 8.40. Comparison of experimental and computed images of dipole A in fig. 8.39 where the arrangement of the dislocations for the computed image corresponds to equilibrium as determined by isotropic elasticity (see text). b is $\pm\frac{1}{2}[10\bar{1}]$, u is $[\bar{1}\bar{1}2]$, ν is 0.32 and ϕ is 90°. B is [616], F is [419], t is 4.1 ξ_{111a}, w is 0.8 and g is $\bar{2}02$.

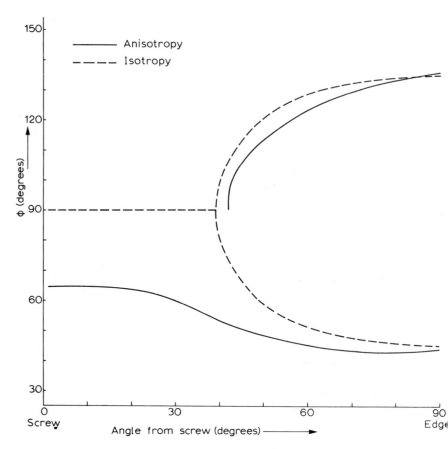

Fig. 8.41. Curves giving the equilibrium angle ϕ for $\pm\frac{1}{2}\langle110\rangle$ dislocations forming dipoles in nickel for isotropic ($\nu = 0.32$) and anisotropic elasticity.

A comparison between the equilibrium configurations of the component dislocations in a dipole in nickel for isotropic and anisotropic elasticity[*] is given in fig. 8.41 where the equilibrium angle ϕ (as defined in fig. 8.36) is plotted as a function of the angle of the dislocation direction from screw orientation. The positions of equilibrium are determined by finding the values of ϕ at which the force of interaction between the component dislocations resolved parallel to their slip planes is zero. This problem can be solved analytically in the isotropic case (Cottrell, 1953) and has been solved numerically

[*] The elastic constans used were c_{11} = 24.65, c_{12} = 14.73 and c_{44} = 12.47 × 10^{11} dyne cm^{-2} (Huntington, 1958).

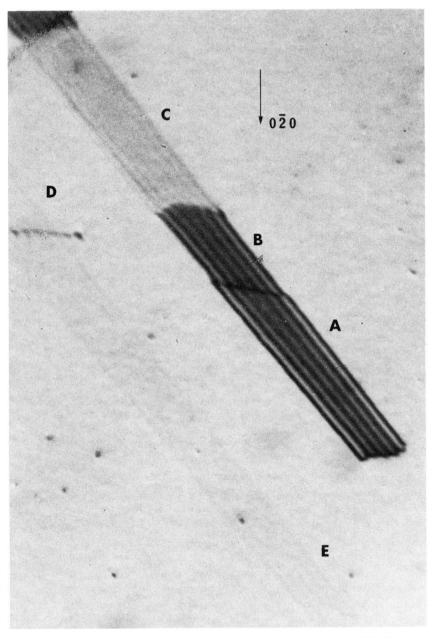

Fig. 8.49. Electron micrograph of a lightly deformed specimen of Cu + 8 at % Si alloy showing faint fringe contrast at C and from D to E associated with faulting on ($\bar{1}\bar{1}1$). **B** is [$\bar{1}$03] and the diffracting vector is indicated. × 60,000.

α which is equivalent to one extrinsic fault, and three overlapping intrinsic faults a value of α equal to an integral multiple of 2π and thus should produce no contrast. However, in reality, faint contrast is observed from three over-lapping intrinsic faults (Humble, 1968a). This is to be expected because the electron waves will not only be altered in phase at each fault in turn but in addition will undergo further phase changes as they propagate between each fault due to their interaction with each other and with the crystal potential between the faults. On this basis, an analysis of the faint contrast produced from three overlapping stacking faults has been made using computed images to determine to what extent such contrast is detectable, and to determine the relation between the contrast and the separation of the faulted planes (Humble, 1968a).

Figure 8.49 shows an example of faint fringe contrast arising from over-lapping faults on ($\overline{1}\overline{1}1$) in a Cu + 8 at% Si alloy. In the extended defect ABC, the region A can be attributed to a single intrinsic fault, the region B to two overlapping intrinsic faults and the region C to three overlapping intrinsic faults. The defect extending from D to E shows similar weak contrast to that at C and can also be shown to consist of three overlapping intrinsic faults.

An observer viewing weak images such as those at regions C and DE in fig. 8.49 will usually adopt more sensitive visibility limits to assimilate the in-formation than when viewing stronger images such as at A and B. The visibility limits used in theoretical micrographs for strong images have generally been 15 % above and 7 % below background intensity. However, it was necessary to find new visibility limits which were suitable for reproducing the detail in the weak images at C and DE. Microdensitometer traces across regions C and DE showed that the intensities of faint details which were just distinguishable by eye were 5 % above and 2 % below background intensity. A grey scale based on these visibility limits was used for computing the contrast from three closely overlapping faults. The computer program used was a modified form of the program TWODIS where the three faulted planes were no longer interconnected but were arranged parallel as shown schematically in fig. 8.50. The three planes LM, NO and PQ are terminated within the crystal with dis-locations at L, O and Q; the separation between the planes LM and NO is x and that between NO and PQ is y.

Figure 8.51 shows computed micrographs for three overlapping intrinsic faults with the diffraction conditions corresponding to fig. 8.49. The different computed images (a)–(k) are for various values of x and y expressed in units of the {111} interplanar spacing d as given in the legend to the figure. The Burgers vectors of the dislocations terminating the faults in fig. 8.51 have been set to zero because preliminary computations showed that the faint fringe contrast was strongly influenced by contrast from the strain fields of the dis-locations. Thus, when comparing faint image contrast in the computed and

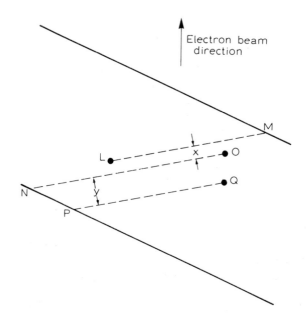

Fig. 8.50. Schematic illustration of the arrangement of three overlapping faulted planes LM, NO and PQ in a tilted foil. The dislocations at L, O and Q are coming out of the page but are not normal to it.

experimental images, regions of the experimental image well removed from the dislocations should be chosen.

In fig. 8.51 the computed images for which $x = y$ (fig. 8.51(a): $x = y = d$; fig. 8.51(e): $x = y = 2d$; fig. 8.51(i): $x = y = 3d$) show fringes which are closely symmetrical about mid-foil. The computed images for which $x \neq y$ show fringes which are asymmetric about mid-foil. The fringes produced for the case where $x = nd$, $y = md$ (where n and m are integers) are reflections about mid-foil of the fringes for the cases $x = md$, $y = nd$. This can be seen by comparing fig. 8.51(b) with 8.51(c), 8.51(d) with 8.51(f), 8.51(g) with 8.51(k) and 8.51(h) with 8.51(j). It will also be noted that the fringes get more intense as x or y increases.

These properties of the faint fringes from three overlapping faults have been used to identify the spacings of the faulted planes in the regions C and DE. It is apparent from fig. 8.49 that the fringes at C are asymmetric about mid-foil and that the fringes at DE are symmetric. The fringes at C are also more intense than those at DE.

Since the fringes at DE are symmetric about mid-foil, they must be due to overlapping faults where $x = y$. These fringes should be compared therefore with those shown in fig. 8.51(a) ($x = y = d$), fig. 8.51(e) ($x = y = 2d$) and fig. 8.51(i) ($x = y = 3d$). The configurations $x = y = 2d$ and $x = y = 3d$ (and any

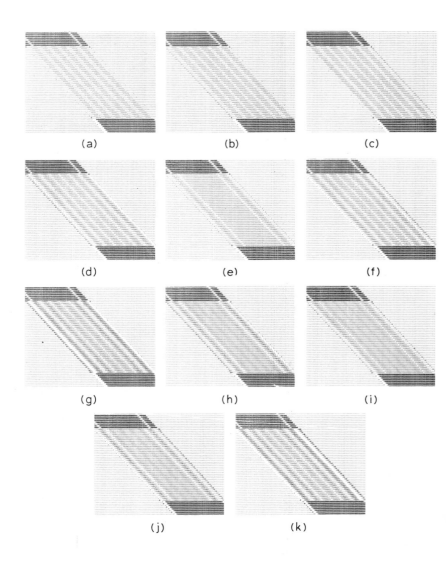

Fig. 8.51. Computed images for the same diffraction conditions as for the micrograph in fig. 8.49. The u of the dislocations is taken as [101] but their Burgers vectors are set to zero. F is [001], t is 6 ξ_{020a} and w is 0.2. Images (a)–(k) are for different spacings x and y of the faulted planes as given below in units of the slip plane spacing:

	(a)	(b)	(c)	(d)	(e)	(f)	(g)	(h)	(i)	(j)	(k)
x	1	1	2	1	2	3	1	2	3	4	5
y	1	2	1	3	2	1	5	4	3	2	1

higher combinations) may be disregarded since they produce contrast which is in excess of 5 % below background intensity, whereas microdensitometer traces show that this is not the case in the experimental image. It was concluded, therefore, that the fringes at D are due to three intrinsic stacking faults on neighbouring slip planes.

A similar comparison of the asymmetry and intensity of the contrast at C in fig. 8.49 with the computed images shown in fig. 8.51 led to the conclusion that the contrast in this case is due to three overlapping intrinsic stacking faults spaced d and $5d$ apart, as can be seen from a comparison of the experimental image with fig. 8.51(g) and (k). The other computed images showing asymmetric fringes in fig. 8.51 do not have the correct topology or are not sufficiently intense, and furthermore, higher combinations of x and y for this case always give rise to fringes which are too intense. The sense of the asymmetry of the fringes enables the further deduction to be made that the spacing of the upper pair of faulted planes is d and the lower pair $5d$ and not vice versa (i.e. the fringes at C compare exactly with fig. 8.51(g) rather than fig. 8.51(k)).

This analysis has illustrated that even when the overlapping stacking faults are on three neighbouring {111} planes, i.e. as close as possible, it is still necessary to take account of the propagation of the electron waves between these planes in order to describe the observed contrast.

8.14. Analysis of partial dislocations and stacking faults on closely spaced planes

In low stacking fault energy alloys $\frac{1}{2}\langle 110 \rangle$ glide dislocations are split into Shockley partial dislocations separated by stacking fault, so that cross slip is a difficult process and slip tends to be confined to well-defined parallel planes. The configurations of dislocations and stacking faults observed in cold worked alloys of this type will thus often be related to interactions between dissociated dislocations slipping on parallel planes. Electron micrographs of deformed alloys usually show a very wide distribution of separations of the partial dislocations. These range from values consistent with a simple balance between the stacking fault energy and the repulsion between the pair of partial dislocations to very extensive separations which may be two orders of magnitude or more greater. These large separations usually involve interactions between pairs of partial dislocations on parallel planes. Figure 8.52, for example, shows a typical area of a lightly deformed Cu + 15.6 at% Al alloy where the defects B, C, D and E are dissociated $\frac{1}{2}\langle 110 \rangle$ dislocations for which the Shockley partial dislocations are closely separated at values consistent with the stacking fault energy of the alloy. These defects show similar contrast to that examined in detail for defect B of ch. 7. Other defects such as A in fig. 8.52 show extensive regions of stacking fault. These defects involve more complex arrangements of partial dis-

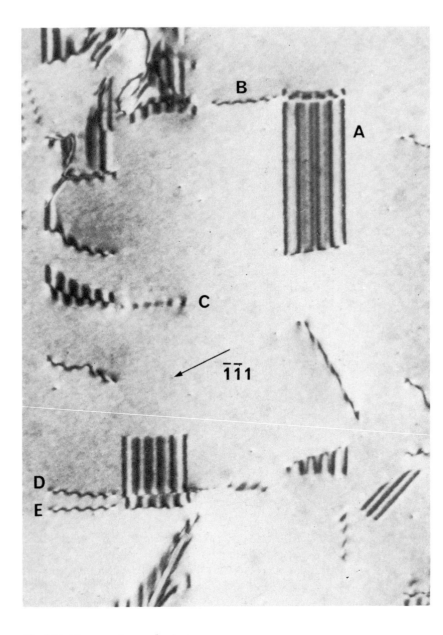

Fig. 8.52. Electron micrograph of a lightly deformed alloy of Cu + 15.6 at % Al showing dislocations dissociated to differing extents. *B* is close to [011] and the diffracting vector is indicated. × 140,000.

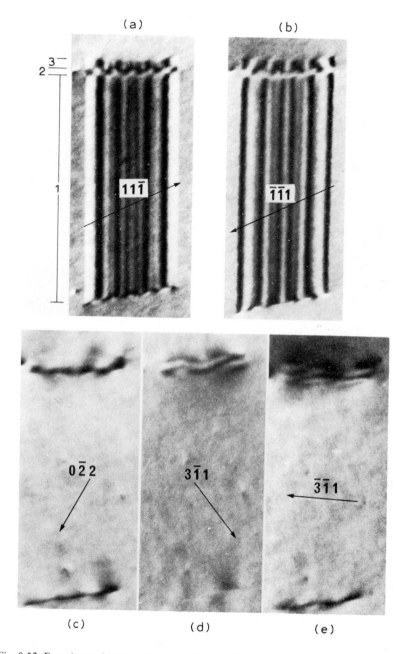

Fig. 8.53. Experimental images of defect A (fig. 8.52) for the diffracting vectors shown. Three regions of fault 1, 2 and 3 are indicated in (a). **B** is close to [011] . × 210,000.

locations which arise from slip of dissociated dislocations on parallel planes under the influence of the applied stress.

In an investigation of the interaction of partial dislocations on parallel planes, complex configurations of the type illustrated by defect A have been analysed using image matching to determine the Burgers vectors of the partial dislocations, the separation of the faulted planes and the separations of the partial dislocations (Clarebrough, Forwood and Morton, 1973).

A set of images of defect A for five different diffracting vectors is shown in fig. 8.53. The defect lies on (111) and it is clear from micrographs (a) and (b) of fig. 8.53 that the fault consists of three regions, 1, 2 and 3, with each region bounded by partial dislocations. The fault intersects the bottom of the foil on the left and the top of the foil on the right. From an inspection of the outermost fringes in the three regions, it can be seen that the lower extensive length of fault, region 1, and the upper narrow region of fault, region 3, show contrast characteristic of intrinsic faulting, whilst the intermediate narrow region of fault, region 2, shows contrast characteristic of extrinsic faulting. The u of the lower dislocation was determined as $[8\bar{1}9]$ and that of the upper dislocations as $[\bar{1}01]$.

The only likely configurations of dissociated dislocations that could give rise to such a region of extrinsic fault contrast within regions of intrinsic fault contrast are ones involving the dissociation of $\frac{1}{2}\langle 110 \rangle$ dislocations on closely spaced (111) planes, so that regions of intrinsic fault overlap as illustrated in fig. 8.54. The possible Burgers vectors of Shockley partial dislocations bounding the three regions of fault on (111) are $\pm \frac{1}{6}[\bar{1}\bar{1}2]$, $\pm \frac{1}{6}[2\bar{1}\bar{1}]$ and $\pm \frac{1}{6}[\bar{1}2\bar{1}]$ and initially the most likely Burgers vectors can be chosen using invisibility criteria for diffracting vectors where $g \cdot R$ is integral. Images corresponding to three such diffracting vectors are given in figs. 8.53(c), (d) and (e). The partial dislocation separating region 1 from the perfect crystal and the partial dislocation separating region 1 from region 2 are in contrast for the diffracting vectors $0\bar{2}2$ and $\bar{3}11$ and out of contrast for the diffracting vector $3\bar{1}1$, suggesting a Burgers vector for these partials of $\pm \frac{1}{6}[\bar{1}\bar{1}2]$. The partial dislocation separating region 2 from region 3 and the partial dislocation separating region 3 from the perfect crystal are in contrast for the diffracting vectors $3\bar{1}1$ and $3\bar{1}1$ and out of contrast for the diffracting vector $0\bar{2}2$, suggesting a Burgers vector for these partials of $\pm \frac{1}{6}[2\bar{1}\bar{1}]$. With the determined line direction of the dislocations taken to be out of the paper in fig. 8.54, the Burgers vectors involved are specifically $\frac{1}{6}[\bar{1}\bar{1}2]$ and $\frac{1}{6}[\bar{2}11]$ which are distributed in each of the four possible configurations in the order indicated in fig. 8.54. It will be seen below that this preliminary designation of the Burgers vectors is confirmed by image computation.

Figure 8.55 shows five experimental images taken under different diffracting conditions for the top end of defect A, together with five matching com-

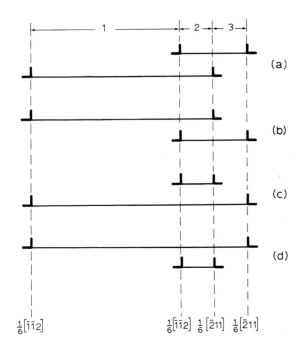

Fig. 8.54. Schematic illustration of possible configurations of partial dislocations and stacking faults for defect A of fig. 8.52.

puted images corresponding to the configuration given in fig. 8.54(a) where the separation of the slip planes Y is 0.01 ξ_{111a} (approximately one {111} interplanar spacing) and the lengths of regions 2 and 3 are 0.55 ξ_{111a} and 0.95 ξ_{111a} respectively. This final set of matching images was obtained by varying the slip plane separation Y and the extent of regions 2 and 3. The agreement between the experimental and computed images in fig. 8.55 confirms the designation made initially from invisibility criteria for the Burgers vectors at the top end of defect A. Confirmation of the Burgers vector assigned to the partial dislocation at the lower end of defect A was also obtained by image matching and matching computed and experimental images for this dislocation were shown earlier in fig. 8.19 of § 8.9.1.

Figure 8.56 shows, for four of the images in fig. 8.55, the influence of varying the slip plane separation Y for constant dimensions of regions 2 and 3. It is clear from a comparison of the experimental and computed images that Y is less than three {111} interplanar spacings and a detailed examination shows that the best agreement between the computed and experimental images is obtained when Y is one {111} interplanar spacing. Figure 8.57 shows for

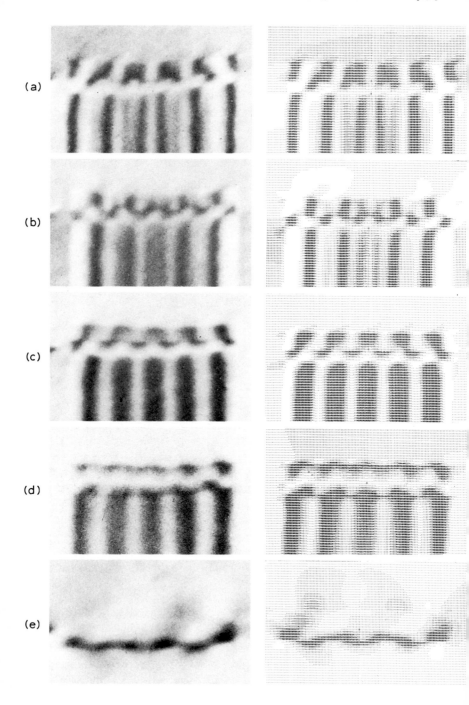

the same four images the effect of varying the dimension of region 2 for a fixed value of the dimension of the combined regions 2 + 3 of 1.5 ξ_{111a} (364 Å) at the optimum value for Y of one {111} interplanar spacing. Again comparison of the experimental and computed images indicates that the best value for the dimension of region 2 is in the range 0.5 to 0.6 ξ_{111a} (121 Å to 146 Å).

Images computed using the configuration of figs. 8.54 (b), (c) and (d) gave equally good agreement with the experimental images provided the same dimensions for regions 2, 3 and the slip plane separation were used. Thus, although it was not possible on the basis of image matching alone to decide between the different configurations of fig. 8.54, it was possible to conclude that the two faulted planes are neighbouring (111) planes and that the dimensions of regions 2 and 3 are (134 ± 15) Å and (230 ± 15) Å respectively.

A distinction between the four possible configurations for defect A depends on the results of calculations of the forces acting on the four partial dislocations when they are arranged in their determined positions, i.e. forces arising from elastic interactions between the dislocations and the tensions of the stacking faults (see, for example, Morton and Forwood, 1973). Such calculations indicate that, for the dimensions of the defect determined by image matching, configuration (a) of fig. 8.54 is the closest to equilibrium and is thus the most likely arrangement for defect A.

Fig. 8.55. Comparison of experimental and computed images of the top end of defect A (fig. 8.52) for five different diffraction conditions as given below:

	B	g	w
(a)	[167]	$\bar{1}\bar{1}1$	−0.25
(b)	[167]	$11\bar{1}$	−0.25
(c)	[167]	$11\bar{1}$	0.45
(d)	[034]	200	0.70
(e)	[155]	$0\bar{2}2$	0.25

F is [259], the separation Y of the slip planes is 0.01 ξ_{111a}, the lengths of regions 2 and 3 are 0.55 ξ_{111a} and 0.95 ξ_{111a} respectively.

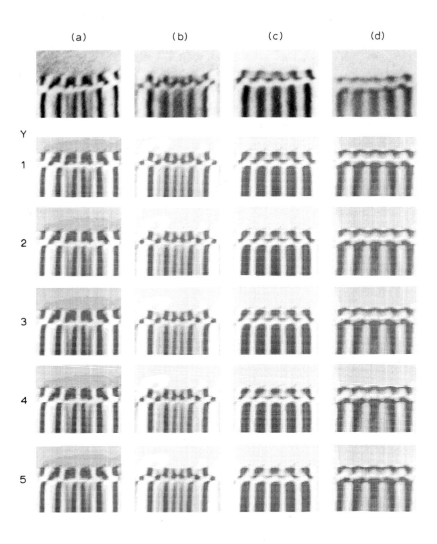

Fig. 8.56. Comparison of experimental and computed images (for the same diffraction conditions as images (a)–(d) of fig. 8.55) showing the influence of varying the slip plane separation Y for the constant dimensions of regions 2 and 3 of 0.55 ξ_{111a} and 0.95 ξ_{111a} respectively. The values of Y, in $\{111\}$ interplanar spacings, are indicated.

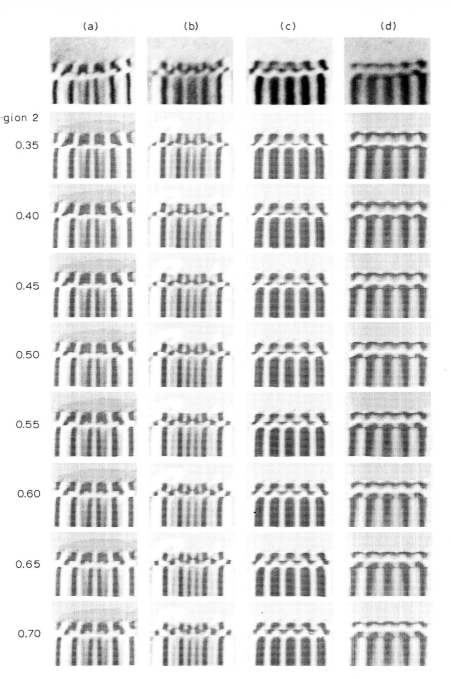

Fig. 8.57. Comparison of experimental and computed images (for the same diffraction conditions as images (a)–(d) of fig. 8.55) showing the influence of varying the dimension of region 2 for a constant value of Y of one $\{111\}$ interplanar spacing and a constant dimension of the combined regions 2 + 3 of 1.5 ξ_{111a}. The dimensions of region 2 in units of ξ_{111a} are indicated.

9 DISCUSSION OF THE APPLICATIONS AND LIMITATIONS OF THE TECHNIQUE

9.1. Introduction

The technique of using computed images to identify defects is both empirical in nature and specific in its application, so that it is impossible to define general rules which will apply to all cases. We can only discuss the applicability of the technique on the basis of our collective experience of its use over the last few years. We will consider the optimisation of experimental conditions and the organisation of the data so that the technique may have the best chance of success. Finally, the limitations of the programs and the theory on which they are based will be considered.

Since this discussion concerns results drawn mainly from our experience, it is necessary to indicate at the outset the scope of this. Our interest has been confined mainly to defects composed of dislocations and stacking faults in metals and alloys. The majority of these have had cubic symmetry (e.g. Cu, Al, Ni, Fe, Ag, Au, β-brass, Cu−Al, Cu−Si) and they have been examined in microscopes operating at 100 kV. We have always endeavoured to set up the experimental conditions so that they approximate as closely as possible to two-beam diffraction and we have usually only concerned ourselves with the bright field micrographs.

9.2. Uniqueness and the amount of information necessary to identify defects

Several assumptions have to be made when using an image matching technique such as the one described here to identify defects. These include the assumptions:

(i) that the theory used to compute the theoretical micrographs is a good approximation to the experimental conditions under which the electron micrographs were obtained;

(ii) that different defects give rise to different and unique sets of theoretical images; and

(iii) that sets of experimental images obtained from different defects are sufficiently different to be distinguished in practice.

Assumptions (i) and (iii) depend on experimental factors which may assume importance from case to case and thus it is not possible in general to say whether they are good or valid. However, there is a good basis for assumption (ii) and this is contained in two papers by Head (1969, b and c). He was able to show that for two-beam or n-beam systematic conditions, if a column approximation is assumed and if there is a direction in the crystal along which the displacements are constant, then (with certain specified exceptions) the component of the displacement field in the direction of the diffracting vector is uniquely specified by the theoretical micrograph which contains intensities but no phase information. It follows that a set of three micrographs of a defect for non-coplanar diffracting vectors is unique to that defect, completely specifies its displacement field and thus uniquely represents it. For the general n-beam case and with the above restrictions, three independent micrographs also serve to uniquely identify a defect, although it is no longer true that there is a direct connection between one micrograph and one component of the displacement field. These conclusions are equally valid for bright and dark field micrographs.

Now let us consider assumption (i). As applied to the image matching technique described in this book, the relevant conditions under which the uniqueness relations hold are those of a two-beam theory using a column approximation, and the existence of a direction in the crystal along which displacements are constant. If these conditions closely represent the situation in the real crystal, if the theoretical micrographs are computed under closely similar diffracting conditions to those for the experimental micrographs, and if the two sets of micrographs are a good match, then it is to be expected that there will be a high degree of correlation between a defect in the real crystal and the matching set of theoretical micrographs, i.e. assumption (i) above will be a good one.

The condition concerning the existence of a direction along which the displacement field is constant can never be exactly true in practice due to the presence of the foil surfaces and because it is also unlikely that the defect will be exactly straight. There is nothing that can be done to reduce the effect of these factors but in our experience they are rarely important.

Good experimental two-beam conditions can usually be achieved with a little manipulation (at least for the common metals and alloys examined at 100 kV). Further, by ensuring that the diffraction patterns are selected from the region of the defect, the diffracting conditions of the computed and experimental micrographs can be made closely similar. We shall see later (§9.4) that the other condition under which the uniqueness relation was obtained, the column approximation, is unlikely to impose a limitation in practice on the correlation between displacement field and image.

Very little is known about the validity of assumption (iii), although it has been our experience that, with one exception (§8.14), we have always been able to identify defects from their experimental images. However, as a guide to the validity of (iii) it is possible to examine the many sets of non-matching theoretical micrographs we have produced in the process of using the technique. A survey of these shows that in most cases they are sufficiently different from each other that the defects, had they existed in reality, could probably have been identified from their experimental micrographs.

Although the image matching technique requires that defects have unique and distinguishable *sets* of images, it is possible, of course, for two different defects to have identical displacement field components in a given direction. In this case, a two-beam micrograph of each of them taken with a diffracting vector along this direction will be identical. Figure 7.4 illustrates this point quite well. It will be seen that in fig. 7.4(e) micrographs 1(ii), 1(iii), 1(v), 1(vi), 3(ii), 3(iii), 3(v) and 3(vi) are all identical *; 1(i) and 3(i) are identical and 1(iv) and 3(iv) are identical. Similar identities hold for the corresponding micrographs in fig. 7.4(f) **.

There are occasions when sets of three micrographs are very similar even if these are taken with non-coplanar diffracting vectors. Compare, for example, micrographs 1(iv) and 3(iv) in fig. 7.4(b), $g = \bar{1}11$; fig. 7.4(e), $g = 20\bar{2}$; and fig. 7.4(h), $g = \bar{2}20$. Compare also the computed micrographs for dislocations having [111] and [010] Burgers vectors in fig. 5.8 for the $0\bar{1}1$, $1\bar{1}0$, $10\bar{1}$ and 020 diffracting vectors. Whilst it is true that there are differences in these sets of micrographs, it would probably entail considerable effort in computing and detailed matching to differentiate between them in practice. Because it is always an aim to create conditions in which the identification procedure is as

---

* In fact, slight differences may be detected in the computed images. These are due to the interpolated calculation of some of the intensities, to the calculation of intensities in columns which are slightly differently placed in the same displacement fields (due to the framing of the micrographs) or to computational inaccuracies. However, it can be shown analytically in this case that these images should be identical (see Appendix).
** These identities occur because the dislocation lines lie along an even-fold axis in the crystal. Under these conditions the displacements due to the edge and screw components of the Burgers vectors are separable (§2.7.2(ii)). Further, in fig. 7.4(e) and (f) the diffracting vector is exactly along the dislocation line so that both the contrast due to the fault and to the edge components of the dislocations is zero. The remaining contrast is due to the screw components and these happen to be the same in the the cases cited above.

simple and as effortless as possible and since, in general, there is no way of knowing in advance how alike sets of micrographs of different defects will be, it is important to collect the experimental information using many different diffracting vectors and not just three or four non-coplanar ones.

If theoretical micrographs are computed for all the possible defects and for all the experimental micrographs, it is likely that the computing time and the effort involved may be excessive. Usually a selection of experimental images is made and theoretical micrographs are computed corresponding to these for all the possible defects. The basis on which the choice of images is made is fairly standard from case to case and takes note of two factors: the set of micrographs selected must contain images taken with at least three non-coplanar diffracting vectors (preferably more) and should include the images with distinct topological features, i.e. the most characteristic images. Such a selection usually results in attention being focussed on six to eight images.

It may also be the case that the number of defects or defect configurations which are possible candidates for the unknown defect is quite large and in these cases a further selection has to be made in the initial stages of the matching procedure. This selection may be done on the basis of the symmetry of the experimental images of the defect (see Appendix), the known deformation behaviour, a currently held hypothesis, or perhaps a theoretical estimate of the relative energy or stability of the defects.

Of course, it is possible that these selection processes result in sets of theoretical micrographs which are too similar and if this is the case, a large amount of effort in detailed matching may well be avoided by increasing the scope of the computations to include other experimental images. In any case, it is suggested that if selections have to be made in order to reduce the preliminary computing to a minimum, when an apparent final match and identification have been made, some of the initially excluded micrographs and possibilities should be computed. This gives added checks and provides greater confidence in the identification.

9.3. Optimisation of the technique

The need for positive identification of defects in crystals usually arises because of their contribution to some physical problem of interest. It is often the case that many examples of a given type of defect exist in a specimen and when this happens, it is obviously advantageous to choose the most suitable ones for detailed examination. Some of the defects may be unsuitable for practical reasons (e.g., they lie in bent or thick areas of the foil) but of the remaining defects it is wise to select those which may be identified with the least effort.

The *ideal* conditions under which a defect or defect configuration may most easily be identified by image matching are as follows. As many different micrographs as possible of the defect should be taken under good two-beam conditions. The images should be as full of character as possible. The micrographs should be taken in beam directions which are as widely spaced as possible (say 30° or 40°) so that the crystallography of the defect and the foil may be determined accurately. Good selected area diffraction patterns should be obtained corresponding to each micrograph so that the diffraction conditions in the region of the defect may be accurately specified. The defect itself should be straight, run right through the foil from one surface to the other at an angle of between 30° and 60°, and be far from other defects.

These ideal conditions may seldom be achieved in practice. The reasons for these being regarded as ideal are given in the following pages and an attempt is made to indicate what magnitude of deviation from these conditions may be acceptable without resulting in too much effort, on the one hand, or a mis-identification on the other.

The matching procedure consists of comparing the topology of the computed and experimental images. The topology of an image is, of course, just the varying pattern of intensity distribution of the image. Thus the image matching technique makes use of relative intensity values (particularly with respect to background intensity) and their distribution over an area in the proximity of the defect. Although the overall intensity of one micrograph of a defect taken under one set of diffracting conditions may be compared with that of another of the same defect taken under a different set of conditions, as far as possible no importance is given to absolute values of intensity *
This is because of the possible inadequacies of the theory where the computed intensities arise from elastically scattered electrons. The occurrence of inelastic scattering processes is represented in the Howie—Whelan theory as absorption, but in fact, many of these 'absorbed' electrons reach the image giving rise to other intensity distributions. However it appears that this effect is either small in magnitude, has a similar topology to that produced by the elastic scattering process **, or produces more or less uniform intensity over the whole of the image ***. Because of these characteristics of inelastic scat-

---

* The only case where absolute intensities have been used in conjunction with image matching is in the identification of overlapping stacking fault configurations (§ 8.13).
** This seems to be so experimentally for most of the inelastically scattered electrons passing through the objective aperture when this is placed around an elastically scattered beam in the usual way (Kamiya and Uyeda, 1961). It also seems to be the case theoretically for plasmon scattering and possibly small-angle, single electron scattering (see for example, Howie, 1970).
*** This seems to be the case for thermal diffuse scattering (e.g. Howie, 1970; Doyle, private communication). Since plasmon scattering, single electron excitation and thermal diffuse scattering are the main forms of inelastic scattering, the statements made above seem to be largely substantiated.

tering, it can be expected that the topology of the image calculated by the Howie–Whelan theory is approximately correct.

Quite often, the most striking and characteristic topological features of an image occur close to the points where the defect intersects the free surfaces of the foil. As discussed earlier in §4.2 (see also §9.5), the displacements around a defect in a real crystal in these regions are not those assumed in computing the theoretical micrographs. It was for this reason that at first we did not use the features of the image close to the surface for image matching, and indeed we are still wary of doing this. However, our experience is that the surface details of an image may be adequately matched in about 90% of the cases we have considered.

The free surfaces impose conditions on the stresses existing there and these affect not only the displacements, but may also act on the defect in such a way that it deviates from the direction which it occupies in the interior of the crystal. Such deviations may not be directly observable, but they will have some influence on the images obtained from the surface regions. This is a possible reason why the matching of surface detail seems to be worst in the case of single dislocations and best in the case of planar defects which are under more geometrical constraints (see for example, the excellent matching obtained for the region where the step in the complex loop meets the surface of the foil in fig. 8.32).

The programs are written for straight defects and indeed depend on this assumption for their speed. Experimentally, it is not possible to know whether a defect is truly straight, since any small departure from linearity may only be detected through its effect on the image. However, there are cases when the images of a defect indicate that it is most certainly not straight and a decision has to be made as to whether its images can be matched adequately by computed micrographs. These decisions are probably dependent both on the degree of elastic anisotropy of the material and on the deviation from linearity of the defect. For materials such as copper, nickel or aluminium, we have successfully matched dislocation images which have a maximum variation in their line direction of about $10°$. The examples of the single dislocation in aluminium in ch. 5 and of the Shockley dislocation in Cu–Al in ch. 7 are cases in point. The examples of sharply bent dislocations in β-brass shown in fig. 8.13 have a variation of their line direction of about $55°$ and it is apparent from the appearance of the images of the two arms of the bend that these could not be adequately matched by a single straight dislocation running in the mean direction. On the other hand, the images of dislocations in β-brass which are apparently straight and which have Burgers vectors of $\langle 1\,1\,1 \rangle$ are very similar for a range of orientation of $5°$ or $10°$ about screw. Thus a curve in such a dislocation of this order of magnitude would not be a serious impediment to matching its image.

The bent dislocations referred to above and shown in fig. 8.13 actually do not extend right through the foil, but both segments intersect the same surface. More commonly, dislocations run right through the foil from one surface to the other. Although dislocations may not end within the interior of the crystal, they may of course terminate where they interact with other dislocations. In general however, the type of defects which may be matched best are those which are straight, do not interact with or come close to other defects and which run right through the foil at an angle of 30°–60° with the surface. The ideal angle is restricted to this range only in as much that it ensures reasonable resolution in a standardly framed micrograph without recourse to computing the image in several parts. The examples used in ch. 5 to illustrate the use of the ONEDIS program, slope through the foil at angles of approximately 63° and 46° and those used in ch. 7 slope at angles of approximately 15° and 19°. In the first case, the images are adequately represented on a standardly framed micrograph or at most on two adjoining micrographs, whereas in the second case the images have been constructed from two or three adjoining micrographs. Thus, if a choice is possible, a defect which slopes through the foil at, say, 45° offers the possibility of identification with about $\frac{1}{2}$ or $\frac{1}{3}$ the computing effort of one which slopes at an angle of 15°.

Although programs could be written to compute the image of a defect parallel to the surface of the foil, the usefulness of the image matching technique in identifying such defects with these programs would be minimal. There are two reasons for this. First, since the defect is at a constant depth in the foil, its image would be the same all along its length. There would be no variations in intensity and no characteristic topology. Secondly, the depth of the defect in the foil would probably have to be measured fairly precisely if the images were to be matched in detail and as we have seen, such measurements (including the thickness of the foil itself) are amongst the least well-known of the parameters.

For similar reasons, it is difficult to match and identify a small segment of dislocation (say one or two extinction distances long) located in the interior of the foil, even if it is sloping at an optimum angle. There is usually too little characteristic topology and its depth in the foil has to be known accurately. Since such small segments can only arise through interactions with other dislocations (e.g., it is part of a polygonal loop or a dislocation network), another and possibly over-riding consideration in trying to match these is the effect of the displacement fields of the adjoining dislocations. However, our experience in matching segments of dislocation whose length is of the order of three or four extinction distances (e.g., the arms of the bent dislocation in fig. 8.13 and the edges of the large polygonal loops in §§8.10 and 8.11) shows that successful matching can be obtained in such cases.

Having chosen a particular example for identification, there are two general ways in which the user can enhance the prospects of the technique. The first of these is to choose suitable images. The advisability of using as many diffracting vectors as possible and the basis on which to make a choice of images to match, has already been discussed. A factor involved in this last point is the character of the images and the operator has a degree of control over this through varying the value of the deviation parameter w. In general, images taken with large positive values of w tend to lack strong characteristic features (see for example, fig. 5.6(b)), whilst images taken with small positive (e.g. fig. 5.6(a) or fig. 5.5(a)) or small negative (e.g. fig. 5.5(c)) values of w have much more character. However, the rate of change of character with w is usually quite large at zero or negative w, so that the value of w needs to be known quite accurately in order to obtain a good matching image. Thus, small or moderate positive values of w are recommended for obtaining characteristic images without the necessity for undue accuracy.

The second way in which the user may enhance the prospects of the technique whilst minimising the total effort, involves the question touched on above, namely the accuracy of the several parameters which enter into the calculation. In general, it can be said that small changes in the parameters produce small changes in the image and, therefore, difficulty is only likely to be encountered in the exceptional cases when an image is particularly sensitive to a particular parameter. The parameters may be considered in two groups: those such as the deviation parameter w, the thickness of the foil t and the anomalous absorption coefficient $\mathcal{A}$, which have a direct and consistent influence on the image, and those such as the defect line direction u, the electron beam direction B and the foil normal F, which in general have a smaller effect on an image except in sporadic cases of high sensitivity. In the rest of this section we try to indicate the ranges of error in the parameters which are generally acceptable and the types of situation in which sensitivity to particular parameters might occur. The information has been collated from our joint experience and as such it is of limited scope. It should be emphasised, therefore, that the following remarks are only intended to be helpful suggestions and in no way constitute a set of rules which apply to all situations.

The electron beam direction B is determined from the Kikuchi line pattern and is usually known to $\pm\frac{1}{2}°$. Although this is more than enough to ensure good matching, it is necessary in order to determine u and F accurately by stereographic analysis. In connection with this parameter, an approximation to be avoided is the substitution of the nearest low order direction for the accurate beam direction determined from the Kikuchi line pattern. An example of how this practice may affect the image is shown for the case of a complex faulted loop in fig. 8.33(c) computed for $B = [011]$ and in fig. 8.33(b) computed for the accurate direction B = [057]. The beam direction [057] is typical of those used in the neighbourhood of [011] in order to set up good two-beam diffraction conditions. Such sensitivity has most often occurred for planar defects where the beam direction is nearly parallel to the plane of the defect or for multi-component defects whose component images interact strongly (for example, the images of dislocation dipoles, figs. 8.43(c), 8.44 and 8.48).

Both u and F are determined by stereographic analysis using micrographs taken with the foil in various orientations. The graphical nature of the method and the restriction to only moderate angles of tilt (up to about ±30°) result in the best accuracy obtainable for these parameters being about ±2°. More commonly it is ±4°. The effect of such variations in the value of u on the image was discussed earlier where it was estimated that variations of this magnitude were unlikely to be serious.

Errors or inaccuracies in the determination of the foil normal can affect the image in two ways. First, they will affect the value determined for t' (THBM), the thickness of the foil in the beam direction. The value of F enters the calculation of t' through the factor $1/\cos\delta$ where δ is the angle between the beam direction and the foil normal. For the angles of tilt available on most microscopes (up to ±30°), $\cos\delta$ is a slowly varying function and thus errors in t' arising from inaccuracies in F are likely to be small. The other way in which F affects the image is by producing a 'shearing' or 'skewing' effect compared with images computed for the case when F and B are coincident (Humble, 1968b). We have observed the degree of shearing to be sensitive to the precise value of F in only one or two cases. These have involved faulted defects and multi-component defects which were shallowly inclined to the foil surface. It was found in these cases that the angle of the fault fringes or the offset of the images changed markedly for variations in F of the order of 3° or 4°.

As mentioned earlier, the parameters w, t and $\mathscr{A}$ have a much more direct and consistent effect on defect images than the sporadic sensitivity caused by u, B or F. Variations in the value of $\mathscr{A}$ usually have a noticeable effect on the enhancement of contrast in the image (that is, the relative sizes of the black and white areas) and can have an effect on the numbers of oscillations in the image (e.g. the appearance of subsidiary fringes in the image of a stacking fault as the value of $\mathscr{A}$ is decreased). The most noticeable effect of t or w on an image, for positive values of w, is the variation in the number of oscillations. In fact as t or w is decreased (say) the topology of the image varies in a more or less cyclic way. This may be seen in fig. 5.2 for sequences of decreasing t at constant w. It may also be seen from fig. 5.2 that over small ranges, t and w are complementary, small increases in t (or w) being approximately compensated by small decreases in w (or t) (cf. the images for $t = 4.38\,\xi_{020}$, $w = 0.50$ and for $t = 4.53\,\xi_{020}$ and $w = 0.45$). Figure 5.2 also illustrates that the areas of extreme contrast in an image tend to be largest at small t or small w.

In addition to the individual sensitivity of images to these parameters, a compound sensitivity has been observed. If any one (or more) of w, t and $\mathscr{A}$ is small * the images have tended to be sensitive to small variations in all three. An example where this sensitivity was usefully employed was in the determination of the anomalous absorption coefficient operating for a 1 1 1 diffracting vector in Cu + 8 at % Si (§ 8.5).

Inaccuracies in w and t arise from inaccuracies in the experimental measurements and also from uncertainties in the values of extinction distance.

Experimental errors in w are straight forward and are due only to errors in measurement of the deviation parameter s from the diffraction pattern. The foil thickness t has usually been estimated by counting fringes or oscillations of contrast in the image and correcting this number (which is the thickness of the foil in the beam direction measured in units of the apparent extinction distance ξ_{ga}) for the effects of w and the tilt of the foil. Although any single measurement is only accurate to about half an oscillation, averaging over several micrographs taken with the same type of diffracting vector enhances the accuracy appreciably. Nevertheless, the foil thickness is probably the least accurate of the experimental parameters and this is the reason that the DELUGE modification is so useful. It will be recalled that this modification enables the user to produce quickly a large number of micrographs of a given defect in foils of different thicknesses.

An additional measure usually applied to the evaluation of t is to scale the values obtained from micrographs with different diffracting vectors to units of one particular extinction distance using extinction distance ratios. This is meant to take account of the fact that the thickness of the foil is constant irrespective of the diffracting vector. Although this procedure is reasonable in principle, in practice it relies on the applicability of the ratios of the theoretical two-beam extinction distances. This brings us to consider therefore the contribution of uncertain values of the extinction distances to inaccuracies in t and w and this in turn requires an appraisal of the validity of the two-beam approximation.

This topic was discussed to some extent in § 2.6. There it was stated that many of the shortcomings in comparing a two-beam theory with an experimental situation can often be accommodated by using a different extinction distance, the apparent extinction distance ξ_{ga}. This artificiality is particularly applicable to two-beam experimental micrographs where, in fact, the n-beam systematic condition is a fuller description of the experimental situation than the two-beam description. In such cases which have been examined in

---

* As a rough guide, the term 'small' implies values of $\mathscr{A} < 0.05$, values of w in the range $0 < w < 0.2$ and values of $t/\xi_g < 3.0$.

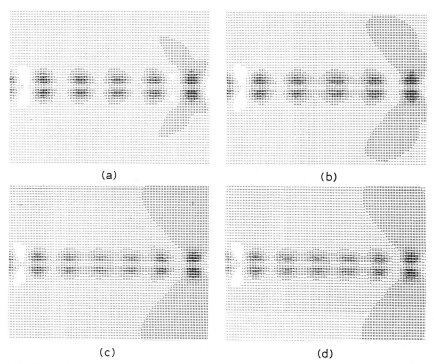

Fig. 9.1. Bright-field theoretical images of a [111] screw dislocation in β-brass computed for two-beams (000, $\overline{1}\overline{1}0$) in (a); three-beams (110, 000, $\overline{1}\overline{1}0$) in (b); four-beams (110, 000, $\overline{1}\overline{1}0$, $\overline{2}\overline{2}0$) in (c), and five-beams (110, 000, $\overline{1}\overline{1}0$, $\overline{2}\overline{2}0$, $\overline{3}\overline{3}0$) in (d). The thickness of the foil is constant (5.0 ξ_{110}) and the deviation from the Bragg condition for the $\overline{1}\overline{1}0$ diffracting vector is the same in all micrographs (0.5). B is [001], F is [001] and the values of extinction distance and anomalous absorption coefficient used in the calculations were:

n	1	2	3	4
ξ_{nn0}	324 Å	693 Å	1446 Å	3000 Å
$\mathscr{A}_{nn0}$	0.1	0.196	0.283	0.345

detail, the value of ξ_{ga} is invariably less than the theoretical value ξ_g. This is illustrated for the case of β-brass in fig. 9.1. Figures 9.1(a), (b), (c) and (d) show the theoretical image of a screw dislocation in β-brass computed for 2, 3, 4 and 5 systematic beams respectively. The micrographs are computed for a constant foil thickness (5 ξ_{110}) and a constant deviation from the Bragg condition for the $\overline{1}\overline{1}0$ diffracting vector ($w_{\overline{1}\overline{1}0} = 0.5$). It will be noticed that the character of the image remains very similar throughout the series although the apparent foil thickness, as indicated by the number of oscillations in contrast, increases from (a) to (d). Thus, apart from the aspect of foil thickness, the micrograph in fig. 9.1(a) is as good for image matching purposes as that in fig. 9.1(d). It can also be observed that there is very little difference be-

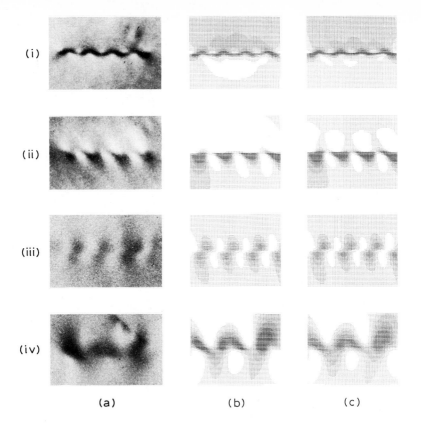

(i)

(ii)

(iii)

(iv)

(a)   (b)   (c)

Fig. 9.2. Four experimental images of a dislocation in aluminium (a), together with matching sets of theoretical micrographs computed on a two-beam approximation (b), and a four-beam systematic approximation (c). b is $\frac{1}{2}[101]$, u is $[135]$, F is $[\bar{2}35]$, and the thickness of the foil was taken to be constant at 1830 Å in (b) and 1760 Å in (c). The nominal two-beam diffracting vectors g are listed below and the corresponding four-beam theoretical micrographs were computed using diffracting vectors $-g$, 000, g and $2g$. The other parameters used in the calculations were:

	g	B	w for (b)	w^* for (c)
(i)	$\bar{1}1\bar{1}$	$[\bar{3}12]$	0.62	0.566
(ii)	$\bar{1}1\bar{1}$	$[\bar{1}12]$	0.64	0.578
(iii)	020	$[\bar{9}08]$	0.60	0.60
(iv)	$0\bar{2}2$	$[\bar{7}33]$	0.67	0.726

n	1	2	3
ξ_{nnn}	620 Å	1690 Å	3410 Å
$\mathscr{A}_{nnn}$	0.059	0.112	0.147
ξ_{2n00}	748 Å	2123 Å	4670 Å
$\mathscr{A}_{2n00}$	0.066	0.125	0.158
ξ_{2n2n0}	1233 Å	4080 Å	12230 Å
$\mathscr{A}_{2n2n0}$	0.086	0.153	0.169

Note that in some micrographs in (a) the contrast is affected by the presence of a nearby dislocation.

* This value of w is for the nominal two-beam diffracting vector.

tween the 4 and 5 beam micrographs, indicating perhaps that the effect on the image of any additional beams would be small. This point has not been checked further because of the increased time for computation, fig. 9.1(c) taking 30 min to compute and fig. 9.1(d), 80 min.

Figure 9.1 concerns theoretical calculations only, but fig. 9.2(a)–(c) illustrates the inter-comparison of a set of experimental images (a) of a dislocation in aluminium with a set of theoretical images computed on a two-beam approximation and with a set of theoretical images computed on a four-beam systematic approximation. In each of the theoretical cases the parameters are identical except for foil thickness and deviation from the Bragg condition and these are within the experimentally measured range. It can be seen that each set provides an adequate match to the experimental images, but whereas each of the micrographs in fig. 9.2(c) took about 30 min to compute, those in fig. 9.2(b) took only about 40 sec. The advantage of being able to use the latter set rather than the former with insignificant changes in image character is obvious.

The many examples of image matching shown throughout this book bear witness implicitly to the empirical fact that most 'two-beam' experimental images can be adequately matched by a two-beam theory. Examples such as those shown in figs. 9.1 and 9.2 explicitly demonstrate the phenomenon and indicate that the major change which has to be made is a simple dimension change, ξ_g to ξ_{ga}. From cases where ξ_{ga} has been determined it appears that the differences between ξ_g and ξ_{ga} and between the ratios of ξ_g and the ratios of ξ_{ga} are sufficiently small that the consequent changes in w and t are within their experimental errors.

It should be mentioned that the concept of an apparent extinction distance has not been applied consistently between t and w. The foil thickness t has usually been obtained by counting oscillations in the experimental images and it is thus measured directly in units of the apparent extinction distance. The dimensionless deviation parameter w on the other hand, is invariably obtained by taking the product of the deviation parameter s with the theoretical extinction distance ξ_g. The advantage of obtaining t and w in this way is that it is the easiest and most straightforward method and the justification of the procedure is that, in general, the differences between ξ_g and ξ_{ga} are small.

We have found two or three cases in which the differences between the theoretical extinction distance and the apparent extinction distance seem to be observable. These cases have involved both the relative values of extinction distances and their absolute values. The example of defect B in ch. 7 involved both these aspects. In that case it was found impossible to obtain adequate matching by scaling foil thickness in the ratios of ξ_g and yet obtain values of the separation S_p of the two dislocations which agreed from micrograph to micrograph. The images were then re-matched with the constraint of scaling foil thickness in the ratios of ξ_g removed and a value of ξ_{ga} was determined for each of the matching pairs of micrographs. This was done by measuring a dimension on the experimental image (between two prominent features) and comparing it with the same measurement on the matching computed micrographs. The latter measurement was obtained in extinction distances using the dimensions of the micrograph, WL and WW and the former measurement was obtained in Ångströms using the magnification of the micrograph. It should be remembered that the magnification of a micrograph is usually difficult to assess because of the variation in magnification with the tilt of the specimen in the microscope. This accounts for the rather large errors in ξ_{ga}.

Following this second procedure for image matching, it was found that better matches could be obtained to the experimental images, and using the values of ξ_{ga} the foil thickness was constant to within acceptable limits and the values of S_p which were obtained were in better agreement. Thus, internal consistency was achieved between the quality of the image matching, the constancy of the foil thickness and the determination of the various critical parameters.

In summary, therefore, in the majority of cases the differences between ξ_g and ξ_{ga} are unimportant for image matching and defect identification, although the aptness of the concept of an apparent extinction distance is one factor responsible for the general excellence of the comparison between theory and experiment. However, it should be emphasised that to obtain the value of a linear dimension in absolute units, the value of ξ_{ga} rather than ξ_g must always be used.

9.4. Limitations in the theory

This section and the following one discuss limitations of the image matching technique arising from limitations in the theory as it may apply to the experimental situation (§9.4) or from limitations due to the specific nature of the programs (§9.5).

The theory of electron diffraction which has been used, is a two-beam theory based on a column approximation. As presented here, the equations describing such a theory (eqs. (2.5)) apply only to centrosymmetric crystals. The parameters used in the equations are based on the diffraction of electrons by a perfect crystal, but the formulation given applies to imperfect or distorted crystals and includes a term in R, the displacement of the atoms from their perfect crystal positions. That is, the displacements due to the presence of defects are assumed to produce only a small perturbation on the perfect crystal parameters. In calculating the displacements due to defects in the crystal, linear anisotropic continuum elasticity theory was used. Each of these limitations will be examined in turn.

Limitations due to the restriction of the theory to two beams were discussed in the previous section. Our experience including the specific examples shown in figs. 9.1 and 9.2 indicate that for two-beam experimental conditions, adequate matching and identification can be carried out using a two-beam theory. It should be emphasised, however, that our experience is limited in the main to microscopes operating at 100 kV, to elements and alloys of low or medium atomic number and to crystals with relatively small unit cells. The possibility of setting up a good experimental approximation to two-beam conditions, and hence the adequacy of matching may be much reduced at high accelerating voltages, or for crystals containing atoms of high atomic number or having large unit cells.

The equations as given in ch. 2 (eqs. (2.5)) describe diffraction in centro-symmetric crystals. In principle, non-centrosymmetry introduces a difference between diffraction with diffracting vectors g and $-g$; i.e. a violation of Friedel's law. In other words, an electron travelling in the direction of the transmitted beam will be diffracted differently (by one side of the diffracting planes) compared with an electron travelling in the direction of the diffracted beam (which is being scattered by the other side of the diffracting planes). This will lead to differences in the extinction and absorption parameters for the transmitted and diffracted directions. Gevers et al. (1966) have pointed out that electrons emerging from a crystal in the transmitted beam will have been reflected an equal number of times from both sides of the diffracting planes and have suggested that the effect of non-centrosymmetry may, there-fore, be averaged out. If this is so, then it might be expected that the effect of non-centrosymmetry on bright field micrographs would be small. Since electrons emerging in the diffracted beam have been scattered an unequal number of times by each side of the diffracting planes, it was suggested that the effects of non-centrosymmetry may be more marked in the dark field image.

Gevers et al. have also shown that the Howie–Whelan equations can be extended to non-centrosymmetric crystals so that there is no restriction in principle to extending the image matching technique to defects in such crystals, but experiments in this area have yet to be done.

The column approximation which is made in the Howie–Whelan theory is such that the resulting equations apply to independent, non-interacting columns in the crystal and hence give independent values of intensity at neighbouring points in the image. As can be seen from expression (2.5), the equations describing a column approximation contain only terms of the form $d\phi/dz$ and ϕ where ϕ is the electron amplitude and z is the coordinate in the direction of the incident beam. The equations which describe a theory of electron diffraction without the limitations of a column approximation, contains terms of the form $\partial\phi/\partial x$, $\partial\phi/\partial y$, $\partial^2\phi/\partial x^2$, $\partial^2\phi/\partial y^2$ and $\partial^2\phi/\partial z^2$ in addition to the terms in $\partial\phi/\partial z$ and ϕ. Howie and Basinski (1968) have investigated the validity of the column approximation *. They indicate that the term in $\partial^2\phi/\partial z^2$ is small since $\partial\phi/\partial z$ is of the order of the extinction distance and relatively constant no matter what the distortion of the crystal. The existence of such a term corresponds physically to electron waves travelling in the $-z$ direction. Neglecting it, therefore, takes cognisance of the fact that in electron diffraction most of the scattering is in the forward direction. The terms in $\partial\phi/\partial x$ and $\partial\phi/\partial y$ are multiplied by the component of the vector $(\boldsymbol{k} + \boldsymbol{g})$ in the x and y directions respectively where $\boldsymbol{k}$ is the incident wave vector of magnitude $1/\lambda$. Since $\boldsymbol{k}$ is very much larger than $\boldsymbol{g}$ and since it is in the z direction, it follows that these x and y components are quite small. Thus their products with $\partial\phi/\partial x$ and $\partial\phi/\partial y$ will also be small unless ϕ changes significantly in the x and y directions over distances of the order of $\theta_B \xi_g$ where θ_B is the Bragg angle. For electron diffraction, $\theta_B \xi_g \lesssim 10$ Å and in most situations it is assumed that variations in ϕ over distances of this magnitude in x and y can only occur due to equally rapid variations of the displacement field $\boldsymbol{R}$. The rapid variations in $\partial\phi/\partial x$ and $\partial\phi/\partial y$ may or may not be reflected as large values of $\partial^2\phi/\partial x^2$ and $\partial^2\phi/\partial y^2$, but in any case, compared with the major term $\partial\phi/\partial z$, these quantities are multiplied by the factor $1/|\boldsymbol{k}|$ and so their effect is small. Thus it would appear that for slowly varying displacement fields $\boldsymbol{R}$, all terms are small compared with $\partial\phi/\partial z$ and the equations reduce to those describing a column approximation. The fact that $\boldsymbol{R}$ is slowly varying for dislocations in the sense meant here, was indicated by calculations of Howie and Basisnski for edge and screw dislocations in an isotropic medium. They found a maximum of 1% difference in intensities computed using a non-column theory compared with those using a column approximation.

Physically, therefore, the validity of the column approximation in electron diffraction depends on the small Bragg angles involved, the predominance of forward scattering, and, for distorted crystals, on the variation of the displacement field being small over distances of the order of 10 Å. In the types of application we have considered, this condition on the displacement field is generally realised except in the region of the core of a dislocation or on passing through a stacking fault. It will be recalled that the interaction of the electron waves with a stacking fault was treated as an interface problem to overcome this difficulty, but due to the continuous nature of the displacement field around a dislocation, the core region of that defect could not be

---

* They have also discussed many of the other aspects of the theory touched on in this section.

treated in a similar way. Thus, since the rates of change of R (i.e. the strains) are large in the neighbourhood of the core, we may expect the column approximation to break down. However, this region of large strain is quite small in extent ($\sim$ 20 Å or so) since for dislocations, the strains fall off inversely with the distance from the centre of the defect. As the observed image of a dislocation extends over a distance of the order of hundreds of Ångströms, the detail from such a small region usually makes a negligible contribution to the overall topology of the image. Figures 8.31 and 8.33 contain experimental and computed images in which features (a fine dark line in fig. 8.31 and a narrow light region in fig. 8.33) within 20 Å of the cores of *two* dislocations are matched quite well. Several other examples could be quoted from ch. 8 in which a critical part of the image (for image matching purposes) is produced by columns passing close to the dislocation core and yet the experimental and computed micrographs agree well in this area.

This observation not only has relevance to the validity of the column approximation, as discussed above, but also has a bearing on the linear continuum approximation used to derive the elastic displacement field R. Near the core, the strains are large so that it is to be expected that the linear theory (Hooke's law) would break down and also, as the centre of the defect is approached, the discrete nature of the lattice becomes more evident. To the authors' knowledge the contrast from dislocations has never been calculated using second-order elasticity theory or atomistic models of the dislocation. However, the same arguments apply here as were used above: namely that the region of the image affected is a relatively small portion of the whole and in cases such as those of figs. 8.31 and 8.33, the approximation seems to be essentially valid even close to the dislocation core.

9.5. Restrictions inherent in the programs

We now consider the limitations arising from the way the theory has been used, rather than the limitations inherent in the basic theory.

In order to achieve the speed of computation of the theoretical micrographs, it was necessary to assume that the linear defects were straight, parallel and of infinite length. It is not possible to apply this computational method to cases where the displacements are markedly affected by a free surface or where the defects are distinctly non-parallel (e.g. a dislocation network), have a three-dimensional nature (e.g. voids, small precipitates or stacking fault tetrahedra) or a small radius of curvature (e.g. small dislocation loops).

As the programs are presented in the following chapter, they are limited to foils of constant thickness. It has already been shown in §4.3.3 that micrograph programs can easily be constructed for defects in tapered foils. However, there are two particular problems associated with such programs.

The first of these concerns the definition and calculation of background intensity. It is clear that if there is a large change in foil thickness in the region of the defect, then the defect image will be superimposed on a background which consists of thickness fringes. Such was the case, for example, for the dislocation shown in fig. 9.2(a). In fact, this defect has been adequately matched and identified using a standard program which assumes a constant foil thickness, thus neglecting the presence of the thickness fringes and any interaction between them and the defect image. However, if the taper of the foil has to be taken into account, then the true value of the normal absorption coefficient will have to be used in the programs *. In addition, some base value of intensity would have to be chosen, so that when the calculated intensities are normalised to this value, the micrograph can be reproduced within the limited photographic range of the grey scale contained in subroutine HALFTN.

In the program for a tapered foil which has been written, the background intensity corresponding to each value of thickness (each column of the micrograph, in this case, since the program corresponds to the generalised cross-section shown in fig. 4.11(b)) is calculated and the image intensities are normalised to these values (column by column). This produces a micrograph with a constant symbol for background intensity which can be handled by HALFTN. It is suitable for cases where a small change in thickness produces a much larger change in the image than in background intensity. This is the case with the image shown in fig. 8.8(b).

The second point which should be mentioned in conjunction with programs concerned with tapered foils is the definition of foil normal. For the type of program illustrated by fig. 4.11(b) the foil normal refers to the normal to the upper surface of the foil, whereas in fig. 4.11(c) the foil normal is to be identified with the normal to the mid-plane in the specimen. The difference between these definitions and between them and the assumptions made in measuring the foil normal experimentally are not generally important. However, it should be borne in mind that the differences they produce in the image may be of the same order (although not of the same kind) as those arising from the taper in the foil. Thus, in writing and using such programs, care should be exercised to obtain compatibility.

Without a doubt, the main limitation inherent in the programs is their

---

* It will be recalled that in programs written for a constant foil thickness, the micrographs are independent of normal absorption which is put equal to the value of anomalous absorption for ease and speed of computation (§ 2.4.1).

restriction to those situations for which a generalised cross-section can be defined, but the speed of the method comes from this restriction. One aspect of the restriction to a generalised cross-section is the neglect of surface relaxations. It was stated in §4.2 that whilst the assumption that the displacements at a free surface are just those calculated for an infinite crystal is unphysical, the presence of a free surface should not be taken to mean that the displacements are zero there. At a free surface only the stresses which act across the surface must be zero; in general the other stresses and the displacements will be non-zero. This problem has been considered by Yoffe (1961) for the case of a dislocation meeting a free surface in an isotropic medium. The expressions for the displacements around a dislocation with arbitrary Burgers vector meeting the surface at an arbitrary angle, are extremely lengthy and complex and theoretical micrographs corresponding to this situation have not been computed. It can be said, however, that in the majority of cases we have considered, the 'no-relaxation' approximation appears to be adequate for image matching purposes. Moreover, since the most characteristic features of an image often originate in regions of crystal near the surface, such features assume a special importance and tend to be used quite frequently in the matching process. As explained earlier (§9.3), at first we were reluctant to do this in view of the assumptions used to compute the theoretical micrographs, but gradually we have come to accept such features as generally reliable. Nevertheless, this is a particular aspect of image matching which has to be continually reviewed from image to image, since some images have been found, particularly those from single dislocations, which could only be poorly matched in the surface regions.

Because of the necessity to define a generalised cross-section, the defects considered must be straight or planar. In the case of multi-component defects, the linear components must be parallel and the planar components must contain a common direction which is parallel to all linear components present. Thus for example the images of non-parallel dislocations, dislocation loops or stacking fault tetrahedra cannot be computed using the present technique, although of course, the images of large defects of this sort can be approximated segment by segment. If the theoretical images of defects for which a generalised cross-section cannot be defined are required in micrograph form, then each intensity point in the image must be the subject of a separate integration through the thickness of the foil. If all the points in one of the micrographs were obtained independently, this would require some 7740 integrations of the equations through the thickness of the foil. This number compares with an equivalent number of 240 integrations for the present way the micrographs are computed, and so, other things being equal, micrographs of non-generalised cross-section defects would need about 30 times more computer time. That is, they would take about 20 minutes each. This is generally unacceptable. Of course, it is possible to use interpolation to obtain the intensities of say one half or one third of the points, but this will only reduce the time for a micrograph by factors of two or three. Thus, in order to compute the micrographs of such defects economically, it would appear necessary to adopt a different approach.

Several authors (Bullough et al., 1971; Thölén, 1970(a) and (b); Hörl, 1971 and Degischer, 1971, 1972) have produced computed micrographs for defects which do not have a generalised cross-section, using different methods of formulating and integrating the two-beam column approximation. It is difficult to make an assessment of the best method in such cases since this will depend upon the type of computer available.

Even when computing images for which a generalised cross-section can be defined, three inter-dependent factors need to be considered in producing micrographs efficiently. These are the characteristics of the computer, the particular form of the two-beam equations chosen and the characteristics of the method of numerical integration. The programs given in ch. 10 represent an optimisation of the last two factors for our computer and these programs can be expected to be reasonably efficient on other computers of the same generation.

10 | COMPUTER PROGRAMS

10.1. Introduction

The computed images used in this book were produced by programs of the type presented in this chapter. These are written in simple FORTRAN and form a basis from which equivalent programs for other computers can be constructed. Some modifications will almost certainly be necessary and sufficient information is given of the structure and conventions of these programs to enable ready adaption. There are two types of modification which may be called for. The first is due to differences between computers such as word length, size, speed, FORTRAN dialect and equipment available for producing a picture from the results of the computation. The second is due to the fact that we do not use a single universal program but rather a family of programs, all similar in the main but each specialised in some particular.

The usual specialisations are to a particular crystal structure (cubic, hexagonal, tetragonal, etc.) and to a particular class of object (one dislocation, two dislocations with stacking faults, four dislocations, etc.). The examples of programs given below start with the simplest, that for one dislocation in a cubic crystal, then illustrate the modifications necessary to change the crystal structure and finally the modifications to change the class of object from one dislocation to two dislocations with stacking faults. This level of specialisation has been found to be a suitable compromise between the effort involved in modifying programs on the one hand and increased speed of computation and simpler data requirements on the other. The general structure of the programs is illustrated in fig. 10.1.

10.1.1. COMPUTER ENVIRONMENT

The programs have been run on a CDC 3600 computer with 32K of core store and extensive peripheral storage on drums, disc files and magnetic tapes. Each computer word is of 48 bits and can contain one number (integer or

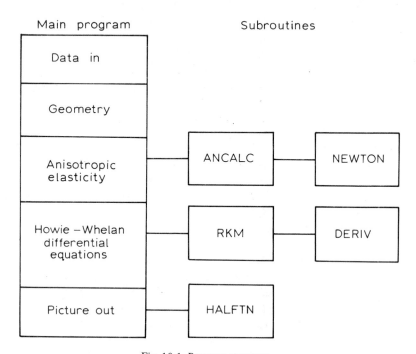

Fig. 10.1. Program structure.

floating point) or two instructions *. Typical instruction execution times are:

Load accumulator	2.00 μs
Store accumulator	1.88 μs
Floating add	4.25 μs
Floating multiply	6.40 μs.

10.1.2. PROGRAM SPEED

The programs have been written for maximum speed of computation, the resulting size of the programs being irrelevant since they easily fit in the available 32K core store. Of the computation time of an image, 90–95% is taken

---

* For floating point numbers the 48 bits are divided into an 11 bit exponent and a 37 bit mantissa, giving 11 decimal digit precision. One alteration, in subroutine NEWTON, may be necessary for computers with less precision.

by the integration of the Howie–Whelan differential equations using subroutines RKM and DERIV (fig. 10.1). This integration time is dominated by
floating point arithmetic so the computation time of an image will be roughly
proportional to the execution time of a typical mixture of floating point
instructions. An appropriate mixture is one of each of the four instructions of
the previous section. These have a total time of 14.5 μs and the corresponding computation time of an image is 40 to 50 sec. Thus a first estimate of the
image computation time on another computer would be the sum of the times
of the corresponding four instructions multiplied by 3×10^6.

The FORTRAN subroutines RKM and DERIV have been written in a form
which causes our FORTRAN compiler to produce the optimum machine code
for speed. No significant increase of speed would have resulted from writing
these subroutines directly in machine code. This would probably also be true
with other efficient FORTRAN compilers.

The parts of the programs dealing with anisotropic elasticity and the
Howie–Whelan differential equations are mainly concerned with complex
quantities. In the interests of speed, the programs are not written in FORTRAN
complex variables but the corresponding real and imaginary parts are handled
separately.

10.1.3. PROGRAM SIZE

As mentioned above, these programs (together with an elaborate operating
system) easily fit in the available 32K core memory. It is estimated that they
would just fit in a memory of half this size (together with a minimal operating
system), that is, in 16K of memory, each word of which can contain one
number or two instructions.

The only simple way to make large reductions in this memory requirement
is if overlay facilities are available. One such scheme would be for subroutines
ANCALC and NEWTON to form one overlay and subroutines RKM, DERIV
and HALFTN to form another, each overlay being used once per computed
image. Further memory saving would result if the main program were divided
into two parts, the first part together with subroutines ANCALC and NEWTON
forming one overlay and the second part with subroutines RKM, DERIV and
HALFTN forming another, each overlay being used once per computed image.
The appropriate place to split program ONEDIS is immediately before card
(ONE 1490), and program TWODIS immediately before card (TWO 1940) *.

10.1.4. PROGRAM OPTIONS

A number of complete programs can be assembled from the various parts

* This notation will be used to refer to card images in the listings of the programs and
subroutines.

given in this chapter. A complete program is composed of the following parts.

(i) For one dislocation: main program ONEDIS (§ 10.2.9) and subroutine DERIV for one dislocation (§ 10.3.4); for two dislocations and stacking faults: main program TWODIS (§ 10.9.3) and subroutine DERIV for two dislocations (§ 10.9.4).

(ii) For cubic crystals: subroutine ANCALC (§ 10.3.1); for non-cubic crystals: modifications to ANCALC and the main program (§ 10.6).

(iii) The equivalent of subroutine HALFTN; this produces a picture from the computed intensities and will be hardware dependent (see § 10.5 for discussion).

(iv) Subroutines NEWTON (§ 10.3.2) and RKM (§ 10.3.3) for all programs.

(v) Optional modification DELUGE (§ 10.8) for an economical scan over a range of foil thickness.

It is recommended that the initial program should be the special test program described in § 10.4.

10.1.5. GENERAL CONVENTIONS

The standard FORTRAN naming convention is used. Variables with names starting with I, J, K, L, M or N are integers, all other variables are real floating point numbers. All variable names are 6 or less characters.

Input data is read from unit MR, a card reader, reading 80 column cards. A blank field on a data card is read as zero under F or I formats. Output is on unit MW, a line printer, printing 135 characters per line, 63 lines per page. The values of MR and MW are set by a DATA statement (ONE 125).

Line printer paper control characters used are:

Blank. Single line feed after printing.

+ No line feed. The next line will print over this one. Used in HALFTN for halftone picture printing.

G Eject to bottom of page before printing. Single line feed after printing. The next line will be printed on the first line of the new page. Used in main program.

Although the CDC 3600 computer uses floating point numbers of 11 decimal digit precision, these programs should be suitable for 7 digit precision computers provided the constant 0.1E−11 on card NEW 270 of subroutine NEWTON is changed to 0.1 E−7.

To be consistent with the simpler FORTRAN dialects, only three-way IF statements are used. If two-way or one-way IF statements are available, they should be used in subroutines DERIV and RKM in the interests of speed.

10.2. Program ONEDIS for one dislocation and cubic crystals

CALLS: Unit MR, card reader, for data cards specifying picture.
Unit MW, line printer, for legend to picture and error messages.
Subroutine ANCALC (data via COMMON/ANCNEW).
Subroutine RKM (data via COMMON/RKMDRV).
Subroutine HALFTN to print a halftone picture.
System function TIMEF, internal millisecond clock.
System function FLOAT, integer to real.
System function SQRT, square root.

10.2.1. GENERAL DESCRIPTION

Program ONEDIS and its associated subroutines calculates and prints a simulated picture of the bright field image of one dislocation as seen in the electron microscope. The crystal containing the dislocation is of cubic symmetry and is elastically anisotropic. The imaging process of the electron microscope is simulated by the Howie–Whelan two-beam, column-approximation theory (Howie and Whelan, 1961).

The data specifying a picture to be computed is on two data cards. The program starts (ONE 130) by reading two data cards (ONE 130–190). It then calculates the geometry of the situation (ONE 200–1130), the anisotropic elastic displacement field around the dislocation (ONE 1140–1480), integrates the Howie–Whelan differential equations to simulate the passage of electrons through the distorted crystal (ONE 1490–2520) printing each of the 60 lines of the picture as it is calculated (ONE 2510) and finally printing a legend under the picture (ONE 2530–2620). It then returns to the start (ONE 2630) to read in the next pair of data cards specifying another picture. The program finally stops (ONE 160) if a first data card is blank. A data card deck will contain $2n + 1$ cards, the first $2n$ cards specifying n pictures and the last card blank to stop the program.

10.2.2. DATA

The layout of each of the two data cards for program ONEDIS is given in tables 10.1 and 10.2. These tables give the columns of the card in which the values of the various parameters are to be punched, the format under which these numbers will be read and the program variables to which they will be assigned. Some default values are also given. These take effect if the corresponding data field is left blank, a blank data field being read as zero.

The first data card starts with the three elastic constants of the cubic crystal, c_{11}, c_{12} and c_{44} *. As the displacement field around a dislocation depends

* For the special case of isotropic elasticity see § 10.7.

TABLE 10.1
Layout of first data card for ONEDIS

Column	Format	Variable	Default	Comment
1–10	F10.0	C11	–	
11–20	F10.0	C12	–	Elastic constants
21–30	F10.0	C44	–	
31–45	15A1	IY	–	15 character message
46–70	25X	–	–	Not used
71–79	F9.0	ANO	0.1	Anomalous absorption
80	–	–	–	Not used

TABLE 10.2
Layout of second data card for ONEDIS

Column	Format	Variable	Default	Comment
1–6	3I2	LB	–	Numerators of Burgers vector $\boldsymbol{b}$
7	X	–	–	Not used
8	I1	LD	1	Common denominator of Burgers vector
9	X	–	–	Not used
10–15	3I2	LU	–	Direction of dislocation line $\boldsymbol{u}$
16	X	–	–	Not used
17–22	3I2	LG	–	Diffracting vector $\boldsymbol{g}$
23	X	–	–	Not used
24–29	3I2	LBM	–	Beam direction $\boldsymbol{B}$
30	X	–	–	Not used
31–36	3I2	LFN	LBM	Foil normal $\boldsymbol{F}$
37–40	F4.0	W	–	Deviation from Bragg condition w
41–44	F4.0	THICK	–	Foil thickness, in units of ξ_g
45–48	F4.0	START	0	Start and finish of integration, in
49–52	F4.0	FINISH	THICK	units of ξ_g, relative to top surface of object
53–54	I2	LPR	1	Grey scale
55–80	26A1	IZ	–	26 character message

on the ratios of the elastic constants and not their absolute values, the three elastic constants can be specified in any convenient units (but the same for all three). For example, the elastic constants of β-brass are

$$c_{11} = 1.291 \times 10^{12} \text{ dyne cm}^{-2}$$
$$c_{12} = 1.097 \times 10^{12}$$
$$c_{44} = 0.824 \times 10^{12}$$

and these could be punched as 1.291, 1.097 and 0.824 or, equally well, as 12.91, 10.97 and 8.24. Following the elastiç constants is a 15 character message, usually used for the name of the material which has these elastic constants. The first card ends with the value of the anomalous absorption coefficient. If this is left blank, the conventional value of 0.1 will be assigned.

The second data card starts with the five vectors: Burgers vector, dislocation line direction, diffracting vector, beam direction and foil normal. Each has a 3I2 format enabling the three components of the vector to be punched as signed one digit integers. The first of these, the Burgers vector, also has a one digit denominator so that $b = \frac{1}{2}[\bar{1}0\bar{1}]$ would be punched as $-1\ +0\ -1/2$. If this common denominator is left blank, the default value of 1 is assigned. The foil normal has the default value of the beam direction, this corresponding to an untilted specimen.

These five vectors are followed by the non-dimensional deviation from the Bragg condition $w = s\xi_g$ and the foil thickness in units of ξ_g *. This thickness is that measured normal to the foil surfaces and *not* the path length of the electron beam through the foil, this latter being a function of the amount the foil is tilted. The next two quantities, START and FINISH, determine the region of the dislocated foil which will be represented in the computed picture. The default values give the standard picture which includes all the dislocation image between the points where the dislocation line intersects the top and bottom surfaces of the foil. The use of START and FINISH to produce magnified or demagnified pictures was explained in §4.3.2. These are followed by an integer specifying one of nine grey scales to be used in printing the picture, and the second data card ends with a 26 character message. The default value of 1 for the grey scale gives the standard exposure and contrast which has been found suitable for most bright field images.

All the data on these two cards, including the messages, is reproduced in the legend to the computed pictures.

The two data cards are read in at the start of the program (ONE 130–190) checking if the first card is blank as a signal to stop. The various default options are then checked and default values assigned where necessary (ONE 220–390). For later convenience, the anomalous absorption is negated (ONE 260).

10.2.3. GEOMETRY

This section (ONE 400–1130) is concerned with the geometry of the dis-

---

* Since the program has been arranged so that the input data, all computations and the output are in non-dimensional form, there is no need in this chapter to distinguish between ξ_g and ξ_{ga} (§ 2.6) and ξ_g will be used throughout.

located foil and the relationship between the four systems of axes which are used to describe it (§4.4). The specification of the object on the data cards by the various vectors and elastic constants is, for convenience, with respect to crystal axes which are the usual cartesian axes (§2.7.2(ii)) used for indexing a cubic crystal. The calculation of the elastic displacement field around the dislocation calls for a dislocation axis system with the 3-axis along u, the dislocation line direction. Vectors (and tensors) given in crystal axes are transformed to dislocation axes by the array of direction cosines DC, where DC(I, J) is the cosine of the angle between dislocation axis I and crystal axis J. The projection of the three-dimensional object into a two-dimensional picture uses generalised cross-section axes with the 2-axis antiparallel to the electron beam direction B and DCX is the direction cosine array connecting this axis system with the crystal axes. The names used for the various vectors when referred to these different systems of axes are given in table 10.3.

The input vectors are first floated (ONE 400–450), the Burgers vector being divided through by its common denominator; the program names of these floated vectors are given in table 10.3.

The direction cosine array DC is then calculated (ONE 460–650), the 3-axis along u (ONE 470), the 1-axis along $B \wedge u$ (ONE 500) and the 2-axis completing a right-handed set (ONE 540). At this stage DC contains direction ratios which become direction cosines on normalisation (ONE 550–650).

The direction cosine array DCX has the 1-axis antiparallel to the 1-axis of DC, the 2-axis anitparallel to B (ONE 670–680) and the 3-axis completing a right-handed set (ONE 720). These operations are followed by normalisation (ONE 730–790).

DATA arrays NP and NQ contain the permutation of indices needed for forming the vector products defining these direction cosines (ONE 110).

Using these direction cosine arrays the vector components in the other axis systems are calculated (ONE 800–910) as in table 10.3. BM and FN are

TABLE 10.3
FORTRAN names of vectors

Vector	Crystal Data	Crystal Floated	Dislocation	Generalised cross-section
b: Burgers	LB/LD	CB	BD	–
u: dislocation line	LU	CU	–	–
g: diffraction	LG	CG	GD	–
B: beam	LBM	CBM	BM	–
F: foil normal	LFN	CFN	FN	FNX
Direction cosines	–	–	DC	DCX

reduced to unit vectors (ONE 960–1000) and their scalar product FNBM
calculated (ONE 1010–1030).

10.2.4. ERROR MESSAGES

In this first part of program ONEDIS there are five error messages which
can occur (ONE 340, 620, 940, 1070, 1120). The printing of each is followed
by GO TO 810 to write the legend of the picture to give a record of the input
data. The program would then return to the beginning to read in the next
data. The messages are:

(i) START AFTER FINISH. A nonsense specification for the part of the
picture to be computed.

(ii) BEAM PARALLEL U. A possible physical situation with the dislocation being viewed end on, but one which this program cannot handle.

(iii) BEAM NOT PERP TO G. In the program the electron beam must be
perpendicular to the diffracting vector.

(iv) U AND FOIL NORMAL NOT ACUTE. The convention used to assign
a direction to the dislocation line is that it shall be acute to the foil normal.

(v) FOIL NORMAL AND BEAM NOT ACUTE. The convention used to
assign a direction to the foil normal is that it shall be acute to the electron
beam direction B.

There are two error messages which can be generated by subroutine
ANCALC (§ 10.3.1) namely NOCONVERGE and REALROOT. These would
also produce a jump to 810 on returning from ANCALC (ONE 1150) since
the variable KRASH would then be non-zero.

10.2.5. ANISOTROPIC ELASTICITY

Most of the elasticity calculations are done by subroutine ANCALC (ONE
1140) and the small part which is in the main program (ONE 1170–1480) is
described in § 10.3.1. At ONE 1480, CN(1)–CN(12) contain the twelve
constants describing the particular displacement field which is to be integrated
to form the computed image.

10.2.6. PICTURE OUTPUT

The remainder of program ONEDIS integrates the Howie–Whelan differential equations to calculate the intensities at 7740 points in the picture (60
lines of 129 points) and transmits these values to subroutine HALFTN which
generates a corresponding picture. The external characteristics of HALFTN
as seen by program ONEDIS are as follows. According to the value of LPR in
the input data (with default value of 1), values of BLACK and WHITE are
chosen (ONE 1490–1750). On calling HALFTN (ONE 1760) with the last
parameter negative, the values of BLACK and WHITE are used to calculate
the grey scale which will be used to relate calculated intensities to printed

symbols. The blackest symbol will be used for intensities less than BLACK, the whitest symbol (blank paper) for intensities greater than WHITE, and intermediate symbols for intermediate intensities. HALFTN is then called with the last parameter zero (ONE 1770) when the grey scale table will be printed, that is the range of intensity which has been allotted to each printed symbol. The line printer paper is then moved to the bottom of the page (ONE 1780–1790) so that the next printing, the picture, starts on the first line of a new page. The call of HALFTN with last parameter positive (ONE 2510) prints one line of the picture, the first three parameters indicating that there are 129 intensity values in the array TB, to be printed as a line of 129 symbols and the Hollerith character in MARK is to be printed at the left-hand margin. This call is repeated 60 times (ONE 1990) for the 60 lines of the picture with MARK blank except for lines 30 and 31 when it is D (ONE 2480–2500), this giving a reference mark on the picture for the core of the dislocation which lies midway between these two lines.

10.2.7. HOWIE–WHELAN DIFFERENTIAL EQUATIONS

Before the actual integration of the differential equations, some quantities associated with the geometry of the picture and the grid of picture points must be calculated. THBM (ONE 1800) is the thickness of the foil in the direction of the electron beam. This is in units of ξ_g. For speed, the differential equations use ξ_g/π as the unit of length and TBP corresponds to THBM in these units (ONE 1810). FRACTN (ONE 1820) controls the magnification of the picture. For the standard picture with the dislocation intersecting the foil surfaces at each margin of the picture, FINISH = THICK and START = 0 and thus FRACTN = 1. Part of this standard picture is magnified so as to fill the line printer page when FRACTN $<$ 1, and when FRACTN $>$ 1 the picture is demagnified to include more than the standard picture. The length WL and height WW of the field of view in the picture are in units of ξ_g. For the standard picture, WL is the projected length of the dislocation (ONE 1840) and this is modified by FRACTN when necessary. WW is related to WL (ONE 1850) by the fact that the picture will be 60 lines of 129 characters, i.e. 59 inter-line spacings at 6 per inch and 128 inter-character spacings at 10 per inch. The integration step size DELT down a column is $\frac{1}{64}$ of the integration distance TBP (ONE 1830) since only alternative points on a picture line are computed, the intermediate points being interpolated. The spacing between picture lines is the spacing DELW between integration columns (ONE 1860). DELT and DELW are in units of ξ_g/π.

The Howie–Whelan differential equations which are integrated are of the form

$$\frac{dT}{dZ} = -\mathscr{A}T + (i - \mathscr{A})S,$$

$$\frac{dS}{dZ} = (i - \mathscr{A})T + (-\mathscr{A} + 2iw + 2\pi i\frac{d}{dZ}(g \cdot R))S, \qquad (10.1)$$

where T and S are the complex amplitudes of the direct and diffracted beams, $\mathcal{A}$ is the anomalous absorption (and normal absorption §2.4.1), w the deviation from the Bragg condition and R represents the distortion of the crystal due to the dislocation. One such pair of equations (with subscript 1 on T and S) is integrated from initial conditions $T_1 = 1$ and $S_1 = 0$. A second pair (for T_2 and S_2) is integrated from initial conditions $T_2 = 0$ and $S_2 = 1$. Each T and S will in general be complex valued. The standard integration subroutine RKM integrates real variables (which it calls Y) and the following identification is made

$$T_1 \rightarrow Y(1) + iY(2) ,$$

$$S_1 \rightarrow Y(3) + iY(4) , \qquad\qquad\qquad\qquad (10.2)$$

$$T_2 \rightarrow Y(5) + iY(6) ,$$

$$S_2 \rightarrow Y(7) + iY(8) .$$

Thus the four complex differential equations become the eight real equations

$$\frac{dY(I)}{dX} = D(I) . \qquad I = 1,8 \qquad\qquad\qquad (10.3)$$

where the functions $D(I)$ (which are contained in subroutine DERIV, §10.3.4) are the real and imaginary parts of the right-hand sides of the Howie–Whelan equations (10.1) and the FORTRAN variable X represents Z, the independent variable.

The first use made of the differential equations is to determine the background intensity transmitted through undistorted crystal (ONE 1870–1980). Strictly this should be done by setting $g \cdot R = 0$ in the differential equations but it is approximated by doing an integration at a large distance from the dislocation where $g \cdot R \simeq 0$. The distance of the integration column from the dislocation line is transmitted to DERIV by CN(29) and this is set at 1000 (ONE 1870), i.e. $1000/\pi$ extinction distances from the dislocation. Initial values of X and Y(1)–Y(8) are loaded, Q is set to zero to indicate that the optimum step size of the integration is unknown and ERROR is set to the permissible error per integration step (ONE 1880–1930). This integration is started with a small step (ONE 1940–1950) which is approximately the optimum size for subroutine RKM and the integration is then continued to the full thickness (ONE 1960–1970). After this integration the bright field background intensity is given by BACK $= |T_1|^2$ (ONE 1980).

The next integrations generate the picture and are repeated 60 times (ONE 1990–2520), once for each line of the picture. For each picture line the integration is in three parts, a first part of 64 steps (ONE 2100–2290), a second part also of 64 steps (ONE 2390–2440) and an intermediate part (ONE 2300–2340) which is only needed if a magnified picture has been specified, and serves to connect the first and second parts. At each of the 64 steps of the second part of the integration, the intensity TB of a picture point is calculated (ONE 2420–2440). The first point of the line (ONE 2450) is calculated as a special case. Between these 65 calculated intensities a further 64 are calculated by linear interpolation (ONE 2460–2470). These 129 intensities are then transmitted to subroutine HALFTN (ONE 2510) for printing as a picture line, which will be prefixed by a blank (ONE 2480) except for the 30th and 31st lines which are prefixed by the letter D (ONE 2490–2500).

    For each line of the picture, the distance of the picture line from the line of the dislocation, which is midway between the 30th and 31st lines, is CN(15) (ONE 2000). This is divided by $\cos \psi$ (ONE 2010) for transmission to subroutine DERIV as CN(29) (§4.4). The positions of the start of the first and second parts of the integration are put in X (ONE 2020) and SURFAC (ONE 2030). Initial beam amplitudes corresponding to $T_1 = 1, S_1 = 0, T_2 = 0, S_2 = 1$ are put in Y(1)–Y(8) (ONE 2040–2070), and X1 set at the start of the first integration (ONE 2080).

    For each of the 64 steps of the first part of the integration (with one possible exception), X1 is incremented by DELT (ONE 2110) and subroutine RKM called to integrate the beams through this increment (ONE 2210). FX(JT, 1)–FX(JT, 4) are then calculated (ONE 2250–2280) such that

$$T_1 [FX(JT, 1) + iFX(JT, 2)] + T_2 [FX(JT, 3) + iFX(JT, 4)] = 1$$

and   (10.4)

$$S_1 [FX(JT, 1) + iFX(JT, 2)] + S_2 [FX(JT, 3) + iFX(JT, 4)] = 0,$$

cf. eqs. (4.1).

    The initial values for the second part of the integration are the values generated by the first part at the position X = SURFAC. These initial values are stored in TEMPY from which they are taken at the start of the second integration (ONE 2360–2370). Two cases can occur; that SURFAC is within the range of the first integration or that it is beyond the range. If it is beyond, then an intermediate integration is necessary continuing from the first part as far as SURFAC (ONE 2300–2340) and this is done if IFLAG is still zero (ONE 2090, 2300). In the other case SURFAC will be passed in one of the 64 steps of the first integration. This special step will be done in two parts, firstly as far as SURFAC (ONE 2150–2190) storing the values there in TEMPY, and then to the end of the DELT increment. IFLAG is set to unity when this occurs and the step in which it will occur is detected

(ONE 2120–2130) by X1 being greater than SURFAC with IFLAG still zero.

The second integration starts from SURFAC (ONE 2350) with initial values from TEMPY (ONE 2360–2370) and proceeds in 64 steps of size DELT (ONE 2390–2410). For each step, TT (ONE 2420–2430) is the square of the modulus of

$$T_1 [\text{FX(JM, 1)} + i\text{FX(JM, 2)}] + T_2 [\text{FX(JM, 3)} + i\text{FX(JM, 4)}] \,,$$

using the FX corresponding to the same number step of the first part of the integration, cf. eqs. (4.5). TT is the bright field intensity which corresponds to a physical beam starting at the position of a step in the first integration with $T = 1$ and $S = 0$ and propagating a distance TBP through the crystal. This is so for the following reasons: corresponding steps in the two parts of the integration are always TBP apart (ONE 2030); the initial conditions (ONE 2040–2070) guarantee that (T_1, S_1) and (T_2, S_2) are independent solutions of the Howie–Whelan differential equations; the Howie–Whelan equations are linear so that all possible solutions can be represented as linear combinations of the independent solutions; the FX are defined as that linear combination which would give $T = 1$ and $S = 0$ at each step of the first part of the integration, and the same linear combination of T_1 and T_2 at a distance TBP further along the integration is used to calculate TT.

This value of TT is normalised by dividing by BACK, the background intensity (ONE 2440) which can be thought of as setting the photographic exposure so that background is always the same shade of grey in the computed picture. No linear combinations need be taken for the first point in the line (ONE 2450) since (T_1, S_1) did start with the desired values of $(1, 0)$.

10.2.8. PICTURE LEGEND

The picture legend contains all information necessary to identify a picture, in the first place when a group of pictures come back from the computer, but also, and more importantly, at any time in the future. In the legend, numerical values are *followed* by the name of the corresponding quantity.

All quantities on the data cards appear in the legend, with default values being printed if any were invoked. The following quantities appear in the legend as on the data cards (their legend names are given here in brackets): c_{11} (C11), c_{12} (C12), c_{44} (C44), b (B), u (U), g (G), B (BM), F (FN), w (W), foil thickness (TH), START (STRT), FINISH (FIN). The message on the first data card appears in the first line of the legend after the elastic constants and the message on the second data card at the end of the second line of the legend. The anomalous absorption coefficient (ANO) appears with a negative sign and the chosen grey scale is recorded by the values of BLACK and WHITE.

The remainder of the legend are quantities which were calculated during the computation. SECS is the computation time in seconds, the internal millisecond clock having been read at the start (ONE 200) and finish (ONE 2530) of the computation. The length (WL) and height (WW) of the picture, in units of ξ_g, give the scale of the picture. The thickness of the foil in the direction of the electron beam (THBM) is also in units of ξ_g and is greater than THICK if the foil is tilted. BACK is the background intensity to which all intensities in the picture have been normalised. It is the exit intensity of the electron beam, for unit incident intensity, from thickness THBM of undistorted crystal with normal absorption equal to anomalous absorption.

10.2.9. LISTING OF PROGRAM ONEDIS

```
      PROGRAM ONEDIS                                                  ONE    10
      DIMENSION LB(3),LU(3),LG(3),LBM(3),LFN(3),IY(15),IZ(26),BD(3),  ONE    20
     1 GD(3),BM(3),FN(3),FNX(3),DCX(3,3),DR(3),DI(3),UR(3,3),UI(3,3), ONE    30
     2 VR(3,3),VI(3,3),CB(3),CU(3),CG(3),CBM(3),CFN(3),TB(129),       ONE    40
     3 TEMPY(8),FX(64,4)                                              ONE    50
      COMMON/RKMDRV/CN(30),X,X1,Y(8),ERROR,SKIP,Q,D(8),ANO           ONE    60
      COMMON/ANCNEW/NEW,ZR,ZI,QR(7),QI(7),KRASH,C11,C12,C44,DC(3,3), ONE    70
     1 C(6,6),PR(3),PI(3),AR(3,3),AI(3,3),ELR(3,3),ELI(3,3),EMR(3,3), ONE    80
     2 EMI(3,3),B(3,3),H(3,3)                                         ONE    90
      COMMON/DATA/NP(3),NQ(3),MM(3),NN(3),L1(6),L2(6),L3(3,3),PY,MR,MW ONE   100
      DATA (NP=2,3,1),(NQ=3,1,2),(MM=1,6,5),(NN=6,2,4),(L1=1,2,3,2,3,1) ONE  110
      DATA (L2=1,2,3,3,1,2),(L3=1,6,5,6,2,4,5,4,3),(PY=3.1415926536)  ONE   120
      DATA (MR=60),(MW=61)                                            ONE   125
   10 READ(MR,20)C11,C12,C44,IY,ANO                                   ONE   130
   20 FORMAT(3F10.0,15A1,25X,F9.0)                                    ONE   140
      IF(C11)30,30,40                                                 ONE   150
   30 STOP                                                            ONE   160
   40 CONTINUE                                                        ONE   170
      READ(MR,50)LB,LD,LU,LG,LBM,LFN,W,THICK,START,FINISH,LPR,IZ      ONE   180
   50 FORMAT(3I2,X,I1,X,3I2,X,3I2,X,3I2,X,3I2,4F4.0,I2,26A1)          ONE   190
      TIME=TIMEF(X)                                                   ONE   200
      CN(14)=2.0*W                                                    ONE   210
      IF(LD)70,60,70                                                  ONE   220
   60 LD=1                                                            ONE   230
   70 IF(ANO)90,80,90                                                 ONE   240
   80 ANO=0.1                                                         ONE   250
   90 ANO=-ANO                                                        ONE   260
      IF(FINISH)120,100,120                                           ONE   270
  100 IF(START)120,110,120                                            ONE   280
  110 START=0.0                                                       ONE   290
      FINISH=THICK                                                    ONE   300
  120 IF(FINISH-START)130,130,150                                     ONE   310
  130 WRITE(MW,140)                                                   ONE   320
      GO TO 810                                                       ONE   330
  140 FORMAT(/,/,20H START AFTER FINISH   ,/,/)                       ONE   340
  150 IF(LPR)170,160,170                                              ONE   350
  160 LPR=1                                                           ONE   360
  170 IF(LFN(1)**2+LFN(2)**2+LFN(3)**2)200,180,200                    ONE   370
  180 DO 190 J=1,3                                                    ONE   380
  190 LFN(J)=LBM(J)                                                   ONE   390
  200 DO 205 J=1,3                                                    ONE   400
      CB(J)=FLOAT(LB(J))/FLOAT(LD)                                    ONE   410
      CU(J)=LU(J)                                                     ONE   420
      CG(J)=LG(J)                                                     ONE   430
      CBM(J)=LBM(J)                                                   ONE   440
  205 CFN(J)=LFN(J)                                                   ONE   450
      DO 210 J=1,3                                                    ONE   460
      DC(3,J)=CU(J)                                                   ONE   470
      K=NP(J)                                                         ONE   480
      L=NQ(J)                                                         ONE   490
  210 DC(1,J)=CBM(K)*CU(L)-CBM(L)*CU(K)                               ONE   500
      DO 220 J=1,3                                                    ONE   510
      K=NP(J)                                                         ONE   520
      L=NQ(J)                                                         ONE   530
  220 DC(2,J)=DC(3,K)*DC(1,L)-DC(3,L)*DC(1,K)                         ONE   540
      DO 270 J=1,3                                                    ONE   550
      Z=0.0                                                           ONE   560
      DO 230 K=1,3                                                    ONE   570
```

```
230    Z=Z+DC(J,K)**2                                           ONE   580
       IF(Z-0.0001)240,240,260                                  ONE   590
240    WRITE(MW,250)                                            ONE   600
       GO TO 810                                                ONE   610
250    FORMAT(/,/,16H BEAM PARALLEL U    ,/,/)                  ONE   620
260    Z=1.0/SQRT(Z)                                            ONE   630
       DO 270 K=1,3                                             ONE   640
270    DC(J,K)=DC(J,K)*Z                                        ONE   650
       DO 280 J=1,3                                             ONE   660
       DCX(1,J)=-DC(1,J)                                        ONE   670
280    DCX(2,J)=-CBM(J)                                         ONE   680
       DO 285 J=1,3                                             ONE   690
       K=NP(J)                                                  ONE   700
       L=NQ(J)                                                  ONE   710
285    DCX(3,J)=DCX(1,K)*DCX(2,L)-DCX(1,L)*DCX(2,K)             ONE   720
       DO 300 J=1,3                                             ONE   730
       Z=0.0                                                    ONE   740
       DO 290 K=1,3                                             ONE   750
290    Z=Z+DCX(J,K)**2                                          ONE   760
       Z=1.0/SQRT(Z)                                            ONE   770
       DO 300 K=1,3                                             ONE   780
300    DCX(J,K)=DCX(J,K)*Z                                      ONE   790
       DO 310 J=1,3                                             ONE   800
       BD(J)=0.0                                                ONE   810
       GD(J)=0.0                                                ONE   820
       BM(J)=0.0                                                ONE   830
       FN(J)=0.0                                                ONE   840
       FNX(J)=0.0                                               ONE   850
       DO 310 K=1,3                                             ONE   860
       BD(J)=BD(J)+DC(J,K)*CB(K)                                ONE   870
       BM(J)=BM(J)+DC(J,K)*CBM(K)                               ONE   880
       FN(J)=FN(J)+DC(J,K)*CFN(K)                               ONE   890
       FNX(J)=FNX(J)+DCX(J,K)*CFN(K)                            ONE   900
310    GD(J)=GD(J)+DC(J,K)*CG(K)                                ONE   910
       IF(LBM(1)*LG(1)+LBM(2)*LG(2)+LBM(3)*LG(3))320,340,320    ONE   920
320    WRITE(MW,330)                                            ONE   930
330    FORMAT(/,/,19H BEAM NOT PERP TO G    ,/,/)               ONE   940
       GO TO 810                                                ONE   950
340    Z=SQRT(FN(1)**2+FN(2)**2+FN(3)**2)                       ONE   960
       X=SQRT(BM(1)**2+BM(2)**2+BM(3)**2)                       ONE   970
       DO 350 J=1,3                                             ONE   980
       BM(J)=BM(J)/X                                            ONE   990
350    FN(J)=FN(J)/Z                                            ONE  1000
       FNBM=0.0                                                 ONE  1010
       DO 360 J=1,3                                             ONE  1020
360    FNBM=FNBM+FN(J)*BM(J)                                    ONE  1030
       IF(FN(3))370,370,390                                     ONE  1040
370    WRITE(MW,380)                                            ONE  1050
       GO TO 810                                                ONE  1060
380    FORMAT(/,/,29H U AND FOIL NORMAL NOT ACUTE    ,/,/)      ONE  1070
390    CONTINUE                                                 ONE  1080
       IF(FNBM)400,400,420                                      ONE  1090
400    WRITE(MW,410)                                            ONE  1100
       GO TO 810                                                ONE  1110
410    FORMAT(/,/,32H FOIL NORMAL AND BEAM NOT ACUTE   ,/,/)    ONE  1120
420    CONTINUE                                                 ONE  1130
       CALL ANCALC                                              ONE  1140
       IF(KRASH)810,430,810                                     ONE  1150
430    CONTINUE                                                 ONE  1160
       DO 440 J=1,3                                             ONE  1170
       DR(J)=0.0                                                ONE  1180
       DI(J)=0.0                                                ONE  1190
       DO 440 K=1,3                                             ONE  1200
       DR(J)=DR(J)+GD(K)*AR(K,J)                                ONE  1210
440    DI(J)=DI(J)+GD(K)*AI(K,J)                                ONE  1220
       DO 450 J=1,3                                             ONE  1230
       Z=DR(J)                                                  ONE  1240
       DR(J)=Z*PR(J)-DI(J)*PI(J)                                ONE  1250
450    DI(J)=Z*PI(J)+DI(J)*PR(J)                                ONE  1260
       DO 460 JA=1,3                                            ONE  1270
       DO 460 L=1,3                                             ONE  1280
       UR(JA,L)=0.0                                             ONE  1290
       UI(JA,L)=0.0                                             ONE  1300
       DO 460 J=1,3                                             ONE  1310
       UR(JA,L)=UR(JA,L)+EMR(JA,J)*H(J,L)                       ONE  1320
460    UI(JA,L)=UI(JA,L)+EMI(JA,J)*H(J,L)                       ONE  1330
       DO 470 JA=1,3                                            ONE  1340
       DO 470 L=1,3                                             ONE  1350
       VR(JA,L)=DR(JA)*UR(JA,L)-DI(JA)*UI(JA,L)                 ONE  1360
```

```
 470    VI(JA,L)=DR(JA)*UI(JA,L)+DI(JA)*UR(JA,L)              ONE 1370
        DO 480 JA=1,3                                         ONE 1380
        DO 480 L=1,3                                          ONE 1390
 480    UR(JA,L)=VR(JA,L)*PR(JA)+VI(JA,L)*PI(JA)              ONE 1400
        DO 490 J=1,3                                          ONE 1410
        CN(J+6)=PR(J)                                         ONE 1420
        CN(J+9)=PI(J)**2                                      ONE 1430
        CN(J)=0.0                                             ONE 1440
        CN(J+3)=0.0                                           ONE 1450
        DO 490 L=1,3                                          ONE 1460
        CN(J)=CN(J)+VR(J,L)*BD(L)                             ONE 1470
 490    CN(J+3)=CN(J+3)+UR(J,L)*BD(L)                         ONE 1480
        GO TO (500,510,520,530,540,550,560,570,580),LPR      ONE 1490
 500    BLACK=0.313                                          ONE 1500
        WHITE=1.154                                          ONE 1510
        GO TO 590                                            ONE 1520
 510    BLACK=0.129                                          ONE 1530
        WHITE=1.253                                          ONE 1540
        GO TO 590                                            ONE 1550
 520    BLACK=0.058                                          ONE 1560
        WHITE=1.340                                          ONE 1570
        GO TO 590                                            ONE 1580
 530    BLACK=0.397                                          ONE 1590
        WHITE=1.462                                          ONE 1600
        GO TO 590                                            ONE 1610
 540    BLACK=0.191                                          ONE 1620
        WHITE=1.866                                          ONE 1630
        GO TO 590                                            ONE 1640
 550    BLACK=0.098                                          ONE 1650
        WHITE=2.280                                          ONE 1660
        GO TO 590                                            ONE 1670
 560    BLACK=0.259                                          ONE 1680
        WHITE=0.959                                          ONE 1690
        GO TO 590                                            ONE 1700
 570    BLACK=0.089                                          ONE 1710
        WHITE=0.869                                          ONE 1720
        GO TO 590                                            ONE 1730
 580    BLACK=0.035                                          ONE 1740
        WHITE=0.809                                          ONE 1750
 590    CALL HALFTN(129,TB,MARK,BLACK,WHITE,-1)              ONE 1760
        CALL HALFTN(129,TB,MARK,BLACK,WHITE,0)               ONE 1770
        WRITE(MW,600)                                        ONE 1780
 600    FORMAT(1HG)                                          ONE 1790
        THBM=THICK/FNBM                                      ONE 1800
        TBP=PY*THBM                                          ONE 1810
        FRACTN=(FINISH-START)/THICK                          ONE 1820
        DELT=FRACTN*TBP/64.0                                 ONE 1830
        WL=THICK*FRACTN*BM(2)/FN(3)                          ONE 1840
        WW=59.0*10.0*WL/(6.0*128.0)                          ONE 1850
        DELW=PY*WW/59.0                                      ONE 1860
        CN(29)=1000.0                                        ONE 1870
        X=0.0                                                ONE 1880
        Q=0.0                                                ONE 1890
        ERROR=0.0001                                         ONE 1900
        DO 610 JK=1,8                                        ONE 1910
 610    Y(JK)=0.0                                            ONE 1920
        Y(1)=1.0                                             ONE 1930
        X1=DELT                                              ONE 1940
        CALL RKM                                             ONE 1950
        X1=TBP                                               ONE 1960
        CALL RKM                                             ONE 1970
        BACK=Y(1)**2+Y(2)**2                                 ONE 1980
        DO 800 JC=1,60                                       ONE 1990
        CN(15)=(FLOAT(JC)-30.5)*DELW                         ONE 2000
        CN(29)=CN(15)/BM(2)                                  ONE 2010
        X=-PY*FINISH/FNBM-(CN(15)*FNX(1)/FNX(2))             ONE 2020
        SURFAC=X*TBP                                         ONE 2030
        DO 620 JK=1,8                                        ONE 2040
 620    Y(JK)=0.0                                            ONE 2050
        Y(1)=1.0                                             ONE 2060
        Y(7)=1.0                                             ONE 2070
        X1=X                                                 ONE 2080
        IFLAG=0                                              ONE 2090
        DO 680 JT=1,64                                       ONE 2100
        X1=X1+DELT                                           ONE 2110
        IF(X1-SURFAC)670,640,640                             ONE 2120
 640    IF(IFLAG)670,650,670                                 ONE 2130
 650    XX1=X1                                               ONE 2140
        X1=SURFAC                                            ONE 2150
```

```
       IFLAG=1                                                        ONE 2160
       CALL RKM                                                       ONE 2170
       DO 660 JK=1,8                                                  ONE 2180
 660   TEMPY(JK)=Y(JK)                                                ONE 2190
       X1=XX1                                                         ONE 2200
 670   CALL RKM                                                       ONE 2210
       DNR=Y(1)*Y(7)-Y(2)*Y(8)-Y(3)*Y(5)+Y(4)*Y(6)                   ONE 2220
       DNI=Y(1)*Y(8)+Y(2)*Y(7)-Y(3)*Y(6)-Y(4)*Y(5)                   ONE 2230
       DNN=1.0/(DNR**2+DNI**2)                                        ONE 2240
       FX(JT,1)=DNN*(Y(7)*DNR+Y(8)*DNI)                               ONE 2250
       FX(JT,2)=DNN*(Y(8)*DNR-Y(7)*DNI)                               ONE 2260
       FX(JT,3)=-DNN*(Y(3)*DNR+Y(4)*DNI)                              ONE 2270
       FX(JT,4)=DNN*(Y(3)*DNI-Y(4)*DNR)                               ONE 2280
 680   CONTINUE                                                       ONE 2290
       IF(IFLAG)720,690,720                                           ONE 2300
 690   X1=SURFAC                                                      ONE 2310
       CALL RKM                                                       ONE 2320
 700   DO 710 JK=1,8                                                  ONE 2330
 710   TEMPY(JK)=Y(JK)                                                ONE 2340
 720   X=SURFAC                                                       ONE 2350
       DO 730 JK=1,8                                                  ONE 2360
 730   Y(JK)=TEMPY(JK)                                                ONE 2370
       X1=X                                                           ONE 2380
       DO 760 JM=1,64                                                 ONE 2390
       X1=X1+DELT                                                     ONE 2400
       CALL RKM                                                       ONE 2410
       TT=(FX(JM,1)*Y(1)-FX(JM,2)*Y(2)+FX(JM,3)*Y(5)-FX(JM,4)*Y(6))**2ONE 2420
      1 +(FX(JM,1)*Y(2)+FX(JM,2)*Y(1)+FX(JM,3)*Y(6)+FX(JM,4)*Y(5))**2 ONE 2430
 760   TB(2*JM+1)=TT/BACK                                             ONE 2440
       TB(1)=(TEMPY(1)**2+TEMPY(2)**2)/BACK                           ONE 2450
       DO 770 JZ=2,128,2                                              ONE 2460
 770   TB(JZ)=0.5*(TB(JZ-1)+TB(JZ+1))                                 ONE 2470
       MARK=1H                                                        ONE 2480
       IF((JC-30)*(JC-31))790,780,790                                 ONE 2490
 780   MARK=1HD                                                       ONE 2500
 790   CALL HALFTN(129,TB,MARK,BLACK,WHITE,1)                         ONE 2510
 800   CONTINUE                                                       ONE 2520
       TIME=(TIMEF(X)-TIME)/1000.0                                    ONE 2530
 810   WRITE(MW,820)C11,C12,C44,IY,TIME,WL,WW,START,FINISH,ANO        ONE 2540
 820   FORMAT(14H TRIBOPHYSICS F5.2,4HC11 F5.2,4HC12 F5.2,4HC44 15A1,F6.10NE 2550
      1,5H SECS F6.2,3H WL F6.2,3H WW F5.2,6H STRT F5.2,5H FIN ,       ONE 2560
      2 F6.3,5H ANO  )                                                ONE 2570
       WRITE(MW,830)LB,LD,LU,LG,LBM,LFN,W,THICK,THBM,BACK,IZ          ONE 2580
 830   FORMAT(1H ,3I2,1H/I1,5HB    3I2,5HU    3I2,5HG    3I2,5HBM   3I2,20NE 2590
      1HFNF7.3,1HWF7.3,4HTHF7.3,4HTHBMF9.3,4HBACK26A1)                ONE 2600
       WRITE(MW,840)BLACK,WHITE                                       ONE 2610
 840   FORMAT(28H PROGRAM ONEDIS  GREY SCALE F5.3,7H BLACK F5.3,6H WHITE)ONE 2620
       GO TO 10                                                       ONE 2630
       END                                                            ONE 2640
```

10.3. Subroutines

10.3.1. SUBROUTINE ANCALC FOR CUBIC CRYSTALS

INPUT   (data via COMMON/ANCNEW):

C11, C12, C44	Elastic Constants
DC	Direction Cosines

(data via COMMON/DATA):

Useful constants and MW, unit number for error messages.

OUTPUT   (data via COMMON/ANCNEW):

C	Elastic Constants
PR, PI	Roots of polynomial
AR, AI	Constants
ELR, ELI	of anisotropic
EMR, EMI	elastic field of dislocation
B, H	
KRASH	Error flag (if non-zero).

CALLED BY: Main program ONEDIS
CALLS: Subroutine NEWTON (data via COMMON/ANCNEW)
          System function ABS, absolute value
          System function SQRT, square root
          Unit MW, line printer, for error message (data via COMMON/
          DATA).

This is a general purpose subroutine for the calculation of the basic constants which specify the elastic field of an infinite straight dislocation in an elastically anisotropic solid. These basic constants are used by the main program ONEDIS to derive the gradient of the displacement field, but as will be pointed out, these same constants can also be used to derive all the elastic properties of the dislocation, e.g. stress, strain and displacement fields, self energy, energy and force of interaction with another parallel dislocation, etc. Reference should be made to Stroh (1958) for the derivation of the formulae which are used, and it will be found that the FORTRAN notation closely parallels the mathematical notation of Stroh. On the other hand, the details of the methods of calculation used in ANCALC bear little resemblance to those suggested by Stroh since his suggestions were made within the framework of hand computation and are usually inappropriate for a digital computer.

The most general anisotropic crystal has 21 independent elastic constants (Nye, 1960). For a cubic crystal these reduce to 3 independent elastic constants which are usually tabulated as c_{11}, c_{12} and c_{44}, and these are defined with respect to cartesian axes which coincide with the crystal axes. However, the theory of the elastic field around an infinite straight dislocation is simplest if dislocation axes are used, with x_3 along the dislocation line, for then all elastic quantities are independent of x_3. The main program supplies ANCALC with the elastic constants C11, C12 and C44 and with the array DC containing the direction cosines between the crystal axes and the desired dislocation axes, DC(J, K) being the cosine of the angle between dislocation axis J and crystal axis K.

ANCALC, like the theory of elasticity, uses two different systems for specifying elastic constants, the four suffix system and the two suffix system. In the four suffix system, which is convenient in the mathematical theory of elasticity and is used by Stroh, there are 81 elastic constants c_{ijkl} with each subscript taking the values 1, 2, 3. In the two subscript system there are 36 elastic constants c_{mn} with each subscript taking the values 1 to 6. The two subscript system is used for the tabulation of experimental values of the elastic constants and is used in ANCALC for convenience because arrays of four dimensions are not available in FORTRAN. The connection between these two systems is that $ij \rightarrow m$ and $kl \rightarrow n$ in the following manner: $11 \rightarrow 1$, $22 \rightarrow 2$, $33 \rightarrow 3$, 23 and $32 \rightarrow 4$, 31 and $13 \rightarrow 5$, 12 and $21 \rightarrow 6$ and this translation is done by the arrays MM, NN, L1, L2, L3 in COMMON/DATA.

ANCALC starts by filling the array D with 36 elastic constant ratios normalised to $c_{44} = 1.0$ (ANC 70–210) and then calculates the array C, the elastic constants relative to the dislocation axes (ANC 220–290). This is most simply done in terms of the four suffix system in which c_{ijkl} is a fourth rank tensor so that the usual tensor rotation relation can be used:

$$c_{ijkl} = DC_{ip} DC_{jq} DC_{kr} DC_{ls} c_{pqrs} . \tag{10.5}$$

In this relation, as in the rest of this section, the summation convention is used for repeated latin subscripts so that it is implied that the right-hand side is summed over the repeated subscripts p, q, r, s.

Stroh's theory first requires finding a vector A_k (see §2.7.2(ii)) satisfying the equations

$$(c_{i1k1} + pc_{i1k2} + pc_{i2k1} + p^2 c_{i2k2})A_k = 0, \quad i = 1, 3 \; [(S7)]^* \tag{10.6}$$

and a non-zero A_k is only possible if p is a root of the sextic equation

$$|c_{i1k1} + pc_{i1k2} + pc_{i2k1} + p^2 c_{i2k2}| = 0 . \qquad [(S8)] \tag{10.7}$$

This determinant, written in full in the two suffix system, is

$$\begin{vmatrix} c_{11} + 2pc_{16} + p^2 c_{66} & c_{16} + p(c_{12} + c_{66}) + p^2 c_{26} & c_{15} + p(c_{14} + c_{56}) + p^2 c_{46} \\ c_{16} + p(c_{12} + c_{66}) + p^2 c_{26} & c_{66} + 2pc_{26} + p^2 c_{22} & c_{56} + p(c_{46} + c_{25}) + p^2 c_{24} \\ c_{15} + p(c_{14} + c_{56}) + p^2 c_{46} & c_{56} + p(c_{46} + c_{25}) + p^2 c_{24} & c_{55} + 2pc_{45} + p^2 c_{44} \end{vmatrix}$$

$$\tag{10.8}$$

and this is multiplied out (ANC 400–680) to find the coefficients of the sextic polynomial. The method used (ANC 650–660) is based on the formula for a symmetric third order determinant:

$$\begin{vmatrix} a & f & e \\ f & b & d \\ e & d & c \end{vmatrix} = abc + 2def - ad^2 - be^2 - cf^2 . \tag{10.9}$$

The coefficients are formed in the arrays QR, QI, real part in QR and

---

* This notation is used to denote the number of an equivalent equation in Stroh (1958).

imaginary part in QI, such that the polynomial is

$$[QR(7) + iQI(7)] p^6 + [QR(6) + iQI(6)] p^5 + \dots + [QR(1) + iQI(1)] = 0.$$
(10.10)

In fact the coefficients are purely real at this point but they become complex later in the process of finding the roots. This polynomial can have no real roots so that the roots occur in complex conjugate pairs. They are found by calls to subroutine NEWTON (ANC 690–930) which finds one root per call and also divides this root out thus reducing the degree of the polynomial by one. The number of coefficients left at each stage is given by NEW, starting at 7 (ANC 700) and a starting approximation to the root is in ZR + iZI. When NEWTON has found a complex root, it returns with it in ZR + iZI and with KRASH left as zero. If it did not find a root in 70 iterations or if the root was real rather than complex then KRASH is set negative or positive, leading to the appropriate error message (ANC 1070–1120). Stroh's theory uses the three roots p_α (α = 1, 2, 3) which have positive imaginary parts and these are stored as PR(α) + iPI(α).

Having found three suitable roots p_α, non-zero vectors A_k can be found which satisfy eqs. (10.6) for each of the p_α. These are called $A_{k\alpha}$ by Stroh and AR(k, α) + iAI(k, α) here. The method which is used (ANC 1140–1450) is that $A_{k\alpha}$ is equal to the cofactor of the element in column k and row α of the determinant (10.8), evaluated with $p = p_\alpha$. Such $A_{k\alpha}$ will certainly satisfy eqs. (10.6), but may not be non-zero in the degenerate case when the dislocation line is perpendicular to a symmetry plane of the crystal (e.g. along $\langle 001 \rangle$ and $\langle 011 \rangle$ in cubic crystals). In this degenerate case all elements in the third row or third column of the determinant (10.8) are zero by symmetry except for $c_{55} + 2pc_{45} + p^2 c_{44}$. A non-degenerate $A_{k\alpha}$ can be ensured by renumbering the p_α so that p_3 is the one which is closest to being a zero of this quadratic (ANC 940–1050).

Stroh then defines:

$$L_{i\alpha} = (c_{i2k1} + p_\alpha c_{i2k2}) A_{k\alpha}, \quad [(S14)]$$
(10.11)

which is calculated (ANC 1460–1590) as ELR(i, α) + iELI(i, α); $M_{\alpha j}$ as the inverse of $L_{i\alpha}$ [(S38)] which is calculated (ANC 1600–1810) as EMR(α, j) + iEMI(α, j); and

$$B_{ij} = \tfrac{1}{2} i \sum_\alpha (A_{i\alpha} M_{\alpha j} - \bar{A}_{i\alpha} \bar{M}_{\alpha j}), \quad [(S40)]$$
(10.12)

which is calculated (ANC 1820–1860) as B(i, j). ANCALC concludes by calculating H(i, j), a quantity not explicitly used by Stroh, as the inverse of B(i, j)

(ANC 1870–1970). Of these matrices B and H are real and symmetric but M, L and A are complex and non-symmetric so the order of the subscripts of the latter is important. It will be noted that ANCALC does not use the Burgers vector of the dislocation but only the elastic constants and the orientation of the dislocation line in the crystal. The matrices A, L, M, B and H are the same for any dislocation with this line direction irrespective of its Burgers vector. The elastic field of a dislocation does of course depend on its Burgers vector b_i (referred to dislocation axes). This is given by Stroh, not in terms of b_i but of a related vector d_i which is defined by

$$b_i = B_{ij}d_j .$$
[(S50)]   (10.13)

However, from the definition of H_{ij} this can be inverted to give

$$d_i = H_{ij}b_j ,$$
(10.14)

and if this is substituted for d_i in Stroh's expressions, the dependence on the Burgers vector is made explicit. If this substitution is made, and defining Z_α as $x_1 + p_\alpha x_2$, then the displacements at the point (x_1, x_2) are given by

$$u_k = \frac{1}{4\pi} \sum_\alpha (A_{k\alpha}M_{\alpha j}H_{ij}b_i \log Z_\alpha) + \text{conjugate complex, [(S45)]}$$ (10.15)

the stresses by

$$\sigma_{i1} = \frac{-c_{44}}{4\pi} \sum_\alpha (L_{i\alpha}p_\alpha M_{\alpha j}H_{ij}b_i Z_\alpha^{-1}) + \text{c.c.,}$$
[(S51)]   (10.16)

and

$$\sigma_{i2} = \frac{c_{44}}{4\pi} \sum_\alpha (L_{i\alpha}M_{\alpha j}H_{ij}b_i Z_\alpha^{-1}) + \text{c.c.,}$$
[(S52)]   (10.17)

and the line energy of the dislocation by

$$E = \frac{c_{44}}{4\pi} H_{ij}b_i b_j \log\frac{r_1}{r_0} ,$$
[(S56)]   (10.18)

where r_0 and r_1 are the conventional inner and outer cut-off radii.

Apart from simple changes of scale, the quantity which appears in the differential equations describing the electron microscope image of a dislocation is $d(g_k u_k)/dx_2$, where g_k is the diffracting vector (referred to dislocation axes). This is calculated in DERIV using constants evaluated in the main program (ONE 1170–1480) but is described here as it follows logically from the quantities described above. From eq. (10.15) we have

$$g_k u_k = \frac{1}{4\pi} \sum_\alpha (g_k A_{k\alpha} M_{\alpha j} H_{ij} b_i \log(x_1 + p_\alpha x_2)) + \text{c.c.},$$
(10.19)

and therefore

$$\frac{d}{dx_2}(g_k u_k) = \frac{1}{4\pi} \sum_\alpha \{(g_k A_{k\alpha} M_{\alpha j} H_{ij} b_i p_\alpha)/(x_1 + p_\alpha x_2)\} + \text{c.c.},$$
(10.20)

or, writing this in real form,

$$\frac{d}{dx_2}(g_k u_k) = \frac{1}{2\pi} \sum_\alpha \frac{x_1 \mathcal{R}(g_k A_{k\alpha} M_{\alpha j} H_{ij} b_i p_\alpha) + x_2 \mathcal{R}(g_k A_{k\alpha} M_{\alpha j} H_{ij} b_i p_\alpha \bar{p}_\alpha)}{x_1^2 + x_1 x_2 (p_\alpha + \bar{p}_\alpha) + p_\alpha \bar{p}_\alpha x_2^2}$$
(10.21)

where $\mathcal{R}$ stands for 'real part of'.

These constants are evaluated in the following sequence using DR, DI, UR, UI, VR, VI as work space:

$$D_\alpha = g_k A_{k\alpha} \qquad \text{(ONE 1170–1220)}$$
$$D_\alpha = g_k A_{k\alpha} p_\alpha \qquad \text{(ONE 1230–1260)}$$
$$U_{\alpha i} = M_{\alpha j} H_{ij} \qquad \text{(ONE 1270–1330)}$$
$$V_{\alpha i} = D_\alpha U_{\alpha i} = g_k A_{k\alpha} p_\alpha M_{\alpha j} H_{ij} \qquad \text{(ONE 1340–1370)}$$
$$\text{UR}_{\alpha i}, = \mathcal{R}(V_{\alpha i} \bar{p}_\alpha) \qquad \text{(ONE 1380–1400)} \quad (10.22)$$
$$\text{CN}(\alpha + 6) = \mathcal{R}(p_\alpha)$$
$$\text{CN}(\alpha + 9) = (\mathcal{I}(p_\alpha))^2, \quad \begin{array}{l}(\mathcal{I} = \text{imaginary} \\ \text{part of})\end{array} \quad \text{(ONE 1410–1480)}$$
$$\text{CN}(\alpha) = b_i \mathcal{R}(V_{\alpha i})$$
$$\text{CN}(\alpha + 3) = b_i \text{UR}_{\alpha i},$$

so that

$$\frac{d}{dx_2}(g_k u_k) = \frac{1}{2\pi} \sum_\alpha \frac{x_1 \text{CN}(\alpha) + x_2 \text{CN}(\alpha+3)}{(x_1 + x_2 \text{CN}(\alpha+6))^2 + x_2^2 \text{CN}(\alpha+9)}.$$
(10.23)

Listing of subroutine ANCALC

```
      SUBROUTINE ANCALC                                          ANC  10
      DIMENSION D(6,6),DR(3,3),DI(3,3),G(9),E(9)                 ANC  20
      COMMON/DATA/NP(3),NQ(3),MM(3),NN(3),L1(6),L2(6),L3(3,3),PY,HR,HW  ANC  30
      COMMON/ANCNEW/NEW,ZR,ZI,QR(7),QI(7),KRASH,C11,C12,C44,DC(3,3),    ANC  40
     1 C(6,6),PR(3),PI(3),AR(3,3),AI(3,3),ELR(3,3),ELI(3,3),EMR(3,3),   ANC  50
     2 EMI(3,3),B(3,3),H(3,3)                                   ANC  60
      DO 30 JA=1,6                                               ANC  70
      DO 30 JB=1,6                                               ANC  80
   30 D(JA,JB)=0.0                                               ANC  90
      D(1,1)=C11/C44                                             ANC 100
      D(2,2)=D(1,1)                                              ANC 110
      D(3,3)=D(1,1)                                              ANC 120
      D(1,2)=C12/C44                                             ANC 130
      D(2,1)=D(1,2)                                              ANC 140
      D(2,3)=D(1,2)                                              ANC 150
      D(3,2)=D(1,2)                                              ANC 160
      D(1,3)=D(1,2)                                              ANC 170
      D(3,1)=D(1,2)                                              ANC 180
      D(4,4)=1.0                                                 ANC 190
      D(5,5)=1.0                                                 ANC 200
      D(6,6)=1.0                                                 ANC 210
      DO 34 M=1,6                                                ANC 220
      I=L1(M)                                                    ANC 230
      J=L2(M)                                                    ANC 240
      DO 34 N=1,M                                                ANC 250
      K=L1(N)                                                    ANC 260
      L=L2(N)                                                    ANC 270
      X=0.0                                                      ANC 280
      DO 33 LP=1,3                                               ANC 290
      Y=0.0                                                      ANC 300
      DO 32 LQ=1,3                                               ANC 310
      LT=L3(LP,LQ)                                               ANC 320
   32 Y=Y+DC(J,LQ)*                                             ANC 330
     1   (DC(K,1)*(DC(L,1)*D(LT,1)+DC(L,2)*D(LT,6)+DC(L,3)*D(LT,5))    ANC 340
     2   +DC(K,2)*(DC(L,1)*D(LT,6)+DC(L,2)*D(LT,2)+DC(L,3)*D(LT,4))    ANC 350
     3   +DC(K,3)*(DC(L,1)*D(LT,5)+DC(L,2)*D(LT,4)+DC(L,3)*D(LT,3)))   ANC 360
   33 X=X+DC(I,LP)*Y                                             ANC 370
      C(M,N)=X                                                   ANC 380
   34 C(N,M)=X                                                   ANC 390
      G(1)=C(5,5)                                                ANC 400
      G(2)=2.0*C(4,5)                                            ANC 410
      G(3)=C(4,4)                                                ANC 420
      G(4)=C(6,6)                                                ANC 430
      G(5)=2.0*C(2,6)                                            ANC 440
      G(6)=C(2,2)                                                ANC 450
      G(7)=C(1,1)                                                ANC 460
      G(8)=2.0*C(1,6)                                            ANC 470
      G(9)=C(6,6)                                                ANC 480
      E(1)=C(5,6)                                                ANC 490
      E(2)=C(2,5)+C(4,6)                                         ANC 500
      E(3)=C(2,4)                                                ANC 510
      E(4)=C(1,5)                                                ANC 520
      E(5)=C(5,6)+C(1,4)                                         ANC 530
      E(6)=C(4,6)                                                ANC 540
      E(7)=C(1,6)                                                ANC 550
      E(8)=C(6,6)+C(1,2)                                         ANC 560
      E(9)=C(2,6)                                                ANC 570
      DO 50 KP=1,7                                               ANC 580
      QR(KP)=0.0                                                 ANC 590
   50 QI(KP)=0.0                                                 ANC 600
      DO 51 KQ=1,3                                               ANC 610
      DO 51 KR=1,3                                               ANC 620
      DO 51 KS=1,3                                               ANC 630
      KT=KQ+KR+KS-2                                              ANC 640
   51 QR(KT)=QR(KT)+G(KQ)*G(KR+3)*G(KS+6)+2.0*E(KQ)*E(KR+3)*E(KS+6)-    ANC 650
     1 E(KQ)*E(KR)*G(KS+6)-E(KQ+3)*E(KR+3)*G(KS+3)-E(KQ+6)*E(KR+6)*G(KS)ANC 660
      DO 52 KP=1,7                                               ANC 670
   52 QR(KP)=QR(KP)/QR(7)                                        ANC 680
      KRASH=0                                                    ANC 690
      NEW=7                                                      ANC 700
      ZR=0.1                                                     ANC 710
      ZI=1.0                                                     ANC 720
      CALL NEWTON                                                ANC 730
      IF(KRASH)70,61,69                                          ANC 740
```

```
61    PR(1)=ZR                                                      ANC  750
      PI(1)=ABS(ZI)                                                 ANC  760
      ZI=-ZI                                                        ANC  770
      CALL NEWTON                                                   ANC  780
      IF(KRASH)70,62,69                                             ANC  790
62    ZR=0.5                                                        ANC  800
      ZI=0.9                                                        ANC  810
      CALL NEWTON                                                   ANC  820
      IF(KRASH)70,63,69                                             ANC  830
63    PR(2)=ZR                                                      ANC  840
      PI(2)=ABS(ZI)                                                 ANC  850
      ZI=-ZI                                                        ANC  860
      CALL NEWTON                                                   ANC  870
      IF(KRASH)70,64,69                                             ANC  880
64    ZR=-ZR                                                        ANC  890
      CALL NEWTON                                                   ANC  900
      IF(KRASH)70,65,69                                             ANC  910
65    PR(3)=ZR                                                      ANC  920
      PI(3)=ABS(ZI)                                                 ANC  930
      ZR=-C(4,5)/C(4,4)                                             ANC  940
      ZI=SQRT(ABS(C(4,4)*C(5,5)-C(4,5)**2))/C(4,4)                  ANC  950
      DO 67 N=1,2                                                   ANC  960
      IF((ZR-PR(N))**2+(ZI-PI(N))**2-(ZR-PR(N+1))**2-(ZI-PI(N+1))**2)ANC 970
     1 66,67,67                                                     ANC  980
66    Z=PR(N)                                                       ANC  990
      PR(N)=PR(N+1)                                                 ANC 1000
      PR(N+1)=Z                                                     ANC 1010
      Z=PI(N)                                                       ANC 1020
      PI(N)=PI(N+1)                                                 ANC 1030
      PI(N+1)=Z                                                     ANC 1040
67    CONTINUE                                                      ANC 1050
      GO TO 74                                                      ANC 1060
69    WRITE(MW,73)                                                  ANC 1070
      GO TO 99                                                      ANC 1080
70    WRITE(MW,71)                                                  ANC 1090
      GO TO 99                                                      ANC 1100
71    FORMAT(/,/,11H NOCONVERGE,/,/)                                ANC 1110
73    FORMAT(/,/,9H REALROOT,/,/)                                   ANC 1120
74    CONTINUE                                                      ANC 1130
      DO 80 K=1,3                                                   ANC 1140
      I=NP(K)                                                       ANC 1150
      L=NQ(K)                                                       ANC 1160
      PRK=PR(K)                                                     ANC 1170
      PIK=PI(K)                                                     ANC 1180
      SQR=PRK**2-PIK**2                                             ANC 1190
      SQI=2.0*PRK*PIK                                               ANC 1200
      DR(1,1)=C(1,1)+PRK*2.0*C(1,6)+SQR*C(6,6)                      ANC 1210
      DR(2,2)=C(6,6)+PRK*2.0*C(2,6)+SQR*C(2,2)                      ANC 1220
      DR(3,3)=C(5,5)+PRK*2.0*C(4,5)+SQR*C(4,4)                      ANC 1230
      DR(1,2)=C(1,6)+PRK*(C(1,2)+C(6,6))+SQR*C(2,6)                 ANC 1240
      DR(2,3)=C(5,6)+PRK*(C(4,6)+C(2,5))+SQR*C(2,4)                 ANC 1250
      DR(3,1)=C(1,5)+PRK*(C(1,4)+C(5,6))+SQR*C(4,6)                 ANC 1260
      DR(2,1)=DR(1,2)                                               ANC 1270
      DR(3,2)=DR(2,3)                                               ANC 1280
      DR(1,3)=DR(3,1)                                               ANC 1290
      DI(1,1)=PIK*2.0*C(1,6)+SQI*C(6,6)                             ANC 1300
      DI(2,2)=PIK*2.0*C(2,6)+SQI*C(2,2)                             ANC 1310
      DI(3,3)=PIK*2.0*C(4,5)+SQI*C(4,4)                             ANC 1320
      DI(1,2)=PIK*(C(1,2)+C(6,6))+SQI*C(2,6)                        ANC 1330
      DI(2,3)=PIK*(C(4,6)+C(2,5))+SQI*C(2,4)                        ANC 1340
      DI(3,1)=PIK*(C(1,4)+C(5,6))+SQI*C(4,6)                        ANC 1350
      DI(2,1)=DI(1,2)                                               ANC 1360
      DI(3,2)=DI(2,3)                                               ANC 1370
      DI(1,3)=DI(3,1)                                               ANC 1380
      DO 80 J=1,3                                                   ANC 1390
      M=NP(J)                                                       ANC 1400
      N=NQ(J)                                                       ANC 1410
      AR(J,K)=DR(I,M)*DR(L,N)-DI(I,M)*DI(L,N)-DR(I,N)*DR(L,M)+DI(I,N)*ANC 1420
     1 DI(L,M)                                                      ANC 1430
80    AI(J,K)=DR(I,M)*DI(L,N)+DI(I,M)*DR(L,N)-DR(I,N)*DI(L,M)-DI(I,N)*ANC 1440
     1 DR(L,M)                                                      ANC 1450
      DO 82 J=1,3                                                   ANC 1460
      NJ=NN(J)                                                      ANC 1470
      DO 82 K=1,3                                                   ANC 1480
      XR=0.0                                                        ANC 1490
      XI=0.0                                                        ANC 1500
      DO 81 L=1,3                                                   ANC 1510
      NL=NN(L)                                                      ANC 1520
      ML=MM(L)                                                      ANC 1530
      YR=C(NJ,ML)+C(NJ,NL)*PR(K)                                    ANC 1540
```

```
         YI=C(NJ,NL)*PI(K)                                          ANC 1550
         XR=XR+YR*AR(L,K)-YI*AI(L,K)                                ANC 1560
 81      XI=XI+YI*AR(L,K)+YR*AI(L,K)                                ANC 1570
         ELR(J,K)=XR                                                ANC 1580
 82      ELI(J,K)=XI                                                ANC 1590
         DO 83 J=1,3                                                ANC 1600
         J1=NP(J)                                                   ANC 1610
         J2=NQ(J)                                                   ANC 1620
         DO 83 K=1,3                                                ANC 1630
         K1=NP(K)                                                   ANC 1640
         K2=NQ(K)                                                   ANC 1650
         EMR(K,J) = ELR(J1,K1)*ELR(J2,K2) -ELI(J1,K1)*ELI(J2,K2)    ANC 1660
        1          -ELR(J1,K2)*ELR(J2,K1) +ELI(J1,K2)*ELI(J2,K1)    ANC 1670
 83      EMI(K,J) = ELR(J1,K1)*ELI(J2,K2) +ELI(J1,K1)*ELR(J2,K2)    ANC 1680
        1          -ELR(J1,K2)*ELI(J2,K1) -ELI(J1,K2)*ELR(J2,K1)    ANC 1690
         DELR=0.0                                                   ANC 1700
         DELI=0.0                                                   ANC 1710
         DO 84 J=1,3                                                ANC 1720
         DELR = DELR  +ELR(3,J)*EMR(J,3)  -ELI(3,J)*EMI(J,3)        ANC 1730
 84      DELI = DELI  +ELR(3,J)*EMI(J,3)  +ELI(3,J)*EMR(J,3)        ANC 1740
         AUMR = DELR/(DELR**2+DELI**2)                              ANC 1750
         AUMI=-DELI/(DELR**2+DELI**2)                               ANC 1760
         DO 85 J=1,3                                                ANC 1770
         DO 85 K=1,3                                                ANC 1780
         X = EMR(J,K)*AUMR -EMI(J,K)*AUMI                           ANC 1790
         EMI(J,K) = EMR(J,K)*AUMI +EMI(J,K)*AUMR                    ANC 1800
 85      EMR(J,K) = X                                               ANC 1810
         DO 86 I=1,3                                                ANC 1820
         DO 86 J=1,3                                                ANC 1830
         B(I,J)=0.0                                                 ANC 1840
         DO 86 K=1,3                                                ANC 1850
 86      B(I,J)=B(I,J) -AR(I,K)*EMI(K,J) -AI(I,K)*EMR(K,J)          ANC 1860
         DO 87 I=1,3                                                ANC 1870
         I1=NP(I)                                                   ANC 1880
         I2=NQ(I)                                                   ANC 1890
         DO 87 J=1,3                                                ANC 1900
         J1=NP(J)                                                   ANC 1910
         J2=NQ(J)                                                   ANC 1920
 87      H(I,J) =  B(I1,J1)*B(I2,J2) -B(I1,J2)*B(I2,J1)             ANC 1930
         DEL=B(3,1)*H(3,1)+B(3,2)*H(3,2)+B(3,3)*H(3,3)             ANC 1940
         DO 88 I=1,3                                                ANC 1950
         DO 88 J=1,3                                                ANC 1960
 88      H(I,J)=H(I,J)/DEL                                          ANC 1970
 99      RETURN                                                     ANC 1980
         END                                                        ANC 1990
```

10.3.2. SUBROUTINE NEWTON

INPUT　　　　(data via COMMON/ANCNEW):

	QR, QI	Coefficients of polynomial
	NEW	Actual number of coefficients
	ZR, ZI	Starting approximation to a root of polynomial = ZR + iZI

OUTPUT　　　(data via COMMON/ANCNEW):

	ZR, ZI	A root of the polynomial
	QR, QI	Coefficients of remainder polynomial
	NEW	Actual number of remaining coefficients
	KRASH	Error flag (if non-zero)

CALLED BY: Subroutine ANCALC

CALLS:　　　System function ABS, absolute value

This subroutine calculates one root of the polynomial whose coefficients are in QR + iQI, starting from the approximation to the root given in ZR + iZI and leaving the found root in ZR + iZI. The actual number of coefficients is given by NEW, i.e. the degree of the polynomial is NEW − 1.

If the polynomial is

$$f(Z) = [QR(1) + iQI(1)] + [QR(2) + iQI(2)]Z + \dots \qquad (10.24)$$

and Z is an approximate root, then Newton's method gives $Z_1 = Z - f(Z)/f'(Z)$ as the next approximation. $f(Z)$ is calculated as XR $+$ iXI, $f'(Z)$ as YR $+$ iYI (NEW 50–200) and $f(Z)/f'(Z)$ as TR $+$ iTI (NEW 220–240). The new approximation to the root is calculated (NEW 250–260) and if the change in the approximate root is sufficiently small (NEW 270), KONVRG is set to one (NEW 280) to indicate that the iteration has converged. A maximum of 70 iterations is allowed (NEW 40) and, if no root has been found, KRASH is given a negative value (NEW 300) as a signal to the calling program.

If a root has been found and KONVRG set to one, the polynomial is evaluated once more and the found root divided out, the coefficients of the reduced polynomial replacing those of the original (NEW 170–180) and the degree of the polynomial reduced by one (NEW 340).

Before returning to the calling program the found root is tested and if it is approximately real then KRASH is set positive (NEW 320–330) as a signal, since the polynomials generated by ANCALC will only have real roots if the elastic constants are physically impossible.

The constant 0.1 E−11 (NEW 270) should be changed to 0.1 E−7 for computers using floating point numbers of 7 decimal digit precision.

Listing of subroutine NEWTON

```
        SUBROUTINE NEWTON                                  NEW    10
        COMMON/ANCNEW/NEW,ZR,ZI,QR(7),QI(7),KRASH          NEW    20
        KONVRG=0                                           NEW    30
        DO 6 KOUNT =1,70                                   NEW    40
        XR=0.0                                             NEW    50
        XI=0.0                                             NEW    60
        YR=0.0                                             NEW    70
        YI=0.0                                             NEW    80
        DO 3 J=1,NEW                                       NEW    90
        TR=ZR*YR-ZI*YI+XR                                  NEW   100
        YI=ZR*YI+ZI*YR+XI                                  NEW   110
        YR=TR                                              NEW   120
        M=NEW+1-J                                          NEW   130
        TR=ZR*XR-ZI*XI+QR(M)                               NEW   140
        TI=ZR*XI+ZI*XR+QI(M)                               NEW   150
        IF(KONVRG)1,2,1                                    NEW   160
   1    QR(M)=XR                                           NEW   170
        QI(M)=XI                                           NEW   180
   2    XR=TR                                              NEW   190
   3    XI=TI                                              NEW   200
        IF(KONVRG)7,4,7                                    NEW   210
   4    F=1.0/(YR**2+YI**2)                                NEW   220
        TR=F*(XR*YR+XI*YI)                                 NEW   230
        TI=F*(XI*YR-XR*YI)                                 NEW   240
        ZR=ZR-TR                                           NEW   250
        ZI=ZI-TI                                           NEW   260
        IF((TR**2+TI**2)/(ZR**2+ZI**2)-0.1E-11)5,5,6      NEW   270
   5    KONVRG=1                                           NEW   280
   6    CONTINUE                                           NEW   290
        KRASH=-70                                          NEW   300
        GO TO 10                                           NEW   310
   7    IF(ABS(ZR)-100000.0*ABS(ZI))9,9,8                 NEW   320
   8    KRASH=NEW                                          NEW   330
   9    NEW=NEW-1                                          NEW   340
  10    RETURN                                             NEW   350
        END                                                NEW   360
```

10.3.3. SUBROUTINE RKM

INPUT   (data via COMMON/RKMDRV):

Y	Initial values of dependent variables of differential equations
X	Initial value of independent variable
X1	Desired final value of X
ERROR	Maximum permissible error in each Y per integration step
Q	Set zero to start an integration. Left non-zero to continue the same integration

OUTPUT   (data via COMMON/RKMDRV):

Y	Final values of dependent variables
X	Final value of independent variable (= X1)
Q	Step size being used.

CALLED BY: Main program ONEDIS

CALLS: Subroutine DERIV (data via COMMON/RKMDRV)

System function ABS, absolute value.

This is a fourth order Runge–Kutta procedure for the integration of a set of 8 simultaneous first order differential equations. It uses the idea of Merson (1957) (see also Lance, 1960) for estimating the truncation error of the integration and automatically choosing the optimum integration step size to satisfy a preassigned accuracy. It integrates the equations

$$\frac{dY_M}{dX} = f_M(X, Y_1, Y_2, ...) \quad M = 1, 8 \tag{10.25}$$

where the functions f_M can be any functions of the independent variable X and the dependent variables Y_M. The specific functions f_M are contained in subroutine DERIV which returns the current values of f_M in D(M) when called (RKM 230, 280, 320, 380, 430).

If Q is an increment in X, then Mersen has shown that the corresponding increment in Y_M is

$$\delta Y_M = \tfrac{1}{2}(K_{M,1} + 4K_{M,4} + K_{M,5}) + O(Q^5), \tag{10.26}$$

where

$$K_{M,1} = \tfrac{1}{3}Qf_M(X, Y_1, Y_2, ...)$$

$$K_{M,2} = \tfrac{1}{3}Qf_M(X + \tfrac{1}{3}Q, Y_1 + K_{1,1}, Y_2 + K_{2,1}, ...)$$

$$K_{M,3} = \tfrac{1}{3}Qf_M(X + \tfrac{1}{3}Q, Y_1 + \tfrac{1}{2}K_{1,1} + \tfrac{1}{2}K_{1,2}, Y_2 + \tfrac{1}{2}K_{2,1} + \tfrac{1}{2}K_{2,2}, ...)$$

$$K_{M,4} = \tfrac{1}{3}Qf_M(X + \tfrac{1}{2}Q, Y_1 + \tfrac{3}{8}K_{1,1} + \tfrac{9}{8}K_{1,2}, ...)$$

$$K_{M,5} = \tfrac{1}{3}Qf_M(X + Q, Y_1 + \tfrac{3}{2}K_{1,1} - \tfrac{9}{2}K_{1,3} + 6K_{1,4}, ...) , \tag{10.27}$$

and an estimate of ϵ, the error in δY_M, is given by

$$5\epsilon = |K_{M,1} - \tfrac{9}{2}K_{M,3} + 4K_{M,4} - \tfrac{1}{2}K_{M,5}| . \tag{10.28}$$

The calling program sets initial values of the variables in X and Y(1)–Y(8), the permissible error per step ϵ in ERROR and the desired final value of X in X1. Subroutine RKM will then integrate the differential equations in suitably sized steps until X attains the value X1, and then returns with X and Y(1)–Y(8) containing the updated values of the variables. The same integration can be continued by setting X1 to a new value and calling RKM. The step size being used by RKM is held in Q so that the integration can continue with the optimum step. At the start of a new integration, the calling program sets Q to zero as a cue to RKM that the optimum step size is unknown (RKM 50).

Within RKM, XT and YT(1)–YT(8) are temporary storage for the initial values of X and Y(1)–Y(8) (RKM 140–160), and the array DT for combinations of the K_M as follows

$$DT(M, 1) = K_{M,1} \qquad \text{(RKM 250)}$$

$$DT(M, 2) = \tfrac{9}{2}K_{M,3} \qquad \text{(RKM 350)}$$

$$DT(M, 1) = K_{M,1} + 4K_{M,4} \qquad \text{(RKM 400)}$$

$$DT(M, 3) = \tfrac{1}{2}K_{M,5} \qquad \text{(RKM 460)}.$$

$$\tag{10.29}$$

LAST is always zero except (RKM 110) when the step in progress would, if successful, increment X to the terminal value X1 and so be the last step of the integration. SKIP is always zero except during the third call of DERIV (RKM 310–330). $K_{M,2}$ and $K_{M,3}$ are both evaluated for the same value of the independent variable and SKIP indicates to subroutine DERIV that any part of f_M which depends only on X need not be re-evaluated and that the last evaluation can be re-used.

The integration step Q is chosen automatically by the following procedure. For each of the Y in turn the right-hand side of eq. (10.28) is evaluated as TEST (RKM 470). This is compared with 5*ERROR (RKM 480) and, if it is greater, then this integration step is abandoned, Q is halved, the previous values of X and Y(1)–Y(8) restored and the step begun again (RKM 570–620). On the other hand, if these eight tests are successful, then the integration is accepted and if, in addition, all eight errors are less than $\frac{1}{32}$ of that specified (RKM 490) then Q is doubled (RKM 540) so that the integration would continue with a larger step-size.

Listing of subroutine RKM

```
      SUBROUTINE RKM                                            RKM    10
      DIMENSION YT(8),DT(8,3)                                   RKM    20
      COMMON/RKMDRV/CN(30),X,X1,Y(8),ERROR,SKIP,Q,D(8),ANO      RKM    30
      LAST=0                                                    RKM    40
      IF(Q)16,1,16                                              RKM    50
    1 Q=X1-X                                                    RKM    60
      SKIP=0.0                                                  RKM    70
      Q15=0.0                                                   RKM    80
      ERHIGH=ERROR*5.0                                          RKM    90
      ERLOW=ERHIGH*0.03125                                      RKM   100
    2 LAST=1                                                    RKM   110
      Q1=Q                                                      RKM   120
      Q=X1-X                                                    RKM   130
    3 XT=X                                                      RKM   140
      DO 4 M=1,8                                                RKM   150
    4 YT(M)=Y(M)                                                RKM   160
    5 IF(Q*1.5-Q15)6,7,6                                        RKM   170
    6 Q2=Q/2.0                                                  RKM   180
      Q3=Q/3.0                                                  RKM   190
      Q4=4.0*Q3                                                 RKM   200
      Q6=Q/6.0                                                  RKM   210
      Q15=Q*1.5                                                 RKM   220
    7 CALL DERIV                                                RKM   230
      DO 8 M=1,8                                                RKM   240
      DT(M,1)=Q3*D(M)                                           RKM   250
    8 Y(M)=DT(M,1)+YT(M)                                        RKM   260
      X=X+Q3                                                    RKM   270
      CALL DERIV                                                RKM   280
      DO 9 M=1,8                                                RKM   290
    9 Y(M)=Q6*D(M)+0.5*DT(M,1)+YT(M)                            RKM   300
      SKIP=1.0                                                  RKM   310
      CALL DERIV                                                RKM   320
      SKIP=0.0                                                  RKM   330
      DO 10 M=1,8                                               RKM   340
      DT(M,2)=Q15*D(M)                                          RKM   350
   10 Y(M)=0.375*DT(M,1)+0.25*DT(M,2)+YT(M)                     RKM   360
      X=XT+Q2                                                   RKM   370
      CALL DERIV                                                RKM   380
      DO 11 M=1,8                                               RKM   390
      DT(M,1)=Q4*D(M)+DT(M,1)                                   RKM   400
   11 Y(M)=1.5*DT(M,1)-DT(M,2)+YT(M)                            RKM   410
      X=XT+Q                                                    RKM   420
      CALL DERIV                                                RKM   430
      DOUBLE=2.0                                                RKM   440
      DO 14 M=1,8                                               RKM   450
      DT(M,3)=Q6*D(M)                                           RKM   460
      TEST=ABS(DT(M,1)-DT(M,2)-DT(M,3))                         RKM   470
      IF(TEST-ERHIGH)12,12,18                                   RKM   480
   12 IF(TEST-ERLOW)14,13,13                                    RKM   490
   13 DOUBLE=1.0                                                RKM   500
   14 CONTINUE                                                  RKM   510
      DO 15 M=1,8                                               RKM   520
   15 Y(M)=0.5*DT(M,1)+DT(M,3)+YT(M)                            RKM   530
      Q=DOUBLE*Q                                                RKM   540
      IF(LAST)20,16,20                                          RKM   550
   16 IF(1.0-(X1-X)/Q)3,2,2                                     RKM   560
   18 Q=Q/2.0                                                   RKM   570
      LAST=0                                                    RKM   580
      DO 19 M=1,8                                               RKM   590
   19 Y(M)=YT(M)                                                RKM   600
```

```
          X=XT                                              RKM   610
          GO TO 6                                           RKM   620
    20    IF(1.0-Q/Q1) 22,22,21                             RKM   630
    21    Q=Q1                                              RKM   640
    22    RETURN                                            RKM   650
          END                                               RKM   660
```

10.3.4. SUBROUTINE DERIV FOR ONE DISLOCATION

INPUT   (data via COMMON/RKMDRV):

CN(1)–CN(12)	Constants of $d(\mathbf{g}\cdot\mathbf{R})/dZ$ for a dislocation
CN(14)	Twice the deviation from the Bragg condition
CN(29)	Coordinate of picture line
X	Independent variable of integration, distance down column
Y	Dependent variables, real and imaginary parts of beam amplitudes
SKIP	Flag to skip evaluation of $d(\mathbf{g}\cdot\mathbf{R})/dZ$
ANO	Anomalous absorption, also normal absorption for convenience.

OUTPUT   (data via COMMON/RKMDRV):

D	Current values of derivatives in differential equations.

CALLED BY: Subroutine RKM

This subroutine returns the current values of the right-hand sides of the Howie–Whelan differential equations when called by subroutine RKM. It is called about 40,000 times during the computation of an image and there can be large speed penalties if it is written inefficiently. The form given here was chosen after examining the corresponding machine code produced by our FORTRAN compiler. It should be optimum for other efficient FORTRAN compilers, but the method of handling the squaring operation (∗∗2) should be examined. If this is translated into a call of a general Nth power subroutine, rather than an in-line multiplication, then the expression for BETA (DER 70–90) would need to be reconsidered. If the process of calling a subroutine is slow, then time would be saved by replacing each of the five calls of DERIV in RKM by a copy of the instructions in DERIV.

The quantity BETA is $2w + 2\pi\, d(\mathbf{g}\cdot\mathbf{R})/dZ$, i.e. $2w + 2\pi\, d(g_k u_k)/dZ$. In the description of subroutine ANCALC it was shown how the form of $d(g_k u_k)/dx_2$ for one dislocation was calculated. Since Z (down the electron beam) and the dislocation axis x_2 are related by

$$x_2 = -Z \cos\psi , \qquad\qquad (10.30)$$

where ψ is the angle between x_2 and the beam direction, then

$$2w + 2\pi \frac{d}{dZ}(g_k u_k) = 2w + \frac{1}{Z}\sum_\alpha \frac{R \cdot CN(\alpha) + CN(\alpha+3)}{(R + CN(\alpha+6))^2 + CN(\alpha+9)} \; , \quad (10.31)$$

where

$$R = \frac{1}{Z}\left(-\frac{x_1}{\cos\psi}\right).$$

In the subroutine the variable Z down the electron beam is the FORTRAN variable X, and CN(29) contains the value of $-x_1/\cos\psi$.

The subroutine starts by calculating BETA, unless SKIP is non-zero (DER 30) in which case the previous value of BETA is re-used. In the calculation of BETA, X is first checked to be non-zero (DER 40) and set very small if it is zero, then R and BETA are calculated in the form described above (DER 60–90). The right-hand sides of the differential equations are then calculated as D(1)–D(8) remembering that ANO is the negative of the anomalous absorption coefficient and that normal absorption is set equal to anomalous absorption.

Listing of subroutine DERIV *for one dislocation*

```
      SUBROUTINE DERIV                                          DER   10
      COMMON/RKMDRV/CN(30),X,X1,Y(8),ERROR,SKIP,Q,D(8),ANO      DER   20
      IF(SKIP)3,4,3                                             DER   30
    4 IF(X)2,1,2                                                DER   40
    1 X=0.00000000001                                           DER   50
    2 R=CN(29)/X                                                DER   60
      BETA=CN(14)+((R*CN(1)+CN(4))/((R+CN(7))**2+CN(10))+(R*CN(2)+ DER   70
    1 CN(5))/((R+CN(8))**2+CN(11))+(R*CN(3)+CN(6))/((R+CN(9))**2+ DER   80
    2 CN(12)))/X                                                DER   90
    3 Z=ANO*(Y(1)+Y(3))                                         DER  100
      D(1)=Z-Y(4)                                               DER  110
      D(3)=-BETA*Y(4)+Z-Y(2)                                    DER  120
      Z=ANO*(Y(2)+Y(4))                                         DER  130
      D(2)=Z+Y(3)                                               DER  140
      D(4)=BETA*Y(3)+Z+Y(1)                                     DER  150
      Z=ANO*(Y(5)+Y(7))                                         DER  160
      D(5)=Z-Y(8)                                               DER  170
      D(7)=-BETA*Y(8)+Z-Y(6)                                    DER  180
      Z=ANO*(Y(6)+Y(8))                                         DER  190
      D(6)=Z+Y(7)                                               DER  200
      D(8)=BETA*Y(7)+Z+Y(5)                                     DER  210
      RETURN                                                    DER  220
      END                                                       DER  230
```

10.4. Special test version of program ONEDIS

This section describes a test run of ONEDIS which should be sufficient to ensure that the program is correct. The program deck consists of main program ONEDIS for cubic crystals (§ 10.2.9) subroutines ANCALC (§ 10.3.1), NEWTON (§ 10.3.2), RKM (§ 10.3.3), DERIV for one dislocation (§ 10.3.4) and the version of HALFTN given in § 10.5 which used only the FORTRAN character set. The following modifications should be made and the program run with the data cards shown here.

Listing of temporary modification to program ONEDIS *for numerical checks*

```
C   TEMPORARY MODIFICATION TO PROGRAM ONEDIS FOR NUMERICAL CHECKS
C•••••••••••••••••••••••••••••••••••••••••••••••••••••••••••••••••••••••
C   INSERT THE FOLLOWING 6 CARDS BETWEEN ONE 1770 AND ONE 1780
        WRITE(MW,591)                                              ONE 1771
591     FORMAT(/,/)                                                ONE 1772
        WRITE(MW,592) ((DC(I,J),J=1,3),I=1,3)                      ONE 1773
592     FORMAT(/,X,3F10.5)                                         ONE 1774
        WRITE(MW,591)                                              ONE 1775
        WRITE(MW,592) (CN(I),I=1,12)                               ONE 1776
C•••••••••••••••••••••••••••••••••••••••••••••••••••••••••••••••••••••••
C   THE FOLLOWING 2 DATA CARDS ARE FOR THE NUMERICAL TEST RUN
C   THEY SHOULD BE FOLLOWED BY A BLANK CARD TO STOP THE PROGRAM
1.291        1.097        .824         BETA BRASS                      0.09
 1 1 1/1 -3 5 5 -1-2 1  1 1 3   0 1 3 0.7 3.0 0.0 3.0 1    TEST MICROGRAPH
C•••••••••••••••••••••••••••••••••••••••••••••••••••••••••••••••••••••••
C•••••••••••••••••••••••••••••••••••••••••••••••••••••••••••••••••••••••
C   THE PREVIOUS CARD IS AN ALIGNMENT GUIDE FOR PUNCHING THE DATA CARDS
C   IT HAS COLUMNS 10,20,30,ETC BLANK
C•••••••••••••••••••••••••••••••••••••••••••••••••••••••••••••••••••••••
C    END  OF  MODIFICATION TO PROGRAM ONEDIS FOR NUMERICAL CHECKS
```

The output which should be obtained is shown in figs. 10.2 and 10.3. It consists of the grey scale table, the array DC which contains the direction cosines of the dislocation axis system, the constants CN(1)–CN(12) which describe the elastic displacement field of the dislocation, and the picture of the dislocation with legend.

The output obtained should be checked against figs. 10.2 and 10.3, making the following allowances. Rounding and truncation errors may change the last figure of any computed number by one unit in the last place. The value of BACK in the picture legend may vary by two or three units depending on the accuracy of the computer. The contours in the picture

TABLE 10.4
Key to test run errors

Error	Fault location
Reproduction of input data in legend	Data cards, ONE 130–190, 2540–2620
DC	ONE 210–650
CN(7)–CN(12)	ONE 660–1140, ANC 10–1130, NEW 10–360, ONE 1420–1430
CN(1)–CN(6)	ANC 1140–1990, ONE 1150–1480
BACK in legend	ONE 1870–1980, RKM 10–660, DER 10–230. Also check THBM, WW and WL in legend
THBM, WW and WL in legend	ONE 660–1130, 1800–1860
Errors in picture	ONE 1990–2520 or HAL 10–740
Grey scale table	HAL 370–740

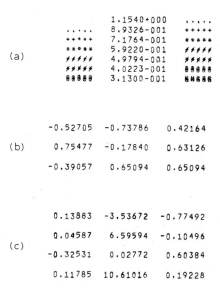

(a)

```
                    1.1540+000     . . . . .
          . . . . . 8.9326-001     + + + + +
          + + + + + 7.1764-001     * * * * *
          * * * * * 5.9220-001     / / / / /
          / / / / / 4.9794-001     / / / / /
          / / / / / 4.0223-001     8 8 8 8 8
          8 8 8 8 8 3.1300-001     H H H H H
```

(b)

```
          -0.52705   -0.73786    0.42164

           0.75477   -0.17840    0.63126

          -0.39057    0.65094    0.65094
```

(c)

```
           0.13883   -3.53672   -0.77492

           0.04587    6.59594   -0.10496

          -0.32531    0.02772    0.60384

           0.11785   10.61016    0.19228
```

Fig. 10.2. Computer output from a test run of ONEDIS showing (a) the grey scale table, (b) the array DC and (c) the constants CN(1)–CN(12).

Fig. 10.3. Computer output from a test run of ONEDIS showing the theoretical image with legend.

where halftone symbols change may move by one position. If on making these allowances the output does not agree with that given, then the sequence of table 10.4 is suggested to localize the area of the program which is probably at fault.

10.5. Subroutine HALFTN

> "HALFTONE. Illustration ... in which the
> lights and shades of the original are represented
> by small or large dots."
> Concise Oxford Dictionary

This subroutine is used to print the computed picture on the line printer. The quality of the picture will depend on the range of symbols available on any particular printer and it is anticipated that most users will want to construct their own version of HALFTN. The listing which is given here is an example which uses only the standard FORTRAN character set from which eight shades of grey can be printed. These characters should be available on all printers and for this reason, this listing of HALFTN was used for the test picture of the previous section. All other pictures in this book used the extensive character set available on the C.S.I.R.O. computers from which eleven shades of grey could be constructed.

Subroutine HALFTN has the parameter list (N, ARRAY, MARK, BLACK, WHITE, JUMP) and performs three different actions depending on whether the last parameter JUMP is negative, zero or positive (HAL 40).

(i) JUMP negative (HAL 440–720). This sets the correspondence between computed intensity and printed shade of grey which will be used in subsequent pictures. The parameters BLACK and WHITE are used to specify the limits of intensity outside which maximum black or maximum white will be printed. Intermediate intensities will be printed in six shades of grey, scaled in suitable logarithmic steps. Once a scale has been set, it remains in force for all subsequent pictures until changed by another call with JUMP negative. The subroutine contains no pre-existing scale so it is essential to set a scale before printing pictures.

(ii) JUMP zero (HAL 370–430). This prints on the line printer a table of the current grey scale. The seven boundary values of intensity are printed in E format flanked by the halftone symbols they separate.

(iii) JUMP positive (HAL 50–360). This prints on the line printer one halftone line of a picture using the parameters N, ARRAY and MARK. The first character of the line is MARK, enabling special lines to be marked. MARK is printed with an A1 format. The values of intensities in the first N locations of the one-dimensional array ARRAY are printed as N halftone symbols, using the current grey scale. N can be in the range 1 to 134. The N

symbols are centred in the middle of the line, specifically in columns
(139–N)/2 to (137+N)/2. MARK is always in column 1. Each picture line is printed
and overprinted.

Returning to the listing (HAL 20) the arrays JX and JXX are used to hold
the characters which will form a picture line, JX being overprinted by JXX.
JA and JAA contain the eight pairs of symbols which give the eight shades
of grey. X contains the seven intensity levels which have been allotted to the
boundaries between the eight shades of grey and this is calculated from the
array Y which contains experimental values of the relative reflectivities of
the printed grey scale.

The grey scale is set up (JUMP negative) starting at HAL 440. The arrays
JA, JAA and Y are filled with characters and values (HAL 480–700) and
the array X is calculated (HAL 710–720). In this expression for X, the variable
F is in effect the photographic contrast and comes from the specified parameters WHITE and BLACK (HAL 470). The variable SENSE has the value +1 if
WHITE is greater than BLACK and the value −1 if WHITE is less than BLACK
(HAL 440–460). The subsequent pictures will be printed as photographic
positives if SENSE is positive or as photographic negative if SENSE is negative.

The grey scale table is printed (JUMP zero) by HAL 370–430.

The printing of a picture line (JUMP positive) starts by checking that N,
the number of intensities to be printed, does not exceed the width of the
paper (HAL 50–80). It then checks that a grey scale has been set (HAL 90–
120). JS and JF are the starting and finishing positions along the printer line
of the N picture points (HAL 130–140), the positions to the left of JS being
filled with blanks (HAL 150–170). The symbols to be printed at the N picture
points are then calculated (HAL 180–310). If the intensity value in ARRAY is
negative (which is physically unreal) then the special letter D will be printed
(HAL 210–240). Otherwise, the intensity is compared with the successive
values in the array X (HAL 250–280) and the corresponding characters selected
(HAL 290–300). The picture line is then printed (HAL 320) and overprinted
(HAL 330), the line printer control character 1H+ meaning no paper movement.

Listing of subroutine HALFTN

```
       SUBROUTINE HALFTN(N,ARRAY,MARK,BLACK,WHITE,JUMP)            HAL    10
       DIMENSION ARRAY(134),JX(134),JXX(134),JA(8),JAA(8),X(7),Y(7) HAL    20
       COMMON/DATA/NP(3),NQ(3),MM(3),NN(3),L1(6),L2(6),L3(3,3),PY,MR,MW HAL  30
       IF(JUMP)190,160,10                                          HAL    40
10     IF(N*(N-135))40,20,20                                       HAL    50
20     WRITE(MW,30) N                                              HAL    60
       GO TO 230                                                   HAL    70
30     FORMAT(8H N WRONG,I15)                                      HAL    80
40     IF(JA(2)-1H,)50,70,50                                       HAL    90
50     WRITE(MW,60)                                                HAL   100
       GO TO 230                                                   HAL   110
```

```
60        FORMAT(18H NO GRAY SCALE SET)                                    HAL   120
70        JS=(137-N)/2                                                     HAL   130
          JF=(135+N)/2                                                     HAL   140
          DO 80 J=2,JS                                                     HAL   150
          JX(J-1)=1H                                                       HAL   160
80        JXX(J-1)=1H                                                      HAL   170
          DO 130 J=JS,JF                                                   HAL   180
          K=J-JS                                                           HAL   190
          Z=SENSE*ARRAY(K+1)                                               HAL   200
          IF(ARRAY(K+1))90,100,100                                         HAL   210
90        JXX(J)=1HD                                                       HAL   220
          JX(J)=1HD                                                        HAL   230
          GO TO 130                                                        HAL   240
100       DO 110 L=1,7                                                     HAL   250
          IF(Z-X(L))110,120,120                                           HAL   260
110       CONTINUE                                                         HAL   270
          L=8                                                              HAL   280
120       JX(J)=JA(L)                                                      HAL   290
          JXX(J)=JAA(L)                                                    HAL   300
130       CONTINUE                                                         HAL   310
          WRITE(MW,140) MARK,(JX(M),M=1,JF)                                HAL   320
          WRITE(MW,150) (JXX(M),M=1,JF)                                    HAL   330
140       FORMAT(1H+A1,134A1)                                             HAL   340
150       FORMAT(2X,134A1)                                                HAL   350
          GO TO 230                                                        HAL   360
160       DO 170 L=1,7                                                     HAL   370
          K=L+1                                                            HAL   380
          Z=SENSE*X(L)                                                     HAL   390
170       WRITE(MW,180) (JA(L),M=1,5),Z,(JA(K),M=1,5),(JAA(L),M=1,5),      HAL   400
         1 (JAA(K),M=1,5)                                                  HAL   410
180       FORMAT(1H+5X,5A1,E13.4,3X,5A1/6X,5A1,16X,5A1)                   HAL   420
          GO TO 230                                                        HAL   430
190       SENSE=1.0                                                        HAL   440
          IF(WHITE-BLACK)200,210,210                                      HAL   450
200       SENSE=-1.0                                                       HAL   460
210       F=(ALOG(WHITE)-ALOG(BLACK))/ALOG(1.7559)                        HAL   470
          JA(1)=1H                                                         HAL   480
          JAA(1)=1H                                                        HAL   490
          Y(1)=1.7559                                                      HAL   500
          JA(2)=1H.                                                        HAL   510
          JAA(2)=1H                                                        HAL   520
          Y(2)=1.5722                                                      HAL   530
          JA(3)=1H*                                                        HAL   540
          JAA(3)=1H                                                        HAL   550
          Y(3)=1.4305                                                      HAL   560
          JA(4)=1H*                                                        HAL   570
          JAA(4)=1H                                                        HAL   580
          Y(4)=1.3167                                                      HAL   590
          JA(5)=1H*                                                        HAL   600
          JAA(5)=1H/                                                       HAL   610
          Y(5)=1.2718                                                      HAL   620
          JA(6)=1H*                                                        HAL   630
          JAA(6)=1H/                                                       HAL   640
          Y(6)=1.1143                                                      HAL   650
          JA(7)=1HO                                                        HAL   660
          JAA(7)=1H*                                                       HAL   670
          Y(7)=1.0000                                                      HAL   680
          JA(8)=1HG                                                        HAL   690
          JAA(8)=1H*                                                       HAL   700
          DO 220 L=1,7                                                     HAL   710
220       X(L)=SENSE*BLACK*Y(L)**F                                        HAL   720
230       RETURN                                                           HAL   730
          END                                                              HAL   740
```

10.6. Programs for other crystal systems

10.6.1. INTRODUCTION

The programs developed in this book have so far been restricted to the computation of images of defects in cubic crystals and this has reflected the major interests of the authors. In the following sections the problem of modifying the programs for other crystal systems is discussed generally

(§ 10.6.2) and, as specific examples, the tetragonal (§ 10.6.3) and hexagonal (§ 10.6.4) crystal systems are considered and modifications to ONEDIS applicable to these systems are given. Procedures for testing programs for non-cubic crystals are outlined in § 10.6.5. In § 10.6.6 there is a brief discussion of the modification, for non-cubic crystals, of programs designed for computing the image of defects more complex than a single dislocation, together with remarks concerning the use of other program modifications such as DELUGE (§ 10.8).

10.6.2. PROGRAM MODIFICATIONS – GENERAL DISCUSSION

It has been pointed out in chs. 2 and 4 that the computation of images of defects are carried out within the framework of two theories: the two-beam dynamical theory of electron diffraction (Howie and Whelan, 1961) and the theory of linear anisotropic elasticity (Eshelby et al., 1953; Stroh, 1958). The first of these theories describes the way in which the electron beam propagates through the crystal containing the displacement field generated by the defect, and this displacement field is itself calculated, using linear anisotropic theory, from the elastic constants of the material and defect characteristics such as the vector u along the dislocation line and the Burgers vector b.

It is the requirements of linear anisotropic elasticity theory which effectively determine the way in which the computer programs are modified to compute the images of defects in non-cubic crystals. Four systems of axes are used in the programs to specify a defect and its geometry. In cubic crystals two of these sets of axes, the crystal axes and the elastic constants axes are coincident, but for non-cubic crystals this need not apply. The elastic constants of any material are measured with respect to a cartesian * axis system and, by convention, the axis system chosen for specifying the elastic constants is related to the crystal axes in the manner defined in: "Standards on piezo-electric crystals" (1949). However, as pointed out previously, the actual calculation of the displacement field of the defect is made simpler in a dislocation axis system. For cubic crystals, since the crystal and elastic constants axes are coincident, the input crystallographic data is already expressed in the elastic constants axis system and is readily converted to the other axis systems used in the programs. When working within the framework of anisotropic elasticity in non-cubic crystals, two approaches are possible: to convert the crystallographic information into the elastic constants axis system and thence readily to the other axis systems involved; or to operate entirely within the axis system defined by the crystal axes and to attempt to solve the elasticity problem in non-cartesian axes. Of these approaches,

---

* As defined previously (§ 2.7.2), a cartesian axis (or coordinate) system is a right-handed set of orthogonal equal unit vectors.

the first is the only reasonable choice and is followed in these programs. This approach is also the most convenient in terms of programming, since in the modification for another crystal system, the bulk of the program remains unaltered, the main modification being the addition of a 'crystallography package' which could be tested before its insertion into the image computation program.

The major alterations then to a cubic program for crystals with non-cubic symmetry are in the main program itself. As indicated in fig. 10.1, it is the main program which contains the geometry required to specify crystal directions and planes in space and then to project features within the crystal so that they appear in the computed image as they would be projected in the electron microscope. A second area of the program requiring alteration to accommodate non-cubic crystal systems is in the subroutine ANCALC ($\S$10.3.1) where the calculations of the constants required to specify the displacement field of the defect are made. Although ANCALC has to a large extent been written generally and thus applies to all crystal systems, the elastic constants array D has been given the form applicable only to a cubic crystal. Further, only the elastic constants c_{11}, c_{12} and c_{44} which define the elastic properties of a cubic crystal have been allotted space for transmission through COMMON/ANCNEW from the main program to ANCALC. Thus, in subroutine ANCALC for non-cubic crystals, allowance must be made for the transmission of the extra elastic constants necessary for any particular crystal system and these elastic constants must be set up correctly in the array D.

In the following discussions of the development of programs for crystal systems other than cubic, the transformation of the components of a vector from one set of axes to another is carried out using matrix methods. The notation and conventions adopted here correspond to those given by Bowles and Mackenzie (1954(a) and (b)) and the reader is referred to their work for a full appreciation of these conventions and the use of the matrix method in axis transformations. The notation and conventions which will be important here can be summerised briefly as follows:

(i) The components of a vector x referred to a basis A are given by the column matrix X where

$$X = \begin{bmatrix} x_1 \\ x_2 \\ x_3 \end{bmatrix}_A , \qquad (10.32)$$

but in order to conserve space the matrix will usually be written

$$X = [x_1\ x_2\ x_3]_A , \qquad (10.33)$$

where the square brackets denote a column matrix and the subscript A, denoting the reference basis, will usually be omitted except when it is necessary to clearly define the reference basis.

(ii) The components of a vector y referred to a basis A*, reciprocal to A, will be expressed as the row matrix

$$Y' = (y_1\ y_2\ y_3)_{A*} \tag{10.34}$$

where the round brackets and the prime denote a row matrix. Usually the prime notation will be omitted, the round brackets alone being sufficient to indicate a row matrix. Again, the subscript notation will only be used when it is necessary to clearly define the reference basis.

Since in the following sections crystal directions will be referred to bases in real space, and hence will be column matrices, whereas the normals to crystal planes will be referred to bases in reciprocal space, and hence will appear as row matrices, the bracket notation adopted conforms with established crystallographic conventions. This distinction is important for the specification of the orientation of the foil. In the following program modifications, for both the tetragonal and hexagonal crystal systems, the choice has been made that, in the input data, the foil orientation will be specified as 'the upward drawn normal to the crystal plane parallel to the foil surface' rather than as 'the upward drawn crystal direction perpendicular to the foil surface'. **. Thus in the conversions from crystal to cartesian coordinates, the foil normal LFN is transformed as a reciprocal lattice vector rather than as a real lattice vector. This choice was made solely because it was considered that such a specification of foil orientation would be the natural choice for readers who usually work with non-cubic crystals. However, some readers who are interested in using the tetragonal and hexagonal programs may prefer to specify foil orientation in the alternative way as the crystal direction perpendicular to the foil surface. For instance, this would almost certainly be the case if the foil orientation is routinely obtained by solving the diffraction pattern obtained from the foil when it is set exactly normal to the electron beam (i.e. when a calibrated tilt stage is set to zero tilt). The foil normal thus obtained corresponds to the zero tilt beam direction and being a vector in real space should be transformed as such in the conversion to cartesian coordinates. This is easily achieved for it merely requires the alteration of one card in modification TETDIS and of two cards in modification HEXDIS. Thus for modification TETDIS, card

---

** This same choice was also made for the cubic system but in that case the two descriptions were identical.

ONE 00430 bearing the statement number 185 would read

CFN(J) = FLOAT(LFN(J))*Z

and for modification HEXDIS, ONE --386 and ONE--410 would become

IFN(J) = LFN(J) − LFN(3) + IN*LFN(4) ,

and

CFN(J) = CFN(J) + OH(J, I)*FLOAT(IFN(I)) ,

respectively.

10.6.3. THE TETRAGONAL SYSTEM – MODIFICATION TETDIS

The general form of the matrix required for specification of the ealstic constants (two suffix notation) in the tetragonal crystal system is given by (Nye, 1960) as:

$$
D = \begin{bmatrix}
c_{11} & c_{12} & c_{13} & 0 & 0 & c_{16} \\
c_{12} & c_{11} & c_{13} & 0 & 0 & -c_{16} \\
c_{13} & c_{13} & c_{33} & 0 & 0 & 0 \\
0 & 0 & 0 & c_{44} & 0 & 0 \\
0 & 0 & 0 & 0 & c_{44} & 0 \\
c_{16} & -c_{16} & 0 & 0 & 0 & c_{66}
\end{bmatrix}
\tag{10.35}
$$

Note that for some tetragonal crystal classes c_{16} is constrained to be zero. The measured elastic constants are specified with reference to cartesian axes chosen such that:

$$
\text{o}x_1 /\!/ a , \quad \text{o}x_2 /\!/ b , \quad \text{o}x_3 /\!/ c ,
$$

where a, b, c are the base vectors of the unit cell of the tetragonal lattice (c being the unique 4-fold axis).

The components of a vector referred to the tetragonal basis are related to its components referred to the cartesian basis in the following way:

$$
[u_1 v_1 w_1]_C = {}_C M_T [uvw]_T ,
\tag{10.36}
$$

where $_C M_T$ is the (3×3) transformation matrix in which the successive columns of the matrix are the components of the tetragonal base vectors relative to the cartesian basis. Thus

$$_C M_T = a \begin{bmatrix} 1 & 0 & 0 \\ 0 & 1 & 0 \\ 0 & 0 & c/a \end{bmatrix} . \tag{10.37}$$

Similarly, the components of the normals to planes in the tetragonal lattice which are most conveniently referred to the reciprocal basis T* can be expressed in terms of the cartesian basis by:

$$(h_1 k_1 l_1)_{C*} = (h k l)_{T*} {}_{T*} M'_{C*} , \tag{10.38}$$

where M' denotes the transpose of the matrix M and C* is the reciprocal basis to C. However, since the bases C and C* are identical and since

$$_{A*} M'_{B*} \equiv {}_A M_B \tag{10.39}$$

eq. (10.38) becomes

$$(h_1 k_1 l_1)_C = (h k l)_{T*} {}_T M_C . \tag{10.40}$$

Since $(_C M_T)(_T M_C) = I$, the identity matrix, it follows that

$$(h_1 k_1 l_1)_C = \frac{1}{a} (h k l)_{T*} \begin{bmatrix} 1 & 0 & 0 \\ 0 & 1 & 0 \\ 0 & 0 & a/c \end{bmatrix} . \tag{10.41}$$

From the form of the transformation matrices $_C M_T$ and $_T M_C$, it is clear that the components of directions and plane normals referred to the cartesian basis, that is the products

$$[u_1 v_1 w_1]_C = {}_C M_T [u v w]_T \tag{10.42}$$

and

$$(h_1 k_1 l_1)_C = (h k l)_{T*} {}_T M_C \tag{10.43}$$

are obtained merely by multiplying the third (c) component of the vectors referred to the tetragonal bases by the ratio c/a for vectors in real space (directions) and by a/c for vectors in reciprocal space (plane normals). This procedure ignores the factors a and $1/a$ in the transformation matrices, but since in general the direction cosines of vectors are required by the geometry of the program, these factors can be ignored. Overlooking these factors may be regarded as defining the unit of distance in the cartesian basis as a. Scalar products, such as $\mathbf{g}\cdot\mathbf{R}$, remain invariant to the transformation to cartesian axes (or to any axis system) since $\mathbf{R}$ and $\mathbf{g}$ are vectors referred to reciprocal bases. This may be seen by combining equations of the form (10.42) and (10.43) to give

$$(\mathbf{g}\cdot\mathbf{R})_C = \mathbf{g}_{T*}(_T M_C)(_C M_T) \mathbf{R}_T \;, \tag{10.44}$$

but since $(_T M_C)(_C M_T) = I$, this becomes

$$(\mathbf{g}\cdot\mathbf{R})_C = (\mathbf{g}\cdot\mathbf{R})_T \;. \tag{10.45}$$

The program modifications to ONEDIS which incorporate the necessary changes for the tetragonal system are described in the following, and a complete listing of modification TETDIS is given at the end of this section.

A. *Modifications to the main program:*

(i) Extra space for the elastic constants c_{13}, c_{33}, c_{66} and c_{16} is allocated in the COMMON/ANCNEW block by adding the card ONE 00091;

(ii) To accommodate the extra elastic constants for tetragonal crystals, the first data card of ONEDIS is replaced by two data cards. The layouts of these cards are given in tables 10.5 and 10.6. The data for each picture is now defined by three cards, the final card still having the layout of table 10.2. The READ statements are modified by replacing ONE 130–140 by ONE 00130–00145;

(iii) The conversion of the input crystallographic data, which is in integer form and referred to the tetragonal bases, to data referred to the cartesian axis system is carried out (ONE 00370–00452) using Z and RRAT as work

TABLE 10.5
Layout of first data card for TETDIS

Column	Format	Variable	Default	Comment
1–10	F10.0	C11		⎫
11–20	F10.0	C12		⎪
21–30	F10.0	C44		⎪
31–40	F10.0	C13		⎬ Elastic constants
41–50	F10.0	C33		⎪
51–60	F10.0	C66		⎪
61–70	F10.0	C16		⎭
71–80	F10.0	RAT	1.0	Axial ratio of unit cell , c/a

TABLE 10.6
Layout of second data card for TETDIS

Column	Format	Variable	Default	Comment
1–10	F10.0	ANO	0.10	Anomalous absorption
11–25	15A1	IY		15 character message
26–80	–	–		Not used

space. Note that RAT, the axial ratio of the tetragonal unit cell is given the default value of 1.0 (ONE 00371). If foil normal is not specified, i.e., if all the LFN components are zero, the foil normal CFN is identified with the beam direction CBM in the cartesian axes (ONE 00440–00452);

(iv) The final modification to the main program sets up new output WRITE statements (ONE 02540–02625) to provide a complete list of the relevant data in the legend.

B. *The modification of subroutine* ANCALC :

(i) As in the main program, extra space for the elastic constants c_{13}, c_{33}, c_{66} and c_{16} is allocated in the COMMON/ANCNEW block (ANC 00065);

(ii) The elastic constants array D is set up for the tetragonal system (ANC 00100–00218).

Listing of modification TETDIS

```
C  MODIFICATION  TETDIS  FOR PROGRAM ONEDIS
C•••••••••••••••••••••••••••••••••••••••••••••••••••••••••••••••••••••
C
C  MODIFICATION OF  PROGRAM ONEDIS
C•••••••••••••••••••••••••••••••••••••••••••••••••••••••••••••••••••••
C  ADD THE FOLLOWING  1   CARD TO THE  COMMON/ANCNEW  STATEMENT
     3 ,C13,C33,C66,C16                                          ONE00091
C•••••••••••••••••••••••••••••••••••••••••••••••••••••••••••••••••••••
C  REPLACE ONE  130 AND ONE  140 BY THE FOLLOWING  4 CARDS
   10     READ(MR,20)C11,C12,C44,C13,C33,C66,C16,RAT             ONE00130
   20     FORMAT(8F10.0)                                         ONE00135
          READ(MR,25)ANO,IY                                      ONE00140
   25     FORMAT(F10.0,15A1)                                     ONE00145
C•••••••••••••••••••••••••••••••••••••••••••••••••••••••••••••••••••••
C  REPLACE ONE  370 TO ONE   450 INCLUSIVE WITH THE FOLLOWING 14 CARDS
  170     IF(RAT)175,175,180                                     ONE00370
  175     RAT=1.0                                                ONE00371
  180     RRAT=RAT-1.0                                           ONE00372
          DO 185 J=1,3                                           ONE00380
          Z=1.0+FLOAT(J/3)•RRAT                                  ONE00381
          CB(J)=FLOAT(LB(J))•Z/FLOAT(LD)                         ONE00390
          CU(J)=FLOAT(LU(J))•Z                                   ONE00400
          CBM(J)=FLOAT(LBM(J))•Z                                 ONE00410
          CG(J)=FLOAT(LG(J))/Z                                   ONE00420
  185     CFN(J)=FLOAT(LFN(J))/Z                                 ONE00430
          IF(LFN(1)••2+LFN(2)••2+LFN(3)••2)190,190,205           ONE00440
  190     DO 200 J=1,3                                           ONE00450
  200     CFN(J)=CBM(J)                                          ONE00451
  205     CONTINUE                                               ONE00452
C•••••••••••••••••••••••••••••••••••••••••••••••••••••••••••••••••••••
C  REPLACE ONE  2540 TO ONE 2620 INCLUSIVE WITH THE FOLLOWING 10 CARDS
  810     WRITE(MW,820)IY,TIME,WL,WW,START,FINISH,ANO            ONE02540
  820     FORMAT(3OH TRIBOPHYSICS PROGRAM ONEDIS    15A1,F6.1,5H SECS F6.2,  ONE02550
          13H WL ,F6.2,3H WW F5.2,6H STRT F5.2,5H FIN F6.3,5H ANO  )  ONE02560
```

```
      WRITE(MW,830)LB,LD,LU,LG,LBM,LFN,W,THICK,THBM,BACK,IZ           ONE02570
830   FORMAT(1H 3I2,1H/I1,5HB      3I2,5HU      3I2,5HG      3I2,5HBM   3I2,2 ONE02580
1HFNF7.3,1HWF7.3,2HTHF7.3,4HTHBMF9.3,4HBACK26A1)                       ONE02590
      WRITE(MW,840)C11,C12,C44,C13,C33,C66,C16,RAT,BLACK,WHITE        ONE02600
840   FORMAT(1X,F6.2,4H C11 F6.2,4H C12 F6.2,4H C44 F6.2,4H C13 F6.2,4H ONE02610
1C33 F6.2,4H C66 F6.2,4H C16 F10.5,7H RATIO ,12H GREY SCALE  F5.3,   ONE02620
      27H BLACK F5.3,6H WHITE  )                                      ONE02625
C•••••••••••••••••••••••••••••••••••••••••••••••••••••••••••••••••••••••
C
C  MODIFICATION OF SUBROUTINE ANCALC
C•••••••••••••••••••••••••••••••••••••••••••••••••••••••••••••••••••••••
C  ADD THE FOLLOWING  1  CARD TO THE  COMMON/ANCNEW  STATEMENT
      3,C13,C33,C66,C16                                              ANC00065
C•••••••••••••••••••••••••••••••••••••••••••••••••••••••••••••••••••••••
C  REPLACE ANC  100  TO ANC  210  INCLUSIVE BY THE FOLLOWING 16 CARDS
      D(1,1)=C11/C44                                                 ANC00100
      D(2,2)=D(1,1)                                                  ANC00110
      D(1,2)=C12/C44                                                 ANC00120
      D(2,1)=D(1,2)                                                  ANC00130
      D(1,3)=C13/C44                                                 ANC00140
      D(2,3)=D(1,3)                                                  ANC00150
      D(3,1)=D(1,3)                                                  ANC00160
      D(3,2)=D(1,3)                                                  ANC00170
      D(3,3)=C33/C44                                                 ANC00180
      D(4,4)=1.0                                                     ANC00190
      D(5,5)=1.0                                                     ANC00200
      D(6,6)=C66/C44                                                 ANC00210
      D(1,6)=C16/C44                                                 ANC00212
      D(2,6)=-D(1,6)                                                 ANC00214
      D(6,1)=D(1,6)                                                  ANC00216
      D(6,2)=-D(1,6)                                                 ANC00218
C•••••••••••••••••••••••••••••••••••••••••••••••••••••••••••••••••••••••
C     END OF MODIFICATION TETDIS
```

10.6.4. THE HEXAGONAL SYSTEM – MODIFICATION HEXDIS

The matrix of elastic constants in the hexagonal system has the form:

$$
D = \begin{bmatrix}
c_{11} & c_{12} & c_{13} & 0 & 0 & 0 \\
c_{12} & c_{11} & c_{13} & 0 & 0 & 0 \\
c_{13} & c_{13} & c_{33} & 0 & 0 & 0 \\
0 & 0 & 0 & c_{44} & 0 & 0 \\
0 & 0 & 0 & 0 & c_{44} & 0 \\
0 & 0 & 0 & 0 & 0 & c'
\end{bmatrix} , \tag{10.46}
$$

where $c' = \frac{1}{2}(c_{11} - c_{12})$ and the elastic constants are referred to the cartesian basis:

$$ ox_3//c, \qquad ox_1//a_1 \quad \text{and} \quad ox_2//c \wedge a_1 , $$

the hexagonal lattice being defined by the base vectors a_1, a_2, a_3 and c, c being the unique 6-fold axis (fig. 10.4).

Various methods have been proposed for the indexing of hexagonal crystals, but in the present modification 4-axis hexagonal (Miller–Bravais) indexing has been used since this system conveys the full symmetry of the hexagonal lattice and it has therefore gained wide acceptance. The reader is

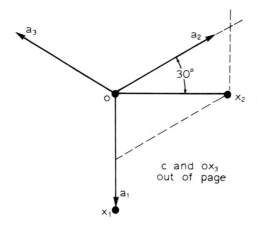

Fig. 10.4. Diagram showing the relationship between the 3-axis hexagonal basis, a_1, a_2 and c; the 4-axis hexagonal basis, a_1, a_2, a_3 and c; and the cartesian basis, ox_1, ox_2, ox_3.

referred to Frank (1965) and Nicholas (1966, 1970) for an appreciation of the 4-axis system and its relationship to other methods of indexing hexagonal crystals. Although the present modification is not directly applicable to data derived using 3-axis hexagonal or orthohexagonal indexing, it is easily converted to 3-axis hexagonal indexing.

In establishing the relationship between the 4-axis hexagonal system and the cartesian axis system used to define the elastic constants, it is convenient first to consider the relationship between the 3-axis hexagonal system and the cartesian system. Figure 10.4 shows a plan view of the basal plane of the hexagonal lattice with c normal to the plane of the paper. From fig. 10.4, with unit distance in the cartesian axes taken as $a = |a_1|$, we have:

$$ox_1 = a_1 ,$$

$$ox_2 = a_1 \tan 30° + a_2/\cos 30° , \qquad (10.47)$$

and

$$ox_3 = (a/c)c ,$$

or, alternatively:

$$a_1 = ox_1 , \qquad (10.48)$$

$$a_2 = -ox_1 \sin 30° + ox_2 \cos 30° , \qquad c = (c/a)ox_3 .$$

From these relationships the transformation matrix relating the components of a vector in the 3-axis hexagonal system to its components in cartesian axes axes is given by

$$
_C M_H = \begin{bmatrix} 1 & -\sin 30° & 0 \\ 0 & \cos 30° & 0 \\ 0 & 0 & c/a \end{bmatrix}
\tag{10.49}
$$

and the inverse matrix is given by

$$
_H M_C = \begin{bmatrix} 1 & \tan 30° & 0 \\ 0 & \sec 30° & 0 \\ 0 & 0 & a/c \end{bmatrix}.
\tag{10.50}
$$

Now for the hexagonal lattice the base vectors of the Miller–Bravais 4-index basis are:

$$
\begin{aligned}
a_1 &= \tfrac{1}{3}[2\bar{1}\bar{1}0]_{4H} = [100]_{3H}\,, \\
a_2 &= \tfrac{1}{3}[\bar{1}2\bar{1}0]_{4H} = [010]_{3H}\,, \\
a_3 &= \tfrac{1}{3}[\bar{1}\bar{1}20]_{4H} = -[100]_{3H} - [010]_{3H}\,, \\
c   &= [0001]_{4H} = [001]_{3H}\,.
\end{aligned}
\tag{10.51}
$$

The relationship between the indices in the 4-axis hexagonal and 3-axis hexagonal systems is, for directions

$$
[u\,v\,t\,w]_{4H} \rightarrow [U\,V\,W]_{3H}
\tag{10.52}
$$

where $U = u - t$, $V = v - t$ and $W = w$, and for planes,

$$
(h\,k\,i\,l)_{4H} \rightarrow (h\,k\,l)_{3H}
\tag{10.53}
$$

noting that for 4-axis indexing, $h + k = -i$ and $u + v = -t$ (Barrett, 1952). It is clear then that the transformation of a vector from 4-axis hexagonal to cartesian axes can conveniently be made in two steps, first the transformation from 4-axis hexagonal to 3-axis hexagonal indexing using eqs. (10.52) and (10.53) and then the transformation from 3-axis hexagonal to cartesian axes using the transformation matrices $_C M_H$ and $_H M_C$. In modification HEXDIS, for clarity and simplicity of programming the transformation is broken into two steps in just this way.

The program modifications required for modification HEXDIS, using 4-axis hexagonal indexing are given below and a complete listing of the HEXDIS modification is given at the end of this section:

A. *The modification of the main program*

(i) The required space for the storage of four components for each of the vectors read in as data is allocated (ONE----20).

(ii) The required space for the storage of the components of the vectors IB, IU, IG, IBM and IFN is allocated (ONE----50).

(iii) The extra elastic constants required for the hexagonal system c_{13} and c_{33}, are allocated space in the COMMON/ANCNEW block (ONE----95).

(iv) The transformation matrices OH and HO are allocated space in the COMMON/DATA block and their components are preset (ONE--102--ONE--108).

It should be noted that OH(3, 3) and HO(3, 3) are preset in the DATA statements to the values applicable to an ideally close-packed hexagonal structure. They are reset later in the program (ONE--370--ONE--374) to the values required by the axial ratio (RAT) of the hexagonal structure being studied and finally restored to the initial values (ONE--414--ONE--416). Thus the default value of RAT is taken to be that corresponding to ideal close packing.

(v) Modified READ and FORMAT statements (ONE--130--ONE--140) are set up for the elastic constants, the axial ratio of the hexagonal unit cell RAT and the anomalous absorption coefficient. The layout of this data card is given in table 10.7.

The READ statement for the crystallographic data is set up for four components for each vector (ONE--190). The layout of this data card is given in table 10.8.

As for ONEDIS. two cards are required to define the data for a picture.

(vi) The input crystallographic data, which is in integer format and is

TABLE 10.7
Layout of first data card for HEXDIS

Column	Format	Variable	Default	Comment
1−10	F10.0	C11		⎫
11−20	F10.0	C12		⎪
21−30	F10.0	C44		⎬ Elastic constants
31−40	F10.0	C13		⎪
41−50	F10.0	C33		⎭
51−60	F10.0	RAT	1.632993162	Axial ratio of unit cell , c/a
61−75	15A1	IY		15 character message
76−80	F5.0	ANO		Anomalous absorption

TABLE 10.8
Layout of second data card for HEXDIS

Column	Format	Variable	Default	Comment
1–8	4I2	LB	–	Numerators of Burgers vector $\boldsymbol{b}$
9	X	–	–	Not used
10	I1	LD	1	Common denominator of Burgers vector
11	X	–	–	Not used
12–19	4I2	LU	–	Direction of dislocation line $\boldsymbol{u}$
20	X	–	–	Not used
21–28	4I2	LG	–	Diffracting vector $\boldsymbol{g}$
29	X	–	–	Not used
30–37	4I2	LBM	–	Beam direction $\boldsymbol{B}$
38	X	–	–	Not used
39–46	4I2	LFN	CBM	Foil normal $\boldsymbol{F}$
47–50	F4.0	W	–	Deviation from Bragg condition w
51–54	F4.0	THICK	–	Foil thickness, in units of ξ_g
55–58	F4.0	START	0	Start and finish of integration, in
59–62	F4.0	FINISH	THICK	units of ξ_g, relative to top surface of object
63–64	I2	LPR	1	Grey scale
65–80	16A1	IZ	–	16 character message

referred to the 4-axis hexagonal basis, is converted to the cartesian axis system (ONE--370–ONE--450). This is done in the following steps:

(a) The components OH(3, 3) and HO(3, 3) are set to the values required by the axial ratio RAT, read in as data or, in default, they are left as preset in the DATA statements (ONE--370–ONE--374).

(b) The conversion from 4-axis hexagonal components (LB, LU, LG, etc.) to 3-axis hexagonal components (IB, IU, IG, etc.) is carried out using IN as work space (ONE--376–ONE--388).

(c) The conversion of the vector components to the cartesian coordinate system is completed in the block of statements ONE--390 to ONE--412, the Burgers vector being divided through by its common denominator LD. If a foil normal is not specified, i.e. all the array LFN is zero, then in cartesian coordinates the foil normal CFN is identified with the beam direction CBM (ONE--420–ONE--450).

(vii) The test for orthogonality of the beam direction LBM and the diffracting vector LG is rewritten in terms of the four components for each of these vectors (ONE--920).

(viii) Modified WRITE statements are set up to provide a complete list of the input data together with some computed parameters in the picture legend (ONE-2540–ONE-2620).

B. *Modification of subroutine* ANCALC

Subroutine ANCALC requires the following modifications for the hexagonal system:

(i) Space is allocated for the transmission of the extra elastic constants c_{13} and c_{33} through the COMMON/ANCNEW block (ANC----65).

(ii) The elastic constants array D is set up for the hexagonal system (ANC--100-ANC--210) *.

Listing of modification HEXDIS

```
C  MODIFICATION  HEXDIS  FOR  PROGRAM  ONEDIS
C•••••••••••••••••••••••••••••••••••••••••••••••••••••••••••••••••••••••
C
C  MODIFICATION OF PROGRAM ONEDIS
C•••••••••••••••••••••••••••••••••••••••••••••••••••••••••••••••••••••••
C  REPLACE ONE    20 BY THE FOLLOWING 1 CARD
      DIMENSION LB(4),LU(4),LG(4),LBM(4),LFN(4),IY(15),IZ(16),BD(3),    ONE---20
C•••••••••••••••••••••••••••••••••••••••••••••••••••••••••••••••••••••••
C  ADD THE FOLLOWING 1 CARD TO THE DIMENSION STATEMENT
    4 ,IB(3),IU(3),IG(3),IBM(3),IFN(3)                                 ONE---55
C•••••••••••••••••••••••••••••••••••••••••••••••••••••••••••••••••••••••
C  ADD THE FOLLOWING 1 CARD TO THE COMMON/ANCNEW STATEMENT
    3,C13,C33                                                          ONE---95
C•••••••••••••••••••••••••••••••••••••••••••••••••••••••••••••••••••••••
C  ADD THE FOLLOWING 4 CARDS TO THE COMMON/DATA AND DATA STATEMENTS
    1 ,HO(3,3),OH(3,3)                                                 ONE--102
      DATA(OH=1.0,0.0,0.0,-0.5,0.8660254038,0.0,0.0,0.0,1.632993162 )  ONE--104
      DATA(HO=1.0,0.0,0.0,0.0,0.5773502692,1.1547005384,0.0,0.0,0.0.0, ONE--106
    1 0.6123724357 )                                                   ONE--108
C•••••••••••••••••••••••••••••••••••••••••••••••••••••••••••••••••••••••
C  REPLACE ONE   130 AND ONE   140 BY THE FOLLOWING 2 CARDS
 10   READ(MR,20)C11,C12,C44,C13,C33,RAT,IY,ANO                        ONE--130
 20   FORMAT(6F10.0,15A1,F5.0)                                         ONE--140
C•••••••••••••••••••••••••••••••••••••••••••••••••••••••••••••••••••••••
C  REPLACE ONE   190 BY THE FOLLOWING 1 CARD
 50   FORMAT(4I2,X,I1,X,4I2,X,4I2,X,4I2,X,4I2,4F4.0,I2,16A1 )          ONE--190
C•••••••••••••••••••••••••••••••••••••••••••••••••••••••••••••••••••••••
C  REPLACE ONE   370 TO ONE   450 BY THE FOLLOWING 28 CARDS
170   IF(RAT)180,180,175                                               ONE--370
175   OH(3,3)=RAT                                                      ONE--372
      HO(3,3)=1.0/RAT                                                  ONE--374
180   DO 182 J=1,3                                                     ONE--376
      IN=J/3                                                           ONE--378
      IB(J)=LB(J)-LB(3)+IN*LB(4)                                       ONE--380
      IU(J)=LU(J)-LU(3)+IN*LU(4)                                       ONE--382
      IBM(J)=LBM(J)-LBM(3)+IN*LBM(4)                                   ONE--384
      IFN(J)=LFN(J+IN)                                                 ONE--386
```

* The relationship given in statement ANC--210 should, for the hexagonal system, actually be as follows:

$$D(6,6) = (C11 - C12)/(2.0*C44)$$

However, when the dislocation line lies along the *c*-axis of the hexagonal crystal, i.e. $u = \pm[0001]$, such an exact specification of $D(6,6)$ leads to a situation where the elasticity becomes essentially isotropic. This will produce difficulties in subsequent computation (see §10.7). To avoid this problem the definition of $D(6,6)$ given in ANC--210:

$$D(6,6) = (C11 - C12)/(2.0*C44)*1.001$$

is used as a very good approximation to exact hexagonal elastic constants but sufficiently inexact to eliminate the problems of isotropic calculations. It should be realised that this deviation from exact hexagonal constants, 0.1%, may need to be larger for computers with more limited accuracy, i.e. with seven rather than eleven significant figures.

```
    182    IG(J)=LG(J+IN)                                                   ONE--388
           DO 185 J=1,3                                                     ONE--390
           CB(J)=0.0                                                        ONE--392
           CU(J)=0.0                                                        ONE--394
           CBM(J)=0.0                                                       ONE--396
           CFN(J)=0.0                                                       ONE--398
           CG(J)=0.0                                                        ONE--400
           DO 185 I=1,3                                                     ONE--402
           CB(J)=CB(J)+OH(J,I)+FLOAT(IB(I))/FLOAT(LD)                       ONE--404
           CU(J)=CU(J)+OH(J,I)+FLOAT(IU(I))                                 ONE--406
           CBM(J)=CBM(J)+OH(J,I)+FLOAT(IBM(I))                              ONE--408
           CFN(J)=CFN(J)+FLOAT(IFN(I))*HO(I,J)                              ONE--410
    185    CG(J)=CG(J)+FLOAT(IG(I))*HO(I,J)                                 ONE--412
           OH(3,3)=1.632993162                                             ONE--414
           HO(3,3)=0.6123724357                                           ONE--416
           IF(LFN(1)**2+LFN(2)**2+LFN(3)**2+LFN(4)**2)190,190,205          ONE--420
    190    DO 200 J=1,3                                                     ONE--430
    200    CFN(J)=CBM(J)                                                    ONE--440
    205    CONTINUE                                                         ONE--450
C*************************************************************************
C  REPLACE ONE   920 BY THE FOLLOWING   1 CARD
           IF(LBM(1)*LG(1)+LBM(2)*LG(2)+LBM(3)*LG(3)+LBM(4)*LG(4))320,340,320ONE--920
C*************************************************************************
C  REPLACE ONE 2540 TO ONE 2620 INCLUSIVE BY THE FOLLOWING 9 CARDS
    810    WRITE(MW,820)IY,TIME,WL,WW,START,FINISH,ANO                      ONE-2540
    820    FORMAT(30H TRIBOPHYSICS PROGRAM ONEDIS    15A1,F6.1,5H SECS F6.2, ONE-2550
           13H WL ,F6.2,3H WW F5.2,6H STRT F5.2,5H FIN F6.3,5H ANO  )       ONE-2560
           WRITE(MW,830)LB,LD,LU,LBM,LFN,W,THICK,THBM,BACK,IZ              ONE-2570
    830    FORMAT(1H 4I2,1H/I1,5H8    4I2,5HU    4I2,5HBM   4I2,            ONE-2580
           15HFN    F7.3,1HW F7.3,2HTH F7.3,4HTHBM F9.3,8HBACK    16A1   )  ONE-2590
           WRITE(MW,840)C11,C12,C44,C13,C33,RAT,BLACK,WHITE                ONE-2600
    840    FORMAT(1X,F6.2,4H C11 F6.2,4H C12 F6.2,4H C44 F6.2,4H C13 F6.2,4H ONE-2610
           1C33 F10.5,7H RATIO ,12H GREY SCALE   F5.3,7H BLACK F5.3,6H WHITE ) ONE-2620
C*************************************************************************

C  MODIFICATION OF SUBROUTINE ANCALC
C*************************************************************************
C  ADD THE FOLLOWING 1 CARD TO THE COMMON/ANCNEW STATEMENT
           3,C13,C33                                                       ANC---65
C*************************************************************************
C  REPLACE ANC  100 TO ANC   210 INCLUSIVE BY THE FOLLOWING 12 CARDS
           D(1,1)=C11/C44                                                  ANC--100
           D(2,2)=D(1,1)                                                   ANC--110
           D(1,2)=C12/C44                                                  ANC--120
           D(2,1)=D(1,2)                                                   ANC--130
           D(1,3)=C13/C44                                                  ANC--140
           D(3,1)=D(1,3)                                                   ANC--150
           D(2,3)=D(1,3)                                                   ANC--160
           D(3,2)=D(1,3)                                                   ANC--170
           D(3,3)=C33/C44                                                  ANC--180
           D(4,4)=1.0                                                      ANC--190
           D(5,5)=1.0                                                      ANC--200
           D(6,6)=(C11-C12)/(2.0*C44)*1.001                               ANC--210
C*************************************************************************
C  END OF MODIFICATION  HEXDIS
```

10.6.5. THE TESTING OF PROGRAMS DEVELOPED FOR NON-CUBIC CRYSTAL SYSTEMS

Programs developed for computation of images of defects in non-cubic crystals should be tested as far as is possible by computing those images of defects which can be predicted theoretically and by using the modified programs to compute standard images such as that given as a test image for program ONEDIS. For testing purposes it is convenient to consider two separate groups of programs, those for the hexagonal and trigonal systems, and those for all other crystal systems. The hexagonal and trigonal crystal systems are distinct from the others in that by suitably specialised input data, all crystal systems except these two may be specialised to cubic symmetry *. For instance, if for the triclinic system, the interaxial angles α, β and γ are put equal to 90° and the base vectors a, b and c are made equal in length, then the symmetry of the system becomes cubic. Further, with suitable adjustment of the input elastic constant data, the elastic constants matrix D can also be made to correspond to the cubic system. Therefore, for all crystal systems except hexagonal and trigonal, it is possible to perform limited tests of the modified program by specialising the data to cubic symmetry and computing the test picture supplied for the cubic system program (§ 10.4).

Programs may be tested additionally by making use of the invisibility criteria for dislocations in anisotropic media (see § 2.7.2(ii) and Appendix). In any crystal system, dislocations of pure edge or pure screw character will be exactly invisible if the line of the dislocation is normal to a mirror plane or is parallel to an even-(2, 4 or 6) fold symmetry axis and both $g \cdot b$ and $g \cdot b \wedge u$ are zero. Thus, except for the triclinic system, it is always possible to select a dislocation (line and Burgers vector) which for a particular set of diffraction conditions can be made exactly invisible. The image of such a dislocation computed from a correctly working program should show only a uniform background.

The hexagonal program is perhaps the simplest program to test since the high symmetry of the hexagonal system imposes special conditions upon the elastic constants. Thus, in any hexagonal crystal, the basal plane (0001) is elastically isotropic in that there is complete rotational elastic symmetry about the c-axis. Therefore, any line in the basal plane is normal to an elastic mirror plane and consequently any pure screw or pure edge dislocation lying in the basal plane will be exactly invisible when both $g \cdot b$ and $g \cdot b \wedge u$ are zero. Secondly, since the c-axis of the hexagonal lattice is a 6-fold axis, pure screw or pure edge dislocations with $u = [0001]$ can also be made exactly invisible. Hexagonal programs can also be tested by adjusting the input elastic constants so that the hexagonal crystal becomes elastically isotropic in all directions (however see § 10.7 for use of programs with isotropic elasticity). When this is done, pure screw or edge dislocations irrespective of their line direction will always be invisible when $g \cdot b$ and $g \cdot b \wedge u$ are both zero.

Testing of programs for the trigonal system can be done by using the general conditions for invisibility in anisotropic crystals for the classes 32, 3m and $\bar{3}$m and further by adjusting the input elastic constants data to specialise

---

* For those crystal structures in the trigonal system which can be conveniently indexed according to rhombohedral axes, it is possible to specialise the situation to one of cubic symmetry by putting $\alpha = \beta = \gamma = 90°$.

the trigonal system to hexagonal symmetry and then using tests applicable to the hexagonal system.

10.6.6. MODIFICATION OF OTHER PROGRAMS FOR NON-CUBIC SYSTEMS

The procedures adopted for modifying ONEDIS for non-cubic crystals apply equally well to the modification of programs such as TWODIS (§10.9) which have been derived for computing images of defects more complex than a single dislocation. Naturally for more complex defects these programs require additional input data to completely specify the crystallography and geometry of the defect. For instance, in TWODIS, up to three faulted planes may be specified as input data as well as the Burgers vectors and the separation of the dislocations. Therefore, the reader wishing to modify such programs for non-cubic crystal systems must be aware of the different crystallographic conventions for specifying crystal directions and the normals to crystallographic planes. The reader must then decide which of these conventions he wishes to build into his program. For example, both modification TETDIS and modification HEXDIS developed for the tetragonal and hexagonal crystal systems respectively, make use of the usual crystallographic convention that crystal directions are indexed with respect to the real lattice while plane normals are indexed with respect to the reciprocal lattice. Thus in modifying TWODIS for other crystal systems, the specification of the faulted, planes would correspondingly be made by the normals to the planes expressed as reciprocal lattice vectors.

The program modification DELUGE (§10.8) which provides an economical scan over foil thickness can, of course, also be applied to programs developed for non-cubic crystal systems. To a large extent the modifications are purely additive. However, it will become clear from a comparison of these modifications that some changes are required to make them completely compatible. For instance, the output statements (ONE 03040–ONE 03060) in the DELUGE modification would need to be altered slightly to make them compatible with the output statements of either modification TETDIS or HEXDIS.

10.7. Isotropic elasticity

It is unwise to use the programs presented here with elastic constants which correspond with *exact* elastic isotropy. Restricting attention to cubic crystals, elastic isotropy corresponds to $c_{11} - c_{12} = 2c_{44}$, so that with this restriction there is only one degree of freedom left in the elastic constants (remembering that the computation depends only on the ratios of the elastic constants). This one degree of freedom corresponds to a choice of Poisson's ratio ν. In terms of Poisson's ratio, the isotropic condition can be written as

$$c_{11}/c_{44} = (2 - 2\nu)/(1 - 2\nu) \, ,$$

$$c_{12}/c_{44} = 2\nu/(1 - 2\nu) \, ,$$

(10.54)

so that if, for example, $\nu = \frac{1}{3}$ then the elastic constants could be $c_{11} = 4$, $c_{12} = 2$ and $c_{44} = 1$ or any other set which are in the same ratio.

For isotropy the sextic equation has three equal pairs of roots and subroutine NEWTON may fail to find them (giving the error message NO-CONVERGE). Even if NEWTON does successfully find all the roots, the subsequent calculations may depend on small differences between large numbers and so may be inaccurate. Only a small shift from exact isotropy is needed to overcome both problems so that for the previous example if $c_{12} = 2$ and $c_{44} = 1$ then $c_{11} = 4.001$ has been found suitable for a computer with 11 figure precision and $c_{11} = 4.01$ should be suitable for 7 figure precision. The change in the computed picture for such small changes in elastic constants will be unnoticeable.

10.8. Modification DELUGE

This optional modification to program ONEDIS stores a selection of the numbers produced during the computation of a picture and after the usual picture has been printed, recalls the stored numbers to produce further pictures with little further integration. These further pictures are for the same defect with the same diffraction conditions but with smaller foil thicknesses (§4.3.3). The time to produce such extra pictures is usually much shorter than that which would be needed to compute them *ab initio* since the arithmetic involved is trivial and the time necessary is essentially that to retrieve the stored numbers and print the pictures. This then gives an economical scan over foil thickness which is valuable in the initial stages of defect identification.

The listing contains instructions as to where cards are to be inserted in program ONEDIS and similar principles would apply to program TWODIS. The modifications are written for storing the numbers on magnetic tape (logical unit 10) but it would be desirable to use storage with the fastest recall, such as main memory, magnetic drums, discs, etc., if such are available and have sufficient capacity. Referring to the listing, it will be seen (ONE 02515) that the arrays FX and FY are saved on tape after each of the 60 lines of the original picture has been computed. Since each of these arrays contains 256 numbers this means that 60 blocks of

512 numbers, a total of 30720 numbers, will be saved and this is the storage capacity which must be provided.

After the usual picture and its legend have been printed, an extra data card is read (ONE 02650) on which NPIX and NDEL have been punched, each with an I2 format. NPIX is the number of extra pictures which are required and if this is zero (e.g. if this data card were blank) then there is an immediate return to the start of ONEDIS (ONE 02670). NDEL specifies the amount the foil thickness will be reduced between successive pictures in units of DELT, the integration step size which was used in the original integration.

An explanation of what pictures will be produced in the deluge is simplest in the case when the usual picture had the standard field of view, that is, with START = 0 and FINISH = THICK. The usual picture then has the dislocation intersecting the upper surface of the foil at the right-hand edge of the picture and intersecting the lower surface at the left-hand edge. All pictures in the deluge series will also have this standard field of view. The foil thicknesses of the series are $\frac{63}{64}, \frac{62}{64}, \frac{61}{64}, \ldots$ of the original foil thickness if NDEL = 1. If NDEL = 2, then only every second thickness in this series is printed, if NDEL = 3 then only every third, etc.. The size of the pictures from left to right shrinks as the foil thickness decreases so that the absolute scale of all pictures in the series is the same.

If the original picture did not have the standard field of view but had been magnified or demagnified, then the deluge series has the following properties. The minimum change in foil thickness (NDEL = 1) is (FINISH – START)/64 and the field of view is such that for each picture the distance of the equivalent START from the upper foil surface and the distance of the equivalent FINISH from the lower foil surface are both kept constant at the values they had in the original picture.

Returning to the listing, a DO loop (ONE 02690–03070) counts the number of pictures to be produced. The tape is rewound (ONE 02710), a new line printer page is started (ONE 02720), the new thickness of the foil in the beam direction is calculated (ONE 02730–02740), and RKM is called to calculate background intensity for this foil thickness (ONE 02750–02820). NCALC is the number of calculated points there will be in each line of the picture (ONE 02830). For each of the 60 lines of the picture (ONE 02850) the appropriate block of numbers is recalled (ONE 02860) and from this the intensities at the NCALC points are evaluated (cf. ONEDIS, ONE 2420–2430) and divided by background (ONE 02870–02930). Intensities at points midway between these calculated points are interpolated (ONE 02940–02960) and the picture line is printed (ONE 02980). The usual legend is then printed after calculating those quantities which change from picture to picture in the series (ONE 02990–03070).

Although this listing is for the specific case of storage on magnetic tape, only trivial changes will be needed for other media. In our case we have used a magnetic drum for storage and have found that each picture in the deluge takes 7 sec to compute as compared to 40–50 sec which would be taken normally.

Listing of modification DELUGE

```
C   MODIFICATION DELUGE FOR PROGRAM ONEDIS
C•••••••••••••••••••••••••••••••••••••••••••••••••••••••••••••••••••
C   ADD THE FOLLOWING 1 CARD TO DIMENSION STATEMENT
C    4  ,FY(64,4)                                              ONE00055
C•••••••••••••••••••••••••••••••••••••••••••••••••••••••••••••••••••
C   INSERT THE FOLLOWING 1 CARD BETWEEN ONE   190 AND ONE   200
      REWIND 10                                                ONE00195
C•••••••••••••••••••••••••••••••••••••••••••••••••••••••••••••••••••
C   INSERT THE FOLLOWING 4 CARDS BETWEEN ONE 2390 AND ONE 2400
      FY(JM,1)=Y(1)                                            ONE02393
      FY(JM,2)=Y(2)                                            ONE02394
      FY(JM,3)=Y(5)                                            ONE02395
      FY(JM,4)=Y(6)                                            ONE02396
C•••••••••••••••••••••••••••••••••••••••••••••••••••••••••••••••••••
C   INSERT THE FOLLOWING 1 CARD BETWEEN ONE 2510 AND ONE 2520
      WRITE(10) FX,FY                                          ONE02515
C•••••••••••••••••••••••••••••••••••••••••••••••••••••••••••••••••••
C   REPLACE ONE 2630 AND ONE 2640 BY THE FOLLOWING 45 CARDS
      READ(MR,850) NPIX,NDEL                                   ONE02650
850   FORMAT(2I2)                                              ONE02660
      IF(NPIX*NDEL)10,10,860                                   ONE02670
860   OVER=FINISH-THICK                                        ONE02680
      DO 930 MPIX=1,NPIX                                       ONE02690
      TIME=TIMEF(X)                                            ONE02700
      REWIND 10                                                ONE02710
      WRITE(MW,600)                                            ONE02720
      OFF=MPIX*NDEL                                            ONE02730
      X1=TBP-OFF*DELT                                          ONE02740
      IF(X1)10,10,870                                          ONE02750
870   X=0.0                                                    ONE02760
      CN(29)=1000.0                                            ONE02770
      DO 880 JK=1,8                                            ONE02780
880   Y(JK)=0.0                                                ONE02790
      Y(1)=1.0                                                 ONE02800
      CALL RKM                                                 ONE02810
      BACK=Y(1)**2+Y(2)**2                                     ONE02820
      NCALC=65-MPIX*NDEL                                       ONE02830
      IF(NCALC)10,10,890                                       ONE02840
890   DO 920 JC=1,60                                           ONE02850
      READ(10) FX,FY                                           ONE02860
      DO 900 NY=1,NCALC                                        ONE02870
      NX=NY-NCALC+64                                           ONE02880
      TT= (FX(NX,1)*FY(NY,1)-FX(NX,2)*FY(NY,2)                 ONE02890
1     +FX(NX,3)*FY(NY,3)-FX(NX,4)*FY(NY,4))**2                 ONE02900
2     +(FX(NX,1)*FY(NY,2)+FX(NX,2)*FY(NY,1)                    ONE02910
3     +FX(NX,3)*FY(NY,4)+FX(NX,4)*FY(NY,3))**2                 ONE02920
900   TB(2*NY-1)=TT/BACK                                       ONE02930
      NINT=2*NCALC-2                                           ONE02940
      DO 910 JZ=2,NINT,2                                       ONE02950
910   TB(JZ)=0.5*(TB(JZ-1)+TB(JZ+1))                           ONE02960
      NDOT=NINT+1                                              ONE02970
920   CALL HALFTN(NDOT ,TB,MARK,BLACK,WHITE,1)                 ONE02980
      WL=WW*6.0*(128.0-2.0*OFF)/(59.0*10.0)                    ONE02990
      THBM=X1/PY                                               ONE03000
      THICK=THBM*FNBM                                          ONE03010
      FINISH=THICK+OVER                                        ONE03020
      TIME=(TIMEF(X)-TIME)/1000.0                              ONE03030
      WRITE(MW,820)C11,C12,C44,IY,TIME,WL,WW,START,FINISH,ANO  ONE03040
      WRITE(MW,830)LB,LD,LU,LG,LBM,LFN,W,THICK,THBM,BACK,IZ    ONE03050
      WRITE(MW,840)BLACK,WHITE                                 ONE03060
930   CONTINUE                                                 ONE03070
      GO TO 10                                                 ONE03080
      END                                                      ONE03090
C•••••••••••••••••••••••••••••••••••••••••••••••••••••••••••••••••••
C   END OF DELUGE MODIFICATION TO PROGRAM ONEDIS
```

10.9. Program TWODIS **for cubic crystals**

10.9.1. INTRODUCTION

In § 10.6 we considered the modifications of the basic ONEDIS program to crystal systems other than cubic. In this section we consider another type of modification, that of changing the object from one dislocation to two parallel dislocations plus three stacking faults. Although this TWODIS program is an extension of ONEDIS, the modifications are too extensive to present as such, and instead a listing will be given of the complete new main program (§ 10.9.3) and the new subroutine DERIV (§ 10.9.4). The card deck will consist therefore of TWODIS (§ 10.9.3); the new subroutine DERIV (§ 10.9.4) and subroutines ANCALC (§ 10.3.1), NEWTON (§ 10.3.2), RKM (§ 10.3.3) and HALFTN (§ 10.5) as before.

For the user, the main change is that a picture is now specified by 3 data cards. The first 2 data cards are identical to those used by ONEDIS and the third carries the extra information necessary to specify the Burgers vector of the second dislocation, its separation from the first dislocation and the characteristics of the three fault planes. If this third data card is left blank, then TWODIS will produce a picture of the one dislocation specified by the first two data cards, and this will be identical with the picture which would be produced by ONEDIS for the same data.

Since the general principles behind TWODIS are the same as have been used in ONEDIS (see ch. 6), and large parts of the program are in fact identical, familiarity with ONEDIS will be assumed and attention concentrated on the additions. The general areas in which additions are necessary are as follows:

(i) the new vectors from the third data card need to be calculated in the various coordinate systems used;

(ii) the elastic displacement field of the second dislocation needs to be calculated and included in DERIV for the integration of the Howie–Whelan equations;

(iii) during this integration, the intersection of the electron beam with the fault planes needs to be detected and appropriate action taken;

(iv) the geometry of this more complicated object and its projection into a two-dimensional picture must be calculated.

As an aid to comparing TWODIS with ONEDIS, the listing of TWODIS has an asterisk in column 76 of those cards which are new or have been substantially changed.

10.9.2. PROGRAM TWODIS

(i) Additional Calls:
System function SIN   : trigonometrical sine
System function COS   : trigonometrical cosine.

TABLE 10.9
Layout of third data card for TWODIS

Column	Format	Variable	Default	Comment
1–6	3I2	LB2	–	Numerators of second Burgers vector
7	X	–	–	Not used
8	I1	LD2	1	Common denominator of second Burgers vector
9–12	F4.0	SEP	–	Separation of dislocations in second fault plane, in units of ξ_g
13–33	3(3I2, X)	LFP	–	Normals to 3 fault planes
34–39	3I2	LS1	–	Numerators of fault vector of first fault plane
40	X	–	–	Not used
41	I1	LQ(1)	1	Common denominator of fault vector of first fault plane
42	X	–	–	⎫
43–48	3I2	LS2	–	⎪
47	X	–	–	⎪
50	I1	LQ(2)	1	⎬ Numerators and denominators of
51	X	–	–	⎪ fault vectors of second and third
52–57	3I2	LS3	–	⎪ fault planes
58	X	–	–	⎪
59	I1	LQ(3)	1	⎭

(ii) Additional Data:

The layout of the third data card is given in table 10.9. The default values take effect if the corresponding data field is left blank, a blank data field being read as zero.

Dislocation 1 is at the intersection of fault planes 1 and 2.

Dislocation 2 is at the intersection of fault planes 2 and 3.

Dislocation 1 is the original dislocation of ONEDIS and is specified on the second data card. Both dislocations are parallel, with their direction u as on the second data card. Their relative positions are given by their common plane (fault plane 2) and SEP, their separation in this plane in units of ξ_g. Fault plane 1 extends from plus infinity to dislocation 1, fault plane 2 from dislocation 1 to dislocation 2, and fault plane 3 from dislocation 2 to minus infinity with respect to the generalised cross-section axis OX_1 (§6.2.1). If a fault plane is not needed then both its normal and fault vector may be left blank on the data card, with the exception that if SEP is non-zero, then the normal to plane 2 must be punched as this is needed to specify the relative positions of the dislocations.

(iii) Additional geometry:

In the first part of the program the vectors, LB2/LD2, LFP, read from the

TABLE 10.10
FORTRAN names of vectors

| Vector | Axes | | | |
| | Crystal | | Dislocation | Generalised |
	Data	Floated		cross-section
Second Burgers	LB2/LD2	CB2	B2D	–
Fault normals	LFP	CFP	FP *	FPX **

* Fault plane 2 only.
** Equivalenced to FP1X, PF2X, FP3X (TWO 90)

additional data card (TWO 260–280) are floated (TWO 520–570) and referred to other systems of axes (TWO 1080–1110). The names used for these vectors are given in table 10.10.

(iv) Additional error messages:

U NOT IN FAULT PLANE "J" (TWO 1470). The common direction of the two dislocation lines must lie in each of the three fault planes.

FAULT PLANE 2 ZERO WITH SEP NONZERO (TWO 2320). If the separation of the two dislocations is non-zero, then the plane in which they are separated (fault plane 2) must be specified.

Although not producing any error message, the quantities VEC1 and VEC2 (TWO 1370–1420) are printed in the picture legend as V1 and V2 for checking purposes. VEC1 is the vector sum of the first Burgers vector and the shears on fault planes 1 and 2 (which meet at the first dislocation). VEC2 is a similar sum for the second Burgers vector and fault planes 2 and 3. Both sums will be a lattice vector for all physically meaningful data (see §6.3.2).

(v) Additional anisotropic elasticity:

Six additional constants CN(21)–CN(26), to specify the displacement field of the second dislocation must be calculated (TWO 1920–1930) for use by subroutine DERIV. These correspond to the constants CN(1)–CN(6) of the first dislocation.

(vi) Howie–Whelan differential equations:

As for ONEDIS there are 60 integrations of the differential equations (TWO 2620–3900), one for each picture line. For each picture line the integration is in three parts, a first part of 64 steps (TWO 3290–3400), a second part also of 64 steps (TWO 3520–3580) and an intermediate part if needed (TWO 3410–3440). The computation of each picture line ends by calling subroutine HALFTN to print the line (TWO 3890), and finally the legend is printed under the picture (TWO 3920–4040).

The three fault planes are handled in the same way as SURFAC in ONEDIS since the problem is the same. In each step of the integration it is necessary to check if any of the four planes (three fault planes and SURFAC) will be intersected. If so, the electron beam is integrated to the plane, appropriate action taken (a phase shift at a fault plane or storage of current variables at SURFAC), and the integration continued to the end of the step. Before starting each of the 60 integrations, the positions at which the four planes will be intersected are calculated (TWO 2800–3180) in the array POS, and each intersection assigned a type in the array ITYPE, fault planes 1–3 being type 1–3 and SURFAC type 4.

Initially the four positions are set large and negative (TWO 2800–2820) and in the subsequent processing, such a large negative position will be used for planes which were not defined in the input data or have already been passed through by the integration. The actual positions of the three fault planes are then calculated in turn (TWO 2850, 2880, 2910) provided certain conditions are met, otherwise they are left as large and negative. For fault plane 1 the conditions are that the integration column is to the left of dislocation 1 (TWO 2830), that the phase shift at the fault (ALPHA (1)) is not zero (this being calculated previously, (TWO 1490–1540), and that the fault plane is not vertical so that FP1X(2) is not zero (TWO 2840). Similar tests are made for the other two fault planes. The fourth position is that of SURFAC (TWO 2950).

These positions are then sorted into the order in which they will be encountered in the integration (TWO 2960–3090). Any or all of these may be encountered in the first part of the integration but only those which come after SURFAC will be encountered in the second part of the integration. For use in the second part of the integration, a copy of those positions which occur after SURFAC is made from POS(1,J) into POS(2,J) (TWO 3100–3180).

Prior to each integration step, in each of the three parts of the integration, it is necessary to examine if any plane will be encountered. This is done by a common block of program (TWO 4060–4280) which is entered from the three parts of the integration (TWO 3310, 3440, 3540) with return according to the value of LINK (TWO 4070). KOUNTF starts at unity (TWO 3260, 3490) and is incremented as each plane is encountered (TWO 4230). On entry to the common block, if all four planes have already been encountered (TWO 4060) there is an immediate return. Otherwise the position of the next plane is checked to see if it falls in the current integration step (TWO 4080–4090). If it does not then there is a return, but if it does then subroutine RKM is called to bring the integration to the plane (TWO 4100–4120) and, according to the type of plane (TWO 4130–4140), there is either a phase shift (TWO 4150–4200) or storage (TWO 4250–4280) and in either case the position is cancelled from the list (TWO 4220).

(vii) Miscellaneous additions:

There are a number of minor changes on going from the one dislocation of ONEDIS which was at the origin of coordinates to two dislocations at equal and opposite displacements from the origin. The components of this displacement are transmitted to subroutine DERIV by CN(17) and CN(30) (TWO 2330–2370). The standard framing of the picture must be increased by an extra amount to include the full length of both dislocations (TWO 2380–2440). It is possible that the positions of the dislocations are such that the integrations would pass exactly through the cores of the dislocations (where $d(\boldsymbol{g}\cdot\boldsymbol{R})/dZ$ becomes infinite) or sufficiently close that the integration becomes very slow and inaccurate. If this is so then the integration column is shifted slightly. The amount of this SHIFT is half a column spacing or $0.01\,\xi_g$, whichever is the smaller (TWO 2470–2490). The position of each integration column CN(15) is compared with the dislocation positions CN(16) and moved if necessary (TWO 2640–2760). Since the dislocations may have any position in the picture their intersections with the foil surfaces are indicated by the letter D replacing half tone symbols within the picture. Subroutine HALFTN prints D for any negative intensity and a filter of tests (TWO 3630–3750) decides if the picture line which has just been calculated should have any D's inserted (TWO 3760–3850). The dislocations are also marked as in ONEDIS by a D in the margin (TWO 3860) unless the integration has been moved, when this is replaced by the letter M (TWO 3870–3880).

10.9.3. LISTING OF PROGRAM TWODIS

```
      PROGRAM TWODIS                                                        TWO    10
      DIMENSION LB(3),LU(3),LG(3),LBM(3),LFN(3),IY(15),IZ(26),BD(3),       TWO    20
     1 GD(3),BM(3),FN(3),FNX(3),DCX(3,3),DR(3),DI(3),UR(3,3),UI(3,3),      TWO    30
     2 VR(3,3),VI(3,3),CB(3),CU(3),CG(3),CBM(3),CFN(3),TB(129),            TWO    40
     3 TEMPY(8),FX(64,4)                                                   TWO    50
     4 ,LB2(3),LFP(3,3),LS1(3),LS2(3),LS3(3),LS(3,3),LQ(3),CQ(3),FP(3)     TWO*   60
     5 ,CB2(3),FP1X(3),FP2X(3),FP3X(3),B2D(3),CFP(3,3),FPX(3,3),VEC1(3)    TWO*   70
     6 ,VEC2(3),ALPHA(3),SINA(3),COSA(3),POS(2,4),ITYPE(4)                 TWO*   80
      EQUIVALENCE (FP1X(1),FPX(1)),(FP2X(1),FPX(4)),(FP3X(1),FPX(7)),      TWO*   90
     1              ( LS1(1), LS(1)),( LS2(1), LS(4)),( LS3(1), LS(7))     TWO*  100
      COMMON/RKMDRV/CN(30),X,X1,Y(8),ERROR,SKIP,Q,D(8),ANO                 TWO   110
      COMMON/ANCNEW/NEW,ZR,ZI,QR(7),QI(7),KRASH,C11,C12,C44,DC(3,3),       TWO   120
     1 C(6,6),PR(3),PI(3),AR(3,3),AI(3,3),ELR(3,3),ELI(3,3),EMR(3,3),      TWO   130
     2 EMI(3,3),B(3,3),H(3,3)                                              TWO   140
      COMMON/DATA/NP(3),NQ(3),MM(3),NN(3),L1(6),L2(6),L3(3,3),PY,MR,MW     TWO   150
      DATA (NP=2,3,1),(NQ=3,1,2),(MM=1,6,5),(NN=6,2,4),(L1=1,2,3,2,3,1)    TWO   160
      DATA (L2=1,2,3,3,1,2),(L3=1,6,5,6,2,4,5,4,3),(PY=3.1415926536)       TWO   170
      DATA (MR=60),(MW=61)                                                 TWO   180
   10 READ(MR,20)C11,C12,C44,IY,ANO                                        TWO   190
   20 FORMAT(3F10.0,15A1,25X,F9.0)                                         TWO   200
      IF(C11)30,30,40                                                      TWO   210
   30 STOP                                                                 TWO   220
   40 CONTINUE                                                             TWO   230
      READ(MR,50)LB,LD,LU,LG,LBM,LFN,W,THICK,START,FINISH,LPR,IZ           TWO   240
   50 FORMAT(3I2,X,I1,X,3I2,X,3I2,X,3I2,X,3I2,4F4.0,I2,26A1)               TWO   250
      READ(MR,60)LB2,LD2,SEP,LFP,LS1,LQ(1),LS2,LQ(2),LS3,LQ(3)            TWO*  260
   60 FORMAT(3I2,X,I1,F4.0,3I2,X,3I2,X,3I2,X,3I2,X,I1,X,3I2,X,I1,X,        TWO*  270
     1 3I2,X,I1)                                                           TWO*  280
      TIME=TIMEF(X)                                                        TWO   290
      CN(14)=2.0*W                                                         TWO   300
      IF(LD)80,70,80                                                       TWO   310
   70 LD=1                                                                 TWO   320
   80 IF(ANO)100,90,100                                                    TWO   330
   90 ANO=0.1                                                              TWO   340
  100 ANO=-ANO                                                             TWO   350
      IF(FINISH)130,110,130                                                TWO   360
```

```
110       IF(START)130,120,130                              TWO   370
120       START=0.0                                         TWO   380
          FINISH=THICK                                      TWO   390
130       IF(FINISH-START)140,140,160                       TWO   400
140       WRITE(MW,150)                                     TWO   410
          GO TO 1350                                        TWO   420
150       FORMAT(/,/,20H START AFTER FINISH   ,/,/)         TWO   430
160       IF(LPR)180,170,180                                TWO   440
170       LPR=1                                             TWO   450
180       IF(LFN(1)**2+LFN(2)**2+LFN(3)**2)210,190,210      TWO   460
190       DO 200 J=1,3                                      TWO   470
200       LFN(J)=LBM(J)                                     TWO   480
210       IF(LD2)220,220,230                                TWO*  490
220       LD2=1                                             TWO*  500
230       DO 270 J=1,3                                      TWO   510
          IF(LQ(J))240,240,250                              TWO*  520
240       LQ(J)=1                                           TWO*  530
250       CQ(J)=LQ(J)                                       TWO*  540
          DO 260  K=1,3                                     TWO*  550
260       CFP(J,K)=LFP(J,K)                                 TWO*  560
          CB2(J)=FLOAT(LB2(J))/FLOAT(LD2)                   TWO*  570
          CB(J)=FLOAT(LB(J))/FLOAT(LD)                      TWO   580
          CU(J)=LU(J)                                       TWO   590
          CG(J)=LG(J)                                       TWO   600
          CBM(J)=LBM(J)                                     TWO   610
270       CFN(J)=LFN(J)                                     TWO   620
          DO 280 J=1,3                                      TWO   630
          DC(3,J)=CU(J)                                     TWO   640
          K=NP(J)                                           TWO   650
          L=NQ(J)                                           TWO   660
280       DC(1,J)=CBM(K)*CU(L)-CBM(L)*CU(K)                 TWO   670
          DO 290 J=1,3                                      TWO   680
          K=NP(J)                                           TWO   690
          L=NQ(J)                                           TWO   700
290       DC(2,J)=DC(3,K)*DC(1,L)-DC(3,L)*DC(1,K)           TWO   710
          DO 340 J=1,3                                      TWO   720
          Z=0.0                                             TWO   730
          DO 300 K=1,3                                      TWO   740
300       Z=Z+DC(J,K)**2                                    TWO   750
          IF(Z-0.0001)310,310,330                           TWO   760
310       WRITE(MW,320)                                     TWO   770
          GO TO 1350                                        TWO   780
320       FORMAT(/,/,16H BEAM PARALLEL U  ,/,/)             TWO   790
330       Z=1.0/SQRT(Z)                                     TWO   800
          DO 340 K=1,3                                      TWO   810
340       DC(J,K)=DC(J,K)*Z                                 TWO   820
          DO 350 J=1,3                                      TWO   830
          DCX(1,J)=-DC(1,J)                                 TWO   840
350       DCX(2,J)=-CBM(J)                                  TWO   850
          DO 360 J=1,3                                      TWO   860
          K=NP(J)                                           TWO   870
          L=NQ(J)                                           TWO   880
360       DCX(3,J)=DCX(1,K)*DCX(2,L)-DCX(1,L)*DCX(2,K)      TWO   890
          DO 380 J=1,3                                      TWO   900
          Z=0.0                                             TWO   910
          DO 370 K=1,3                                      TWO   920
370       Z=Z+DCX(J,K)**2                                   TWO   930
          Z=1.0/SQRT(Z)                                     TWO   940
          DO 380 K=1,3                                      TWO   950
380       DCX(J,K)=DCX(J,K)*Z                               TWO   960
          DO 410 J=1,3                                      TWO   970
          B2D(J)=0.0                                        TWO*  980
          FP(J)=0.0                                         TWO*  990
          DO 390  K=1,3                                     TWO*1000
390       FPX(J,K)=0.0                                      TWO*1010
          BD(J)=0.0                                         TWO  1020
          GD(J)=0.0                                         TWO  1030
          BM(J)=0.0                                         TWO  1040
          FN(J)=0.0                                         TWO  1050
          FNX(J)=0.0                                        TWO  1060
          DO 410 K=1,3                                      TWO  1070
          B2D(J)=B2D(J)+DC(J,K)*CB2(K)                      TWO*1080
          FP(J)=FP(J)+DC(J,K)*CFP(K,2)                      TWO*1090
          DO 400 L=1,3                                      TWO*1100
400       FPX(J,L)=FPX(J,L)+DCX(J,K)*CFP(K,L)               TWO*1110
          BD(J)=BD(J)+DC(J,K)*CB(K)                         TWO  1120
          BM(J)=BM(J)+DC(J,K)*CBM(K)                        TWO  1130
          FN(J)=FN(J)+DC(J,K)*CFN(K)                        TWO  1140
          FNX(J)=FNX(J)+DCX(J,K)*CFN(K)                     TWO  1150
410       GD(J)=GD(J)+DC(J,K)*CG(K)                         TWO  1160
          IF(LBM(1)*LG(1)+LBM(2)*LG(2)+LBM(3)*LG(3))420,440,420   TWO  1170
```

```
420      WRITE(MW,430)                                                    TWO 1180
430      FORMAT(/,/,19H BEAM NOT PERP TO G    ,/,/)                       TWO 1190
         GO TO 1350                                                       TWO 1200
440      Z=SQRT(FN(1)**2+FN(2)**2+FN(3)**2)                               TWO 1210
         X=SQRT(BM(1)**2+BM(2)**2+BM(3)**2)                               TWO 1220
         DO 450 J=1,3                                                     TWO 1230
         BM(J)=BM(J)/X                                                    TWO 1240
450      FN(J)=FN(J)/Z                                                    TWO 1250
         FNBM=0.0                                                         TWO 1260
         DO 460 J=1,3                                                     TWO 1270
460      FNBM=FNBM+FN(J)*BM(J)                                            TWO 1280
         IF(FN(3))470,470,490                                             TWO 1290
470      WRITE(MW,480)                                                    TWO 1300
         GO TO 1350                                                       TWO 1310
480      FORMAT(/,/,29H U AND FOIL NORMAL NOT ACUTE    ,/,/)              TWO 1320
490      IF(FNBM)500,500,520                                              TWO 1330
500      WRITE(MW,510)                                                    TWO 1340
         GO TO 1350                                                       TWO 1350
510      FORMAT(/,/,32H FOIL NORMAL AND BEAM NOT ACUTE   ,/,/)            TWO 1360
520      DO 550  J=1,3                                                    TWO*1370
         Z=LS2(J)                                                         TWO*1380
         IF(FP2X(2))530 ,530 ,540                                        TWO*1390
530      Z=-Z                                                             TWO*1400
540      VEC1(J)=FLOAT(LS1(J))/CQ(1)+Z/CQ(2)+CB(J)                       TWO*1410
550      VEC2(J)=-Z/CQ(2)-FLOAT(LS3(J))/CQ(3)+CB2(J)                     TWO*1420
         DO 580  J=1,3                                                    TWO*1430
         IF(LU(1)*LFP(1,J)+LU(2)*LFP(2,J)+LU(3)*LFP(3,J))560 ,580 ,560   TWO*1440
560      WRITE(MW,570 ) J                                                 TWO*1450
         GO TO 1350                                                       TWO*1460
570      FORMAT(/,/,22H U NOT IN FAULT PLANE ,I2,/,/)                    TWO*1470
580      CONTINUE                                                         TWO*1480
         DO 590  J=1,3                                                    TWO*1490
         M=LG(1)*LS(1,J)+LG(2)*LS(2,J)+LG(3)*LS(3,J)                     TWO*1500
         Z=M/LQ(J)                                                        TWO*1510
         ALPHA(J)=2.0*PY*(FLOAT(M)/CQ(J)-Z)                             TWO*1520
         SINA(J)=SIN(ALPHA(J))                                           TWO*1530
590      COSA(J)=COS(ALPHA(J))                                           TWO*1540
         CALL ANCALC                                                      TWO 1550
         IF(KRASH)1350,600,1350                                          TWO 1560
600      CONTINUE                                                         TWO 1570
         DO 610 J=1,3                                                     TWO 1580
         DR(J)=0.0                                                        TWO 1590
         DI(J)=0.0                                                        TWO 1600
         DO 610 K=1,3                                                     TWO 1610
         DR(J)=DR(J)+GD(K)*AR(K,J)                                       TWO 1620
610      DI(J)=DI(J)+GD(K)*AI(K,J)                                       TWO 1630
         DO 620 J=1,3                                                     TWO 1640
         Z=DR(J)                                                          TWO 1650
         DR(J)=Z*PR(J)-DI(J)*PI(J)                                       TWO 1660
620      DI(J)=Z*PI(J)+DI(J)*PR(J)                                       TWO 1670
         DO 630 JA=1,3                                                    TWO 1680
         DO 630 L=1,3                                                     TWO 1690
         UR(JA,L)=0.0                                                     TWO 1700
         UI(JA,L)=0.0                                                     TWO 1710
         DO 630 J=1,3                                                     TWO 1720
         UR(JA,L)=UR(JA,L)+EMR(JA,J)*H(J,L)                             TWO 1730
630      UI(JA,L)=UI(JA,L)+EMI(JA,J)*H(J,L)                             TWO 1740
         DO 640 JA=1,3                                                    TWO 1750
         DO 640 L=1,3                                                     TWO 1760
         VR(JA,L)=DR(JA)*UR(JA,L)-DI(JA)*UI(JA,L)                       TWO 1770
640      VI(JA,L)=DR(JA)*UI(JA,L)+DI(JA)*UR(JA,L)                       TWO 1780
         DO 650 JA=1,3                                                    TWO 1790
         DO 650 L=1,3                                                     TWO 1800
650      UR(JA,L)=VR(JA,L)*PR(JA)+VI(JA,L)*PI(JA)                       TWO 1810
         DO 660 J=1,3                                                     TWO 1820
         CN(J+6)=PR(J)                                                    TWO 1830
         CN(J+9)=PI(J)**2                                                 TWO 1840
         CN(J)=0.0                                                        TWO 1850
         CN(J+3)=0.0                                                      TWO 1860
         CN(J+20)=0.0                                                     TWO*1870
         CN(J+23)=0.0                                                     TWO*1880
         DO 660 L=1,3                                                     TWO 1890
         CN(J)=CN(J)+VR(J,L)*BD(L)                                       TWO 1900
         CN(J+3)=CN(J+3)+UR(J,L)*BD(L)                                   TWO 1910
         CN(J+20)=CN(J+20)+VR(J,L)*B2D(L)                               TWO*1920
660      CN(J+23)=CN(J+23)+UR(J,L)*B2D(L)                               TWO*1930
         GO TO (670,680,690,700,710,720,730,740,750),LPR                TWO 1940
670      BLACK=0.313                                                     TWO 1950
         WHITE=1.154                                                     TWO 1960
         GO TO 760                                                       TWO 1970
```

```
680      BLACK=0.129                                              TWO 1980
         WHITE=1.253                                              TWO 1990
         GO TO 760                                                TWO 2000
690      BLACK=0.058                                              TWO 2010
         WHITE=1.340                                              TWO 2020
         GO TO 760                                                TWO 2030
700      BLACK=0.397                                              TWO 2040
         WHITE=1.462                                              TWO 2050
         GO TO 760                                                TWO 2060
710      BLACK=0.191                                              TWO 2070
         WHITE=1.866                                              TWO 2080
         GO TO 760                                                TWO 2090
720      BLACK=0.098                                              TWO 2100
         WHITE=2.280                                              TWO 2110
         GO TO 760                                                TWO 2120
730      BLACK=0.259                                              TWO 2130
         WHITE=0.959                                              TWO 2140
         GO TO 760                                                TWO 2150
740      BLACK=0.089                                              TWO 2160
         WHITE=0.869                                              TWO 2170
         GO TO 760                                                TWO 2180
750      BLACK=0.035                                              TWO 2190
         WHITE=0.809                                              TWO 2200
760      CALL HALFTN(129,TB,MARK,BLACK,WHITE,-1)                  TWO 2210
         CALL HALFTN(129,TB,MARK,BLACK,WHITE,0)                   TWO 2220
         WRITE(MW,770)                                            TWO 2230
770      FORMAT(1HG)                                              TWO 2240
         Z=SQRT(FP(1)**2+FP(2)**2)                                TWO*2250
         IF(Z)810 ,780 ,810                                       TWO*2260
780      Z=1.0                                                    TWO*2270
         FP2X(1)=1.0                                              TWO*2280
         IF(SEP)790,810 ,790                                      TWO*2290
790      WRITE(MW,800)                                            TWO*2300
         GO TO 1350                                               TWO*2310
800      FORMAT(/,/,36H FAULT PLANE 2 ZERO WITH SEP NONZERO,/,/)  TWO*2320
810      PT=SEP*FP(2)/Z                                           TWO*2330
         SL=-SEP*FP(1)/(Z*BM(2))                                  TWO*2340
         CN(16)=PY*PT/2.0                                         TWO*2350
         CN(17)=PY*SL/2.0                                         TWO*2360
         CN(30)=CN(16)/BM(2)                                      TWO*2370
         EXTRA=ABS(SL+PT*FNX(1)/FNX(2))                           TWO*2380
         DIVISR =BM(3)/BM(2)-FNX(3)/FNX(2)                        TWO*2390
         THBM=THICK/FNBM                                          TWO 2400
         TBP=PY*THBM                                              TWO 2410
         FRACTN=(FINISH-START)/THICK                              TWO 2420
         DELT=PY*FRACTN*(THBM+EXTRA)/64.0                         TWO*2430
         WL=((THICK*BM(2)/FN(3))+EXTRA/DIVISR)*FRACTN             TWO*2440
         WW=59.0*10.0*WL/(6.0*128.0)                              TWO 2450
         DELW=PY*WW/59.0                                          TWO 2460
         SHIFT=DELW/2.0                                           TWO*2470
         IF(SHIFT-0.01)830 ,820 ,820                              TWO*2480
820      SHIFT=0.01                                               TWO*2490
830      CN(29)=1000.0                                            TWO 2500
         X=0.0                                                    TWO 2510
         Q=0.0                                                    TWO 2520
         ERROR=0.0001                                             TWO 2530
         DO 840 JK=1,8                                            TWO 2540
840      Y(JK)=0.0                                                TWO 2550
         Y(1)=1.0                                                 TWO 2560
         X1=DELT                                                  TWO 2570
         CALL RKM                                                 TWO 2580
         X1=TBP                                                   TWO 2590
         CALL RKM                                                 TWO 2600
         BACK=Y(1)**2+Y(2)**2                                     TWO 2610
         DO 1340 JC=1,60                                          TWO 2620
         CN(15)=(FLOAT(JC)-30.5)*DELW                             TWO 2630
         MOVE=0                                                   TWO*2640
         Z=CN(15)-CN(16)                                          TWO*2650
         IF(SHIFT-ABS(Z))870 ,870 ,850                            TWO*2660
850      CN(15)=CN(16)+SHIFT                                      TWO*2670
         IF(Z)860 ,900 ,900                                       TWO*2680
860      CN(15)=CN(16)-SHIFT                                      TWO*2690
         GO TO 900                                                TWO*2700
870      Z=CN(15)+CN(16)                                          TWO*2710
         IF(SHIFT-ABS(Z))910 ,910 ,880                            TWO*2720
880      CN(15)=-CN(16)+SHIFT                                     TWO*2730
         IF(Z)890 ,900 ,900                                       TWO*2740
890      CN(15)=-CN(16)-SHIFT                                     TWO*2750
900      MOVE=1                                                   TWO*2760
910      XXX=CN(15)+CN(16)                                        TWO*2770
         YYY=CN(15)-CN(16)                                        TWO*2780
```

```
       CN(29)=CN(15)/BM(2)                                          TWO 2790
       DO 920 J=1,4                                                 TWO*2800
       POS(1,J)=-10000.0                                            TWO*2810
 920   ITYPE(J)=J                                                   TWO*2820
       IF(YYY)950,950,930                                           TWO*2830
 930   IF(ALPHA(1)*FP1X(2))940,950,940                              TWO*2840
 940   POS(1,1)=CN(17)-(CN(15)-CN(16))*FP1X(1)/FP1X(2)              TWO*2850
 950   IF(XXX*YYY)960,980,980                                       TWO*2860
 960   IF(ALPHA(2)*FP2X(2))970,980,970                              TWO*2870
 970   POS(1,2)=-CN(15)*FP2X(1)/FP2X(2)                             TWO*2880
 980   IF(XXX)990,1010,1010                                         TWO*2890
 990   IF(ALPHA(3)*FP3X(2))1000,1010,1000                           TWO*2900
1000   POS(1,3)=-CN(17)-(CN(15)+CN(16))*FP3X(1)/FP3X(2)             TWO*2910
1010   STARTA=PY*(EXTRA/2.0-(THRM*EXTRA)*FINISH/THICK)-CN(15)*      TWO*2920
      1  FNX(1)/FNX(2)                                              TWO*2930
       SURFAC=STARTA+TBP                                            TWO*2940
       POS(1,4)=SURFAC                                             TWO*2950
       DO 1040 J=1,3                                               TWO*2960
       LUCK=0                                                      TWO*2970
       DO 1030 K=1,3                                               TWO*2980
       IF(POS(1,K)-POS(1,K+1))1030,1030,1020                        TWO*2990
1020   Z=POS(1,K+1)                                                TWO*3000
       POS(1,K+1)=POS(1,K)                                          TWO*3010
       POS(1,K)=Z                                                  TWO*3020
       ISTORE=ITYPE(K+1)                                           TWO*3030
       ITYPE(K+1)=ITYPE(K)                                          TWO*3040
       ITYPE(K)=ISTORE                                             TWO*3050
       LUCK=-1                                                     TWO*3060
1030   CONTINUE                                                    TWO*3070
       IF(LUCK)1040,1050,1040                                       TWO*3080
1040   CONTINUE                                                    TWO*3090
1050   LSWTCH=0                                                    TWO*3100
       DO 1100 J=1,4                                               TWO*3110
       IF(ITYPE(J)-4)1060,1080,1060                                 TWO*3120
1060   IF(LSWTCH)1070,1090,1070                                     TWO*3130
1070   POS(2,J)=POS(1,J)                                           TWO*3140
       GO TO 1100                                                  TWO*3150
1080   LSWTCH=-1                                                   TWO*3160
1090   POS(2,J)=-10050.0                                           TWO*3170
1100   CONTINUE                                                    TWO*3180
       X=STARTA                                                    TWO*3190
       X1=X                                                        TWO 3200
       IFLAG=0                                                     TWO 3210
       DO 1110 JK=1,8                                              TWO 3220
1110   Y(JK)=0.0                                                   TWO 3230
       Y(1)=1.0                                                    TWO 3240
       Y(7)=1.0                                                    TWO 3250
       KOUNTF=1                                                    TWO*3260
       N=1                                                         TWO*3270
       LINK=1                                                      TWO*3280
       DO 1130 JT=1,64                                             TWO 3290
       X1=X1+DELT                                                  TWO 3300
       GO TO 1390                                                  TWO*3310
1120   CALL RKM                                                    TWO 3320
       DNR=Y(1)*Y(7)-Y(2)*Y(8)-Y(3)*Y(5)+Y(4)*Y(6)                 TWO 3330
       DNI=Y(1)*Y(8)+Y(2)*Y(7)-Y(3)*Y(6)-Y(4)*Y(5)                 TWO 3340
       DNN=1.0/(DNR**2+DNI**2)                                     TWO 3350
       FX(JT,1)=DNN*(Y(7)*DNR+Y(8)*DNI)                            TWO 3360
       FX(JT,2)=DNN*(Y(8)*DNR-Y(7)*DNI)                            TWO 3370
       FX(JT,3)=-DNN*(Y(3)*DNR+Y(4)*DNI)                           TWO 3380
       FX(JT,4)=DNN*(Y(3)*DNI-Y(4)*DNR)                            TWO 3390
1130   CONTINUE                                                    TWO 3400
       IF(IFLAG)1150,1140,1150                                      TWO 3410
1140   X1=SURFAC                                                   TWO 3420
       LINK=3                                                      TWO*3430
       GO TO 1390                                                  TWO*3440
1150   X=SURFAC                                                    TWO 3450
       X1=X                                                        TWO 3460
       DO 1160 JK=1,8                                              TWO 3470
1160   Y(JK)=TEMPY(JK)                                             TWO 3480
       KOUNTF=1                                                    TWO 3490
       N=2                                                         TWO*3500
       LINK=2                                                      TWO*3510
       DO 1180 JM=1,64                                             TWO 3520
       X1=X1+DELT                                                  TWO 3530
       GO TO 1390                                                  TWO*3540
1170   CALL RKM                                                    TWO 3550
       TT=(FX(JM,1)*Y(1)-FX(JM,2)*Y(2)+FX(JM,3)*Y(5)-FX(JM,4)*Y(6))**2  TWO 3560
      1 +(FX(JM,1)*Y(2)+FX(JM,2)*Y(1)+FX(JM,3)*Y(6)+FX(JM,4)*Y(5))**2   TWO 3570
1180   TB(2*JM+1)=TT/BACK                                          TWO 3580
```

```
          TB(1)=(TEMPY(1)**2+TEMPY(2)**2)/BACK                      TWO 3590
          DO 1190 JZ=2,128,2                                        TWO 3600
 1190     TB(JZ)=0.5*(TB(JZ-1)+TB(JZ+1))                           TWO 3610
          MARK=1H                                                   TWO 3620
          STAGR=EXTRA/DIVISR                                       TWO*3630
          LSTAG=STAGR*129.0/WL                                     TWO*3640
          DELL=DELW/2.0+0.00000001                                 TWO*3650
          EFP2X1=FP2X(1)/SQRT(FP2X(1)**2+FP2X(2)**2)               TWO*3660
          EFNX1=FNX(1)/SQRT(FNX(1)**2+FNX(2)**2)                   TWO*3670
          IF(ABS(XXX)-DELL) 1210,1210,1200                         TWO*3680
 1200     IF(ABS(YYY)-DELL) 1210,1210,1330                         TWO*3690
 1210     IF(FP2X(2))1220,1230,1240                                TWO*3700
 1220     IF(EFP2X1-EFNX1) 1250,1270,1260                          TWO*3710
 1230     IF(SEP) 1270,1270,1280                                   TWO*3720
 1240     IF(EFP2X1+EFNX1) 1260,1270,1250                          TWO*3730
 1250     IF(CN(15)) 1290,1330,1300                                TWO*3740
 1260     IF(CN(15)) 1300,1330,1290                                TWO*3750
 1270     TB(1)=-1.0                                               TWO*3760
          TB(129)=-1.0                                             TWO*3770
          GO TO 1310                                               TWO*3780
 1280     TB(1)=-1.0                                               TWO*3790
          TB(129-LSTAG)=-1.0                                       TWO*3800
 1290     TB(LSTAG+1)=-1.0                                         TWO*3810
          TB(129)=-1.0                                             TWO*3820
          GO TO 1310                                               TWO*3830
 1300     TB(1)=-1.0                                               TWO*3840
          TB(129-LSTAG)=-1.0                                       TWO*3850
 1310     MARK=1HD                                                 TWO*3860
          IF(MOVE)1320,1330,1320                                   TWO*3870
 1320     MARK=1HM                                                 TWO*3880
 1330     CALL HALFTN(129,TB,MARK,BLACK,WHITE,1)                   TWO 3890
 1340     CONTINUE                                                 TWO 3900
          TIME=(TIMEF(X)-TIME)/1000.0                              TWO 3910
 1350     WRITE(MW,1360) C11,C12,C44,IY,TIME,WL,WW,START,FINISH,THICK,THBM,  TWO*3920
         1VEC1                                                     TWO*3930
 1360     FORMAT(3H   ,F5.2,4HC11 F5.2,4HC12 F5.2,4HC44 15A1       TWO*3940
         1    ,F6.1,5H SECSF6.2,3H WLF6.2,3H WWF5.2,6H STRT F5.2,5H FIN     TWO*3950
         2F7.3,2HTHF7.3,4HTHBM3F6.2,2HV1 )                         TWO*3960
          WRITE(MW,1370)LB,LD,LU,LG,LBM,LFN,W,ANQ,BACK,BLACK,WHITE,VEC2     TWO*3970
 1370     FORMAT(3H   312,1H/I1,5HB    312,5HU    312,5HG    312,5HBM  312,  TWO*3980
         12HFNF7.3,4HW   F6.3,5HANO  F6.3,6HBACK  F5.3,7HBLACK  F5.3,7HWWHITE TWO*3990
         2  3F6.2,2HV2 )                                           TWO*4000
          WRITE(MW,1380)LB2,LD2,SEP,LFP,LS1,LQ(1),LS2,LQ(2),LS3,LQ(3),IZ    TWO*4010
 1380     FORMAT(3H   312,1H/I1,4HB2  F5.2,5HSEP  312,5HFP1  312,4HFP2 312,  TWO*4020
         1 5HFP3  312,1H/I1,5HSH1  312,1H/I1,5HSH2  312,1H/I1,5HSH3  26A1,   TWO*4030
         2 12HTWODIS TRIBO )                                       TWO*4040
          GO TO 10                                                 TWO 4050
 1390     IF(KOUNTF-5)1410,1400,1400                               TWO*4060
 1400     GO TO (1120,1170,1150),LINK                              TWO*4070
 1410     IF(X1-POS(N,KOUNTF))1400,1420,1420                       TWO*4080
 1420     IF(X-POS(N,KOUNTF))1430,1430,1460                        TWO*4090
 1430     XX1=X1                                                   TWO*4100
          X1=POS(N,KOUNTF)                                         TWO*4110
          CALL RKM                                                 TWO*4120
          IP=ITYPE(KOUNTF)                                         TWO*4130
          GO TO (1440,1440,1440,1470),IP                          TWO*4140
 1440     Z=Y(3)                                                   TWO*4150
          ZZ=Y(7)                                                  TWO*4160
          Y(3)=Y(3)*COSA(IP)-Y(4)*SINA(IP)                        TWO*4170
          Y(7)=Y(7)*COSA(IP)-Y(8)*SINA(IP)                        TWO*4180
          Y(4)=Y(4)*COSA(IP)+Z*SINA(IP)                           TWO*4190
          Y(8)=Y(8)*COSA(IP)+ZZ*SINA(IP)                          TWO*4200
 1450     X1=XX1                                                   TWO*4210
          POS(N,KOUNTF)=-9000.0                                    TWO*4220
 1460     KOUNTF=KOUNTF+1                                          TWO*4230
          GO TO 1390                                               TWO*4240
 1470     DO 1480 JK=1,8                                           TWO*4250
 1480     TEMPY(JK)=Y(JK)                                          TWO*4260
          IFLAG=1                                                  TWO*4270
          GO TO 1450                                               TWO*4280
          END                                                      TWO 4290
```

10.9.4. SUBROUTINE DERIV FOR TWO DISLOCATIONS

ADDITIONAL INPUT (data via COMMON/RKMDRV):

CN(17)   Component of displacement of dislocation 1 from coordinate origin in direction of integration. Displacement of dislocation 2 is −CN(17).

CN(21)–CN(26)   Constants of numerator of $d(\mathbf{g}\cdot\mathbf{R})/dZ$ for dislocation 2. Constants of denominator as for dislocation 1.

CN(30)   Component of displacement of dislocation 1 from coordinate origin normal to direction of integration in the same units as CN(29). Displacement of dislocation 2 is −CN(30).

This listing is a simple extension of subroutine DERIV for one dislocation (§ 10.3.4). The expression for BETA has the elastic displacement field of the second dislocation added (DER 160–180). Since each half of BETA refers to that dislocation as origin, it is necessary to correct for the displacement of the dislocation from the coordinate origin (DER 40, 70, 80, 110).

Listing of subroutine DERIV *for two dislocations*

```
        SUBROUTINE DERIV                                              DER    10
        COMMON/RKMDRV/CN(30),X,X1,Y(8),ERROR,SKIP,Q,D(8),ANO          DER    20
        IF(SKIP)7,1,7                                                 DER    30
1       X11=X-CN(17)                                                  DER    40
        IF(X11)3,2,3                                                  DER    50
2       X11=0.000000001                                               DER    60
3       R1=(CN(29)-CN(30))/X11                                        DER    70
        X22=X+CN(17)                                                  DER    80
        IF(X22)6,5,6                                                  DER    90
5       X22=0.000000001                                               DER   100
6       R2=(CN(29)+CN(30))/X22                                        DER   110
        BETA=CN(14)                                                   DER   120
        1+(((R1*CN(1)+CN(4))/((R1+CN(7))**2+CN(10)))+((R1*CN(2)+CN(5))/(( DER  130
        2R1+CN(8))**2+CN(11)))+((R1*CN(3)+CN(6))/((R1+CN(9))**2+CN(12)))) DER  140
        3 /X11                                                        DER   150
        4+(((R2*CN(21)+CN(24))/((R2+CN(7))**2+CN(10)))+((R2*CN(22)+CN(25))/DER 160
        5((R2+CN(8))**2+CN(11)))+((R2*CN(23)+CN(26))/((R2+CN(9))**2+CN(12)))DER 170
        6))/X22                                                       DER   180
7       Z=ANO*(Y(1)+Y(3))                                             DER   190
        D(1)=Z-Y(4)                                                   DER   200
        D(3)=-BETA*Y(4)+Z-Y(2)                                        DER   210
        Z=ANO*(Y(2)+Y(4))                                             DER   220
        D(2)=Z+Y(3)                                                   DER   230
        D(4)=BETA*Y(3)+Z+Y(1)                                         DER   240
        Z=ANO*(Y(5)+Y(7))                                             DER   250
        D(5)=Z-Y(8)                                                   DER   260
        D(7)=-BETA*Y(8)+Z-Y(6)                                        DER   270
        Z=ANO*(Y(6)+Y(8))                                             DER   280
        D(6)=Z+Y(7)                                                   DER   290
        D(8)=BETA*Y(7)+Z+Y(5)                                         DER   300
        RETURN                                                        DER   310
        END                                                           DER   320
```

10.10. Dark field pictures

It is simple to change the computer programs to compute dark field intensities but not so simple to print these intensities as a picture. Taking program

ONEDIS for example, it is only necessary to replace Y(1) by Y(3), Y(2) by
Y(4), Y(5) by Y(7) and Y(6) by Y(8) in the expressions for BACK (ONE
1980) and TT (ONE 2420–2430) and to replace TEMPY(1) by TEMPY(3)
and TEMPY(2) by TEMPY(4) in the expression for TB(1) (ONE 2450). The
array TB will then contain dark field intensities divided by dark field background. The problem now is, in photographic terms, with what exposure and
contrast should this picture be printed so that the significant parts of the
picture are successfully reproduced within the limited ability of the line
printer? For bright field pictures it is fortunate that a standard combination
of exposure and contrast is almost always suitable. No such automatic
choice can be suggested for dark field pictures because of their much greater
variability and a human decision on individual cases is often necessary.

APPENDIX

A.1. Introduction

This section describes how the symmetry properties of images can be used to minimise the amount of computing necessary for defect identification. Attention will be confined to dislocations and stacking faults in crystals in general, in centrosymmetric crystals, and to cases involving elastic symmetry.

The number of guesses for which theoretical micrographs are to be computed may be reduced initially by recognising the defect as being of a particular type (e.g. a single dislocation, dislocations bordering a stacking fault, a dislocation dipole, a dilation, etc.). This is usually done by considering the symmetry exhibited by the experimental images (e.g. for a dipole see § 8.12 and for a dilation see § 8.4) in conjunction with other factors such as specimen history, and usually no specific computations are required at this stage.

Having made a series of informed guesses, images are computed for each guess. In general, the images for each guess are unrelated and each has to be obtained by a specific individual computation. However, there are occasions when the images for two or more guesses are related in a predictable way, so that in such cases a single computation can be applied to several guesses. The only relation we have used to make this kind of prediction is that the images corresponding to different guesses are identical either directly, or after a rotation of one image through $180°$ in its plane. We will now discuss the conditions when different defects produce identical sets of images.

Consider two similar crystals of thickness t containing defects where the displacement function in the first crystal is $R_1(Z)$ and in the second crystal is $R_2(Z)$ where Z is measured in the direction of electron flow from the top surface of each crystal. If the two displacement functions differ only by a constant displacement R_0 corresponding to a rigid body motion of one crystal, (i.e. $R_1(Z) = R_0 + R_2(Z)$) then under the same diffracting conditions, the two crystals will give identical sets of images. Howie and Whelan (1961) showed that for centrosymmetric crystals, if $R_1(Z) = R(Z)$ and $R_2(Z) = R_0 - R(t - Z)$ then for the same diffracting conditions the two crystals will give identical sets of bright field images.

In the case of two-beam diffraction theory, since the displacement function always occurs in conjunction with the diffracting vector g, the conditions for identical images may be re-stated as follows. If

$$g_1 \cdot R_1(Z) = g_2 \cdot (R_0 + R_2(Z)), \tag{A.1}$$

then images from the two crystals are identical provided all other diffraction conditions are equal. Similarly, bright field micrographs of centrosymmetric crystals are identical if:

$$g_1 \cdot R_1(Z) = g \cdot R(Z),$$
$$g_2 \cdot R_2(Z) = g \cdot (R_0 - R(t \cdot Z)). \tag{A.2}$$

In the formulation of the diffraction theory, the function $g \cdot R$ is useful for considering the contrast from defects such as stacking faults, but for other defects, such as dislocations, we have found it more useful to consider the function $\beta' = g \cdot dR/dZ$. In terms of β' it can be seen from eq. (A.1) that images from the two crystals are identical if:

$$g_1 \cdot R_1'(Z) = g_2 \cdot R_2'(Z). \tag{A.3}$$

In the case of centrosymmetric crystals it can be seen from eq. (A.2) that if

$$\beta_1'(Z) = g \cdot R'(Z),$$
$$\beta_2'(Z) = g \cdot R'(t - Z), \tag{A.4}$$

then the bright field images will be identical.

It will now be shown how relations (A.1) to (A.4) can be used to predict the conditions when identical images occur for dislocations, stacking faults and several dislocation-stacking fault configurations.

A.2. Single dislocations

In discussing the conditions under which the images of single dislocations

are identical, we will be concerned with the displacement function β' and therefore interest will be centered on relations (A.3) and (A.4).

Consider first relation (A.3), which is a general result for all crystals, as it
applies to two similar crystals each containing a dislocation having a common
line direction with Burgers vectors b_1 and b_2. Since we are considering the same
type of defect in each crystal, $R'_1(Z)$ and $R'_2(Z)$ have the same functional form.
Clearly, there will be several instances when diffracting vectors g_1 and g_2 can
be found to satisfy eq. (A.3) so that individual micrographs of the two dislocations will be identical. However, a general result, when sets of images of
the two dislocations are identical, occurs when $b_1 = b_2$ or $b_1 = -b_2$. The first
case is trivial since it represents the same dislocation in the same crystal under
the same diffracting conditions ($g_1 = g_2$). In the second case the displacement
functions in the two crystals will be equal and opposite i.e. $R'_1(Z) = -R'_2(Z)$
and it follows that eq. (A.3) is only satisfied when $g_1 = -g_2$. Thus, for any
crystal, a dislocation with Burgers vector $+b$ imaged with a diffracting vector
$+g$ has an identical image to a parallel dislocation with Burgers vector $-b$
imaged with a diffracting vector $-g$. This result is illustrated diagrammatically
in fig. A.1 where the image of a dislocation is denoted by ⌐⌐⌐⌐⌐⌐⌐ and the
direction of the dislocation line in this diagram and all subsequent diagrams of
this type is from left to right.

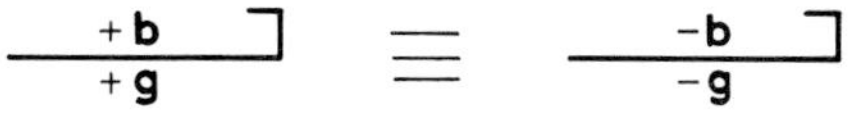

$$\underline{\quad\quad +\,b\quad\;\;\rceil} \quad\quad = \quad\quad \underline{\quad\quad -\,b\quad\;\;\rceil}$$
$$\overline{\quad\quad +\,g\quad\quad} \quad\quad\quad\quad \overline{\quad\quad -\,g\quad\quad}$$

Fig. A.1

This result is seldom of use for images of isolated dislocations, but is utilised
in deducing the symmetry properties of dislocation-stacking fault configurations.

Let us now investigate the symmetry properties of the images of single dislocations in centrosymmetric crystals using relation (A.4). Figure A.2 shows
two identical crystals of thickness t containing dislocations with a common line
direction and with Burgers vectors b_1 in (a) and b_2 in (b). Consider a plane i_1
in the first crystal such that the point where the dislocation intersects it is a
distance d from the top surface, and a plane i_2 in the second crystal such that
the point of intersection of the dislocation with the plane is a distance d above
the bottom surface of the crystal. These two planes are shown separately in
fig. A.3 (a) and (b). The displacement function β' in such planes for a dislocation in an anisotropic crystal is given by eq. (4.23) as:

$$\beta' = \cos\psi \sum_\alpha \frac{P_\alpha X_1 + Q_\alpha X_2 \cos\psi}{(X_1 + R_\alpha X_2 \cos\psi)^2 + (S_\alpha X_2 \cos\psi)^2} \qquad [(4.23)]$$

where the axes X_1 and X_2 are indicated in fig. A.3 and the point of intersection

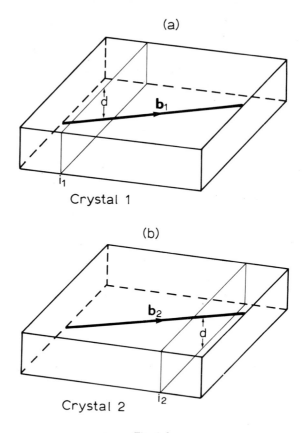

Fig. A.2

of each dislocation with each plane is taken as origin. To be compatible with
the form of the expression (A.4), we will consider the form of β' in each plane
with respect to axes X and Z whose origin is situated at the top of the foil

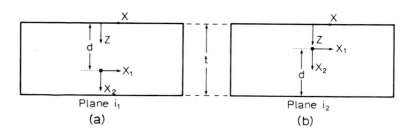

Fig. A.3

such that for crystal 1, $X_2 = Z - d$ and $X_1 = X$, and for crystal 2, $X_2 = Z - (t - d)$ and $X_1 = X$. Then for crystal 1:

$$\beta'_1(Z) = \cos \psi \sum_\alpha \frac{P_{1\alpha}X + Q_{1\alpha}(Z - d) \cos \psi}{(X + R_{1\alpha}(Z - d) \cos\psi)^2 + (S_{1\alpha}(Z - d) \cos\psi)^2} \qquad (A.5)$$

and for crystal 2:

$$\beta'_2(Z) = \cos \psi \sum_\alpha \frac{P_{2\alpha}X - Q_{2\alpha}((t - Z) - d)\cos \psi}{(X - R_{2\alpha}((t - Z) - d)\cos\psi)^2 + (-S_{2\alpha}((t - Z) - d)\cos\psi)^2}$$

$$(A.6)$$

Equations (A.5) and (A.6) have the form of eq. (A.4) if in eq. (A.6):

$$P_{2\alpha} = -P_{1\alpha}; \; Q_{2\alpha} = -Q_{1\alpha}; \qquad (A.7)$$

$$R_{2\alpha} = R_{1\alpha}; \; S_{2\alpha} = S_{1\alpha}; \qquad (A.8)$$

and X is replaced by $-X$. $\qquad (A.9)$

Thus, for planes such as i_1 and i_2, eqs. (A.7)–(A.9) are the conditions that must be satisfied for the bright field images of crystals 1 and 2 to be identical.

R_α and S_α depend only on the direction of the dislocation in the crystal and the elastic constants so that eqs. (A.8) are always satisfied. By comparing eqs. (4.23) with (10.21):

$$P_\alpha = \mathcal{R}(g_k A_{k\alpha} M_{\alpha j} H_{ij} b_i p_\alpha)$$

and $\qquad (A.10)$

$$Q_\alpha = \mathcal{R}(g_k A_{k\alpha} M_{\alpha j} H_{ij} b_i p_\alpha \bar{p}_\alpha),$$

where $\mathcal{R}$ denotes 'the real part of'. The terms $A_{k\alpha}$, $M_{\alpha j}$, H_{ij}, p_α and $\bar{p}_\alpha$ depend only on the direction of the dislocation in the crystal and the elastic constants and therefore are the same in crystals 1 and 2. However, by an appropriate choice of the diffracting vector g, (components g_k) or the Burgers vector b (components b_i), eqs. (A.7) can be satisfied. That is, for the same diffracting vector g, eqs. (A.7) are satisfied if the Burgers vector in crystal 1 is $+b$ and that in crystal 2 is $-b$. Alternatively, for the same Burgers vector b, eqs. (A.7) are satisfied if the diffracting vector in crystal 1 is $+g$ and that in crystal 2 is $-g$.

The condition (A.9) means that the intensities for crystal 1 resulting from the plane i_1 in fig. A.3(a) going from left to right across the image are the same as those for crystal 2 resulting from the plane i_2 in fig. A.3(b) but going from right to left. This, together with the fact that the planes i_1 and i_2 were chosen in the crystals to be symmetrically disposed about the centre of the dislocation lines, means that, when eqs. (A.7)–(A.9) are satisfied, the entire image from crystal 1 will be identical with that from crystal 2 only when one image is rotated in its plane through $180°$ with respect to the other. Thus the following relations hold between sets of bright field images from single dislocations in centrosymmetric crystals.

For any given diffracting vector g, the image of a dislocation with Burgers vector $+b$ is identical with that of a dislocation with Burgers vector $-b$ after a rotation of $180°$. This is illustrated diagrammatically in fig. A.4:

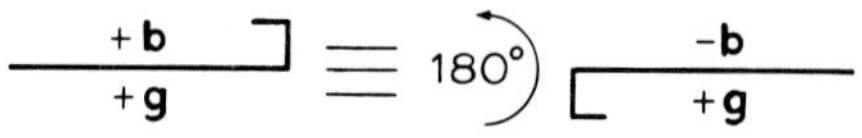

Fig. A.4

For a dislocation with any given Burgers vector b, its image for a diffracting vector $+g$ is related to its image for a diffracting vector $-g$ by a rotation of $180°$ (fig. A.5):

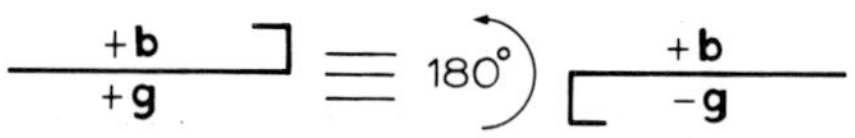

Fig. A.5

The result expressed in fig. A.4 enables a reduction to be made in the number of theoretical micrographs computed when matching dislocations in centrosymmetric crystals since only one sign of the Burgers vector need be considered. This was used in ch. 5. The property illustrated in fig. A.5 is one of the symmetry properties which distinguishes a dislocation from other defects and so may be used in the initial classification of the type of defect. An experimental demonstration of this property was given in fig. 5.10.

A.3. Single stacking faults

The conditions which are most convenient for establishing the relations between images of stacking faults are those given in eqs. (A.1) and (A.2). Due to the simpler form of the displacement field for a stacking fault compared with that for a dislocation, the relations between images will be merely quoted in this case.

From eq. (A.1), the image of a stacking fault with displacement vector $+R$ imaged with a diffracting vector $+g$ is identical with that of a similar fault in an identical crystal where the displacement vector is $-R$ imaged with $-g$.

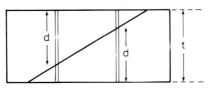

Fig. A.6

Figure A.6 shows a cross-section of a stacking fault on an inclined plane in a centrosymmetric crystal. By considering points on the fault which are equidistant from the centre of the foil, it is apparent from eqs. (A.2) that the bright field intensities arising from columns passing through these points are identical. Therefore the bright field images of stacking faults in centrosymmetric crystals are symmetric about mid-foil.

In the examples which follow, these two results for stacking faults are always used in conjunction.

A.4. Relations between dislocation–stacking fault images

The results obtained for isolated dislocations and stacking faults can be used to predict when the images of composite dislocation–stacking fault configurations are identical. Three particular examples which have been used in this book are given for bright field images of centrosymmetric crystals. The diagrammatic form of presentation used previously will be continued where, in each diagram, the dislocation line direction is from left to right and the image of a stacking fault is denoted by diagonal shading.

A.4.1. A PARTIAL DISLOCATION BORDERING A STACKING FAULT

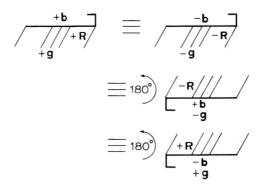

Fig. A.7. Equivalences of bright field images of a partial dislocation bordering a stacking fault in a centrosymmetric crystal. These relations were used in § §7.2 and 8.9.1.

A.4.2. A PARTIAL DISLOCATION SEPARATING FAULTS WITH EQUAL BUT OP-POSITE DISPLACEMENT VECTORS

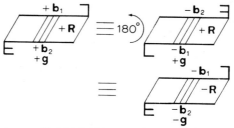

Fig. A.8. Equivalence of bright field images of a partial dislocation separating faults with equal but opposite displacement vectors in a centrosymmetric crystal. This relation was used in § 8.9.2.

A.4.3. TWO PARTIAL DISLOCATIONS BORDERING A STACKING FAULT

Fig. A.9. Equivalences of bright field images of two partial dislocations bordering a stacking fault in centrosymmetric crystals. The relation involving the rotation of 180° was used in § 7.3.

A.5. The symmetry of dislocation dipole images

The relation expressed in fig. A.9 involving the rotation of 180° can be used to show that bright field images of dislocation dipoles in centrosymmetric crystals possess a centre of inversion. Figure A.10 expresses the relation given by fig. A.9 for the case of a dipole, i.e., $R = 0$, $b_1 = -b_2 = b$, where it can be seen that the dipole images are identical after a rotation of 180°.

Fig. A.10

However, the defects shown on each side of the identity sign in fig. A.10 are identical and, since the diffraction conditions are the same, their images must also be identical. The only condition which allows the images to be identical with and without a rotation of 180° is that they possess a centre of

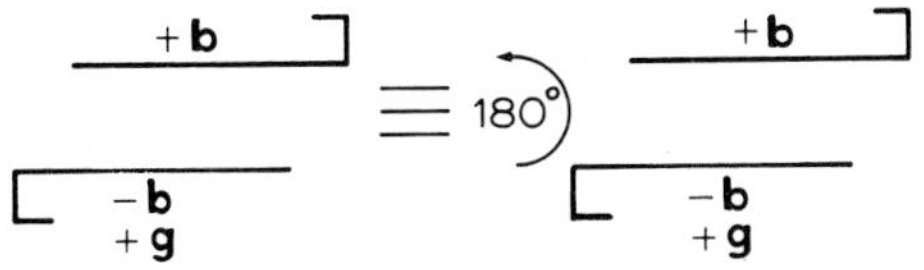

Fig. A.11

inversion. Thus fig. A.10 would in fact be represented by fig. A.11.

This property is one which can be used to make an initial identification of the type of defect (see § 8.12).

A.6. The effect of elastic symmetry on dislocation images

A further reduction in the number of guesses can sometimes be made in the case of a dislocation lying along an elastic symmetry direction. Dislocation images have some predictable properties when their line directions are normal to an elastic symmetry plane, or parallel to an even-fold rotation axis of the crystal[*]. These conditions are fairly restrictive and specific, but of course, the relations between images deduced on the basis of elastic symmetry can be used in conjunction with the identities already given to further extend their usefulness.

When a dislocation is parallel to an elastic symmetry direction, the displacement field is separable into two components of which one depends on the edge component of the Burgers vector and the other on the screw component. In such cases a suitable choice of diffracting vector g can make one of the components invisible. In particular, when g is parallel to u, the edge component of the displacement field is exactly invisible, and when g is normal to u, the screw component of the displacement field is exactly invisible.

In the special cases when the dislocation is pure screw or pure edge, one of these choices of diffracting vector will make it exactly invisible, thus facilitating its identification. Conversely, if the dislocation is visible under these conditions, it is neither pure screw nor pure edge and these possibilities need not be considered in computing theoretical micrographs. These conditions were employed during the identification of the partial dislocations lying along ⟨110⟩ directions bordering steps in complex loops (§ 8.11). For dislocations which lie along elastic symmetry directions further reductions in computing can be made when the dislocations are visible for diffracting vectors which are parallel or normal to the dislocation line. For example, in those micrographs where g is parallel

---

[*] The situation involving predictable properties of dislocation images discussed in § 8.2 is not included here since it is too restrictive to be of practical use.

to u, only the screw component of the displacement field contributes to the images, so that Burgers vectors which have the same screw component produce identical images and therefore only one of these need be computed. Similarly, for those micrographs where g is normal to u, only the edge component of the displacement field contributes to the image so that Burgers vectors which have the same edge component produce identical images. In § 9.2 attention was drawn to instances where these conditions occurred in fig. 7.4, and in that example several images were computed which were unnecessary.

REFERENCES

Andrews, K.W., D.J. Dyson and S.R. Keown, 1967, Interpretation of Electron Diffraction Patterns (Hilger and Watts Ltd., London).

Art, A., R. Gevers and S. Amelinckx, 1963, Phys. Stat. Sol. 3, 697.

Barnes, R.S., 1954, Acta Met. 2, 380.

Barrett, C.S., 1952, Structure of Metals (McGraw-Hill, New York).

Blank, H. and S. Amelinckx, 1963, J. Appl. Phys. 34, 2200.

Bowles, J.S. and J.K. Mackenzie, 1954a, Acta Met. 2, 129.

Bowles, J.S. and J.K. Mackenzie, 1954b, Acta Met. 2, 138.

Broom, N. and P. Humble, 1969, Phil. Mag. 19, 639.

Bullough, R., D.M. Maher and R.C. Perrin, 1971, Phys. Stat. Sol. B43, 689.

Chadderton, L.T., 1964, Proc. Roy. Soc. A280, 110.

Clarebrough, L.M., 1969, Aust. J. Phys. 22, 559.

Clarebrough, L.M., 1971, Aust. J. Phys. 24, 79.

Clarebrough, L.M., C.T. Forwood and A.J. Morton, 1973, Crystal Lattice Defects (in press).

Clarebrough, L.M. and A.J. Morton, 1969a, Aust. J. Phys. 22, 351.

Clarebrough, L.M. and A.J. Morton, 1969b, Aust. J. Phys. 22, 371.

Clarebrough, L.M., R.L. Segall and M.H. Loretto, 1966, Phil. Mag. 13, 1285.

Coker, E.G. and L.N.G. Filon, 1957, Photoelasticity (Cambridge University Press), p. 299.

Cottrell, A.H., 1953, Dislocations and Plastic Flow in Crystals (Clarendon Press, Oxford), p. 47.

Darwin, C.G., 1914, Phil. Mag. 27, 315, 675.

Degischer, H.P., 1971, The World through the Electron Microscope, Metallurgy V (JEOL Ltd.), p. 63.

Degischer, H.P., 1972, Phil. Mag. 26, 1137.

Dingley, D.J. and K.F. Hale, 1966, Proc. Roy. Soc. A295, 55.

Doyle, P.A. and P.S. Turner, 1968, Acta Cryst. A24, 390.

Escaig, B., 1963, Acta Met. 11, 595.

Eshelby, J.D., W.T. Read and W. Shockley, 1953, Acta Met. 1, 251.

Fisher, P.M.J., Acta Cryst., to be published.

Forwood, C.T. and P. Humble, 1970, Aust. J. Phys. 23, 697.

France, L.K., C.S. Hartley and C.N. Reid, 1967, Metal Science J. 1, 65.

France, L.K. and M.H. Loretto, 1968, Proc. Roy. Soc. A307, 83.

Frank, F.C., 1951, Phil. Mag. **42**, 809.

Frank, F.C., 1965, Acta Cryst. **18**, 862.

Gevers, R., H. Blank and S. Amelinckx, 1966, Phys. Stat. Sol. **13**, 449.

Hall, C.R. and P.B. Hirsch, 1965, Proc. Roy. Soc. **A286**, 158.

Hashimoto, H., A. Howie and M.J. Whelan, 1960, Phil. Mag. **5**, 967.

Hashimoto, H., A. Howie and M.J. Whelan, 1962, Proc. Roy. Soc. **A269**, 80.

Head, A.K., 1967a, Aust. J. Phys. **20**, 557.

Head, A.K., 1967b, Phys. Stat. Sol. **19**, 185.

Head, A.K., 1969a, Physics of Strength and Plasticity (M.I.T. Press, Cambridge Massachusetts) p. 65.

Head, A.K., 1969b, Aust. J. Phys. **22**, 43.

Head, A.K., 1969c, Aust. J. Phys. **22**, 345.

Head, A.K., 1969d, Aust. J. Phys. **22**, 569.

Head, A.K., M.H. Loretto and P. Humble, 1967, Phys. Stat. Sol. **20**, 521.

Hearmon, R.F.S., 1956, Advances in Physics **5**, 323.

Hirsch, P.B., 1965, International Conference on Electron Diffraction and the Nature of Defects in Crystals, Melbourne, Pergamon, New York) p. J–4.

Hirsch, P.B., A. Howie and M.J. Whelan, 1960, Phil. Trans. **A252**, 499.

Hirsch, P.B., A. Howie, R.B. Nicholson, D.W. Pashley and M.J. Whelan, 1965, Electron Microscopy of Thin Crystals (Butterworths, London).

Hirth, J.P. and J. Lothe, 1968, Theory of Dislocations (McGraw-Hill, New York).

Hörl, E.M., 1971, Crystal Lattice Defects **2**, 71.

Howie, A., 1963, Proc. Roy. Soc. **A271**, 268.

Howie, A., 1970, Modern Diffraction and Imaging Techniques in Material Science, eds. S. Amelinckx et al. (North-Holland, Amsterdam) p. 331.

Howie, A. and Z.S. Basinski, 1968, Phil. Mag. **17**, 1039.

Howie, A. and M.J. Whelan, 1961, Proc. Roy. Soc. **A263**, 217.

Howie, A. and M.J. Whelan, 1962, Proc. Roy. Soc. **A267**, 206.

Howie, A. and P.R. Swann, 1961, Phil. Mag. **6**, 1215.

Humble, P., 1968a, Phys. Stat. Sol. **30**, 183.

Humble, P., 1968b, Aust. J. Phys. **21**, 325.

Humble, P., 1969, Aust. J. Phys. **22**, 51.

Humphreys, C.J. and P.B. Hirsch, 1968, Phil. Mag. **18**, 115.

Humphreys, C.J., A. Howie and G.R. Booker, 1967, Phil. Mag. **15**, 507.

Huntington, H.B., 1958, Solid State Phys. **7**, 213.

International Tables for X-ray Crystallography, 1962, Volume III, (Kynoch, Birmingham) p. 232.

Kamiya, Y. and R. Uyeda, 1961, J. Phys. Soc. Japan **16**, 1361.

Lance, G.N., 1960, Numerical Methods for High Speed Computers (Iliffe, London),

Lazarus, D., 1948, Phys. Rev. **74**, 1726.

Lazarus, D., 1949, Phys. Rev. **76**, 547.

Loretto, M.H. and L.K. France, 1969, Phil. Mag. **19**, 141.

Maher, D.M., R.C. Perrin and R. Bullough, 1971, Phys. Stat. Sol. **B43**, 707.

McManus, C.M., 1963, Phys. Rev. **129**, 2004.

Merson, R.H., 1957, Conf. Proc. Data Processing and Automatic Computing Machines (W.R.E. Salisbury, Australia) p. 110/1–110/26.

Metherell, A.J.F., 1967, Phil. Mag. **15**, 763.

Metherell, A.J.F. and M.J. Whelan, 1967, Phil. Mag. **15**, 755.

Morton, A.J. and L.M. Clarebrough, 1969, Aust. J. Phys. **22** , 393.

Morton, A.J. and C.T. Forwood, 1973, Crystal Lattice Defects (in press).

Morton, A.J. and A.K. Head, 1970, Phys. Stat. Sol. 37, 317.

Nicholas, J.F., 1966, Acta Cryst. 21, 880.

Nicholas, J.F., 1970, Phys. Stat. Sol. A1, 563.

Nordstrom, T.V. and S. Amelinckx, 1967, Phys. Stat. Sol. 24, K121.

Nye, J.F., 1960, Physical Properties of Crystals (Clarendon Press, Oxford).

Radi, G., 1970, Acta Cryst. A26, 41.

Read, W.T., 1953, Dislocations in Crystals (McGraw-Hill, New York) p. 131.

Schapink, F.W. and M. de Jong, 1964, Acta Met. 12, 756.

Seeger, A. and G. Wobser, 1966, Phys. Stat. Sol. 17, 709.

Silcock, J.M. and W.J. Tunstall, 1964, Phil. Mag. 10, 361.

Silcox, J. and P.B. Hirsch, 1959, Phil. Mag. 4, 72.

Smith, G.H. and R.E. Burge, 1962, Acta Cryst. 15, 182.

Standards on Piezoelectric Crystals, 1949, Proc. Inst. Radio Eng. 37, 1378.

Stroh, A.N., 1958, Phil. Mag. 3, 625.

Teutonico, L.J., 1968, Phil. Mag. 18, 881.

Thölén, A.R., 1970a, Phil. Mag. 22, 175.

Thölén, A.R., 1970b, Phys. Stat. Sol. A2, 537.

Thompson, N., 1953, Proc. Phys. Soc. B66, 481.

Tunstall, W.J. and P.J. Goodhew, 1966, Phil. Mag. 13, 1259.

Whelan, M.J. and P.B. Hirsch, 1957, Phil. Mag. 2, 1303.

de Wit, G. and J.S. Koehler, 1959, Phys. Rev. 116, 1113.

Yoffe, E.H., 1961, Phil. Mag. 6, 1147.

Yoon, D.N. and A. Bienenstock, 1968, J. Appl. Phys. 39, 356.

SUBJECT INDEX

Only the more significant FORTRAN names used in the programs have been included in this index. FORTRAN variables are confined to Chapters 4, 6 and 10.